1998

Reconstructing women's wartime lives

MANCHESTER
UNIVERSITY PRESS

For Sarah

Reconstructing women's wartime lives

Discourse and subjectivity in oral histories of the Second World War

Penny Summerfield

Manchester University Press

Manchester and New York

distributed exclusively in the USA by St. Martin's Press

Published by Manchester University Press
Oxford Road, Manchester M13 9NR, UK
and Room 400, 175 Fifth Avenue, New York, NY 10010, USA

Distributed exclusively in the USA by
St. Martin's Press, Inc., 175 Fifth Avenue, New York, NY 10010, USA

Distributed exclusively in Canada by
UBC Press, University of British Columbia, 6344 Memorial Road, Vancouver, BC, Canada V6T 1Z2

British Library Cataloguing-in-Publication Data
A catalogue record for this book is available from the British Library

Library of Congress Cataloging-in-Publication Data applied for

ISBN 0 7190 4460 X *hardback*
       0 7190 4461 8 *paperback*

First published 1998

05 04 03 02 01 00 99 98   10 9 8 7 6 5 4 3 2 1

Typeset in Sabon with Frutiger
by Northern Phototypesetting Co Ltd, Bolton

Printed in Great Britain
by Bell and Bain Ltd, Glasgow

Contents

Illustrations

Abbreviations

AID	Aeronautical Inspection Directorate
AIF	Australian Imperial Force
ATA	Air Transport Auxiliary
ATS	Auxiliary Territorial Service
CD	Civil Defence
CSO	Central Statistical Office
GI	private soldier in US Army – acronym of Government Issue
GPO	General Post Office
M-O	Mass-Observation
MOI	Ministry of Information
MOLNS	Ministry of Labour and National Service
NAAFI	canteen for Service personnel – acronym of Navy, Army and Air Force Institutes
PRO	Public Record Office
RAF	Royal Air Force
REME	Royal Electrical and Mechanical Engineers
ROF	Royal Ordnance Factory
SMT	Scottish Motor Transport
WAAF	Women's Auxiliary Air Force
WLA	Women's Land Army
WRNS	Women's Royal Naval Service
W/T	Wireless/Telegraph

Preface and acknowledgements

Oral history is a demanding methodology as well as one which raises complex theoretical issues. The investment of time and energy required both of interviewers and of those interviewed is necessarily considerable, and the creation in this way of the historical data to be studied differentiates oral history from document-based historical research. The engagement in verbal, face-to-face dialogue with living people is enormously attractive to a wide variety of researchers, who include schoolchildren, family and community historians, as well as academics like myself. But oral history also demands, via the processes of transcribing tape-recorded interviews, and summarising, indexing and closely scrutinising them, a dialogue with texts which brings oral history back within the frame of more traditional historical methods – almost. One of the differences is that the researcher herself or himself has a more salient place within the construction of oral history narratives than in the production of a document from the past. His or her subjectivity becomes, of necessity, part of the study.

These reflections led me to engage with my own subjectivity, and to ask myself why I have had such an enduring interest in the Second World War, which has been a principal subject of my research since 1974. It seems appropriate to preface this book with a personal account of its (distant) pre-history. (You will find more about its recent history in the opening chapter.)

I was born in London in 1951. I grew up aware of wartime bomb damage which still made a visual impact in the 1950s. There were fascinating holes between buildings, bounded by walls on which fireplaces, doorways and even wallpaper were still visible. The craters at the bottom were threaded with secret paths and softened by self-seeded buddleia, brambles and willowherb. The fact that people once lived in the houses which were now spaces was not a source of fear to me. My imagination was preoccupied with the playgrounds created by the destruction, rather than the lives lost or damaged. The war was also woven into conversation. It was still a common reason for not having things, such as a Noah's Ark toy ('they haven't made things like that since the war'), or a house to ourselves (my parents rented the upstairs of a house and shared that with my aunt, 'because it was hard to find anywhere to live after the war'). It was also an explanation for members of the family possessing certain things, such as another aunt's hens which squawked and smelt in her back garden ('you couldn't get eggs in the war'), the army blankets under which we slept, my father's naval duffle coat and my mother's square-necked Wren 'white fronts' (which I wore at primary school as overalls). It was a source above all of stories which to me aged four or five sounded exciting and romantic, no doubt because my own origins were implicated in them. I loved hearing about my parents meeting in Scotland when my father was in the Navy and my mother in the Wrens, and about the good times they had with their friends, some of whom used to turn up periodically to see us, wreathed in cigarette smoke and smelling of travel and adventure.

The war was undoubtedly glamorised (in spite of the privations which it caused) in my eyes. I did not have to live through its atrocities. Although my parents talked to me when I was older about the Belsen concentration camp and about the atomic bombs which ended the war, and although I remember experiencing acute terror at about the age of eleven about the prospect of a future nuclear war, these horrors were at a distance from the youthful, confident tales of war which I had absorbed when little. At the age of four or five I wondered whether everyone went through 'the war' as they reached adulthood; the fact that National Service was required of young men until 1963 may have contributed to my confusion. My parents were Labour voters and my mother saved with the Co-operative Wholesale Society. From an early age I linked the war with positive moves towards a better society. One of my grandfathers had been an insurance collector in the 1920s and 1930s, in very poor districts of Manchester where families suffering the effects of the Slump and the Depression found it hard to find a few pennies a week to insure themselves against poverty, death or disaster. I grew up understanding that the post-war Labour government had passed laws which, rightly, made the job he had done unnecessary because now everyone would be cared for by the state from the cradle to the grave. The war, it seemed, was a necessary precursor to this welcome development.

It was in the main my mother who taught me these things, which were later transformed, as I became a student and then an academic, into critical historical questions about war and social change. As in many children's experience, it was the women of my family who had the habit of frequent, casual story-telling and reminiscence. My mother sketched for me the place of the war in my father's life, but looking back it was her war in which I participated imaginatively and her angle of vision which I shared. Perhaps I was trying to reach my father in the first piece of research I did on the Second World War, which was an exploration of politics within the British armed forces, focused on the army education schemes of 1939 to 1945.[1] On the other hand, in the mid-1970s I was just emerging from learning history as a male story. I was becoming aware of gender as a neglected area of study, of the excitement of the recovery of women in history and of the development of new types of feminism through which to interpret women's place in the past. In 1975 I gave a seminar paper on the army education project, and after it a fellow woman graduate student asked tentatively: 'what about servicewomen?' Her question sent me back to my mother, or at least to the range of women's experiences of the Second World War, some so different from hers, amongst which her stories belonged.

In the first chapter of this book I discuss the more recent personal and intellectual origins of the project on which this book is based, that is, since 1977 rather than 1951. I also address theoretical issues concerning the use of oral history as something other than a colour-ful adjunct to histories based on more conventional sources. The discussions I have had with a number of colleagues about these issues, and the comments they have made on drafts of the first chapter, have been invaluable. I should like to thank in particular Tess Cosslett for her careful, critical reading of two quite different drafts, three years apart, of chapter 1, and also Rosemary Deem, Oliver Fulton, Annette Kuhn and Elizabeth Roberts for their reactions to one or the other draft. Special thanks are due to Penny Tinkler who read and commented on the chapters on parents and on masculini-ties, to Gail Braybon and to Oliver Fulton for responding to an early version of the chapter on war work and feminine identity, to Har-riet Bradley for reactions to the chapter on discourses of women's work, and to Claire Duchen for her thoughts on the concluding chapter on personal change. Angela Woollacott's thoughtful formal commentary on a paper based on the chapter on masculinities, at the Berkshire Conference on the History of Women in 1996, strengthened my resolve to pursue the relationship between discourse and subjectivity in memories of the war. As this indicates, parts of the book have been 'tried out' as papers at conferences and seminars in Britain and other countries, and the debates which have taken place in these settings have shaped the book's development. I should like to acknowledge the following organisations for giving me the opportunity to talk about the research, and to thank the participants for their contributions to those discussions: the Economic History Society UK, the Manchester Women's History Group, the Royal Historical Society, the Scottish Labour History Society, the Social History Society UK, the Women's History Network UK, and abroad the 1996 Berkshire Conference on the History of Women at Chapel Hill, North Carolina, the Beatrice Bain Research Group and the Consortium for the Study of Education and Society both at the University of California at Berkeley, the War and Society Seminar at the University of Paris XIII, and the Women's International Network on Gender and Society based at Nijmegen. I also appreciate invitations to give seminar papers on the project at the universities of Warwick, Bristol, Cardiff, Sheffield Hallam and of course at my own university, Lancaster. The interviews could not have been done without the financial support of the Economic and Social Research Council,[2] analysis of them would have been a slower process without a two-term sabbatical from teaching and administration, and it would have taken place in less delightful circumstances in the absence of the generous offer of a Visiting Fellowship at the Centre for the Study of Higher Education at University of California, Berkeley, for all of which I am very grateful.

I said earlier that oral history becomes a text, or set of texts, through the transformative processes of transcription, summarising and indexing. I should like to thank Bridget Cook and Roz Platt for their careful transcriptions, Maggie Lackey for turning my notes into readable summaries, and Angela Gelston for using the NUDIST qualitative data analysis computer package to enter indexing. The use of electronic means of manipulating the oral history transcripts was an experiment well worth undertaking, although my advice to anyone thinking about it is to keep it simple, at least in the first instance. The forty-two transcripts used here were in fact indexed twice. The first time, in a flush of enthusiasm at the discovery of this powerful electronic tool, my research associate Nicole Crockett and I indexed in great complexity all that the women said about work

and training, in preparation for writing an end-of-grant report for
the Economic and Social Research Council, which sponsored the
original research. We did more than was needed: three or four
broad categories (such as 'pre-war employment', 'wartime training',
'wartime employment', 'post-war work') would have been more
useful than the sixty-odd fine divisions we made (such as 'wartime
training/government training centres/skills learned' and 'wartime
training/government training centres/skills learned/skills used post-
war'). In order to undertake the interpretative work on which my
reanalysis of the oral histories for this book was based, I indexed the
transcripts again, this time under just fifteen broad headings.[3] The
fine subdivisions and cross-referencing which packages like
NUDIST make possible evolved in my head, from close study of the
transcript extracts in each category. I found it unnecessary to return
to the computer screen to inscribe these connections electronically,
although I acknowledge that in the presence of a bigger data set
than my own forty-two transcripts, to do so might well be helpful.
I used the indexed extracts on each theme for initial analysis, with
the summaries and the original transcripts beside me for reference
as I wrote. I also returned periodically to the spoken word on the
tapes, and consulted my own research notes and diaries and those
of the other two researchers (who had both by now left Lancaster),
in order to understand the tone and inflexion of what was said, and
the circumstances in which it was spoken.

A project like this is of course not a one-person enterprise,
although I take sole responsibility for the particular interpretation
offered in this book.[4] I am indebted to Nicole Crockett and Hilary
Arksey, both of whom were committed researchers, prepared to
undertake long and difficult journeys and to cope with a wide variety of social interactions, in order to interview the women who
agreed to talk about their memories of the 1940s. Above all I want
to thank those women themselves, who by entrusting us with their
personal accounts have enriched both the social history of the
1940s and our understandings of the meaning and significance of
oral history.

This is not a book that I have wanted to finish writing, even
though I know that my partner Oliver Fulton and my children, Sam
and Sarah Easterby-Smith and Chloe Summerfield, all of whom
have been wonderful sources of encouragement throughout, are
glad that I have! The same must be true of Vanessa Graham of

Manchester University Press, whose patience and support I would also like to acknowledge. The satisfaction and sheer pleasure of working with, contextualising and interpreting the oral histories on which the book is based have been enormous. I therefore release it into the public domain with a sense not of finality and closure, but of possibilities yet unrealised. I hope that it will make a difference both to historical conceptualisations of British women in the 1940s, and to the way that oral history is used. I look forward to watching the ripples.

Notes

1 P. Summerfield, 'Education and Politics in the British Armed Forces in the Second World War', *International Review of Social History*, 26, 2 (1981) pp. 133–58.

2 Economic and Social Research Council grant number R000 23 2048, 1990–92, project title 'Gender, Training and Employment 1939–1950, An Historical Analysis'.

3 These headings were: family; work; maturation; then and now; horror; sexuality; marriage; narrative consciousness; uniform and dress; friendship; education; leisure; gender relations; class relations; 'race'. Indexing electronically meant that in order to study what all the interviewees had said about any one of these themes, it was possible to print out all the relevant extracts from every transcript at the touch of a button.

4 The end-of-project report was planned by Nicole Crockett and myself and written up by me after the end of the project: P. Summerfield, 'Gender Training and Employment 1939–1950, An Historical Analysis', Report to the ESRC on Grant Number R000 23 2048, 1992. See also P. Summerfield, 'The Patriarchal Discourse of Human Capital: Training Women for War Work 1939–1945', *Journal of Gender Studies*, 2, 2 (1993), pp. 189–205. For a joint publication on one aspect of the project see P. Summerfield and N. Crockett, '"You Weren't Taught That With the Welding": Lessons in Sexuality in the Second World War', *Women's History Review*, 1, 3 (1992), pp. 435–54.

'Women's Services' (1940–41) by Feliks Topolski

Chapter 1

Gender, memory and the Second World War

Reconstructing Women's Wartime Lives is about women's personal experiences and subjective understandings of the Second World War. It is also about history and spoken memory. The book develops the argument that oral history, that is the telling of life stories in response to a researcher's enquiries,[1] is not a simple one-way process, but involves a set of relationships all of which are pervaded by gender. These include a dialogue between the present and the past, between what is personal and what is public, between memory and culture.

This chapter explores the problematic from which the book developed, and traces a path through four debates. One is about women, war and social change, another concerns personal testimony as a historical source, a third is about the production of memory and the fourth is about gender and memory. The chapter seeks to develop an understanding of memories of wartime as gendered products of an interplay between discourse and subjectivity, and so to establish the conceptual framework within which to explore the reconstruction of women's wartime lives in the rest of the book.

Women, the Second World War and social change

In 1977 I spoke to an adult education group about women's experiences of the Second World War. I had just discovered Mass-Observation's (M-O) 1943 publication *War Factory*, the report of a researcher's participant observation in a factory making radar equipment during the war.[2] Drawing on *War Factory* I suggested that the war did little to alter women's position within the sexual division of labour at work or at home. Contrary to histories of women doing 'men's' skilled work in wartime,[3] I argued that the war heralded an acceleration of the pre-war development of routine, monotonous, low status factory work for women. Rather than taking up war work with patriotic enthusiasm, wartime women endured state direction and were motivated mainly by material concerns. My talk emphasised women workers' alienation from war work, lack of identification with the war effort, and continuity of expectations regarding their private and public relationships with men and the relative position in their lives of home and work.[4]

Two women in the audience took great exception to my account.

They were both working-class women from the midlands in their late fifties or early sixties, who had done war work in the Second World War, one of them in the Armed Forces. They recalled their own desire to join the war effort, their pride in their work and their sense of the war as a special and different period in their lives. Their angry response to my paper was a warning to me that interpreting, and generalising about, women's subjective responses to the war was problematic. Even though I had evidence (the M-O survey) to support my argument, their version was hardly 'wrong': it was true for them, it was their memory of the war. My reaction as a young historian in 1977 was to retreat from trying to interpret women's wartime 'consciousness' directly. I decided instead to explore policy, notably the government's efforts to control the employment of women in wartime, as an alternative way of gauging the extent of wartime change for women, which (I have to admit) would leave me less exposed to contradiction.

This research, first published in 1984 as *Women Workers in the Second World War*, confirmed the absence of the kinds of change which would have profoundly altered gender relations at work or at home. To summarise, the changes in the employment of women during the war involved continuity with pre-war trends. These included the expansion of women's employment in clerical work and in process industries like electrical engineering and food manufacture, and the decline of the traditional areas of women's employment such as the textiles industries and domestic service. Women's wartime access to 'men's work' was extremely limited. The biggest changes were the shift in the profile of women workers to include more older, married women, and the participation of larger numbers of women in regions of Britain like north-east England, where few had previously been employed. The wartime government took very cautious steps to facilitate the recruitment of women workers by alleviating the responsibilities associated with their domestic roles, such as shopping and childcare. The demands of production indicated a need for the development of such policies, but the outcome was constrained by an opposing concern to maintain conventional gender relations and the accompanying distribution of domestic work. Although there was some assistance, for example the provision of wartime nurseries for some of the children of women war workers, most women had to find their own solutions to the problems of combining war work with domestic tasks. Part-time working arrangements, which were enormously extended in the 1950s and 1960s, constituted the main wartime 'solution' to these problems.[5]

Government agencies were constrained to take account of women's attitudes and behaviour in order both to develop the policies that mobilised women for war work, and to maintain the stability and productivity of the (increasingly female) wartime workforce.[6] Material within the official archives brought my study of the development of wartime policies back to the issue of how women experienced, or were perceived to experience, wartime changes. Ministerial channels of information included the Women's Consultative Committee of the Ministry of Labour, on which sat women's representatives such as Members of Parliament, trade union leaders and members of voluntary organisations, and the Wartime Social Survey, which conducted questionnaire surveys for the Central Office of Information. From outside government, Mass Observation, which claimed to have special access to popular feeling, worked to obtain what it regarded as better data, and campaigned to draw it to the attention of the government.[7] Mass Observation's superiority, it claimed, arose from its ability to tap the words of the people it observed, sometimes by recording their overheard conversations, sometimes by direct discussion or interview.

War Factory was just such a piece of research. It was undertaken by a researcher who worked incognito in a factory, and it was written up in a style designed to warn the government and all those concerned with war production of the inefficiencies consequent upon managerial failures to inform and inspire the workforce. On a wider scale M-O's network of observers, panellists and diarists provided intimate and detailed evidence of their own and other people's attitudes and moods, and its archive is rich in such material. In its publications, including *War Factory*, M-O presented the data to the public with a strong authorial hand.[8] The Mass-Observer who collected it, Celia Fremlin, was a young Oxford graduate.[9] In the book, she interpreted the words of the workers she had observed and the effects on the war effort of their behaviour, both from the perspective of her own reactions to factory work and workers, and within the framework of the campaign to enhance the war effort, 'the war to win the war',[10] in which M-O took a leading part. Her book is imbued with her own subjectivity and the political purpose behind the investigation. Had she given a paper based on her research to 'her' factory women, she too might have been contradicted.

The study of wartime policy, then, returned me to the difficulties of accessing and interpreting accounts of women's subjective responses to their wartime experiences. Developments within both feminism and academia in the 1970s and 1980s, made the task increasingly urgent. Interest in women 'speaking for themselves' grew enormously with the feminist rebirth associated with the Women's Liberation Movement of the late 1960s. That movement was in itself largely based on women's collective discoveries of the many ways in which the personal was political. The sharing of experience, and the reinterpretation of that experience in the light of new feminist theories, was of major importance in popularising the movement and sustaining its momentum. This commitment embraced the past as well as the present. Women's personal testimony, whether in written autobiography or in oral history interviews, was seen as a vital part of the recovery of women's hidden history.[11]

Interest encompassed women's experiences of life in the past generally, but the concentration on the twentieth century necessitated by the age of the women available to be interviewed, drew attention to the periods of the two world wars. From the 1970s to the 1990s, there was a persistent if sporadic growth in the publication of women's personal accounts of the war.[12] Interviewing projects were undertaken by groups seeking to present women's history through popular media, such as theatre, television and museum displays, as well as by librarians building up archives, by school and community groups exploring the history of the locality and by academics and students seeking data for research projects and dissertations. These developments were stimulated by the simultaneous growth of oral history, both as a community activity and as a branch of the new social and labour history, committed to 'history from below'.[13]

The profile of the wars was enhanced by expectations, derived from academic and popular historical works that the wars had reduced inequality between British men and women, at least temporarily. Of these accounts, probably the most optimistic about the transformative effects of the war on gender relations, echoed in popular and academic accounts subsequently, were those of Alva Myrdal and Viola Klein, published in the 1950s and 1960s. Myrdal and Klein wrote that during the Second World War 'sex discrimina-

tion in matters of employment almost disappeared' and that there
was a wartime 'reorganization of working conditions to meet the
needs of women workers' which amounted to nothing less than 'a
social revolution'.[14]

The book which Gail Braybon and I wrote together and published in 1987 belonged in the context of the new feminist interest
in women's experiences as a basis for women's history. It drew on
autobiographical and oral history records for its comparison of
women's experiences in the two world wars. It registered the discrepancy between evidence that gender relations were not permanently altered by either war, which was its academic argument,[15]
and personal accounts which emphasised the significance of participation for individual women, from which its title *Out of the Cage*
was drawn. The common theme of this evidence was that the war
offered access to opportunities beyond the sheltered and domestic
ones which women who felt they had been 'let out of the cage' had
hitherto accepted as their lot. Our scepticism about the transformation thesis was shaken by the personal testimony, as (looking back)
the confrontation at the adult education meeting in 1976 suggested
that it would be. But there are two caveats. First, some women said
that although life changed profoundly for them as women during
the war, they did not feel that they became equal with men as a
result of the war. These accounts reconstructed wartime changes in
women's identities which had a positive effect on gender relations
but which did not involve the removal of the gender hierarchy.
Second, not all the personal testimony which we collected suggested
that the war had a transformative effect. On the one hand, some
women said that the war made very little impact on them, or indicated that they were indifferent towards wartime change. These
accounts supported the idea of continuity rather than change (as
M-O's 1943 evidence had done).[16] On the other hand, there were
accounts which intimated that war marked the intensification of
gender differences. In these, women spoke of resisting the wartime
assault on gender roles, and of using the war as an opportunity to
assert conventional femininity.

Testimony of this second kind was used by other historians to
support a stronger argument, about not just the continuity but the
intensification of sex segregation as a result of the war. For example, Harold Smith drew on autobiography and survey reports to
support the view of a commentator at the end of the war that

women 'fervently wish themselves back into their pre-war way of life' at the end of the war. Smith's interpretation of such evidence was that 'the war's most important legacy for women was a strengthening of traditional sex roles rather than the emergence of new roles'.[17] Smith's argument was a social-historical version of J. B. Elshtain's philosophical one, that wars, by creating or enlarging a specific military role for men, have historically polarised rather than equalised gender identities and relations.[18] But as far as women's subjective responses were concerned, this polarisation thesis, as much as either the continuity or the transformation theses, could only be constructed by ignoring some evidence, or by denying read-ings of it which suggested a more ambiguous and contingent picture of women's desires and preferences.[19]

A new project on wartime training and employment which I undertook with a research associate, Nicole Crockett, and a student researcher, Hilary Arksey, in the early 1990s, confirmed the variety of responses women had to the war and the difficulties of interpret-ing them.[20] The objective of this project was to find out whether wartime training made a difference to women's labour market posi-tion during and after the war. Scrutiny of policy records showed that there were strong material reasons, which were urged by mem-bers of training institutions and by women's rights advocates, to train women to high levels of skill to take the place of men. But for-midable interest groups including employers' organisations and trade unions ranged themselves against such a possibility. The Min-istry of Labour and National Service initially dismissed any skills training for women as unnecessary. It came round to the idea of giving women intensive, relatively high-level training due to the growing wartime skills shortage. Then, in response to the difficul-ties of obtaining employment for women at levels appropriate to their training, the ministry reduced training provision for women to brief, general courses in 'machine minding'.[21]

The variety of experiences of wartime training which these shifts in policy and practice indicated were evident in the accounts of the forty-two women interviewed as part of the project. The women were selected from four broad occupational categories of wartime work: manual and non-manual, military and civilian. None of the women who were trained for work defined as 'men's work' in the military (whether manual, such as aircraft maintenance, or non-manual, such as meteorology) experienced continuity of occupation after the war. The work histories of only two of the women who were trained for civilian war jobs which were regarded as 'men's work' revealed changes that outlasted the war. One worked as an engineering draughtswoman (non-manual work) and the other as a gauge-tester (manual work). The draughtswoman felt that she was denied opportunities for which her training equipped her, and withdrew from the labour market on her marriage in 1948. The gauge-tester found that her work had been redefined as 'women's work' when she returned to it two years after the war. Women who received various types of clerical training, in civilian or military settings, on the other hand, experienced more continuity and mobility. Their wartime training, which fitted them for an increasingly feminised area of work, did bestow upon them long-term benefits.[22]

The thesis that wartime changes promoted continuity in gender relations was (once again) supported, this time by scrutiny of a particular aspect of wartime employment policy which had been overlooked in earlier studies, in combination with evidence of personal work histories. But the oral history interviews also constituted a new set of personal testimonies which was more extensive and comparable than the data used by previous historians, including Harold Smith on the one hand, and Braybon and myself on the other.[23] The oral history interviews provided a new opportunity to explore the subjective meanings of the war to women. These data, it appeared, would throw light on the debate about the effects of the Second World War on women's subjective sense of themselves as women, and hence on the issue of how the war affected gender identities and gender relations.

However, the different ways in which women presented their wartime lives within the interviews, and the variety and complexity of the feelings and attitudes revealed, suggested that clear answers would emerge only if the selectivity and denials of previous contributions to the debate were repeated. The experiences of the forty-two women interviewed form the basis of this book, but before we turn to them we must explore further the relationship between personal accounts and historical interpretations. In the next section of this chapter we shall investigate the methodological and theoretical problems of using accounts of experience as the basis for writing about social change.

Personal testimony as a historical source

Denise Riley was probably the first feminist historian to make the problems of using accounts of 'lived experience' explicit. Her analysis led her to abandon the attempt to use personal testimony in the writing of history. She was followed by other leading scholars, including Joan Scott with whom she worked, whose theorising about experience, discourse and agency divided the world of women's history.

Riley developed her methodological and theoretical critique of the use of accounts of personal experience, through, as it happens, her work on wartime and post-war understandings of the mother-child relationship. She undertook this work in the context of the debates among feminists of the 1970s and early 1980s about the route to liberation. Marxist-feminists argued that paid work (even when it was exploitative and alienated) and socialised forms of domestic work, paved the way from the patriarchal oppression of women in the home towards women's equal participation in the class struggle and eventual emancipation as women and as workers. Riley recorded the frustration, incomprehension and use of such concepts as 'collusion' and 'false consciousness' which greeted the absence of evidence that women were seeking paid work and freedom from domesticity.[24] This was especially so for a period like the Second World War, when such 'liberating' changes were apparently within women's reach.[25] Denise Riley confessed that she shared the assumption that the war offered opportunities which women needed and wanted, but that her certainty was shaken when she could not find the history of feminist agitation for nurseries and work which she had expected. As a result she felt herself,

> oscillating between two explanatory models: the one of saying, 'Women really did want to work, they did want nurseries; if we read the responses to these flat questionnaires correctly, we can surely decipher these wishes; or we can uncover the buried evidence of meetings, demonstrations and petitions to reveal their wants.' And the second of saying, 'Well, no wonder women were, on the whole, indifferent: what else, given these political conditions and these circumstances of work, could these women have done in 1945?'[26]

Riley saw the problem initially as one of historical methodology and later as one of theoretical perspective. She posed the question of whether there was a historical method which could be used to dis-

cover 'why and how people produce particular formulations about
what they want'.[27] Her answer was negative. Contemporary
wartime surveys were unreliable because they used loaded questions
which produced ambiguous answers. Riley did not trust personal
accounts, such as autobiographies or oral histories, either.

> The trouble with the attempt to lay bare the red heart of truth beneath
> the discolourations and encrustations of thirty-odd years on, is that it
> assumes a clear space out of which voices can speak – as if, that is,
> ascertaining 'consciousness' stopped at scraping off history. That is
> not, of course, to discredit what people say as such, or to imply that
> considering the expression of wants is pointless. The difficulty is that
> needs and wants are never pure and undetermined in such a way that
> they could be fully revealed, to shine out with an absolute clarity, by
> stripping away a patina of historical postscripts and rewritings.[28]

These ideas led Riley to her later theoretical position, informed by
post-structuralism, on women's history. She (with Joan Scott)
argued against the use of 'women' as a category, the record of whose
experiences might reveal women's consciousness. Instead of working with a taken-for-granted category such as women, at root
defined in essentialist terms based on biology, the object of study
should be the discourses by which, as part of a dynamic process,
such a category was established.[29] Gender, as a constituent of social
relations, as a way of thinking and as a set of social identities, argued
Scott, is constantly constructed and reconstructed by powerful
sources which define women and men and control the parameters
of possibility in their lives.[30]

   This approach deeply upset the world of women's history,
because it sounded like a recipe for abandoning the focus on
women, individually and collectively, which was so central to the
'recovery' of women from and for history in the 1970s. It appeared
to recommend the study of discourses about women, produced by
powerful institutions, rather than women's words and women's
actions themselves.[31] The historiographical tradition of treating
women as the objects of history, operated upon, perceived by and
controlled by those with power, was criticised by advocates of
women's history in the 1970s for its tendency to accept hostile and
belittling accounts of women and to portray them as victims.[32] One
of the objectives of women's history, as we saw in the previous section, was to enable women to speak for themselves. Woman-centred

sources, within which women were subjects rather than objects, would, it was hoped, provide access to the hidden history of women's negotiation and resistance of such subjugating forces. In short, the aim of women's history was to discover women's agency in history. Scott's theoretical position appeared to reject such an endeavour; it seemed to deny agency. The opposition was understandable.

The post-structuralist position may, however, have more to offer those seeking to use personal testimony as a historical source than appears at first sight. The arguments of Scott, Riley and other post-structuralist feminists including Judith Butler rest on the importance of language within social relations. We are dependent upon language for understanding who we are and what we are doing. The meanings within language are cultural constructions collectively generated, historical deposits within the way we think, which constitute the framework within which we act. Judith Butler has written, 'construction is not opposed to agency; it is the necessary scene of agency, the very terms in which agency is articulated and becomes culturally intelligible'.[33]

Women 'speaking for themselves' through personal testimony are using language and so deploying cultural constructions. The debate about experience and agency has hinged on the degree of freedom an individual possesses in constructing her own account of personal experience. Scott's position is that no one's personal testimony represents a truth which is independent of discourse. Historians who base their work on accounts of 'lived experience', claiming that such accounts give access to a social reality apart from the controlling forces of the social relations in which their subjects are implicated, falsely separate discourse and experience: experience cannot exist outside discourse, agency cannot exist independently of language.[34] Applied to the history of women in the Second World War, this means that accounts of lived experience, or in Riley's words of 'consciousness' and 'what people say as such'[35] should not be considered outside the discursive constructions of the aspect of wartime life to which that testimony refers, be it the mother-child relationship, family life, war work, post-war expectations or whatever.

There is surely theoretical space here for the study of the relationship between cultural constructions and consciousness, which could throw considerable light on both. The difficulty Riley defined in 1983 as one of 'scraping off history' and thereby removing the 'discolourations and encrustations' which affect the way people speak about the past, can be redefined. Instead of being halted by the 'patina of historical postscripts and rewritings' which affect memory over time, these layers of meaning can become part of the object of study. Since cultural working and reworking precede and accompany events, as well as continuing after them, cultural constructions form the discursive context not only within which people express and understand what happens to them, but also within which they actually have those experiences. Scott's statements, 'it is not individuals who have experience, but subjects who are constituted through experience' and 'experience is a linguistic event', do not have to foreclose the study of experience, but set a new historical agenda.[36] The objective of the historian working with personal testimony becomes, in the words of Kathleen Canning, 'to untangle the relationships between discourses and experiences by exploring the ways in which subjects mediated or transformed discourses in specific historical settings'.[37]

Important to those endeavouring to redeploy post-structuralist concepts in such ways is the argument that subjectivities are rarely constituted through a single and unified dominant discourse. The Second World War was a period in which, in Britain, unifying discourses of, for example, the collective war effort, wartime national unity and post-war reconstruction were particularly strong. It is possible to imagine that discursive dominance might be greater in a social and political setting such as that of war than at other times, but it seems unlikely it is ever complete, that absolute conformity between the way people think and the discourse is ever achieved. Luisa Passerini suggests that even in a totalitarian political context, where considerable efforts are made by the state to ensure that everyone thinks alike, subordinate as well as dominant discourses feed collective memory. Such proliferation is particularly characteristic of democracies, in which the principles of 'free choice' and 'free speech' (however imperfectly realised) are central to economic and political ideology.[38] Furthermore, discourses may have different meanings for different social groups. In particular gender differentiates discourse. In the Second World War, as we shall see, the war effort, national unity and post-war reconstruction meant different things for men and women, as well as for those of different social class and colonial status.

Feminist scholars who make a special study of subjectivity suggest that subjectivities are formed by conjunctions of numerous differ-entiated discourses, some of which may be subordinate or even sub-versive and which may contain contradictory conceptualisations of identity. This approach, which has been applied to auto/biography rather than oral history, allows subjects some opportunity for selec-tion or rejection of the discursive understandings of themselves and their societies available to them. It seeks to unite, theoretically, dis-course and individual consciousness. The Australian cultural sociol-ogist Bronwyn Davies, for example, proposed that the relationship between women and subjectivity works in the following way: 'When I talk about the experience of being "a woman", I refer to the experience of being assigned to the category female, of being discursively, interactively and structurally positioned as such, and of taking up as one's own those discourses through which one is con-stituted as female'.[39] Davies explored how her own youthful subjec-tivity was formed in relation to powerful romantic narratives of the heroism bestowed on young women through caring. Graham Dawson's work on his subjective relationship as a boy to public con-structions of the 'soldier hero' is a parallel study in the context of constructions of masculinity.[40] Feminist scholars urge, however, that femininity is particularly unstable and problematic. The prolifera-tion and confusion of discourses of femininity makes it especially difficult for women to attach themselves to an identity: 'The dis-courses through which the subject position "woman" is constituted are multiple and contradictory. In striving to successfully constitute herself within her allocated gender category, each woman takes on the desires made relevant within those contradictory discourses. She is however never able to achieve unequivocal success at being a woman'.[41]

As this quotation suggests, feminist scholarship on subjectivity implies that femininity is more fragile than masculinity, which is constituted in less discursively contradictory ways. But studies of masculinity suggest that discourses of masculinity are also fractured and insecure. In particular, it is argued, the alignment of boys and young men with a masculine identity and the power it supposedly bestows is an unstable process, complicated by the effects of social class, race and region.[42] Historians of masculinity have argued that masculine power is constantly reasserted, through a variety of cul-tural forms, because of its volatility. The relative security of mascu-line identities is upheld by the relatively powerful position of men

within their primary social reference groups, at home, at work and
in all-male associations (such as clubs, pubs and trade unions).[43] But
men's dominant position in any of these contexts is not guaranteed.
Paid work, for example, cannot offer secure self-sufficiency, because
of the possibilities of competition from rival groups of workers such
as women, and of unemployment. It is certainly ahistorical and
inaccurate to regard masculinity as 'unrelieved villainy ... unitary,
fixed in time and oppressive in equal degree'.[44] Nevertheless, historians of masculinity agree that an organising principle of the dominant forms of British masculinity in the nineteenth and twentieth
centuries has been the assertion of masculine superiority over the
'other'.[45] 'Others' have included homosexual men, young men, subordinated ethnic groups, children and, routinely, women. The
power of dominant masculinity to define the parameters of identity
and behaviour possible to women, and hence to regulate them, con-
tributes to the special fragility of feminine subjectivities.

In the context of the Second World War, the contradictory character of the discourses constituting 'woman' is particularly visible.
This 'total' war stimulated a rhetoric concerning 'the people', all of
whose efforts had to be mobilised. Within this process, contradictory demands were placed on women. They were required both to
be at home, keeping the home fires burning as they watched and
waited for their menfolk to return from the front, and they were
required to 'do their bit' in the war effort, in a paid or voluntary
capacity. They were expected to be carers and mothers, but they
were also under pressure to be soldiers and workers. There were
demands for women to wear dresses and look feminine, but also to
put on uniforms, the wartime emblems of citizenship, which
restrained the visible signs of feminine difference. They were represented both as loyal citizens and as treacherous subversives.[46]

As far as men were concerned, the war highlighted tensions not
so much within their roles (as was the case for women) but between
the different identities available to men, most obviously, in the context of the intensive military mobilisation of men, between combatants and non-combatants. As well as being discursively constructed,
through, for example, wartime films, popular literature and government policies, feminine identities were assessed from across the
gender boundary which they marked. Various forms of male
approval and disapproval, for example chivalry at one extreme and
harassment at the other, confirmed wartime feminine performances

as appropriate or condemned them as unacceptable. While still acknowledging the greater determining power of masculine constructions of femininity, it is reasonable to suppose that masculine identities have been validated, historically, by women in parallel ways.

Just as it is important to acknowledge that there is not likely to be a single discourse at any one time which directly determines consciousness, so it is the case that as well as drawing upon the available cultural constructions we contribute to them. The idea that there is some sort of feedback loop between personal accounts and discourse is suggested by theorists of popular memory. Graham Dawson, drawing on work by Richard Johnson, maps a 'cultural circuit' between on the one hand private and local and on the other public and national cultural products. He gives the example (usefully for us) of soldiers' stories. Privately and locally told stories of soldiering are not crudely determined by the public and national forms, and can and do influence those cultural productions. But the 'general-public forms', which present stories in more abstract and generalised terms of heroism and national identity than the local variants 'may come to have an apparent life of their own, independent of any particular, concrete historical conditions, constituting a tradition of recognizable public forms that tends both to define and to limit imaginative possibilities'.[47] Thus local and particular accounts cannot escape the conceptual and definitional effects of powerful public representations.

The use of personal testimony in the writing of history, then, is not as theoretically unsound as Riley's 1983 doubts appear to suggest. Nor is the study of 'experience' as valueless as readers of Scott might suppose. However, it is vital to understand personal testimony as inter-subjective in the first of two senses. (We shall explore the second in the next two sections of this chapter.) Personal narratives draw on the generalised subject available in discourse to construct the particular personal subject. It is thus necessary to encompass within oral history analysis and interpretation, not only the voice that speaks for itself, but also the voices that speak to it, the discursive formulations from which understandings are selected and within which accounts are made. We shall explore in the chapters that follow how the multiple discourses concerning women's wartime lives were 'taken up' by women recounting their experiences, and were deployed by them in constituting themselves retrospectively as wartime women. Chapter 2 discusses the tension between the wartime discourse of the young woman as a free agent at the disposal of the state and pre-war discourses of the dutiful daughter of dominant parents, and examines women's application of these constructions to themselves in relation to entering war work. Chapter 3 investigates women's uses of the discourse of the appropriate feminine response to the war effort, divided as this was between the idea of women's heroic engagement in warfare and the image of women stoically enduring the pressures and privations of a war waged by men, well behind the lines. In chapter 4 we explore the interplay between dominant popular constructions of 'true' masculinity in wartime and women's remembered perceptions of the men with whom they worked. Chapter 5 investigates the relevance of the discourse of national unity to women's reconstructions of their relationship with other women. Chapter 6 discusses the uses made of discourses of women and work, by women when tracing their own work histories. Finally chapter 7 looks at discursive constructions of the effects of the Second World War on women, and examines women's take-up of these accounts of war and personal change in their own narratives.

We have established that personal narratives are the products of a relationship between discourse and subjectivity. We have argued that personal testimony is inter-subjective in the sense that a narrator draws on the generalised subject available in discourse to construct the particular personal subject. But the personal accounts collected through oral history are also inter-subjective in other ways. The memory texts on which the book is based are products of relationships between subjects and their audiences, and also between those subjects and the performance models available to them. The next two sections look at the way the processes of eliciting oral histories interact with the production of memory and at the effects of gender on both.

The production of memory: achieving 'composure'

An important aspect of the theory of subjectivity developed by Graham Dawson, and hinted at in Bronwyn Davies' reference to the subject constantly 'striving to successfully constitute herself' within the framework of discourse, concerns the production of memory. Dawson uses the term 'composure' to describe this, playing on the double meaning of the verb 'to compose' to explore the twin processes of creating accounts of experiences and achieving personal composure, or equilibrium, through constituting oneself as the subject of those stories. Composing stories about oneself is 'a cultural practice deeply embedded in everyday life, a creative activity in which everyone engages'.[48] A necessary part of this process is the establishment, within these stories, of an acceptable self. Public memory (or discourse) is not drawn upon indiscriminately in the production of personal memory, 'the story that is actually told is always the one preferred amongst other possible versions'. This is because the purpose of telling is to produce both a coherent narrative, and 'a version of the self which can be lived with in relative psychic comfort, to enable in other words, subjective composure to be achieved'.[49] An important addition to Dawson's useful formulation is the point that, since discourses tend to be multiple, contradictory and fractured, the narrator must also find words for what discourses marginalise or omit.

Approaches which use theories of subjectivity and of 'composure' have made relatively little impact on British oral history, which remains in theory and in practice on the whole wedged in the framework within which it developed in the 1970s. This framework is bounded on one side by a methodological defensiveness provoked by the attacks upon oral history of practitioners of empirical social science. To rebut charges of anecdotalism, a preoccupation with the markers of 'objective' social science, such as sampling techniques, representativeness, validity and the problem of triangulation, characterise British discussions of oral history method.[50] On the other side, British oral history is bounded by its original commitment to 'history from below', to giving a voice to the voiceless, to empowerment and social change.[51] The subjectivity of oral histories is acknowledged as the source of the 'richness' of such data, but, paradoxically, the problems of how to understand and interpret the subjectivities revealed have been much less discussed than the 'validity' of oral accounts of the past as historical data.[52]

Exceptionally in the British context, Alistair Thomson's work on the life stories of Australian veterans of the First World War draws on popular memory theory, particularly the concepts of the 'cultural circuit' and of 'composure', to develop a different approach to understanding the formation of memories from that of traditional British oral historians. Thomson emphasises the interaction

between personal accounts and the 'public legend' of the Anzacs
(soldiers who joined the Australian and New Zealand Army Corps
and fought with the Australian Imperial Force (AIF) in France and
Flanders in the First World War).[53] The 'legend' enabled veterans to
compose stories about themselves which affirmed their self-worth,
through its emphasis on comradeship, endurance, personal worth
and national identity, especially in the context of a shift in 'the
Anzac legend' in the 1970s and 1980s to accommodate the horrors
of the trenches. Memory was stimulated by the appearance of new
audiences interested in the surviving subjects of the legend, for
example companions in old people's homes, children for whom the
First World War was on the school syllabus and oral historians. But,
argues Thomson, the legend also displaced and marginalised some
experiences and understandings in the cause of creating a 'homoge-
neous Anzac identity defined in terms of masculine and national
ideals'.[54] As well as showing that the legend was not a straightfor-
ward product of Anzac soldiers themselves, oral history in Thomson's hands provided an opportunity for veterans to compose
versions of themselves which included these publicly excluded and
marginalised experiences. We shall shortly return to the issue of
composure and discourse in order to read gender into it.

First, though, we need to consider the contribution of psychologists of reminiscence to the understanding of 'composure'. Psychologists agree that ageing and reminiscence (the telling of stories
about the past) are strongly linked. Peter Coleman's special contribution has been to identify two types of reminiscence, or, in
Dawson's language, processes of composure. One involves the 'life
review', in which individuals engage in making sense of and inte-
grating their lives. The review process may make the narrator feel
good, as integration is achieved, or it may provoke distress,
expressed for example in tears, in the inability to stop talking or in
the inability to say anything at all, because it leads to confrontation
of disturbing periods of life and unresolved issues. In contrast, the
second type of reminiscence identified by Coleman, is oriented to
the 'maintenance of self esteem'. This is a different strategy from the
(risky) life review; in it the narrator seeks to maintain a sense of self-
hood by reiterating stories which prove their worth and the value of
the past in their lives. Coleman characterises the two strategies of
composure thus: 'the former task is that of the explorer who in the
face of death tests the validity of a life as it has been lived, the latter

that of the conserver who holds on to well established proofs of worth and value'.[55] Both types of reminiscence are in his view strategies for coping with the losses that are an inevitable part of ageing. Not everyone can use them: for some people the process is too personally painful, the possibilities for guilt and grief are too great; in other cases the process is too inter-personally uncomfortable and the narrator can gain a sense of self-worth only at other people's expense.

In an oral history project like ours, as opposed to the kind of incidental reminiscence to which Coleman refers, it is quite unlikely that narrators would be at either of the extremes indicated above, because of the process of self-selection which had taken place prior to the interview. Our interviewees had initially responded to the piece we placed in the magazine by writing to us, indicating that they had memories of wartime work and training which they wanted to share. Those we contacted with a view to arranging an interview could change their minds about participating: when it came to making final arrangements several were simply 'not available'. However, even within the interview group it was possible to identify the two types of reminiscence. Those evidently involved in the process of life review (for example Mary Mackenzie and Caroline Woodward, whom we shall meet in the next chapter) were engaged in a struggle with memory. They were visibly and audibly trying to work out whether what they did during the war, in relation to, for example, their parents and their choice of war work, was right, and to resolve any pain which those memories caused them. Narratives oriented to the maintenance of self-esteem differed in two ways. Either they were more assured, as in the case of some of the 'heroes' whom we shall meet in chapters 3 and 4, such as Ann Tomlinson and Felicity Snow, who told 'epic' war work stories of triumphing against the odds. Alternatively they were more guarded, as in the cases of some of those, such as Peggy Peters who appears in chapter 5, who did not open up in response to our invitations to reflect upon their wartime experiences, but preferred to reiterate a version that evidently satisfied them.

Coleman's typology is undoubtedly useful. However, it may be misleading to regard its categories as watertight, in the sense of suggesting that an interviewee consistently occupies one or other of its subject positions. Some interviewees moved between them, depending on which part of their lives they were talking about and whether they had talked about it before. Notably, some of the women who drew on the idea of women's heroic war contribution composed stories about their wartime selves which clearly constituted proofs of 'worth and value' and maintained their self-esteem. But when talking about the late 1940s and 1950s the same women appeared to be less certain about which public discourse to use in relating their personal experiences, and more anxious in general about the validity of this part of their lives.[56] The presence of an interviewer asking questions which prompted them to move from a 'safe' to a less safe part of their life history, rather than simply to reminisce, was crucial. We need now to consider, therefore, the issue of audience.

Coleman and Dawson both argue that the real or imagined audience for reminiscence and for everyday stories is vital to the effort to achieve subjective composure. This is at the heart of the second definition of the inter-subjectivity of oral history that I shall use here. The process of the production of memory stories is always dialogic or inter-subjective in the sense that it is the product of a relationship between a narrator and a recipient subject, an audience. Coleman says simply 'there is an interplay between what people are able to tell about their lives and what they perceive to be of interest to their audience'.[57] Dawson elaborates further. Subjective composure depends upon social recognition, which provides confirmation that the 'self and world figured in a narrative' are not completely socially disconnected, are not fantasies that exist only in the mind of the narrator, but belong within 'shared, collective identities and realities'.[58] Audiences, or publics, vary. Hence 'the social recognition offered within any specific public will be intimately related to the cultural values that it holds in common, and exercises a determining influence upon the way a narrative may be told and, therefore, upon the kind of composure that it makes possible'.[59]

Dawson's formulation relates to the everyday production of narratives about the self, but it is highly relevant to oral history in which stories which reconstruct large parts of a person's past life are told. The audience for such stories is not a casually composed private one, of family and friends, but is public and research-oriented, whether the researchers are local schoolchildren, community oral historians or university academics whose work has a national and international reach.

The specific composition of the oral history audience, then, has salience for the oral histories collected. It is therefore appropriate to describe briefly the identities and values of the three researchers involved in the project on which this book is based. We were aged between 30 and 40, and were at various stages of academic life. Hilary, a mature student, was undertaking the project as part of her B.A. degree in Independent Studies. Nicole, who had just successfully completed her Ph.D. in History and Sociology, was employed as a Research Associate. I was at the time a Senior Lecturer and Co-Director of Women's Studies. In our everyday interactions we all drew on the language of post-1970s feminism, in relation for example to women's rights to equal opportunities at work and to resist oppressive behaviour from men wherever it might occur. Moreover, the academic work specific to each of us was informed by feminist concerns and concepts. Hilary's other project work included a study of the feminisation of clerical work and an exploration of sexual harassment in the office.[60] Nicole's thesis was on the distribution of power within nineteenth-century Scottish households, in relation to women's positions within the industrial workforce.[61] I have already described the part of my own intellectual biography which relates to studies of the effects of the Second World War on gender relations.

We all went into the interviews committed to, in Katherine Anderson's words, enabling women to 'tell their own stories as fully, completely and honestly as they desire'.[62] We had our own agreed agenda, defined by the research proposal for which the grant was awarded: we had to find out what jobs and training the women had done before, during and after the war. We took with us an interview schedule on small cards, consisting of some direct questions and numerous prompts, to which we added freely in dialogue with our interviewees. We hoped and expected that women would be able to talk within this framework, about what really mattered to them in their wartime pasts. We tried to present ourselves as open, friendly, relaxed, non-hierarchical and nice-to-talk-to.[63] Each of us bore markers of other identities (for example I was eight months pregnant when we started interviewing in September 1991, Hilary had been an office worker and teacher of secretarial skills before becoming a university student, Nicole had strong non-academic interests in film, television and journalism). All three of us were white and heterosexual. We inevitably carried with us the discursive orientations of the academic context in which we were working: indeed, they were announced by the Lancaster University letterhead which we used to confirm the interview arrangements and to thank the participants afterwards. As we shall see in later chapters, some of the interviewees referred to our subject positions, emphasising aspects of their own subjectivities in relation to them.

Just as we were, inevitably, actively constructing identities for ourselves in conducting each interview, so too our interviewees were devising appropriate performances in their meetings with us. Kristina Minister argues that the oral history interview occupies a position at the interface of the private and the public. It is ostensibly private in that it is usually one-to-one and takes place in the respondent's own home, or some other place where interviewer and interviewee can meet by themselves. But even though it is thus set up as an occasion for intimate exchanges, Minister argues that interviewees 'make the inference' that what is expected of them is 'a public performance ... for a ghostly audience'.[64] They are under pressure, after all, to perform for a stranger as a narrative subject, to constitute themselves orally, as Marie-Françoise Chanfrault-Duchet puts it, 'as the subject and hero of a narrative aiming to communicate an experience laden with signification'.[65] Our interviewees' assumption that they were delivering their stories into the public domain was indicated in part by the preparations they had made, and in part by the way they spoke. There was evidence that respondents had tidied and cleaned the parts of the house used for the interview, that they had dressed smartly as if for a relatively formal occasion, and most of them had prepared refreshments. Hilary kept a record of everything she was offered during her seven interviews. They included: tea or coffee, chocolate brownies, shortbread biscuits topped with pink sugar; tea, Rich Tea biscuits; lunch of salmon pâté and toast, bran biscuits and cheese, chocolate cake and coffee; lunch of quiche and salad (apologies for no wine); coffee and chocolate biscuits and a sandwich; lunch of meat salad, dessert (lemon mousse and cream) and grape juice; cup of tea.[66]

Our interviewees commonly revealed their awareness of the hidden requirement that they become the narrative subject of the oral history interview, in expressions of anxiety about their ability to produce a coherent autobiographical account of relevance to our project. Comments like 'I don't think I've anything very interesting to say' and lack of confidence about being able to remember were common. Some interviewees seemed at first committed to giving a public account, taking care for instance over technical terms and referring in formal ways, which they dropped as they relaxed, to close relatives and friends. Others indicated their hesitancy about becoming a narrative subject, by waiting to be asked rather than offering their own contributions. Many interviewees checked out the relevance of what they found themselves wanting to say as they went along, by asking questions like 'You don't want to hear this?', 'Haven't you heard enough?', 'I don't know if this is of any interest?'[67] They were, of course, encouraged by the interviewer to continue. Some had prepared notes or found photos, certificates and other memorabilia which indicated prior thought about the kind of narrative they wanted to tell. Family chronologies (the relationship of births, deaths and marriages to the course of the war) were readily remembered by most respondents, whereas dates punctuating work histories (for example, starting and finishing war work) were more taxing to respondents' memories. The special efforts which some respondents made to find evidence which related their personal histories to the formal, public calendar were another indicator of their awareness of their relatively public performance.

Gender and the production of memory

We have argued in the previous section that inter-subjectivity, understood as the relationship between the narrator and his or her audience, is a necessary and inescapable part of the production of memory. The social recognition offered by an audience and the degree of continuity between the cultural values of narrator and audience affect the narrative produced. Those working with popular memory theory, such as Dawson and Thomson, and on the psychology of reminiscence, such as Coleman, do not pay particular attention to the ways in which gender may intersect with these processes. Feminist scholars, on the other hand, particularly oral historians, have focused greater and more anxious attention on this type of inter-subjectivity. The feminist understanding of gender as constitutive of social relations in which power is unevenly distributed suggests that gender must affect any social interaction including both the specific relationship between investigator and subject and more general socio-linguistic processes.

Feminist discussion of the first of these two issues, the relationship between the interviewer and the subject, is based on a critique of conventional social science for its tendency to ignore the research relationship, and particularly the subject position of the researcher, in the name of 'objective' research.[68] The feminist argument is informed by the political aim of avoiding the reproduction of relations of domination and subordination, of colonisation and disempowerment, in social research. This requires the conceptualisation of the research relationship as a more equal one, in which interchanges affect both participants. The researcher influences and is influenced by her subjects. In Jennifer Robinson's words, 'an absolutely necessary process of engagement and mutual transformations of subjectivities [accompanies] the process of naming and mapping others'.[69]

Feminist scholars have recognised that the ideal of equality between academic researchers and their subjects is impossible to achieve.[70] The researcher cannot escape her or his institutional position as a representative of 'an arm of a society that wants to collect information about its components, its different processes, and its past'.[71] Feminist oral historians advocate instead ways of mitigating the power imbalance in the relationship, in three main ways: first, by seeing the interview as a sharing of experience; second, by placing themselves in a subjective position within the interview; and third, by giving interviewees some responsibility for the project. The definition of inter-subjectivity used in feminist oral history, then, is an elaboration of the concept of the necessary interplay between narrator and audience used in popular memory theory. It is not a 'given' but has to be achieved. Feminist inter-subjectivity is about the mutual exchange of subject positions through dialogue. There are obviously a number of problems, both practical and epistemological, with such an imperative.

Kristina Minister urges researchers to place 'themselves in a subjective position within the project' and to make sure that 'narrators are free to take some responsibility for the project'.[72] But Minister does not expect completely shared occupation of each position. The researcher herself will make only limited, anecdotal, autobiographical contributions.[73] Indeed, Miriam Zukas has remarked that interviewees are more likely to be interested in who else an interviewer has interviewed and what the research is for than in intimate aspects of her life.[74] Although Mary Stuart gives a moving example of a personal awakening to a part of her own past, as a result of admitting her own subjectivity into the interviewing process, the main purpose of her interviews was still to facilitate the process of 'composure' in the interviewees, rather than in herself.[75] Kristina Minister's suggestions for reducing the power imbalance (such as that the interviewer should adapt her dress style and linguistic performance) seem to be less about levelling the hierarchy than about the interviewer composing a self which enables her to demonstrate some shared values with her respondents, and so to constitute for them a facilitating audience.[76] Respondents' perceptions of researchers are not likely to be of someone 'level' with them, in any case, by virtue of, for example, age, social class, ethnicity, region, education, occupational identity and other markers of difference. The extent to which Minister advocates the participation of respondents in the research project is also in practice limited. The researcher nurtures, assists and validates the narrator's interpretative role, but ultimately the work of interpretation and analysis, and the time and skills necessary to do it, are her own.

There were noticeable differences in the readiness of our interviewees to develop a relationship with the interviewer beyond the frame of the interview. All our interviewees were in their late 60s or older, and all had retired from paid work. But widows and divorcees were on the whole the more hospitable to the researchers, and the keenest to detain us in conversation not necessarily related to the interview, establishing greater intimacy.[77] Married women with husbands at home, especially one with a disabled husband, were the most pressed for time and some (though not all) were inclined to be more businesslike and concentrate only on what they understood the research topic to be. These women's husbands were salient to the development of an inter-subjective relationship within the interview. One or two husbands, when spoken to by the researcher, indicated they had no idea that their wives had 'done anything' during the war, some clearly thought their own experiences more worthwhile recording than their wives', some were present at the interview and monitored or corrected what their wives said, and some were evidently proud of what the interview revealed their wives had done and wanted a record for the family: a photograph, a video, or a copy of the tape or transcript.[78] Other husbands were unseen presences apparently waiting to reclaim their wives from the researcher, referred to by interviewees in hushed tones as restrictive or even oppressive influences on their lives in the past and the present.[79] Husbands' responses were relevant both to

women's behaviour in the interview and to the women's constructions of the war, as a time that was pivotal for most women of this
age group (their median date of birth was 1922), in the transition to
an existence informed by the discourses of home-making which
these husbands symbolically and materially embodied.

Minister recommends that researchers should develop the relationship with their interviewees by arranging several meetings.[80]
Numerous meetings demand the commitment of considerable
resources of time and also money if interviewees live at any distance
from the researcher. The expense of using the method is increased
by the need to produce a transcript of the spoken word, a memory
text, on which to work interpretatively. The funding of the project
on which this book is based did not stretch to more than one interview with each of the forty-two respondents, lasting on average
ninety minutes. We interviewed a diverse group of women, in order
to explore commonalities and differences in experience and feeling,
and as a result the interviewees were scattered across England,
Wales and Scotland. Although the researchers had made contact by
letter and telephone beforehand, and we had thus established rap-
port with our interviewees, we sacrificed the benefits of multiple
meetings for those of the number and diversity of our interviewees.

Feminist oral historians also recommend that interviewers should
encourage openness in their respondents by guaranteeing their
anonymity.[81] Bestowing anonymity is another problematic aspect of
the methodology. It is done to protect respondents from public
recognition, but it contradicts the feminist objective of using oral
history as a vehicle for women to speak for themselves, to gain a
place in history. Most of the interviewees did not take up our offer
of anonymity, suggesting that they expected such public recognition
to follow the interview. But in the process of engaging with their testimony for the purpose of writing this book, I decided to give all our
respondents pseudonyms for reasons to do with my own part in
writing about their pasts. I wanted to protect them from the embar-
rassment which my mediation between their words and 'the public'
might cause. Anonymity screens interviewees from the ultimate
manifestation of the power imbalance in the oral history relationship, the historian's interpretation and reconstruction in the public
form of print of intimate aspects of their lives.

Such issues have been of great concern to feminist oral historians
and, as Mary Stuart has remarked, a 'self righteous tone' often char-

acterises discussions of them.[82] An explanation of this heavy investment in the ethical objectives of feminist oral history is that it is not
simply about commitment to reducing the power imbalance
between researcher and interviewee, but is mainly (and connect-
edly) about facilitating interiority in interviews. We need to return
to the relationship between discourse and the production of
memory to understand this stress on the intimate and the private in
feminist oral history. Is it mere voyeurism, or is it a political
response to the gendered power relations which pervade socio-linguistic exchanges?

Chanfrault-Duchet argues that the interviewer must allow himself or herself to be drawn into the narrative in such a way as to
facilitate the production of 'a narrative focused upon the inner self'
of the respondent, rather than one 'focused upon the social self
viewed in relation to its past'.[83] In this 'real narrative' the interviewee 'has been able to organise her (or his) memory in such a way as
to give it coherence and significance' overcoming 'the communication frame of the interview'. If this does not occur, the interviewer
is at fault for being too deeply 'imprisoned within the framework of
positive sciences'.[84] Thus, notwithstanding her critique of the inap-
propriateness of positivism (that is the deduction of unitary truths
from the collection of objective data) for oral history, Chanfrault-
Duchet, like other feminist oral historians, is oriented to producing
'better' history. The proper tapping of intimate accounts of
women's lives will achieve greater accuracy, truth and authenticity.
It is oral history's mission to release women's 'honest voices'.[85] Oral
history focused on interiority will counter the collection of 'unreliable and invalid information' about women.[86]

These arguments imply that the public framing of the meaning of
experience (the creation of general or public discourse), takes place
within male norms of action and control. Built into them are
notions about gender difference and inequality which locate women
within a particularly disadvantaged subject position. A consequence
of this discursive positioning for popular memory is that women are
a social group whose generation of personal narratives is not perceived by those in control of socio-linguistic processes, at either a
local and particular or a general and national level, as having the
same legitimacy as men's. Furthermore, as we have seen, gender
relations mean that the construction of feminine subjectivity takes
place under special duress. Women are the targets of multiple mes-

sages and are thereby confronted with a confusing range of discursive options within which to try to frame their own experience.[87] In short, if and when women do express themselves, they find it hard to be heard.

This understanding draws on the perception of the anthropologist Shirley Ardener, that women's expression of their experience as women is 'muted' when it differs from dominant, normative constructions of gendered experience. The North American oral historians Anderson and Jack relate this muting to the dialogue of an oral history interview in the following way. Women may talk about their lives from two perspectives, 'one framed in concepts and values that reflect men's dominant position in the culture, and one informed by the more immediate realities of a woman's personal experience'. However, concepts for the expression of experiences which do not 'fit dominant meanings' may not be available, with the result that women may 'mute their own thoughts and feelings when they try to describe their lives in the familiar and publicly acceptable terms of prevailing concepts and conventions'.[88]

The feminist theory of muting can be related to the concept of the 'cultural circuit' in popular memory theory. The muting of women's words implies that within the cultural circuit men's stories are returned more readily to the discursive formulation of popular or collective memory than are women's. This does not mean that popular accounts of, for example, Anzac experiences of the First World War are 'accurate' or 'complete'. As we saw in the previous section, Alistair Thomson's work shows that many aspects of Anzac experience have been 'muted'. But it does mean that Anzac memories in the form of the 'legend' are present in and salient to popular culture in a way that stories of, for example, Australian farm women of the First World War, or for that matter British women's experiences of the war of 1939–45, are not. Women's experiences are, routinely, omitted from public accounts of the construction of national identity through military activity, and hence from accounts of war, which is reproduced as (inevitably) predominantly masculine. Several of the women interviewed as part of our project commented on the amnesia within popular culture about women's wartime contribution. This began during the war with, for example, the omission of a place for the Women's Land Army in the VE Day parades. It continued, we were informed, with the absence of understanding that among the older women of the 1980s and 1990s were those who as young women in the war had, for example, transmitted secret messages or built and repaired aeroplanes.[89] Women's protests in the press on the occasion of the fifty-year commemorations of the D-Day landings in 1994 registered women's annoyance that these occasions for remembrance almost entirely ignored the involvement of women in the events of June 1944.[90]

Thomson, researching the relationship of a legend about men and war to men's memories of their wartime experiences, could frame his account within a 'myth and reality' structure. The legend is the myth and by the right use of oral history individual participants can be helped to 'tell it as it really was'. This framework suggests that 'legends' which deny conflict and celebrate dominant values, for example those concerning nationhood and masculinity, will always be produced about the past. The purpose of oral history is to rescue individuals from the generalising force of legends and expose them for the fabrications that they are. Feminist oral historians who subscribe to 'muting' share this objective. The particular relevance of oral history for giving women a voice grew out of the understanding that, conducted according to male norms rather than with feminist insights, oral history would 'confirm the prevailing ideology of women's lives and rob women of their honest voices'.[91]

However, a simple myth-and-reality approach is in danger of seeking to do what Riley identified as impossible, that is to scrape off the patina of history to get at the red heart of truth. It moves us away from the insights of popular memory theory about the interaction of public and personal accounts. The 'cultural circuit' suggests that personal accounts are in their own ways fictive or constructed, as are public accounts, because they are woven from available ways of understanding which suit the individual in relation to his or her own sense of self, and his or her audience's expectations at the time of telling. As we have seen, not all past experience, particularly women's, has been 'legendised', but there do not have to be legends for there to be discourses which shape and make sense of, or deny, experience.

It is reasonable to suppose that the muting of women by male power is not inevitable and universal, but varies according to social context, both on the scale of political systems and ideologies and in relation to the specific context of the performance of memory.[92] Kristina Minister and the Black oral historian, Gwendolen Etter-Lewis, suggest that women find it particularly hard to turn themselves into narrative subjects because girls and women, and Black people of both sexes, are consistently discouraged from engaging in public speaking performances.[93]

Their point relates to the more formal opportunities for public address, which certainly appear to be dominated by white middle-class males, in Europe and North America. It overlooks, however, the proliferation of performance models for communicating private stories in public settings which are available to women. The most obviously relevant one to our project is the women's magazine, since we advertised for women to write to us about their memories of wartime training and work through a popular women's magazine aimed at the over-60s, *Woman's Weekly*. This magazine frequently requests its readers to write in and encourages a confessional style, implying that the norm in the magazine is to regard any aspect of the private lives of readers as suitable matter for public consumption.[94] In addition women have everyday experience of a variety of public/private interviews. They see interviews on television, hear them on the radio, experience medical interviews, they are interviewed when claiming benefits, applying for further or higher education, for jobs, at confession if they are Catholics, and may have participated in a number of different types of therapeutic interview. The nature and extent of self-exposure in the different interview modes listed above varies, but they all offer models for autobiographical telling. While spoken memory is, as we have argued, discursively constituted, so, too, memory performances are culturally mediated. Women come to oral history interviews with experience of a range of confessional occasions from which they are likely to select a model that seems most appropriate and with which they are most comfortable in the circumstances. In this there is likely to be wide variation.

It was not always the case that interviewer and interviewee shared an understanding about the performance entailed in an oral history interview. Some of our respondents inclined towards the model of the market research interview rather than the confession. There was a single case of a respondent who appeared not to wish to reminisce, and not to constitute herself as a narrative subject. Since our agreed interview style was not compatible with the 'yes/no' answers with which this respondent evidently felt more comfortable, both interviewer and interviewee were left feeling uncomfortable and dissatisfied. Nicole noted on her summary of the interview, 'I found this a particularly difficult interview to conduct. [Eleanor Matthews] found it hard to remember things and found some of my questions very silly'. Since Mrs Matthews' letter spoke warmly of her 'very interesting and worthwhile job feeding our Air Crews' as a cook in the Women's Auxiliary Air Force (WAAF), and ended 'I look forward to hearing from you', it seems reasonable to suppose that the interview was not what she had expected, that there was an inter-subjective clash of values which did not facilitate the process of memory and narration in her case. Fortunately for the project she was the only respondent for whom what we were doing appeared not to make sense.

At the other extreme, at least four of our interviewees had at some time previously experienced oral history interviews. Two of them had appeared in a video recording and two in previously published books, thus they were also aware of the public form which their testimony might eventually take.[95] All four were confident that they had a story of interest to tell and they were relaxed and spoke fluently. Producing their narratives evidently helped maintain their self-esteem, and they were also willing to be reflective. These four women in particular, but also others among our interviewees, had a high level of understanding of the interview's dual purpose, namely to encourage the construction of a private and personal account of wartime experiences, as well as to facilitate a contribution to a public project designed to discover commonalities and differences in women's memories of the war.

The formulations in this chapter, of the relationship between gender, subjectivity, inter-subjectivity and discourse, indicate the approach to oral history which informs this book. They enable us to avoid the trap identified by Riley of assuming that there ever could be 'a clear space out of which voices can speak', and on the other hand they free us from a concern exclusively with discourse. When we collected accounts of women's wartime lives through interviews, the three of us were both asking women to remember various aspects of the war, and inviting recall of the various understandings of a woman's relationship to war occasioned by the discourses in which they were represented at the time and have been since. We also constituted a particular audience for the narratives constructed. Our variable receptivity towards the stories we were told extended degrees of social recognition to our interviewees and encouraged or discouraged the self-composure in which, in composing their narratives, they were engaged. This book explores how both the discursive constructions of experiences that were available during the war and have been since, and the social interactions within the oral history interviews themselves, were being used by those interviewed to understand and explain their wartime subjectivities, and to reconstruct their wartime lives.

Notes

1 For definitions of oral history, see T. Lummis, *Listening to History. The Authenticity of Oral Evidence* (London, Hutchinson Education, 1987), pp. 21–3; S. Caunce, *Oral History and the Local Historian* (London, Longman, 1994), p. 7ff; G. Hitchcock and D. Hughes, *Research and the Teacher. A Qualitative introduction to School-Based Research* (London, Routledge, 1989), pp. 128–9 attempt the most succinct definition: 'Oral history might be said to be the study and investigation of the past by means of personal recollections, memories, evocations, or life stories, where the individuals talk about their experiences, life-styles, attitudes and values to a researcher ... Oral history ... deals specifically with what people say about the past as they have experienced and seen it ... The oral history interview is solicited by the researcher, taking the form of a face-to-face encounter with an individual'.

2 Mass-Observation, *War Factory* (London, Gollanz, 1943). The adult education event was organised by Coventry Workers' Education Association, Trade Union Branch, on 29–30 October 1977, at The Charterhouse, London Road, Coventry.

3 See for example A. Marwick, *Britain in the Century of Total War: War, Peace and Social Change 1900–1967* (London, The Bodley Head, 1968), pp. 291–4.

4 See P. Summerfield, 'Women Workers in the Second World War', *Capital and Class*, 1, 1 (1977), pp. 27–42.

5 Published as P. Summerfield, *Women Workers in the Second World War. Production and Patriarchy in Conflict* (London, Croom Helm, 1984; 2nd ed. Routledge, 1989).

6 According to the Central Statistical Office, in 1939 women formed 26.8% of the total workforce in civilian employment and in 1944 39%. However, the percentages underestimate the proportion of women, since the Central Statistical Office (CSO) counted two part-timers as one worker and did not include domestic servants: CSO, *Fighting with Figures. A Statistical Digest of the Second World War*

(London, HMSO, 1995), p. 38, Table 3.3.

7 P. Summerfield, 'Mass-Observation: Social Research or Social Movement?', *Journal of Contemporary History*, 20, (1985), pp. 439–52.

8 P. Summerfield, 'Mass-Observation on Women at Work in the Second World War', in L. Stanley (ed.), 'En/gendering the Archive: Mass-Observation Among the Women', *Feminist Praxis*, 37 and 38 (1992), pp. 35–49.

9 A. Calder and D. Sheridan, *Speak for Yourself. A Mass-Observation Anthology, 1937–49* (London, Jonathan Cape, 1984), pp. 198–9.

10 A. C. H. Smith, *Paper Voices. The Popular Press and Social Change 1935–1965* (London, Chatto and Windus, 1975).

11 See M. Stuart, 'You're a Big Girl Now: Subjectivities, Oral History and Feminism', *Oral History* (Autumn 1994), p. 56.

12 Collections based on oral history interviews include B. Anderson, *We Just Got On With It. British Women in World War II* (Chippenham, Picton Publishing, 1994); M. Nicholson, *What Did You Do in the War, Mummy? Women in World War II* (London, Chatto and Windus, 1995); K.Price, *What Did You Do in the War, Mam? Women Steelworkers at Consett during the Second World War* (Newcastle upon Tyne, Open University Northern Region, December 1984); P. Schweitzer, L. Hilton and J. Moss (eds) *What Did You Do in the War, Mum?* (London, Age Exchange, 1985). There are also a great many written wartime memoirs by women, some of which have been published and many of which are archived in the Documents Section of the Imperial War Museum in London.

13 The authoritative and comprehensive account of the origins and development of oral history is Paul Thompson's *The Voice of the Past, Oral History* (Oxford, Oxford University Press, 1988; 1st pub. 1978). In the late 1960s and 1970s oral history in Britain had a radical mission, to research the undocumented history of subordinate social groups. A major inspiration for British oral history was that it would unearth a radical working-class political culture and class consciousness. This was paralleled in feminist history by the commitment to discovering a feminist subculture.

14 A. Myrdal and V. Klein, *Women's Two Roles. Home and Work* (London, Routledge and Kegan Paul, 1956; 2nd ed. 1968), pp. 52–4

15 This was consistent with our earlier work: see Summerfield, *Women Workers in the Second World War*; G. Braybon, *Women Workers in the First World War: The British Experience* (London, Croom Helm, 1981).

16 Elizabeth Roberts comes down firmly on the side of the continuity thesis. She emphasises that the war made little or no impact on her oral history respondents in her survey of the period 1940–70. 'The

war itself ... did not figure prominently in the oral evidence'. Most of the men in her sample 'returned to their previous occupations' or never left them, and as far as women were concerned 'the war had only a limited effect on the history of women in the labour market, as almost all of those doing war work lost their jobs at the end of the war; indeed, they expected to do so': E. Roberts, *Women and Families. An Oral History 1940–1970* (Oxford, Blackwell, 1995), pp. 17–18 and 115–16.

17 H. L. Smith, 'The Effect of the War on the Status of Women', in H. L. Smith (ed.), *War and Social Change. British Society in the Second World War* (Manchester, Manchester University Press, 1986), p. 225.

18 J. B. Elshtain, *Women and War* (Brighton, Harvester, 1987).

19 P. Summerfield, 'Women, War and Social Change: Women in Britain in World War II', in A. Marwick (ed.), *Total War and Social Change* (London, Macmillan, 1988), pp. 95–118.

20 Economic and Social Research Council grant number R000 23 2048, 1990–92, project title 'Gender, Training and Employment 1939–1950, An Historical Analysis'.

21 P. Summerfield, 'The Patriarchal Discourse of Human Capital: Training Women for War Work 1939–1945', *Journal of Gender Studies*, 2, 2 (1993), pp. 189–96.

22 *Ibid.*, pp. 196–205.

23 It was more comparable in the sense that a relatively large and diverse sample of women was interviewed using the same set of prompts and questions in a semi-structured format within a few months of each other.

24 D. Riley, *War in the Nursery. Theories of the Child and Mother* (London, Virago, 1983), pp. 191–2.

25 J. Mitchell, *Psychoanalysis and Feminism* (Harmondsworth, Penguin, 1975), pp. 227–8.

26 D. Riley, *War in the Nursery*, pp. 190–1.

27 *Ibid.*, p.190.

28 *Ibid.*, p.191.

29 D. Riley *'Am I That Name?' Feminism and the Category 'Women' in History* (London, Macmillan, 1988).

30 J. W. Scott, 'Gender: A Useful Category of Historical Analysis', in J. W. Scott (ed.), *Feminism and History* (Oxford, Oxford University Press, 1996), pp. 152–80.

31 See, for example, Joan Hoff, 'Gender as a Postmodern Category of Paralysis', *Women's History Review*, 3, 2 (1994), pp. 149–68 and the ensuing debate in *Women's History Review*, 5, 1 (1996). A more measured response, welcoming many aspects of the reconceptualisation of history proposed by Riley and Scott, for instance the focus on the dis-

cursive construction of power and the understanding of politics as the contestation of meaning, came from Catherine Hall. But she, too, had reservations about the disappearance of the subject from history: 'The deconstructionist death of the subject, even a de-centred version, can lead to a loss of any notion of agency. The post-structuralist critique of the old humanist illusion of autonomous individuals acting in the world, together with an insistent emphasis on the categories which allow the construction of identities can, when driven to the limits, result in a curious loss of feeling in historical writing ... Do we really think about ourselves only as subjects interpolated in a discursive field? Is it not also vital to think about the ways in which individuals and groups are able to challenge meanings and establish new inflections which expand the terrain?': C. Hall, 'Politics, Post-Structuralism and Feminist History', *Gender and History*, 3, 2 (1991), pp. 204–10.

32 Examples include S. R. Johansson, '"Herstory" as History: A New Field or Another Fad?', in B. A. Carroll, *Liberating Women's History. Theoretical and Critical Essays* (Chicago, University of Illinois Press, 1976), pp. 401–27, and J. Lewis, 'Women Lost and Found: The Impact of Feminism on History' in D. Spender, *Men's Studies Modified. The Impact of Feminism on the Academic Disciplines* (Oxford, Pergamon Press, 1981), pp. 55–72.

33 J. Butler, *Gender Trouble: Feminism and the Subversion of Identity* (London, Routledge, 1990).

34 Scott's argument with Linda Gordon about Gordon's book *Heroes of Their Own Lives* clarifies her position: see J. W. Scott, *Book Review, of Heroes of Their Own Lives: The Politics and History of Family Violence* (New York, Viking, 1988) by Linda Gordon, and 'Response to Scott' by Linda Gordon, *Signs*, 15, 4 (1990), pp. 848–53. Gordon argued that women who suffered domestic violence in late nineteenth-century New England produced their own narratives of violence, and so found ways of protecting themselves from both abusive men and intrusive welfare workers. Scott claimed that Gordon was saying that only the welfare workers operated within the discursive realm, whereas their clients' words represented a truth independent of discourse, based on lived experience. The women who had suffered violence were subjects whose agency and capacity for resistance were determined within the discursive framework of the welfare agencies concerned. Their words could not represent a 'truth' outside the discourse of scientific rescue. Whatever agency they had was not an attribute of an autonomous individual but a 'discursive effect'. The women beneficiaries of welfare were not free from the constructions of themselves used by welfare workers. They had agency, but not (as Gordon was arguing) independently of the welfare system with which

they were interacting. I am grateful to Pamela Cox for drawing my attention to this debate.

35 Riley, *War in the Nursery*, p. 191

36 J.W. Scott, 'Experience', in J. Butler and J. W. Scott, *Feminists Theorize the Political* (London, Routledge, 1992), pp. 26, 34.

37 K. Canning, 'Feminist History After the Linguistic Turn: Historicizing Discourse and Experience', *Signs: Journal of Women in Culture and Society*, 19, 2 (1994), pp. 373–4. Kathleen Canning describes 'redeploying' post-structuralist concepts in relation to her work on the discourses of social reform and the experiences of female textile workers in late-nineteenth and early twentieth-century Germany, in such a way as to 'rewrite … the notions of agency, subjectivity, and identity'.

38 L. Passerini, 'Introduction', in L. Passerini (ed.), *Memory and Totalitarianism* (Oxford, Oxford University Press, 1992).

39 B. Davies, 'Women's Subjectivity and Feminist Stories', in C.Ellis and M. G. Flaherty, *Investigating Subjectivity. Research on Lived Experience* (London, Sage, 1992), p. 54.

40 G. Dawson, *Soldier Heroes, British Adventure, Empire and the Imagining of Masculinities* (London, Routledge, 1994).

41 Davies, 'Women's Subjectivity and Feminist Stories', p. 55

42 M. Roper and J. Tosh, *Manful Assertions: Masculinities in Britain since 1800* (London, Routledge 1991), pp. 16–18.

43 J. Tosh, 'What Should Historians do with Masculinity? Reflections on Nineteenth-Century Britain', *History Workshop*, 38 (1994), pp. 179–202.

44 Roper and Tosh, *Manful Assertions*, p. 10.

45 *Ibid.*, pp. 1–2.

46 On these contradictory wartime feminine identities, see P. Summerfield, '"The Girl that Makes the Thing that Drills the Hole that Holds the Spring …" Discourses of Women and Work in the Second World War', in C. Gledhill and G. Swanson (eds), *Nationalising Femininity: Culture, Sexuality and the British Cinema in the Second World War* (Manchester, Manchester University Press, 1996). On representations of women as wartime subversives see A. Lant, *Blackout. Reinventing Women for Wartime British Cinema* (Princeton, Princeton University Press, 1991), ch. 2.

47 Dawson, *Soldier Heroes*, p.25.

48 *Ibid.*, p. 22.

49 *Ibid.*, pp. 22–3. Luisa Passerini has a similar argument, suggesting that perception may be complex until the individual settles on one particular perspective and establishes it 'in the niche of memory': Passerini, 'Introduction', in Passerini, *Memory and Totalitarianism*, p. 13.

50 Thompson, *The Voice of the Past*; Lummis, *Listening to History*. See

also Roberts, *Women and Families*, p. 3, where she summarises (while not debating) oral history's assumed vulnerabilities: 'It is not intended to discuss here its potential or its limitations. It is perhaps permissible to observe that all history contains bias, there are omissions, distortions and ambiguities in all primary historical sources, whether they be written or oral. There is also bias in the historian, because he or she has to select material and construct arguments, processes which are inevitably affected by her own experiences and preconceptions as well as by conscious choice.'

51 See for example S. Humphries, *The Handbook of Oral History. Recording Life Stories* (London, Inter-Action Trust, 1984), p. x: 'Most history has been written "from above", from the perspective of the powerful, privileged few. In re-writing history "from below", oral history can create a more accurate and authentic picture of the past. It can give back to people a sense of the historical significance of their own lives and make the practice of history more exciting and available to all.' Examples of oral history work so informed include M. Chamberlain, *Fenwomen: A Portrait of Women in an English Village* (London, Virago, 1975) and *Growing Up in Lambeth* (London, Virago, 1989); A. Davies, *Leisure, Gender and Poverty: Working-Class Culture in Salford and Manchester 1900–1939* (Buckingham, Open University Press, 1992); S. Humphries, *Hooligans or Rebels? An Oral History of Working-Class Childhood and Youth 1889–1939* (Oxford, Blackwell, 1981); E. Roberts, *A Woman's Place. An Oral History of Working-Class Women 1890–1940* (Oxford, Basil Blackwell, 1984); Roberts, *Women and Families*.

52 Feminist oral historians in Britain have made a start, however, notably Stuart, 'You're a Big Girl Now', pp. 55–63. See also J. Bornat, 'Is Oral History Auto/biography?', in *Lives and Works*, a special edition of *Auto/Biography*, 3, 2 (1994), especially p. 27 where she seeks to explain oral historians' omission of explorations of subjectivity. 'Perhaps because we gave ourselves a strongly instrumental, empowering tradition oral historians have found it more difficult to put our own selves into accounts ... We can only benefit from a deeper focus on the self and the personal.' Oral historians in Italy and in North America have taken up these issues. See, for example, A. Portelli, 'The Peculiarities of Oral History', *History Workshop*, 12 (1981), pp. 96–107; J. Sangster, 'Telling our Stories: Feminist Debates and the Use of Oral History' *Women's History Review*, 3, 1 (1994), pp. 5–28, in which she argues 'for a feminist oral history which is enlightened by post-structuralist insights but firmly grounded in a materialist-feminist context'.

53 A. Thomson, *Anzac Memories. Living with the Legend* (Oxford, Oxford University Press Australia, 1994). The purpose of his book is

to expose the public account of the Anzacs as a construction, produced from 'the preconceptions and ideals of its narrators, according to the requirements and constraints of different media, and in relation to the social and political demands of the AIF and Australian society': p. 215.

54 Thomson, *Anzac Memories*, p. 215. Examples of 'sharp' areas of Anzac experience which the legend had rubbed smooth included tensions between officers and men, the post-war disillusionment of many soldiers, and soldiers' understandings of war as big business.

55 P. Coleman, 'Ageing and Life History: The Meaning of Reminiscence in Late Life', in S. Dex (ed.), *Life and Work History Analyses: Qualitative and Quantitative Developments* (London, Routledge, 1991), p. 140.

56 Compare, for example, Ann Tomlinson's account of joining the Women's Royal Naval Service (WRNS) in chapter 3 and her story of the relationship between motherhood and paid work in her life in chapter 6.

57 Coleman, 'Ageing and Life History', p. 121.

58 Dawson, *Soldier Heroes*, p. 23.

59 *Ibid.*

60 Hilary Arksey, 'Black Coat to White Blouse Worker' and 'Respectability in the Office', (B.A. dissertations, Lancaster University, 1992).

61 Nicole Crockett, 'Home at Work: Households and the Structuring of Women's Employment in Late Nineteenth Century Dundee', (unpublished Ph.D. thesis University of Edinburgh, 1991).

62 K. Anderson and D. C. Jack, 'Learning to Listen: Interview Techniques and Analyses', in S. B. Gluck and D. Patai, *Women's Words. The Feminist Practice of Oral History* (London, Routledge, 1991), p. 18.

63 The by now classic argument for such an approach to interviewing is A. Oakley, 'Interviewing Women: A Contradiction in Terms', in H. Roberts (ed.), *Doing Feminist Research* (London, Routledge and Kegan Paul, 1981).

64 K. Minister, 'A Feminist Frame for the Oral History Interview', in Gluck and Patai, *Women's Words* pp. 28, 29.

65 M.-F. Chanfrault-Duchet, 'Narrative Structures, Social Models, and Symbolic Representation in the Life Story', in Gluck and Patai, *Women's Words*, p. 79, note 8.

66 H. Arksey, Project Diary, Gender, Training and Employment ESRC project, Lancaster University, 1991–92 (copy in possession of author).

67 Economic and Social Research Council project R000 23 2048, 'Gender, Training and Employment 1939–1950', interviews: Beryl Bramley (244), Helena Balfour (560), Myrna Wraith (34). The figures

in brackets refer to the text unit numbers added to the transcripts by the computer package (NUDIST) which we used to help index and sort the interviews by theme. Each paragraph of a transcript constituted a text unit. The numbers have been invaluable aids to data retrieval. Henceforth, when referring to interviews I shall cite only the name (pseudonym) of the interviewee and text unit numbers.

68 See, for example, S. Reinharz, *Feminist Methods in Social Research* (Oxford, Oxford University Press, 1992).

69 J. Robinson 'White Women Researching/Representing "Others": From Anti-Apartheid to Post-Colonialism?', in A. Blunt and G. Rose (eds), *Writing Women and Space: Colonial and Postcolonial Geographies* (New York, Guilford Press, 1994).

70 Judith Stacey, 'Can There Be a Feminist Ethnography?', in Gluck and Patai, *Women's Words*, pp. 111–19.

71 Chanfrault-Duchet, 'Narrative Structures, Social Models', p. 78.

72 Minister, 'A Feminist Frame for the Oral History Interview', p. 36.

73 *Ibid.*, pp. 37, 39.

74 M. Zukas 'Friendship as Oral History: A Feminist Psychologist's View', *Oral History*, 21, 2 (1993), p. 78.

75 M. Stuart, '"And How Was It For You, Mary?"': Self, Identity and Meaning for Oral Historians', *Oral History*, 21, 2 (1993), pp. 80–3.

76 The adaptations of personal style could obviously misfire if suspected of being some sort of disguise.

77 Sometimes this led to revelations of pain and suffering which the researcher might not feel equal to dealing with. For instance one interviewee told Hilary prior to the interview about the physical and verbal abuse she had suffered at the hands of her husband and her suspicions that he had abused their daughter. Hilary was so stunned that she avoided all mention of the woman's marriage in the interview, even though the interviewee had brought up the subject unbidden at lunch. Another interviewee described to me her experience of a violent husband fully on tape.

78 Examples included the husbands of Marianne Lloyd, Estelle Armitage and Marion Paul. Mr Paul corrected Marion's terminology, for example interrupting her story about being issued with her uniform in a 'huge room' with 'that would have been the stores' (179). One couple took a photograph of Nicole Crockett in action as interviewer.

79 Beryl Bramley spoke like this about her husband's wish that she should not go into the Forces; Greta Lewis did so about her husband wanting her home from the Forces. In both cases the husbands were sitting in other rooms in the house.

80 Minister, 'A Feminist Frame for the Oral History Interview', p. 36.

81 Gluck and Patai, *Women's Words*, Introduction, p. 4, note 2.

82 Stuart, 'You're a Big Girl Now', p. 61.

83 Chanfrault-Duchet, 'Narrative Structures, Social Models', p. 78.

84 *Ibid.*, p. 91, note 8.

85 Anderson and Jack, 'Learning to Listen', pp. 16–17

86 Minister, 'A Feminist Frame for the Oral History Interview' p. 31.

87 Bronwyn Davies suggests that the discourses of femininity are more contradictory than those of masculinity, quoting Helene Cixous to make her point that women are in a no-win situation as far as achieving an acceptable feminine identity is concerned. Women have 'always occupied the place reserved for the guilty (guilty of everything, guilty of every turn: for having desires, for not having any; for being frigid, for being "too hot"; for not being both at once; for being too motherly and not enough; for having children and for not having any; for nursing and for not nursing …)': Davies,'Women's Subjectivity and Feminist Stories', p. 55.

88 Anderson and Jack, 'Learning to Listen, p. 11. Carolyn Heilbronn is frequently cited as a source of inspiration to biographers to search for stories that lie beyond the 'constraints of acceptable discussion'. See C. Heilbronn, *Writing a Woman's Life* (London, The Women's Press, 1989), p. 30. The Italian philosopher/historian Louisa Passerini is often credited with being the first to urge on oral historians the need to listen for and interpret women's silences and contradictions as part of the endeavour to gain access to the deeper meanings of what women are saying. See S. Geiger, 'What's So Feminist about Women's Oral History?', *Journal of Women's History*, 2, 1 (1990), p. 174.

89 Katharine Hughes, a wireless-telegraphist in the WRNS during the war, said, 'Even my son, I sometimes say something. Well he laughs, "No not you Katie, you couldn't do this, you couldn't do that"' (246) and later 'It's only since the war, when I've read things and I've thought, "Oh God" you know "they don't realise what women did". They're talking about now what the Wrens do, but they don't talk about what the Wrens used to do before.' (330). Helena Balfour, who worked in an aircraft factory during the war, described the reactions of a group of men at a social club to her statement 'I was an aircraft fitter', when she was asked to speak to the members about her wartime experiences. 'Well you see they just all giggled and laughed and I said, you see that's the same reaction that I get from my grandson, from my family, or anybody else that hasn't lived, you know, through these things … I think it irritates me slightly that they think women can't do that kind of job – I drew them up. But you see, I think young people should really find out about these things, you know.' (364, 368)

90 L. Noakes, 'Gender and British National Identity in Wartime: A Study

of the Links Between Gender and National identity in Britain in the Second World War, the Falklands War, and the Gulf War', unpublished D.Phil. thesis, University of Sussex, 1996, pp. 3–5.

91 Anderson and Jack 'Learning to Listen', pp. 16–17.

92 The process of muting, proposed here as part of gender relations, is paralleled in other power relations. The Italian philosopher and historian Luisa Passerini's work on the fascist period in Italy demonstrated the muting effect that political forms could have. Her interviews with Italian political militants revealed that they treated the fascist period as a gap in their lives about which they were unable to speak, while non-political interviewees tended to recall it as a period in which nothing in particular had happened, and which was, for that reason, unworthy of attention. Passerini's interpretation of these different types of 'silence' was that they were produced by the way that 'Fascism ... accentuated the gap between the political sphere and daily private life, thus creating wounds in the tissue of memory, which could not easily recompose what had been forcefully separated': Passerini, 'Introduction', p. 13. Passerini regarded as 'almost derisory' the 'naive claim of oral history in its early decades, to simply give voice to those who had been silenced by history'. Oral historians were deluding themselves if they imagined they could instantly repair those memory wounds: *ibid.*, p. 16.

93 Minister, 'A Feminist Frame for the Oral History Interview', p. 31; G. Etter-Lewis 'Black Women's Life Stories: Reclaiming Self in Narrative Texts', in Gluck and Patai, *Women's Words*, p. 48. (Current usage is to give Black a capital to indicate respect for the claim to Black identity and rejection of racism by people of a wide range of minority ethnicities living in Britain, and I have followed this practice throughout the book.) Minister writes: 'a formidable double bind ties women's tongues in the oral history situation, posing a contradiction between expectations that they will seek out and name their meaningful life experience and that they will do so in a public context'. Analogously men may find it hard to adopt anything but a public performance mode in which they communicate the 'facts' of their meaningful life experiences. I have evidence from an earlier project of a man refusing to talk about anything 'personal', e.g. family background, marriage, children; he understood the interview to be about his school and college education, and he evidently wished to 'compose' only the identity of the academically successful schoolboy and student: P. Summerfield, Oral History of Schooling Project, Joseph Scott Transcript, February 1986, p. 1.

94 We in fact contacted two women's magazines with information about the project, *Woman's Weekly* and *Woman*: see Appendix 1. *Woman's*

Weekly published a letter about our project from Nicole Crockett in its issue of 23 July 1991, on page 3 under the caption 'Lovely to Hear from You'. It produced over 350 replies. *Woman* magazine published a brief announcement of the project, under the caption 'Where Are They Now?' on a double spread headlined 'You and Us'. This produced only four replies. There is a fuller description of the double page spreads on which the letter and the announcement appeared in the respective magazines, and a brief discussion of the reasons for the enormous difference in response, in Appendix 1.

95 Ann Tomlinson and Sadie Bartlett had been interviewed before for other publications; Estelle Armitage and Nadia Beale had appeared in a video recording, *Caribbean Women in World War II*, made by the AV Unit of the London Borough of Hammersmith and Fulham.

Film still from *Millions Like Us*, 1943

Chapter 2

Daughters reconstruct their parents:
mothers, fathers and wartime mobilisation

A life story has to have a starting-point. In our interviews we followed the conventional opening of autobiography, by asking first about birth and parentage. Such a beginning invites the delineation of the subject position of daughter or son prior to any other, and establishes the child's relationship with his or her parents as a theme which may run through the narrative. The women interviewed for this book varied in their responses to our invitation to reconstruct themselves in relation to their parents before talking about their wartime experiences. Some confined themselves to brief details of date and place of birth and parents' occupations, and made only brief references, in response to questions, to the attitudes of their families of origin to their participation in war work. Others repeatedly revisited the theme of their familial relationships, and spoke of them at length, suggesting that it was impossible for them to explain what they had done in the war without setting it in this context. Some of the accounts fitted snugly within identifiable pre-war and wartime discourses of the filial relationship. Other women's constructions of themselves as daughters revealed a complex interplay between rival versions of that relationship. The new identities for young single women which became available in the Second World War heightened, in their accounts, pre-existing ambivalence about, or frustration with, the role of daughter, or stimulated new anxieties. The war sometimes, but not always, featured as the setting for the resolution of these tensions within their filial narratives.

The mobilisation of young women for war had the effect of disrupting the pre-war discourse of the daughter. The 1930s construction of the obedient subject of parental will competed with a wartime discourse of the independent young woman at the disposal of the state. Against the background of military crisis, Blitz and growing labour shortage in 1940 to 1942, the young woman was identified in official policy as a crucial alternative source of labour to that of the five million men conscripted to the Armed Forces, and the boundary between the public and the private was redrawn to include her within the public persona of the war worker. Wartime citizenship for young single women came to mean leaving home if necessary to take up war work of some kind, in industry, civil defence, the women's auxiliary services to the Armed Forces, on the land or in voluntary work.

The young woman was treated in official policy as a mobile unit of female labour, highly desirable in the eyes of the state. Her mobility was defined in contrast to the relative immobility of married women (who were assumed to have husbands to look after) and the complete immobility of mothers of children under 14 (anchored by their maternal responsibilities). From April 1941 women aged 21, later extended downwards to 18 and upwards to 24, were required to register at Employment Exchanges whence they could be directed (with the force of compulsion if necessary) to useful war work. And in December 1941 women aged 20 to 30 could be called up, that is conscripted to the women's military auxiliaries.[1] The forty-two women interviewed were inescapably affected by these regulations and by the expectations of the young woman and her family contained within them. Their median age was 18 in 1940, 23 in 1945. All but two were single in 1941, and none had any children.[2] All but two were living with at least one of their parents in that year, the two married women included. The possibilities for a young single woman to live alone or with friends rather than family in the 1930s were extremely limited.[3]

Although it was trading on the well-established social habit of young women working, the government's decision to apply compulsion to young women represented a considerable intervention into the realm of private life. The government was usurping private decision-making about whether and where to work. The Ministry of Labour and National Service displayed some sensitivity towards the individual young woman, with regard to this expropriation. Instructions to interviewing officers at Employment Exchanges indicated that a process of negotiation was to take place so that each woman would feel 'that she is the last person in the world likely to require compulsion and that she is only too ready to do voluntarily what is in the national interest'.[4] The Employment Exchanges were required to be respectful of women's qualms. However, in dealing directly in this way with young women, they treated them as free agents, contradicting older understandings of a young woman's embedded place within her family.

Some of those advising the government on the recruitment of women had doubts about the wisdom of this construction. For example, Mary Sutherland, Chief Women's Officer of the Labour Party, tried to alert the Ministry of Labour to the idea that a young woman was differently positioned from a young man within the web of family relations. In a letter of September 1941 she wrote, 'It is really very important to get the right publicity, and the right kind of approach to the young women – and their parents – for, whether reasonable or unreasonable, it is just a fact that the general attitude to the "conscription" of women is different from the attitude to the conscription of men. In a question that needs to be handled with great wisdom, the Press has added to the difficulties.'[5]

The gender difference that she pointed out linked 'young women – and their parents'. It referred to customary differences in the authority exercised over boys and girls in a family, and implied that parents were readier to relinquish control of their sons than their daughters to the state. Sutherland wanted the government to confront this issue in an address that acknowledged the conventional relationship of parents and daughters. But the kind of publicity that she wanted was apparently not forthcoming. Parents were evidently expected to include abrogation of the control of daughters among the many wartime sacrifices urged upon them in propaganda posters and government-sponsored films (for example saving rather than spending, making do with short supplies, taking in evacuees, forgoing journeys, etc.), and the press had readily taken up this idea. Indeed, the government had considerable influence upon the media in wartime, particularly on film-makers, over whom they exercised material as well as ideological controls.[6] A parent who tried to prevent his or her daughter leaving home for war work, like Celia's father in the film *Millions Like Us* (1943), was depicted as selfish, unreasonable and cantankerous. The parents of the seven young women who joined the ATS in the film *The Gentle Sex* (1943) were all portrayed as non-obstructive, even if they were allowed some emotional responses, such as sorrow at the moment of separation.[7] The message was simple. The patriotic parent would let a daughter go wherever the state required.

Antonia Lant demonstrates that representations of the more general wartime disintegration of the family, as well as reassurances about its eventual reconstruction, abounded. Before women were 'called up' for war service in 1941, men (some fathers as well as sons) had been conscripted and children evacuated. In filmic constructions of the wartime family, Lant argues, 'absence is simply a condition of war'[8] and the reconstitution of the British nuclear family was presented as war's compensatory objective. In other words, parents had been prepared during the early years of the war for the further disintegration of the family resulting from the departure of their daughters, although in accomplishing this loosening of the framework of the family, government promised to avoid complete destruction by the conservation of the mother as an immovable (officially an 'immobile') cornerstone.

However, as Mary Sutherland indicated, the wartime government's view of the young woman as independent, contradicted other contemporary representations. Penny Tinkler's recent research on girls' magazines from 1920 to 1950 indicates that parental authority over teenage girls and young women was upheld in magazines addressed to all social groups throughout the period. There were some important changes in the depiction of familial relationships, which wove new threads into the fabric of the discourse. Girls' lives were represented as becoming less exclusively domestic: a wider variety of training and careers was opening up, the scope for physical activity was growing, and the idea that marriage should follow training and paid work was gaining ground. Representations of interactions between daughters and parents were also undergoing change: mothers and daughters were depicted as more sisterly and companionate; parental, particularly paternal, styles of authority that involved force and an absence of communication were regarded as old-fashioned. Nevertheless, Tinkler argues that the right and responsiblity of parents to decide what a daughter might do was not questioned and that 'Independence and adventure were unlikely to be consistent with parental expectations of daughters'.[9] Maternal and paternal roles remained highly stereotyped in the magazines. A daughter was expected to assimilate to her mother's domestic role as she grew up. She was depicted as accomplishing the transition particularly rapidly if her mother was absent through illness or death, in which case it was her duty to undertake the full weight of domestic tasks. Fathers were both relatively absent and mostly silent. Their ultimate authority remained absolute. Tinkler writes: 'Both middle-class and working-class fathers were represented in the fiction as the final arbiters of power within the family; they established the rules and regulations of the home, which were administered by their wives.'[10]

As we have seen, in wartime such arrangements were challenged. The state now rivalled the father as the final arbiter of power over members of his family. Mobilisation policy sought to exempt the 18 to 24-year-old woman from 'the rules and regulations of the home' and subject her instead to those of the state. The government was apparently reluctant to address explicitly the potential clash between parental authority and its own, but the issue could not be ignored altogether. The Ministry of Information enlisted the support of magazines such as *Girls' Own Paper* and *Miss Modern* to encourage girls to join the war effort. Tinkler found that stories in these magazines on the theme of mobilisation depicted girls confronting adult resistance to their war participation, suggesting that this was a common experience of readers. But editors did not allow such representations to depict *parental* opposition to daughters' mobilisation, displacing it on to more distant family members such as uncles and aunts. Tinkler writes: 'It seems that these magazines were trying to identify with the problems of their readers and influence the parents of these girls without posing a direct challenge to parental authority or suggesting disrespect of them.'[11]

Cultural constructions of the parent-daughter relationship in the Second World War, then, were adjuncts of the idea of the patriotically disintegrating family. The state required the daughter herself to be freed from the pre-war hold of her identification with her mother's role and responsibilities within the home. The consent of fathers to the abrogation of their authority by the state was assumed. This new construction of familial dynamics, however, rivalled and did not completely replace prior versions of a daughter's duties and her parents' rights and responsibilities towards her.

In the construction of themselves as daughters in their wartime stories, the women interviewed in the 1990s had at their disposal not only these rival wartime understandings, but in addition later challenges to the construction of the daughter as dutiful and domestic. The youthful rebellions of the 1960s challenged authority in general, particularly parental authority, and generated a language of independence from the family.[12] The feminist movement of the 1970s carried with it a critique specifically of the domestic mother who passed on her own oppression to her daughter.[13] Thirty-six of the forty-two women interviewed became mothers themselves during or after the war, and had therefore had experience of devising their own parental performances. They did so in the context of the strengthening of some of the earlier trends identified by Tinkler, such as the emphasis on companionate mother-daughter relationships, the growing unacceptability of the use of physical sanctions by parents against children, and the expectation that fathers should, while retaining their authority, become more approachable and communicative. What is more, the period from the 1940s to the present day has seen a huge popularisation of the ideas of Freud and post-Freudians such as Melanie Klein, concerning the significance of childhood experiences in the formation of a person's psyche. The idea that the ways in which parents care for their children, and affirm or deny their desires and capacities, have an enormous effect on the sort of person that child becomes, underpins not only many forms of therapy, but everyday ways of thinking about the self.[14] Initiating interviews by asking about parents, suggested (albeit inexplicitly) the therapeutic possibilities commonly understood to be inherent in a discussion of childhood, as well as tapping into the variety of discursive constructions of the daughter-parent relationship outlined above.

Free agents

The construction of the self as the free agent of wartime employment policy was a discourse which some of the women interviewed readily took up as their own. In marked contrast to the idea of young women being deeply embedded within their families, the 'free agents' represented themselves as individuals who were almost completely detached from their parents.

For example, Ann Tomlinson described making her own decisions after leaving school. Her father, a bank manager, believed that girls should have a good education and wanted his four daughters to become medical doctors, but on leaving school in 1938 with the qualifications for university entry, Ann was undecided about what she did want to do. Aware of the unstable international situation she deferred her university place, took a shorthand and typing course while living with an aunt in Edinburgh, and then worked as a secretary first for the Observer Corps and then in London for the BBC. A sister suggested that she should join the WAAF as a barrage balloon operator but Ann recalled rejecting the suggestion: 'I didn't want to be a uniformed person like everybody else, in a regiment of women. I wanted to be an individual and do my own thing.'[15] In 1942, however, she changed her mind and joined the WRNS.

Asked what her parents thought about this succession of decisions between the ages of 18 and 21, Ann was dismissive. She explained that her mother (who was 56 in 1942) 'was elderly and not very well. She had arthritis very very badly. They were retired. They were rather remote from me, because I had run my own life after leaving school in a big way, and they were not really into giving me advice about things. They accepted what I did and I think probably weren't particularly surprised that I would want to do these various things'.[16] The language Ann used to describe herself as a young adult, 'I wanted to ... *do my own thing*', 'they were not *into* giving advice' was the language of youthful independence of the 1960s and 1970s, with which she assumed the interviewer would be in tune. It was as if these concepts gave expression to Ann's quest for independence in a way that language of the 1940s could not have done.[17]

Another interviewee who registered detachment from her parents, reflected on her emotional distance from them more explicitly. Barbara Wilson depicted herself as an unwanted appendage to the family, about whom everyone was at a loss. As the fifth child who arrived seven years after her nearest sibling, when her mother 'thought she had finished', Barbara believed that her birth was 'a great mistake'.[18] She was sent to boarding school but, unlike Ann, described herself as rather a failure there, achieving School Certificate only at the second attempt. Back at home she drifted into secretarial training and art classes, following which in desperation her parents sent her to Kingston Technical College to study art: 'nobody knew what to do with me'.[19] But the college course was a turning-point in Barbara's account, in that she now started to decide what she wanted for herself, namely a qualification: 'to train for something, not just do like a finishing course'.[20] She embarked on a course on interior design, but her new-laid plans were shattered by the call-up in 1942, when she was 19. As a middle-class young woman, she decided that she would have to join the WRNS, the most socially select of the available options, and quickly volunteered (since the WRNS did not take conscripts). Barbara spoke of her family taking very little interest in this process. After all, nobody had known what to do with her and now the state was relieving them of their responsibilities. But her parents were tolerant rather than rejecting: 'the family never stopped me. Our family wouldn't have stopped us doing anything we wanted to do I think'.[21]

These women were from relatively well-off middle-class backgrounds. But class alone evidently did not endow women with a sense of independence. Among the women who spoke of themselves as 'free agents', there were also women from working-class and lower middle-class families, who grew up under greater economic duress. Some of them were the daughters of widowed parents. For example, Ivy Jones' father, a cellarman and at one time a publican in Cardiff, was frequently unemployed in the 1930s, and died in 1943. The family required Ivy to get a job as soon as she left school at 16 in 1939. But Ivy said that she made decisions about her future with little reference to her family after her father's death. She was distant from her mother, 'I probably didn't really understand how she was feeling at the time'. Ivy explained her mother's ready acceptance of her decision to join the WAAF in terms of reducing pressure on the household: 'we were pretty crowded at home anyway'.[22]

It might seem hardly surprising that daughters such as Ivy, required to be economically self-sufficient from their teens, recalled making decisions about their wartime jobs without reference to their widowed fathers or mothers. However, their accounts were at odds with contemporary popular magazines' constructions of the responsibilities to the household of daughters of lone parents. As we shall see shortly, they were also markedly different from the accounts of other women in the sample who had grown up in similar circumstances. A possible explanatory factor is education. All the women who depicted themselves as 'free agents' had been to academic schools for girls, even though the daughters of single parents had been constrained to leave school before fulfilling their educational ambitions. The alternative discourses of femininity available in academic girls' schools contributed to, without completely endorsing, the identity of the independent woman. Such schools did not wholly reject the domestic role, but headmistresses of girls' high schools cautiously encouraged the kind of independence needed for academic success and the passage to higher education and professional status.[23] More emphatically, in fiction and biography, inter-war feminists such as Virginia Woolf, Vera Brittain and Winifred Holtby deplored the subordination of intellectually aspiring young women to domestic demands, and celebrated their liberation from them.[24] The identity of the independent and self-sufficient person was available to the relatively well-educated (and academically successful) young woman. The ideology of the educated woman does not, however, entirely explain these subjectivities. We shall meet other women from similar educational backgrounds who recon-

structed their youthful relationships with their parents in terms
more consistent with the conventional construction of parental
authority.

Supportive parents

The women whose stories we have considered so far depicted themselves as untrammelled by their families in their decisions about war
work. There were also women who spoke of their families' greater
involvement in the process by which they put themselves at the disposal of the state. Some of these accounts revealed families which
not only offered no resistance to daughters' participation, but
actively encouraged them to join up, as the patriotic thing to do.
The portrayal of parents in these accounts converged with official
constructions in films such as *The Gentle Sex*, of familial support for
the state's bid for daughters to be at its disposal.

These women remembered unity between themselves and their
parents over discontinuing their current work or training, and leaving home if need be, to join the war effort. Their narratives are characterised by an emphasis on the involvement of other members of
the family, notably mothers and brothers, in the war effort. Their
families were self-conscious about their own identities and had a
strong sense of agency, and their values were consistent with those
of the wartime state. For example, Marianne Lloyd characterised
her family as 'strong minded, individual ... a good strong Welsh
influence'.[25] The manifestation of a family tradition of enterprise
and determination in the children was applauded, rather than being
seen as a threat to parental authority.

Her mother, a factory worker in Birmingham in the 1920s and
1930s, herself took up war work, becoming a welder. Her father, a
window cleaner, had been frequently unemployed between the wars
and was suffering from the early stages of muscular dystrophy in the
war years. It was vital that all members of the family earned their
keep. But although Marianne's parents had already paid for her
office training after she left school at 14, they supported her
wartime departure from the office to train as a draughtswoman.
Economically the family would not be worse off, since Marianne
earned as much, even while at the Government Training Centre, as
she had as a secretary. But family support went further than this.
Marianne related her choice of draughtsmanship to her father's

love of drawing and described her parents (as well as her fiancé) actively helping her through the demanding training course.[26]

Pam Wootton's account also emphasised parental support for her choices, and in addition gave a greater place to patriotism within the family as a motivator. Her mother, who had taken in outwork such as brush-making in the 1920s and 1930s when times were hard for the family, was doing war work when Pam decided to volunteer for the WRNS in 1942.[27] Pam's mother appears in the account as her role model. Because she was 'working on aircraft parts' Pam felt a growing desire to leave the office where she worked and also have 'something to do with aircraft'.[28] Pam's father, a union official, had earlier encouraged her to stay at her central school to get School Certificate, but he was absent from her account of her choice of war work, which was located in relation to her mother's patriotic contribution, and to the fact that all her brothers were in the Forces. As a young single woman, she, like them, had the option of greater 'mobility' than her mother. She described unanimous family support for her membership of the WRNS.

The educational experiences of this group of women were less consistent than those of the 'free agents'. Only one had a high school education, one attended a central school (which offered an advanced elementary education), another a trade school, a fourth a commercial school for office training and two had simply completed a standard elementary school education. There is little consistency in the social class positions of their fathers either. Their fathers' occupations ranged from farmer to window cleaner. A more important factor is perhaps that most of their mothers did paid work, ranging from café proprietor to factory worker. But rather than class, gender or education being separable as important influences, the strongest common feature of these accounts is their construction of solidaristic families with relatively companionate parents, who supported their daughters' ambitions, and also respectably aligned themselves with the needs of the state in wartime.

Authoritarian parents

The parents of the 'free agents' did not (could not) stop them doing what they wanted in wartime, and 'supportive parents' accepted and supported the idea that their daughters should 'do their bit'. But numerous women recalled quite different interactions with their families over joining the war effort.

Several women who remembered being keen to assume the identity of the mobile woman evoked obstructive parental styles based on polarised patriarchal and matriarchal power. These gendered types of control had special characteristics which were destabilised by wartime pressures in different ways. Fathers were accustomed to dominate both daughters and wives, so as to limit their sphere of activity primarily to the home. Mothers in such households wanted daughters to grow up in their own image, that is primarily home based, obedient to male demands, and subject to their mothers' guidance and control.

Janice Brunton represented her parents in such a way. 'My father said no' was a refrain in her interview, used with reference to all her educational and occupational ambitions after leaving elementary school in Liverpool at the age of 14 in 1936, including her desire to train as a nurse in wartime. Janice believed that her father (a landscape gardener) exercised similar control over her mother 'but there was no question of opposing', 'women in those days seemed to submit to their husbands' views'.[29] In any case, Janice's mother did not want her daughter to leave home either. However, this stasis was disrupted in the war, by Janice's successful (if unwitting) exploitation of a contradiction in her father's position. Patriotism was characteristic of men like him, with conservative views of social life generally (including gender relations). The extension of patriotism to include releasing daughters for war service contradicted his values concerning the patriarchal control of women at home in wartime. In spite of the numerous times her father had thwarted her ambitions, Janice was successful when she made a further bid for freedom in 1941. 'I said could I go in the Air Force and he thought about it and he said yes'.[30]

Janice could not explain this surprising acquiescence. The concealment of his thoughts and feelings was central to her father's authoritarian style. Instead of giving a reason, Janice told a story of her father's reactions to her first appearance home on leave, late one night: 'I can always remember him coming down and he just went like this [feeling the fabric of her uniform] and said "oh that's a nice bit of stuff". He had great tears in his eyes you know. But that was the only way I knew he really had feelings'.[31] It was also the only time in her narrative that he showed her any sort of approval. The story enables one to hazard a reconstruction of Janice's father's decision-making process. Janice was her father's only child. He himself was not in a position to give patriotic service to the state and he had no son to offer. The military position of Britain in the war was at a low point in 1941, and the labour shortage was acute. Mr Brunton therefore reconciled himself to letting go of his hitherto tight control of his daughter. The outcome of his inner tussle over whether to allow her to join the WAAF ('he thought about it and he said yes') was to place patriotism and the needs of the state over his own patriarchal authority. Janice's return in uniform, symbol of both his vicarious patriotism and his personal sacrifice, provoked his unique show of emotion towards her.

Janice was not, however, blessed with complete family approval. The consent given by her father for her departure to the Forces was directly contrary to her mother's expectations that she would remain within the feminine sphere of their home, in part as a buffer to the pressures of life with her patriarchal husband. 'My mother was devastated. I think she cried for three days … because my father was not all that he should have been, drank too much, and I think my mother had built her life around me and knew how much she was going to miss me'.[32] Janice's mother, submissive to her husband's views, did not find a way of using wartime changes to make her own life more satisfying. Mrs Brunton's matriarchal power was undermined by her husband's uncharacteristic permissiveness towards his daughter, unaccompanied by any slackening of his domination of his wife. Janice returned repeatedly in her account to her own guilty satisfaction at making her escape, and her various attempts to make amends to her mother.[33]

In other accounts matriarchal mothers used the war to make their own bids for freedom, while still blocking those of their daughters. Joan Stanton believed that her father, a decorative artist working at a fashionable London store, had terminated her mother's career as a pianist, on marriage, and both parents consistently thwarted her own ambitions. Her parents pushed her into secretarial training, frustrating her ambitions first to become a nurse and later to join the WRNS.[34] Joan's father then evacuated Joan and her mother to Cheltenham, when their London house was bombed in 1940. Joan, living with her mother who continued to stop her joining the Services, was sent to a succession of secretarial jobs by the local Employment Exchange. Joan's mother, on the other hand, succeeded not only in maintaining her control of her daughter ('she rather wanted me under her thumb'), but also in extending her own sphere of action in wartime.[35] Mrs Stanton became a voluntary nurse, which was evidently permissable in the eyes of her husband, as a patriotic and voluntary contribution to the war effort, and so did not upset the patriarchal marriage. Joan, on the other hand, in contrast both to her mother and to Janice Brunton, was not able to exploit the requirements of the wartime state in order to obtain her own preferences, against parental restraint.

Janice, Joan and other women who depicted their families in similar ways, characterised their parents as 'Victorian', drawing on the construction in girls' magazines that such styles of parenting were outdated in the 1930s and 1940s. Their accounts evoke the image of the family in the inter-war novels of Ivy Compton-Burnett, which, as Alison Light comments, 'offer us the family as an anatomy of authoritarianism', a prison in which women, and particularly mothers, were the 'most enthusiastic warders'.[36] In these accounts parents decided the course of their daughters' lives without consulting them, and the daughters were powerless to resist. Janice encapsulated this in her statement: 'I suppose the training we received when I was young – you accepted what your parents – even if you didn't agree with it, you accepted what your parents said'.[37]

In other accounts daughters represented themselves as more rebellious than Janice's formulation of filial obedience implied. Some women described successfully eroding their parents' opposition to them leaving home for war work;[38] others depicted open conflict. But in a number of cases daughters were reconciled specifically with fathers because their new roles both appealed to their fathers' patriotism (as in Janice's case) and, when the daughters were doing 'masculine' war work such as flight mechanic or driver, constituted grounds for a new rapprochement between father and daughter. For example Heather McLaren's Glaswegian working-class parents both opposed her going into the WAAF: 'they just didn't like the idea of me being away in the Services, away from home'.[39] Heather eventually volunteered for the WAAF without telling them, presenting them with a *fait accompli* about which they were extremely disapproving. But as with Janice, so with Heather, her appearance at home in uniform appealed to her father's patriotism, 'he was as proud as punch then … he was telling everyone what I was doing' which was initially crewing a barrage balloon.

Later, when Heather was training to be a flight mechanic, her father
(himself a railway carriage builder) contributed a new tool to her
tool kit every time she came home on leave.[40] Basking in his new
interest in her, Heather (who described herself as 'the black sheep'
of the family) could afford to ignore her mother's continuing
doubts about her departure.

A daughter's wartime bid for paternal approval was not always
successful, however. Beryl Bramley was the daughter of a controlling father, a chemist who worked for the Bleachers' Association,
and a distant mother who had never done paid work.[41] Beryl's
authoritarian father approved of educational opportunities for girls,
and sent her to a prestigious academic school, but was deeply disappointed with her inability to live up to his academic expectations.
She failed School Certificate because she could not pass the mathe-
matics component, 'he could not understand why his daughter was
so stupid' and he was 'appalled' by her subsequent choice of hairdressing as a job (even though she trained at a high-class establishment).[42] In the early stages of the war he found her a clerical job at
the factory he was now managing, but she moved voluntarily to
work as a riveter on the shop floor, and then persuaded her parents
to let her leave home to train for the Aeronautical Inspectorate. The
technical training demanded hard work, and Beryl was delighted to
find that she was successful. 'I actually got 92 per cent and that was
from the whole school ... and I was so proud of myself. I remember
when I told my father, I couldn't stop telling him because I never
had anything more than about 75 before'. He does not appear to
have responded warmly, however: 'He was very quiet, but ... he
just, I mean if he spoke to you, you fell through the floor, that sort
of person. You know, you were so thrilled that he'd condescended
to say anything to you of any interest'.[43] Beryl's war work did not
produce the rapprochement with her father that she evidently
desired, and her narrative continued to emphasise his critical stance
towards her and her inability to penetrate his reserve.[44]

The emphasis on a father's approval of a daughter's war work
could leave, as we have seen in the case of Janice Brunton, a disappointed mother in the shadows of the account.[45] Fathers on the
whole exercised the dominant influence (extending even from the
grave in one case[46]), over what a daughter should do in wartime,
consistent with contemporary constructions of fathers as 'the final
arbiters of power within the family'.[47] Such accounts poignantly

evoked the precarious sources of matriarchal power in marriages based on conventional ('Victorian') gender divisions. Mothers' power was both considerable and fragile, because of its contingent character. It was considerable in orienting the upbringing of daughters towards the reproduction of wifely and maternal roles. But it was contingent upon their husbands' support for this process, and crumbled when husbands withdrew support, as some of them did in response to daughters' insistence upon taking up the alternative identities urged upon young women by the wartime state.

The social class position of parents with these marital and parental styles was diverse, suggesting that they characterised a family culture which crossed class boundaries. The occupations of five of these fathers were working- or upper working-class (for example brick-maker, chief mechanic). Those of the other seven were middle- or lower middle-class (for example senior civil servant, shopkeeper). The patriarchal style of these men required non-working wives, and mothers had either ceased paid work on marriage or their daughters thought they had never been employed. A common characteristic of these restraining families was their completeness as conventional family units. Both parents were alive at the start of the war. Fathers were not unemployed, sick or disabled, and their wives did not 'need' to go out to work. Fathers' masculine identities as heads of families were intact.

Paternal dominance was not incompatible with giving girls an academic education when that was consistent with the class position of the family (as in the cases of Joan Stanton and Beryl Bramley). But these accounts differed from those of the other well-educated and well-off women we have discussed above. The shared experience of these daughters was of parental disapproval of their aspirations and the rejection of their suggestions for specific types of war work. When interviewed in their seventies, these women reviewed with bitterness the denials they had experienced in their teens and twenties, as well as reflecting on the extent to which the war had enabled them to obtain their desires, be they training, jobs or parental approval.

Family solidarity against the state

The emphasis in the accounts of the women discussed so far was on welcoming the new opportunities which the war appeared to offer.[48]

The drama in the stories of authoritarian parents hinged on daughters' triumph or defeat in the family conflict over their participation in the war effort. In contrast, the desires of another group of women were not congruent with the expectations of the state that they would join up, and their parents supported their desire not to do so. The kinds of families they evoked were similar to the authoritarian ones discussed above, in that parents endeavoured to control their daughters' lives. But there were two major differences. First, the daughters of these controlling fathers and mothers did not reconstruct their parents as oppressive. The second difference was that, unlike some of the authoritarian parents discussed above, these families did not accept the construction of daughters' involvement in war work as a patriotic contribution which justified her departure from home. On the contrary, parents and daughters stood united against disruption of family life and relationships implied by the encroachments of the state. This did not mean that these families were in other ways unpatriotic or anti-war. Their values simply did not alter from those of opponents of the conscription of women, which the feminist Labour MP Edith Summerskill critically summarised thus in 1942: 'That women should be afforded the maximum protection and that conscription would interfere with the sanctity of the home'.[49]

Evelyn Mills, for instance, depicted her family as an enclosed world with its own values: 'Mum and Dad were never the type that would go out and leave us or anything like that you know. Their main thing was the family'.[50] This meant among other things that her father, the superintendent of the Council yard of a London borough, exercised uncontested control over his daughters' choice of jobs. He worked with Evelyn against the encroachments of the state both in relation to her schooling (taking her away early) and when she was called up in 1942. She constructed a different position for him in wartime, however, than in 1938 when he defied the educational authorities and found Evelyn a job. He was now on the sidelines, an inevitable consequence of the superordinate power of the state over the father in wartime. Evelyn had to attend her call-up interview at the Employment Exchange alone. All her father could do was to vet the options with which she was presented, take her to the Admiralty and wait while she took a typing test which she failed, and encourage her to accept the offer of a job there as a duplicator operator, because it would mean she did not have to leave home.

This was just what she wanted. Far from the family disappearing from her account once Evelyn had started her war work, as it did in many other cases, 'Dad and Mum' continued to feature, providing her with physical and emotional protection and safety. Dad met her from the underground station, Mum had meals ready for her whether she was working days or nights, and put her to bed in the air raid shelter. Mum and Dad also made sure she obtained her release from the job when she became ill and returned to her old job close to home. Evelyn's interpretation of the considerable parental control she described was of kindly guidance. She spoke approvingly of it, contrasting her acceptance of her parents' authority with the impetuousness of youngsters today.[51] Only the second part of Janice Brunton's statement 'even if you didn't agree with it, you accepted what your parents said' applied to young women like Evelyn. She simply did not recall disagreeing with her parents.

Ethel Singleton hinted that she might have done, but nevertheless described approvingly a family in which her lorry driver father made the crucial decisions about her education, training and paid work. Ethel's parents made her leave school as soon as she was 14 in 1935 in spite of the fact that, as she put it, 'I loved school, I cried when I had to leave'.[52] However, Ethel made it clear that she came to appreciate her parents' alternative view of education. 'My father believed in you learning as much as you can', not from books but from participation in the labour market.[53] Her father paid for his daughter to take training in office skills on leaving school, and then to learn sewing (her mother had been a tailoress before marriage), as part of a deliberate strategy to accumulate what would now be called a portfolio of skills, to maximise her employment opportunities. Like Evelyn Mills' father, Mr Singleton reacted defensively in relation to his daughter when war was declared, advising the 18 year old to 'get close to home'. This prompted her to leave the sewing rooms where she had been working for five years, and take a job her mother found for her as a shop assistant, where the family believed she might be safe from state direction because she was 'in food'.[54] In the event she was not protected from call-up. In 1941 the state broke Ethel's family's control of her career when she 'had to register with the twenties', and reluctantly entered war work in an engineering factory.[55] Ethel felt that up to this point she had been 'sheltered' by her parents, but she now constructed herself as doing the sheltering. On her own at the Employment Exchange she rejected possibilities of working away from home in, for example, the Land Army or nursing because 'my father was working away a lot and mum had two little boys and I thought, you know, it was my duty to stay near as possible to her'.[56] The protectiveness was mutual, in that while Ethel supported her mother in this way, she was well cared for at home during her period as a welder.

In such accounts fathers were patriarchs and mothers were domestic, but daughters did not resent these arrangements or perceive them as conflictual. On the contrary, in their experience such relationships had advantages for young women. The family in which a conventional sexual division of labour and authority appeared to its subjects to operate benignly was a source of support, affection and welcome protection. The wartime state in contrast was a relatively hostile force, anonymous and uncaring, and destructive of these positive bonds. Some historians have argued that a culture of suspicion of state intervention has characterised some sectors of the working class.[57] But the social class profile of the fathers of daughters who gave such accounts was no more consistent than that of restraining authoritarian fathers, ranging from working class (for example lorry driver) to lower middle class (shop keeper) and middle class (naval photographer). Mothers, like those rebelled against in the restraining families, had mostly ceased paid work on marriage. Indeed assumptions about gender relations were similar in both sorts of family. Daughters were allowed, subject to parental approval, educational and work opportunities which were consistent with the family's social position. The daughters concerned were not younger (and therefore arguably in greater need of protection) either. The median date of birth of the daughters in these families was 1921, meaning that they were slightly older than the daughters who resented their authoritarian parents, whose median date of birth was 1922, the same as the 'free agents'. In contrast the daughters of parents who supported their involvement in war work were younger than those in any of these groups. Their median date of birth was 1923/24. The major difference between the resentful and acquiescent daughters of authoritarian parents was that in the accounts of the latter, fathers, although dominant, did not oppress their wives and daughters. On the contrary, the recurrent motif in these reconstructions of family interactions (in sharp contrast to accounts of subordinating fathers) was of the approval and support which fathers gave their daughters, while at the same time determining what they should do with their lives.

Authoritarian lone mothers

There were, on the other hand, families within which mothers rather than fathers dominated. Some women described their mothers as family heads, due to the undermining of their fathers' power by death, desertion, disability or long-term absence. Nationally in 1939, 18,500 or 4 per cent of all ever-married women were widows, and 5,400 or 1.1 per cent of ever-married women were divorced.[58] The numbers with unemployed, invalid or absent husbands were uncounted. In the 1930s and 1940s, as in the 1990s, single parenthood meant in general poverty for women (whatever their social class origins) and their children. As we have seen, the daughter in a household which did not conform to the supposed patriarchal norm of the male breadwinner and domestic wife was constructed in popular magazines as her mother's second-in-command, her main source of support.

Some of the most disturbed and disturbing interviews of the forty-two were with women who recalled the experience of being required to provide such support for a lone mother. The painful process of life review and the use of the interview as a quasi-therapeutic occasion were visibly at work in these women's attempts to reconcile their understandings of a daughter's duty towards her mother with their sense of having been exploited, economically and emotionally. In the two accounts to which I shall refer in depth, such mothers' economic responsibility for their families endowed them with quasi-patriarchal power which overpowered a daughter's scope for independent decision-making. Wartime events worked in one case to neutralise and in the other to intensify a mother's power.

Even though the events of Mary Mackenzie's childhood prefaced her wartime experiences by some years (she was born in 1921), Mary felt an urgent need to relate them in detail before talking about her experiences in the WAAF. In an account almost unbroken by questions or prompts she poured out her story, eventually pausing to dismiss the tears trickling down her face with the statement 'excuse me, I have blocked tear ducts and I start crying every so often'.[59]

Mary Mackenzie's story was of a father who was slowly being paralysed by Parkinson's disease and of a hard-pressed mother. He had ceased to work in 1928, when Mary was 7, and the eleven children including a Down's syndrome daughter were supported by Mary's mother, who made and sold cooked meat products from the family home in Brighton. The family requirements, for example that Mary bought the meat for her mother's business and minced it early every morning, cared for her disabled sister after school, and went to work as soon as she was 14, conflicted with Mary's interest and proficiency in school subjects and activities such as swimming, dancing and singing. Mary commented 'I loved school. I never wanted to leave school, I really really loved school. I was heartbroken when I had to leave'.[60]

Mary's departure from school in 1935 was the consequence of a bitter row with her mother hinging on an apparently trivial event. It concerned the destruction of Mary's swimming cap by her handicapped sister, for which Mary blamed her mother to her face, whereupon her mother exploded: 'You're not going swimming, you're getting a job.'[61] The intense emotion that Mary still felt about the incident suggests a reading of it as deeply significant: the swimming cap symbolised Mary's relative freedom and mobility; Mary's accusation to her mother suggested her anger about the lack of support she received for the activities which represented escape from a constraining home life and which she loved; her mother's fury spoke of her own need to control the clever daughter who might dance or swim away from her. Within three days of the row, Mary's mother had removed her from school, disregarding the forthcoming events in Mary's school life, which included both commitments (performing country dancing) and the celebration of Mary's achievements (receiving a certificate of scholarship).[62] Instead of participating in these events, Mary, at her mother's insistence, worked as an assistant at a local bakery, too ashamed of her abrupt departure from school to take up the offer of a half holiday to collect her certificate.

Mary's narrative was one of shame and loss, emotions which pervaded her account of her relationship with her parents. It was also one of fear and pride. The fear was of failing her mother by becoming unemployed, and the pride was in her success as a supplementary wage earner: 'I mean I was never out of work for a day, from the time I left school until I joined the WAAF'.[63] Mary evoked her

fear in stories such as one of being dismissed from her first job
because a new regulation forbade under-18 year olds from working
the hours required of her. Mary remembered saying to her boss 'I
can't go home. I can't tell my mother that I've got the sack' as a
result of which one of the other bakery assistants found her another
job and took Mary home to explain the situation to her mother.[64]
Maternal approval was required for each job change, as in 'I asked
my mother if I could go and work for [a boarding house keeper]. I
mean I wasn't going to be out of work at all'.[65] Mary's mother gave
approval for local jobs, even though badly paid ones like shop assistant, domestic servant and waitress were all that Mary could get,
given her truncated education. But she turned down Mary's request
to join the Services, which would have meant both low pay and
absence from home.

The turning-point in Mary's narrative, leading to her joining the
WAAF, involved profound family losses, which precipitated the
slackening of her mother's hold upon Mary. In September 1940 the
family home and business was bombed. This disastrous event, which
Mary described in harrowing detail, altered family relationships.
Mary's mother who 'always did everything' suffered from concus-
sion and was suddenly dependent on Mary to find the family somewhere to live, to obtain what compensation she could, and to set up
a new home.[66] Mary found the new role difficult. She did not succeed in obtaining compensation for the business or the family pos-
sessions, all of which were lost. However, having moved her parents
to a house on a new estate with other members of the family living
nearby, she took steps to get right away from the domestic disaster
that home had become. Her account emphasised the deflation of
her mother's authority and the almost complete paralysis of her disabled father: they were both now powerless to stop her. Mary's
'mother wasn't happy' about her joining the WAAF, but her reaction was: '"Well if that's it, you'd better go". And that was it. You
see my father didn't say much at all. He could hardly speak by this
time and he could hardly move'.[67] Mary's reflections on her emotionally self-preserving decision were (like Janice Brunton's) guilty:
'I suppose in a way I was selfish, because I didn't realise just the way
they were' (in other words the incapacitating effect of the bombing,
particularly on her mother).

Nevertheless, the responsibility Mary assumed for the family was
considerable. Her years of financial support as a young woman

worker were extended when she entered the WAAF. She wanted to arrange for the payment of a dependants' allowance to her parents, but when this proved impossible she signed a declaration stating that she would make a voluntary contribution to them which the WAAF deducted from her pay. As a result Mary never received more than half pay while she was in the Service.[68] Even so Mary chastised herself for insouciance in the interview: 'I was just one of the young stupid ones at that time'.[69]

Once Mary had volunteered for the WAAF she was 'away within a week'. As far as her narrative was concerned the sundering from her stressful and demanding home life represented by this departure was complete. In sharp contrast to her initial narrative, tightly bound up with her relationship with her mother, the next part, concentrating on life in the WAAF, was not concerned with her parents at all. Her one brief reference to them evoked the healing power of their patriotic response to her appearance in uniform, in a similar way to Janice Brunton's account of her father's rare show of emotion towards her when she came home on leave. In Mary's story it was her draconian mother whose hard exterior momentarily melted: 'They were very very proud of me, and you know she loved to meet me and see friends walking me down the road and what have you'.[70]

The resentment that Mary felt about her mother's part in shaping her early working life, structured her story of freeing herself from her family's dependence upon her, and putting herself at the disposal of the state. Another similarly emotional account of a hard-pressed mother who exerted decisive control over her daughter's job choices differed from Mary's in that this mother also took charge of her daughter's participation in war work. Caroline Woodward's mother perceived the economic advantage of a daughter going into munitions work, and pre-empted the state's direction of her daughter, to ensure that Caroline got such a job. Caroline found the reconstruction in the interview of the stressful relationship painful, telling a story of rejection and exploitation by a mother whose authority she regarded as absolute. But like Mary, Caroline was insistent that she wanted to continue with her narrative. The story was, for her, a necessary part of her account of doing war work as well as being central to a process of life review that she evidently wanted to undertake, in spite of the distress it caused.[71]

Caroline Woodward's father was intermittently unemployed

between the wars and, as a soldier, was absent in the Second World War. Caroline described Mrs Woodward's perpetual struggle to support her nine children on peacetime doles, low wages and the wartime serviceman's wife's allowance. To ease the family burden, Mrs Woodward had sent the 5-year-old Caroline away from Edinburgh in 1930, to live with her grandparents in Croydon. There she stayed throughout her school years but as soon as she was 14, in 1939, Caroline was required to return to her mother, who found her a succession of jobs. Caroline emphasised that her mother's motives were entirely economic: 'I went into Macvitie's biscuit – well I had to, my mother couldn't – well she didn't have the money to keep us', 'my mum was needing me … moneywise'.[72] Her mother then removed her from the biscuit factory and sent her into domestic service. Breaking down in tears in the interview Caroline said, 'I didn't like that at all', implying that the trigger for her distress was the memory of the abrupt change from the affection of her grandparents to the brusque and instrumental treatment she received from her mother, particularly being dispatched into domestic service. After a break during which she left the room, Caroline insisted on carrying on with the interview. She explained how, after a further job change, her mother decided that she should go into better-paying munitions work lest she was snatched away by the state, and 'put away in the Forces' where she would not be much use to her mother.[73]

Caroline's account reconstructed a mother who saw how the requirements of the state could be used to her own and the family's advantage. She made Caroline volunteer for a job at Fountain Bridge engineering factory where she became a welder: 'my mother said actually you'll get more money there. She was thinking about herself. Aye, I was good to my mother'.[74] Indeed, Caroline remembered fabulous wages of £9 or £10 a week, all of which she handed over to her mother, receiving back just ten shillings (50p) pocket money: 'I was never well off – my mother was!'.[75] Mrs Woodward treated Caroline as if she were the hen that was laying the golden egg, ensuring that 'I got my sleep', although Caroline still had to help in the house and could not go out much.[76] 'I was good to my mother' was a refrain in Caroline's interview. The statement was ironic in that Caroline felt she had no choice but to be 'good' to her. 'I just took it, I never had any quarrels about it'.[77] Caroline was helpless before her mother's will, while simultaneously knowing that her mother did not respect her submissiveness. 'My mother just died two year ago last April. She was 90 and I'd never answered her back in my life', 'I hadn't got enough gumption as my mother would say'.[78] At the same time there was a defensive pride in her account and a reluctance to admit explicitly to the grievance she strongly implied. 'I've not got a grudge, she was a good mother, but you felt sometimes you never had a minute to yourself'.[79] Caroline, like Mary Mackenzie, understood herself not only to be under her mother's authoritarian thumb, but also to be morally bound to her. As the girls' magazines emphasised, a girl's duty was to help her mother through domestic crisis and exigency. To have refused to do so would have been not only personally traumatic, but deeply socially reprehensible.

Supportive lone mothers

The daughters of controlling lone mothers evidently desired both freedom to make their own decisions, and maternal support and approval, while still conforming to the contemporary construction of the 'responsible daughter'. But their relationships with their needy mothers were incompatible with either freedom or approval, at least for as long as mothers were capable of exerting control. Other daughters of lone mothers did not evoke such polarised relationships. Outlining their family circumstances could still be painful, expecially when it involved remembering the death or desertion of their fathers. But rather than finding in the interview an outlet for suppressed hostility towards their mothers, these daughters drew on the model of the 'responsible daughter' who supported her mother within a mutually caring and relatively 'sisterly and companionate' relationship.

For these daughters the war posed the dilemma of how they could sustain the support they wanted to give their mothers, while at the same time responding to the requirements of the wartime state. Some remained at home, taking local civilian work of sufficient importance to the war effort to exempt them from being sent away. For example, Moira Underwood was 31 years old when the war began and had worked as a hairdresser since she was 14, living throughout with her mother who was widowed in 1928. Moira weighed her desire to join the war effort against her need to care for her mother. She explained her special sense of responsibility to her, in relation to a traumatic experience at the age of 8, when Moira witnessed an accident in which she believed her mother to have drowned. Moira subsequently developed a nervous condition. She felt that disagreements between her parents, who evidently had a stormy relationship worsened by her father's chronic gambling, focused on how best to deal with her condition. Mr Underwood died in 1928, following which Moira assumed considerable responsibility for her mother: 'she wasn't very strong and I had to look after her. My sister was at home, but she wasn't very good at looking after my mother – I had to do it!'.[80] In wartime Moira chose to work at a filling factory, Risley Royal Ordnance Factory (ROF), where she campaigned for special travel grants so that train fares did not eat into wages because 'I had my mother as well'.[81] She eventually changed jobs so that she would not have to move her mother nearer Risley when the special travel arrangements came to an end. Moira expressed only concern for her mother. She would not have taken a decision about wartime work which would have involved financial risk or geographical moves.

Other such daughters did not resist when the state called upon them to leave home and serve in the Armed Forces, and were not restrained by their mothers, but (like Mary Mackenzie) these daughters took steps to protect their mothers' standards of living. For example, Kate Lomax's father had deserted the family when Kate was 10, in 1929. Kate evoked him in the interview with a great deal of pain, speaking of being overcome with speechlessness and weeping on the few occasions on which she met him after he had left home. Kate's brothers helped make sure that she could continue her schooling to the age of 16, when she recalled proudly getting a clerical job which enabled her to bring £2 a week home to her mother.[82] On joining the WAAF, she 'signed up' her mother as a dependant with the result that Kate herself received only ten shillings of her pay each week. The rest, including rises resulting from promotion, was sent to her mother, who took jobs when she could as a private nurse. Kate expressed no resentment about being 'good to her mother' in this way, which she presented as entirely voluntary. In the interview she gave expression to her feelings for her mother in a description of her departure for the WAAF on the train. Peeping over the top of the newspaper which concealed her own sorrow, she saw from the train window the tiny figure of her mother, standing at the end of their alley and watching the train as it passed over the bridge, 'with the biggest handkerchief possible, wiping the tears away'.[83] The only regrets that Kate expressed in the interview were that she married and moved away from her mother and her old job at the end of the war.[84]

Conclusion

These intimate glances into family dynamics in the period of the 1920s and 1930s and the war years, focusing on interactions over the specific issue of daughters' contributions to the war effort, suggest some surprising answers to some of the bigger questions raised earlier. They reveal a range of styles of parenting and family cultures, and an interaction in daughters' responses to them with discursive constructions of a daughter's relationship with her parents. To summarise, some daughters found it possible to be the 'free agents' of official policy. Other daughters recall families which conformed to wartime propaganda, in which parents actively supported their daughters' ambitions to join the war effort. In contrast, women who remember a family struggle over this issue reconstructed parents who were in the habit of repressing all their daughters' desires, and of controlling them in an authoritarian style which was being increasingly criticised in popular magazines and literature. Those among them who achieved their own aims remember doing so by co-opting the support of dominant fathers against mothers, whose subordination was, by this process, emphasised. But this was not the only story about authoritarian parents. In another variant of this type of family, daughters and parents stood united against the encroachments of the state upon fathers' power, and daughters spoke approvingly of fathers who were the 'final arbiters' in their families. Daughters of mothers who were heads of families also had more than one tale to tell. Needy mothers were portrayed in popular culture as requiring their daughters' support. But while in some accounts such mothers exercised painfully remembered control and offered little emotional succour in return, in others they were recalled as the subjects not only of daughterly responsibility, but also of mutual affection.

There were no simple determinants. It was not the case that, for example, all middle-class fathers were perceived by their daughters as domineering, or that all lone mothers were oppressive, or that all working-class fathers resisted state intervention. Nor did the age of daughters in wartime determine the way they remember being treated by their parents. Rather, the chapter charts the process by which women's family narratives positioned the self in relation to discursive constructions of wartime possibilities for young women. It reveals what different positions meant for the identity of 'daughter'. While independence was assumed or determinedly pursued by some, continuing dependency within the family was sought by others, and ways of continuing to fulfil daughterly obligations by yet others. The war had no single effect on the place of daughters within familial gender relations, although the discourse of participation put under pressure the conventional position of the protected and passive 'daughter of the house'.

The potential for the interview to become a confessional or therapeutic occasion, in respect of the reconstruction of parents by their daughters, was huge. It was enhanced inter-subjectively, by the commitment of the interviewers to asking not only about what happened, but also about how experiences felt and what they meant to narrators. The appearance of the interviewers as apparently independent women themselves may also have stimulated responses related to that subject position. The extent to which the interview developed as therapy no doubt depended upon the women's willingness, or need, to revisit conflict in their interactions with their parents, and to relive the concomitant anger and guilt. Ultimately, however, parents had a place in these narratives only in as far as they were important for the wartime identities which the women were composing. We shall explore these identities further in the next chapter.

Notes

1 H. M. D. Parker, *Manpower. A Study of War-time Policy and Administration* (London, HMSO, 1957), p. 113. Women were given some choice in theory, in particular between joining the women's auxiliary forces and going into industry, but the Ministry of Labour and National Service in practice exercised considerable direction according to labour supply needs.

2 The two who were married before compulsory war service was introduced were Beryl Bramley, who married in 1940, and Greta Lewis, who married in 1941.

3 The two who were living apart from their parents were Ann Tomlin-

son and Helena Bruce. Ann left home when she was 18 in 1938 and lived in succession with an aunt in Edinburgh, with a vicar and his wife in Humby and with relatives in London, while doing varous different types of training and work. She was evacuated to Shipley on Thames in 1941 and lived in accommodation provided by the British Broadcasting Corporation for which she was by now working as a secretary. Helena was a much more reluctant exile from the family home. She described being 'turfed out' of home and sent into residential domestic service when she was 14, to ease the pressure on her widowed father (29, 89). (Figures in brackets after names of interviewees refer to text unit numbers in the interview transcripts.)

4 Public Record Office (PRO) Lab 26/130, WCC5, Draft Instruction to Interviewers, 4 April 1941. Employment Exchange officers were told, nevertheless, that it was 'an advantage if a girl attends for interview with an open mind and without preconceived ideas based on rather bare information as to the type of work she wants'. See PRO Lab 26/130, WCC14, May 1941.

5 PRO Lab 26/130 WCC, 'Additional points raised by Miss Sutherland' for consideration at meeting on 13 September 1941.

6 See S. Harper, 'The Years of Total War: Propaganda and Entertainment', in C. Gledhill and G. Swanson (eds), *Nationalising Femininity: Culture, Sexuality and the British Cinema in the Second World War* (Manchester, Manchester University Press, 1996), pp. 192–3. 'On the one hand, it [the Ministry of Information] could exert influence on film producers by controlling supplies of film stock, and by releasing stars and key technicians from military service. On the other hand, it effectively subsidised compliant producers by giving them administrative and practical support. The Ministry of Information (MOI) also established an "Ideas Committee" which organised informal discussions between its own personnel and hand-picked directors and scriptwriters co-opted from the Screenwriters' Association. The Ideas Committee discussed topics which were aligned to government propaganda policy; and as far as is known, all the committee members were male'.

7 For a discussion of these films see A. Lant, *Blackout. Reinventing Women for Wartime British Cinema* (Princeton, Princeton University Press, 1991), pp. 89–113; J.Thumim, 'The Female Audience: Mobile Women and Married Ladies', in Gledhill and Swanson, *Nationalising Femininity*, pp. 240–4.

8 Lant, *Blackout*, p. 47.

9 Tinkler, *Constructing Girlhood. Popular Magazines for Girls Growing Up in England 1920–1950* (London, Taylor and Francis, 1995), p. 121.

10 *Ibid.*

11 *Ibid.*, p.109

12 See, for example, D. Cooper, *The Death of the Family* (Harmondsworth, Penguin Books, 1971).

13 N. Friday, *My Mother Myself. The Daughter's Search for Identity* (London, Fontana, 1979, 1st pub. in the USA, 1977); S .Rowbotham and J. McCrindle (eds), *Dutiful Daughters* (London, Allen Lane, 1977); L. Heron (ed.), *Truth Dare or Promise* (London, Virago, 1984).

14 For a discussion of some of the psychoanalytic theories underpinning these ideas see G. Dawson, *Soldier Heroes. British Adventure, Empire and the Imagining of Masculinities* (London, Routledge, 1994), ch. 2 and J. Mitchell *Psychoanalysis and Feminism* (Harmondsworth, Penguin, 1975) part 2.

15 Ann Tomlinson (47, 53). Specifically she wanted to earn money 'so that I could buy nice clothes' (51) and hence determine her own identity.

16 Ann Tomlinson (75).

17 Ann's couching of her account in these rather jaunty terms may also, of course, have been a way of concealing tensions with her parents, just as her departure at the age of 18 literally evaded them. Other versions of her life story evoked a series of rejections: she was not the boy her parents had longed for, her departure to boarding school at the age of 8 was deeply unhappy, and returning home (especially in the absence of her older sisters) was marred by her parents' quarrels. Ann Tomlinson is a close relative of the author, who grew up with these stories of unhappy home life. In fact they were more often repeated than stories of Ann's happy and highly successful life in the WRNS on which the interview focused.

18 Barbara Wilson (4).

19 Barbara Wilson (27).

20 Barbara Wilson (37).

21 Barbara Wilson (76). A third woman, Joyce Greaves, presented herself in similar terms of detachment. Joyce depicted her middle-class, suburban parents as having little understanding of what the war effort involved, but of accepting their daughter's participation because 'everybody that was young did something' (40, 93). She drew on the official language of labour mobility to explain her departure from the Ambulance Service for the WAAF: 'It left room for a married woman to do the job I was doing, without her having to move away' (79).

22 Ivy Jones (197, 195).

23 Tinkler, *Constructing Girlhood*, pp. 97–8; P. Summerfield, 'Cultural Reproduction in the Education of Girls: A Study of Girls' Schooling

in Two Lancashire Towns', in F. Hunt, *Lessons for Life. The Schooling of Girls and Women 1850–1950* (Oxford, Basil Blackwell, 1987), pp. 149–70; C. Arscott *et al.*, *The Headmistress Speaks* (London, Kegan Paul, Trench, Trubner & Co, 1937). Arguably headmistresses sought to replace, in academically successful girls, dependence on the family with dependence on the school and later college.

24 V. Woolf, *A Room of One's Own* (London, The Hogarth Press, 1929) and *Three Guineas* (London, The Hogarth Press, 1938); W. Holtby, *The Crowded Street* (London, Collins, 1924) and *South Riding. An English Landscape* (London, Collins, 1936); V. Brittain, *Testament of Friendship. The Story of Winifred Holtby* (London, Macmillan & Co Ltd, 1940).

25 Marianne Lloyd (101).

26 Marianne Lloyd (128).

27 Pamela Wootton (21, 37).

28 Pamela Wootton (149).

29 Janice Brunton (16, 59).

30 Janice Brunton (75).

31 Janice Brunton (174).

32 Janice Brunton (168).

33 Janice Brunton (168): 'I felt dreadful about it, but I suppose I suddenly realised that I'd got to do something to change the pattern of my life'. She also spoke of refusing an envied posting to Stanmore in preference for an unglamorous one to Preston, so that she could go home to her mother 'as often as I could' to 'try to make it up' (168), and described the painful homesickness she felt initially in the WAAFs, and her inability to express it in tears, as the other new recruits were doing (480).

34 Joan Stanton (42, 96, 51).

35 Joan Stanton (42, 47).

36 A. Light, *Forever England. Femininity, Literature and Conservatism Between the Wars* (London, Routledge, 1991), p. 39.

37 Janice Brunton (59).

38 For example, Marion Paul described gradually weaning her parents from their initial 'no absolutely not' position about her leaving her office job for the ATS.

39 Heather McLaren (214).

40 Heather McLaren (220).

41 Beryl Bramley (5, 13).

42 Beryl Bramley (57, 78).

43 Beryl Bramley (145, 567).

44 Beryl Bramley (545).

45 A similar case to that of Janice Brunton, was that of Margaret Gray.

She depicted her home life as stiflingly 'enclosed' (34). She was required to stay at home 'keeping my mother company' after leaving high school, and became determined 'to make the break from home', specifically from her mother. She first managed to obtain a war job in a local telephone exchange, and then joined the ATS in 1942, volunteering to become a driver. This appealed to her previously restrictive father, who was 'very keen on cars' (16), and who had 'been in the First World War and he was rather proud of us' [his two sons and daughter, all of whom were by 1942 in uniform] (138). As to her mother, on the other hand, 'I think it made her very sad' (140).

46 Estelle Armitage's mother, in Kingston, Jamaica, was plagued with worries when Estelle volunteered (in her words) as a 'coloured' colonial, to go to England with the ATS. Mrs Armitage's doubts were overruled by the rest of the family, who supported Estelle's desire to go abroad in the name of their late father's colonial patriotism. 'You were always brought up, you know, England was your mother country ... my father was strict you know about England, Rule Britannia and all this business' (19).

47 Tinkler, *Constructing Girlhood*, p. 121.

48 An exception was Barbara Wilson, one of the 'free agents', who joined the WRNS without reference to her parents, but who expressed resentment against compulsory war service because it was a disruption to her training in interior design.

49 E. Summerskill 'Conscription and Women', *The Fortnightly*, 151 (March 1942), p. 209.

50 Evelyn Mills (4).

51 Evelyn Mills (259).

52 Ethel Singleton (15).

53 Ethel Singleton (25, 29).

54 Ethel Singleton (31, 47).

55 Ethel Singleton (53).

56 Ethel Singleton (76).

57 For example (with reference to specifically to educational policy) S. Humphries, *Hooligans or Rebels? An Oral History of Working-Class Childhood and Youth 1889–1939* (Oxford, Blackwell, 1981).

58 Central Statistical Office, *Fighting with Figures. A Statistical Digest of the Second World War* (London, HMSO, 1995), Table 1.4.

59 Mary Mackenzie (64).

60 Mary Mackenzie (18, 22).

61 Mary Mackenzie (30).

62 Mary Mackenzie (34).

63 Mary Mackenzie (32).

64 Mary Mackenzie (69).

65 Mary Mackenzie (75).
66 Mary Mackenzie (108).
67 Mary Mackenzie (113).
68 Mary Mackenzie (191).
69 Mary Mackenzie (113). Mary's account of her interview at the WAAF recruiting office in Brighton emphasised the practice of those seeking to mobilise women of (unwittingly) encouraging them not to think about home and parents. The vignette reveals the interactive process by which officials constructed young women as 'free agents'. 'This officer said "well we're desperately wanting waitresses. If you could be trained as a waitress, we would take you. You'll be away within a week". So I said "well I am a waitress now as it happens" ... and she said "we'll have you in a week, but you'll have to learn. It's not the same type of waitressing you do in a shop ..." I said "I'm quite willing to try. I want to go because I've lost my home, my parents are not the same, I want to go into the Air Force" so she said "Fine"': Mary Mackenzie (111).
70 Mary Mackenzie (114).
71 In her letter in response to the piece in the woman's magazine Caroline wrote 'looking forward to being visited', the only respondent to be quite so oncoming. Letter and form 25 June 1991.
72 Caroline Woodward (48, 54).
73 Caroline Woodward (89).
74 Caroline Woodward (123).
75 Caroline Woodward (350).
76 Caroline Woodward (386).
77 Caroline Woodward (362).
78 Caroline Woodward (502, 80).
79 Caroline Woodward (524).
80 Moira Underwood (137).
81 Moira Underwood (326).
82 Kate Lomax (156).
83 Kate Lomax (220).
84 Kate Lomax (758, 772).

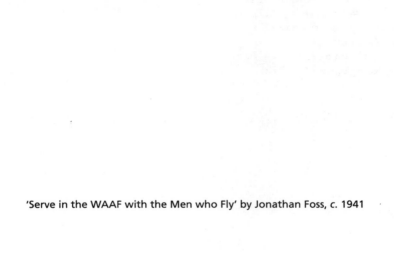

'Serve in the WAAF with the Men who Fly' by Jonathan Foss, c. 1941

Chapter 3

'Heroes' and 'stoics':
war work and feminine identity

The previous chapter explored women's memories of their interactions with their parents over what a daughter should do in wartime. The wartime identities to which women aspired, or which they rejected, were indicated obliquely in their accounts of parents' responses to the possibility that they would do war work. These narratives deployed, on the one hand, official versions of the obligations of the young woman to the wartime state, and on the other older understandings of the familial duties of daughters. This chapter explores further the official construction of the identity of the young woman war worker, and investigates its salience to women invited in the 1990s to reconstruct their wartime selves.

Images of women's participation in war work concentrated on the young single woman actively engaged in work which was publicly useful. The figure of this woman strode, in full colour, through the pages of wartime books such as *British Women Go To War* (1943) written by the popular writer and broadcaster J. B. Priestley to support the mobilisation of women. Her image was also lavishly used in government recruitment posters, and by advertisers. The identity constructed for the woman war worker in these sources was exciting and attractive, although, as we shall see shortly, her heroism was circumscribed.

The woman war worker was presented as performing tasks which were exceptional for women, such as driving a jeep, guiding carthorses, or beckoning women into factories producing aeroplanes and tanks.[1] She wore distinctive dress, the uniforms of the three auxiliary military services or the land army, factory overalls or dungarees. Her heroism resided in her public service, undertaken not for personal gain but for the greater good, marked by the idealistic expressions of the women whose photographs were selected for use in propaganda material.[2] A young woman's heroism was also indicated by the 'unfeminine' settings in which she was required to work and the signs that she was performing successfully there. Both by virtue of her obviously public role, and by her proximity to military action, the woman war worker was stepping out of the conventionally feminine sphere and into a more masculine world than the one to which she normally had access. And, because of the special wartime need and justification for her entry to this world, she was not officially derided for taking up such public roles, as she was in parallel circumstances, for example when demanding the parliamentary vote.[3] On the contrary, she was congratulated for doing so:

BOVRIL 'doffs the cap' to the splendid women of Britain ...

The way in which women are tackling unaccustomed, strenuous and often dangerous war work, has won, and deserved, wide-spread admiration. As mechanics, as bus conductors, lorry drivers and porters, as W.R.N.S., A.T.S., W.A.A.F., land girls and nurses, their record of service is itself the most eloquent tribute to the women of Britain. Bovril acclaims their fine spirit, and makes a practical contribution to their supply of strength and energy.

HOT BOVRIL CHEERS![4]

Since the end of the Second World War there has not been any equivalent celebration of women's presence in unusual types of employment. The wars in which Britain has been involved from the 1950s to the 1990s (for example the Korean War, the Falklands War, the Gulf War) have not impinged on the domestic economy in the same way, either in removing a substantial part of the male population to fight, and to be supported while doing so, or in requiring a large part of the country's productive capacity to be turned over to the manufacture of weapons. These post-war wars have been represented as almost entirely male enterprises, the images associated with them are of male aggressors, and war heroism has been emphatically military and male. As Lucy Noakes demonstrates, the evocation of the Second World War in public discourse in both the Falklands and the Gulf wars did not encompass women war workers.[5] Its purpose was to validate the continuity of a concept of 'Britishness' based on the defence of democracy by the valour and heroism of young British men.

The eclipse of the celebration of the heroic woman war worker in representations of war since 1945 helps to explain the anger expressed by some women about the private and public neglect, or even obliteration, of experiences of women's war participation.[6] It also places in context the surprise and fascination which the occasional rerunning of heroic images of women in the Second World War has evoked.[7] Some of the 350 women over 60 who enthusiastically responded to the small piece which we placed in *Woman's Weekly*, asking for women who remembered their training and work in the Second World War to contact us, wrote with a sense of mission about informing the world (especially the younger generation) of what they had done in the war. They wanted women's wartime heroism to be collectively recognised, implicitly acknowledging that the story of women's part in the war effort had become a muted discourse.[8]

However, the construction of the heroic image of women during the Second World War was heavily qualified by notions of femininity. The heroism of the single woman lay in her freedom to serve her country. But both her 'freedom' and her 'service' were circumscribed. Her freedom was the result of her not being what a woman was expected to become, a wife and mother. As we have seen in the previous chapter, women who came into these categories were not expected to be available for war work in the unconditional way in which young single women were: the housewife and mother must remain the 'cornerstone' of the home and hence the nation.[9] The labour shortage dictated that nevertheless the government called upon wives and mothers to contribute to the war effort, but strictly as volunteers, not under compulsion.

In contrast, the young single woman who had not (yet) assumed the classic responsibilities of an adult woman, was assumed to be 'mobile', and was required by law to go to the work to which the government sent her. However, her service was not given to the nation on equal terms with that of men. It was mediated by the process defined by M. R. and P. L.-R. Higonnet as 'gender displacement'. As men moved into wartime military roles at the front or just behind it, women were required to do work previously reserved for men. But since the new roles for men were more highly valued than those now acquired by women, the dynamic of gender subordination was not profoundly altered in spite of these changes.[10]

In Britain in the Second World War young single women were required to substitute for men in roles which were defined as supportive and supplementary. They became, for example, members of auxiliary military services, replacing men in non-combatant jobs so that they could fight, and supplying them with the goods and services they needed in order to do so. Or they became 'dilutees' in industry, taking over part of a man's job to release him for more skilled work or to become a soldier. Or they were drafted into farming as Land Girls, part of a youthful 'army' of women who supplemented the more seasoned and experienced labour of 'real' agricultural workers. Or they backed up firefighters and rescue and demolition men by working on ambulances or switchboards in Civil

Defence. Women released men from 'deskwork', 'groundwork', and 'routine tasks' in the 'backroom' for more direct and masculine involvement in the war effort, without ever becoming combatants themselves.[11] Furthermore, women's role in these jobs (which might be relatively prosaic but were nevertheless normally jobs which men did) was temporary.

The development of a series of recruitment posters by Jonathan Foss neatly sums up women's place in the process of war mobilisation. Early in the war Foss designed a poster for the Air Ministry called 'Volunteer for Flying Duties' addressed to men employed as ground personnel in the Royal Air Force (RAF) to encourage them 'to volunteer for duties in the air ... to let them know it was possible to do so'.[12] He placed a photograph of a pilot 'chosen from hundreds of suitable idealistic types' against a blue sky with the round RAF symbol on a flag behind his head 'in the place where a halo would go in a traditional painting'. Foss explained his design thus, 'In my serious mood these men were patriots and heroes ... saints even'.[13] Two years later, Foss designed a poster to encourage women to volunteer for the WAAF, entitled 'Serve in the WAAF with the men who fly'. He simply added to the beatified pilot a photograph of an equally idealistic-looking WAAF. She was slightly superimposed upon him, her gaze fixed not on the pilot (symbol in wartime of desirable manhood) but out of the picture at the same abstract goal (Victory, Peace) on which his sights were set. She shared his space, but on the ground not in the air, and he retained sole possession of the halo.

The woman in 'Serve in the WAAF', although in uniform, exuded considerable feminine charm. Women were constructed as being available for 'men's' work, only in so far as they were unmarried, and only for the duration of the war. Simultaneously they were constantly reminded of the need to preserve some aspects of the peacetime norms of femininity, even while they deviated from traditional gender roles. Advertisers and magazine editors advised women that they should maintain their femininity in masculine settings as a matter of morale. For example O'Do Ro No warned women to 'Stop the Rot' of underarm perspiration: 'However hard you work, however thick your uniform, O'Do Ro No will give you complete protection'[14] and other advertisers of a wide range of cosmetics and clothing urged that 'beauty is a duty' in wartime.[15] J. B. Priestley reassured his readers that 'Women do not stop being women because they have started work in a factory or may be doing a job formerly done by a man'.[16] Similarly Peggy Scott emphasised that the masculinising effects of war work went no deeper than the uniform. Not only was there continuity beneath the surface in women's gentle, maternal nature, but there were no permanent changes in the role she wanted for herself either: 'when the war is over the job will not be so much her concern as the home'.[17]

These popular representations constructed women's participation in war work as heroic, but contingent and temporary. Special courage, effort and self-sacrifice were expected of the woman who stepped across the gender boundary into war work. However, she would not be in direct contact with military action, and she would remain for just as long as that action lasted. Afterwards she would relinquish the job to a man, and replace her heroic wartime identity with a conventionally feminine one, centred on the functions considered natural to her. Heroism was demanded of single women as a national duty in wartime, but for women it involved not only superhuman effort, but (unlike men) doing what did not come 'naturally' in gender terms. Heroic status was intersected by gender, and the potential for achieving it was circumscribed by femininity. This discursive construction was redolent with contradictions productive of instability. On the one hand the idea of women participating heroically in the war effort could produce distrust and even fear in those with a preference for conventional gender relations. On the other, the limitations imposed on women's capacity for heroism could be a source of frustration for women who saw no reasons to remain within the gendered definition of their part in the war effort.

The women interviewed for this book were young and all but two were single in 1941, the year in which the recruitment of women to the war effort intensified. As such they were the targets of wartime propaganda and conscription, and were exposed to the constructions of women's participation discussed above. The memories which questions about call-up and war service evoked in the interviews reveal a range of responses to the dominant representations of women's role in the war, and expose some of its instabilities.

Heroic narratives

Some accounts conformed closely to the heroic image of women's call up and participation in the war effort, especially in terms of taking on a man's role. The phrase 'doing your bit' was widely used to express this identification.[18] For example, an urgency about getting involved in the war effort pervaded Moira Underwood's account of her call-up. In 1939, Moira, born in 1908, was, as we saw in the previous chapter, supporting her widowed mother and herself by her job as a hairdresser in Manchester. Although Moira felt that her responsibility to her mother came first, she was determined to join the war effort. Her anxiety to do war work was prompted by a desire *not* to be in the classic feminine position of non-combatant. Moira expressed this through her recollections of crippled ex-servicemen after the First World War, selling such things as writing paper and brushes door to door.

> And they used to look at you and say 'I fought for you. I gave my, I nearly gave my life for you' and I used to feel so awful, you know. I thought if ever we have another war, I'm not going to have anybody telling me that. I'm going to say 'yes I did my bit too' you know. And that was why I was keen to give up hairdressing and do a war job you know. So that's how I landed at Risley.[19]

Her determination not only to 'do her bit' but to distance herself from the non-combatant woman who did not risk her life in the war, led her to Risley ROF, near Warrington, 'a very dangerous place to work', where explosives were packed into bullets and shells, and detonators were fitted.[20] Moira, first a shopfloor worker and then a storekeeper at Risley, relished and took pride in the work. 'I felt I was doing a good job', she said.[21] To Moira 'doing her bit' involved working in a setting where not only male but female lives, including her own, were risked for future generations.

A similar desire to get as close to combat as possible coloured other accounts. Some of the women constructed themselves as sisters following in the footsteps of military brothers, giving expression in this way to their desire to cross the gender boundary.[22] For example, Felicity Snow modelled her own participation in a 'masculine' type of war work on the wartime role of her brothers. Felicity went straight into the office of 'a big ammunition factory' when she left school at 14 in 1939, but she was not satisfied with this non-combatant role, giving an explicit reason for wishing to do a man's job:

> Well I had my brother killed in 1942 in one of the bombing raids of the Halifax bombers over Germany and that made me think I'd try

and step in his shoes. You have these ideas when you're young, you get
– we were all very patriotic in those days and I think I thought I was
wasting my time just working in an office. I thought I could do more
for the war effort by going into the Air Force ... I thought I'd be able
somehow to do my bit instead of him.[23]

She asked to be a flight mechanic in the WAAF, emphasising that this
was the only job she wanted, and relating it to her identification
with her dead brother, 'my brother Sid always worked on motorbikes and I'd always been outside helping him in the garden, taking
the engine to pieces'.[24]

Others were equally emphatic that they wanted the sorts of jobs
that brothers did. Pam Wootton wanted to 'be where my brothers
were, out in the field' and made clear her determination to get a
more heroic job than typical women's work. She volunteered for
the WRNS: 'We were called to see what we wanted to do in the
Wrens ... I wanted to be an A.T. driver – no vacancies for A.T. drivers. I didn't want to be a cook. I didn't want to be a steward ...
They suggested air mechanic, "wow, yes please. That'll do me fine".
An air mechanic I became'.[25] She developed a passion for the work,
'I loved hydraulic systems', and had a strong sense of contributing
to the war effort: 'You worked as hard as you could ... we felt that
we were being useful'.[26]

There was apparently no resistance from employers or the
Employment Exchange to Moira, Felicity or Pamela's deliberate
choice of 'masculine' war work. But one of the contradictions of the
heroic construction of the woman war worker was that it was not
universally accepted. The images of the idealistic woman serving
with the men who waged war, directed principally at women themselves, were assumed to be based on a shared understanding, even a
consensus, about what was required of women in wartime. But
wider social support did not always exist in practice. We have
reviewed the resistance of some parents in the previous chapter, and
young women's current employers also raised objections in some
cases. More surprisingly, there is evidence that bias against directing
women to 'masculine' jobs existed within the selection and appoint-
ing authorities themselves. Several women told of encountering
opposition to a desire to take up a particular form of war service
which they had selected because they believed it was both a useful
public role and would give them great personal satisfaction.

Women who volunteered for the women's auxiliaries of the armed services found, as Pam Wootton hinted, that they were frequently invited to commit themselves to various types of women's work. The determination of some of them to obtain a heroic wartime role was expressed in their accounts of rejecting such suggestions and insisting on a 'masculine' option, as Pam did.[27]

The account which gave the most dramatic rendering of a story of resistance to determined efforts to deflect her from a heroic wartime role was that of Ann Tomlinson. Ann left a job as a secretary in the BBC to volunteer for the WRNS to train as a mechanic in the Fleet Air Arm in 1941, because she felt the BBC job was 'cushy', and because she wanted to do something 'that little bit different, I was still seeking some sort of individual cachet'.[28] She was quite determined to leave her typewriter and cross the gender boundary into work 'as near to the front line as most women would get'.[29] She took private lessons in electronics and mechanics in order to prepare herself for the role she wanted. However, once in the Wrens she was dismayed to find that she had been sent for initial training to a centre for secretarial work. 'I was absolutely horrified because my whole being was set upon joining the Fleet Air Arm as an air mechanic. So I made a fuss.'[30] Other young women joined her, and a Senior Wren Officer came to warn them against deserting gender-conformist roles. Ann reconstructed the lecture this officer gave them:

> She said, 'This job that you're wanting to do is dirty, difficult, out of doors in the most appalling weather, in snow, in sleet, in rain, in cold winter, in hot summer. You're always out of doors. You are working all the time with men. You might be perhaps the only girl on the airfield doing that kind of work ... It is a job where you would have to carry heavy things. You might have to go up in the aeroplane to test the apparatus ... You have a very arduous training course ahead of you. You really need to have some fairly high school qualifications' ... but what impressed most of us was the heavy work, the dirty work, the awful weather we would have to be in.[31]

The heroism of Ann's account was sharpened by the fact that, at the end of the lecture, only she and one other young woman remained 'determined to go through with this'. The training was every bit as tough as the officer had alleged, 'it was a gruelling course but incredibly interesting' and did indeed turn typists into mechanics.[32] Ann trained as an electrician, and recalled the immense satisfaction of becoming 'qualified to sign', meaning that she conducted daily inspections and signed a book to certify that there were no faults in the aeroplane's electrical system and it was fit to fly. 'This was a most marvellous moment. You know, you really felt, you really felt just so proud to be able to do this.'[33] Ann was emphatic that her job put her 'in almost what I would consider a fighting capacity, or at least enabling the fighting to go on', so it was crucial to the war effort.[34]

Such women redefined in the interviews their youthful commitment to the discourse of the woman war worker. The exceptionality of their desires should not be overlooked. Educational initiatives of the 1970s, 1980s and 1990s, which aimed to reduce the inequalities between the sexes in educational, training and employment choices, have found young people's gendered preferences a major obstacle. Young men and young women have demonstrated a redoubtable desire to prepare for work which conforms to gender norms, rather than that which is exceptional for their sex.[35]

The women we have been discussing, on the other hand, were recalling an insistence to do work which was exceptional for women. They had particular difficulties when they came before the authorities with skills and experience in 'women's work' (such as cook, waitress, machine operator) which fitted them for an available war job. The enormous expansion of clerical work since 1900, and its feminisation, stimulated by each war, meant that it was especially difficult for women with experience of clerical work to escape it in the war.[36] Ann Tomlinson, a qualified secretary, is a case in point. Others included Margaret Gray. She wanted to become an ATS driver but her job as a switchboard operator in the General Post Office was both a 'reserved occupation' and therefore difficult to leave, and fitted her for work in the Royal Corps of Signals, that is the communications branch of the Army. In the end Margaret's insistence paid off: 'they allowed me to go and do my driving training, as I was very keen on it' and she recalled her great pride in developing the ability to drive and maintain a range of vehicles including motorbikes and three-ton lorries.[37] Similarly Kate Lomax explained that her boss at the town hall was reluctant to let her leave, and that when she joined the WAAF she had to 'fight for photography', both because she had previously been a clerk and because 'they said that it was a man's job'.[38] Kate, like others, rejected a 'desk

job' and relished the 'masculine' skills she learned and the responsibility of reconnaissance photography. She said she liked it because it
involved 'knowing that the – I wasn't failing anybody ... knowing
that it was a front line job'.[39]

In the foregoing stories, the women got their way after insisting
that they should be allowed to be wartime heroes, to conform to the
recruitment images that they saw around them demanding that
women replace men for the duration. These were epic narratives, in
which resistance to the hero's rightful quest was the result of prejudice, either against women in general, or against the occupational
and skills transition these women wanted to make for the sake of
the war. Barriers crumbled in the face of their valiant determination.

Some women with similar aspirations, however, told of not getting their way. For example, Marion Paul, a wages clerk in the office
of a coal mine near Doncaster at the start of the war, spoke of how
she really wanted to become a driver, but the response at her interview in the ATS was, '"Oh yes, what have you been doing?". So I
said "well I've always done clerical work", so she said, "oh yes, well
we do need rather a lot of clerical workers"' and Marion found herself being trained as a Regimental Clerk for the Royal Electrical and
Mechanical Engineers, doing the kind of personnel and wages work
she had formerly done in the mines office.[40] Nevertheless, however
disappointed she may have been at the time, Marion felt released by
her escape into the Army from the oppressive mines office and her
restrictive parents. She was confident that she made an important
contribution in spite of not getting the more glamorous job she had
sought. As in the cases of Felicity Snow and Pamela Wootton, a
brother's fate was the bench-mark for Marion's feelings about the
job. Marion's brother was invalided out of the army with a shrap-
nel wound in 1943: 'I felt very much that I was doing my bit, I was
taking my brother's place'.[41]

In retrospect it seems plausible, given the system of 'reservations'
which maintained in skeletal form the gender segregation of labour
during the war, that civilian employers as well as military authorities might have had grounds for resisting women's insistence on
gender atypical jobs. The demand for women to work in 'women's
work', as factory assemblers, or as clerks, cooks, waitresses and
stewards, in civilian as well as military organisations, was high
throughout the war. It was, indeed, higher than wartime propa-

ganda acknowledged. A survey undertaken in 1942 into the slow pace of recruitment to the ATS, found that women were put off by a stress on the Army's need for women to fill traditional jobs. Since potential recruits responded better to appeals for women to train for more technical and adventurous jobs, the advertising followed this path.[42] The official construction of the heroic woman war worker had evidently become part of popular thinking. It was returning (via the cultural circuit) to haunt those trying to manage the wartime labour supply rationally by placing women with experience of any of the kinds of 'women's work', for which there was a high demand, into similar wartime jobs. Indeed one of the criticisms voiced within the counter-discourse of wartime radicalism in 1941–42 was of 'square pegs in round holes', that is of unsuitable war work placements, as well as of people being moved away from jobs near home, while others were drafted in from afar to take the jobs they had vacated.[43] As far as the interviewees we have discussed so far were concerned, the official constructions of an exceptional role for women in wartime remained part of their subjective understandings. They relived in the interviews their determination to acquire for themselves the wartime identities which matched those understandings. The resistance they encountered when they volunteered for these jobs represented a dramatic discovery of the persistence of the gendered structuring of the labour force into the war. They recalled determinedly challenging it, at a time when there appeared to be public approval for such defiance.

Some women wished to take further the possibilities opened up in the name of patriotism by the wartime process of gender displacement. Indeed the constraints imposed on women's heroism by the requirements that women should serve and support rather than engage directly in combatant roles were in tension with the idealism of some of those who responded positively to the call to serve 'in almost ... a fighting capacity'.[44] But, as Di Parkin has discussed, there was an official prohibition on women bearing arms or firing weapons.[45] Although women could make lethal weapons, prepare them for use, aim them and service them, they were not allowed to use them for their intended purpose. An experiment on a mixed anti-aircraft battery under General Pile, where women were permitted to 'man the guns' was short-lived because of disapproval in the War Office, in Parliament and in the Cabinet.[46] But some women experienced this prohibition as highly contradictory. Greta Lewis, who was responsible for the height and range calculations that enabled anti-aircraft guns to be targeted on enemy aircraft, curled her lip when she spoke about the equipment issued to women for the purpose of guarding the gun emplacement: 'we used to be at the gates, you know how men go on guard, they have a gun don't they? We didn't have a gun, we had a stick. "Stick guard" they called it!'.[47] Heather McLaren remembered having to guard the barrage balloon which she crewed in a similar manner: 'We took over from the RAF and the men had rifles and we had truncheons to defend ourselves!'.[48] The logic of thus rendering the women guards, as well as the positions they were guarding, more vulnerable, was a ludicrous dimension of gender differentiation.

The ban on women using weapons was also remembered, and resented, by other women. Amy O'Connor expressed intense patriotism and impatience with her non-combatant role on an ATS switchboard. She left domestic service enthusiastically to join the ATS, and as a signals operator, she said, 'I felt I was doing my bit, I was helping England, yes, England, my country right or wrong'.[49] But she would have liked to have taken her commitment further. She expressed passionately anti-Nazi sentiments in the interview, leading to the statement: 'I'm bloodthirsty you know. They could have given me a gun and I would have gone, I would. I'd have gone out with a gun. There were quite a few of us asked, could we go out with the men? Could we take guns? They wouldn't let us'.[50]

Yvette Baynes also recalled the prohibition. She did not seek a 'heroic' war job, but worked as a secretary close to home, supporting her widowed mother, throughout the war. But she did volunteer for the Home Guard when a company was formed at her workplace in Birmingham in 'probably 1942 or 1943'.[51] The Home Guard, originally the Local Defence Volunteers, was formed in May 1940 as a volunteer organisation to prepare for and resist invasion. Yvette remembered that the men in her unit wanted women 'to help them with the clerical side', but nevertheless the five women who joined for this purpose wore a uniform and went through the same training as the men, until the unit was abruptly disbanded:

> We had to learn to track down the enemy if there was an invasion and the enemy came over. We had to learn what to do in such an event and we were going to use rifles, but then suddenly they disbanded the Home Guard and we just didn't touch a rifle.

Hilary: Do you wish that you had?
YB: Yes I do really – I think it would have been a good experience.[52]

Yvette attributed the end of her membership of the Home Guard to a lack of the organisation's cost-effectiveness, and did not connect it with the gendering of combat. However, the political history of the Home Guard (which would have been obscure to Yvette at the time) reveals sustained controversy concerning women's membership. There was considerable agitation for it by, among others, Dr Edith Summerskill, Labour MP and equal rights feminist, from the summer of 1940, but it was steadfastly resisted by the War Office, backed by the Cabinet. At length, in June 1943, limited membership was granted. 'Older' women could be 'nominated' for support duties by recognised organisations. These strictly non-combatant 'nominated women' were issued with no more uniform than a 'badge brooch'.[53] However, there is evidence that other women (including, it seems, Yvette Baynes) formed their own Women's Home Defence Units and joined the Home Guard, before the ban was lifted. They wore uniforms and trained to use guns, neither of which they were ever officially permitted. This trend provoked a crackdown by the War Office as early as November 1941, when *The Times* reported:

> The War Office has sent an order to all Home Guard units that the training of women as unofficial Home Guard units has not been authorized. Weapons and ammunition in the charge of the Army or of Home Guard units must not be used for the instruction of women and the use of the name Home Guard is not permitted.[54]

Yvette's experience suggests that the War Office had to renew its commitment to keeping women out of the Home Guard, and weapons out of women's hands, repeatedly. Her unit, with its commitment to equal training (if not identical functions) for men and women, was acting outside the official remit. It was formed and closed down, in Yvette's memory, sometime in 1942 or 1943, whereas women were officially allowed to join only in the second half of 1943, and the official stand-down did not occur until December 1944, by which time Yvette had moved to a different employer.[55]

The government's resistance to women's involvement in the Home Guard can be explained in terms of the prohibition on arming women, while the larger issue of women and combat concerns the construction of gender identities. If women were to defend themselves, their homes and their children against an invader, they needed to be trained and equipped with weapons. But arming women was unacceptable in national defence and offence, because of the resilience of the dominant construction of femininity: women were life-givers, not life-takers; in wartime men must fight for and defend the vulnerable women and children of the motherland. Gender stability depended upon this construction, which was upheld against all challenges, no matter how starkly it contradicted the experience of women mobilised for war, and the rhetoric which contributed to their mobilisation.[56]

The women discussed so far, who volunteered enthusiastically for gender atypical war work, expressed, as we have seen, their desire to get as close to battle as they could: 'out in the field', 'in the thick of it', 'in ... almost a fighting capacity', in 'a front line job'.[57] Their memories of the pleasures of wearing wartime uniform reinforced their 'composure' as heroes. They might choose to put on silk cami-knickers under their uniforms, instead of the regulation 'black-outs', but they relished the battledress, the overalls and the dungarees with which they were issued for work, alongside the skirts and tunics which constituted 'service dress'.[58] Women in trousers were still an unusual sight in the 1940s. The 'masculine' work dress which these women wore willingly not only afforded them much-appreciated comfort and physical freedom. It also indicated their apparent assimilation to the ranks of men, and so symbolised their heroic wartime role.[59] One of the women described having her hair cut by an army barber, in the short-back-and-sides style of the soldier. Several spoke with pleasure of its feminised equivalent, the wartime 'liberty cut'.[60] They nevertheless described lavish use of lipstick and face powder, traditional markers of femininity. As with cami-knickers, so with cosmetics, for these women the creative synthesis of 'masculine' and 'feminine' styles produced a wartime feminine identity predicated upon agency for women within the national struggle.

These women cherished memories of their participation in the war effort in ways which transgressed conventional gender identities, and used the interviews as opportunities to achieve public recognition. Women who spoke in this way about their wartime participation formed the majority of those interviewed, twenty-four out of forty-two. They were a socially diverse group: eight came from working-class families, eleven from the lower middle class and six from the middle class. Indeed the wartime discourse which they took up and made their own was intended to induce the feeling of national unity, of pulling together across the demarcations of social class as well as those of gender. These women's constructions of their relationships with their parents were also varied.[61] 'Heroes' belonged within all the different types of family relationship that we observed in the previous chapter, with one notable exception. None of those who recalled enthusiastically joining up described their parents as sheltering them from the unwelcome demands of the state. It would have been inconsistent for them to have done so since to them those demands were not unwelcome.

Stoic accounts

However, daughters who did accept their parents' protection, as well as other women scattered through the various types of daughter–parent relationship we have discussed, spoke with far greater caution about adopting a heroic wartime identity. Even amongst the group motivated to respond to the piece in *Woman's Weekly* asking for memories of wartime training and work, and who agreed to be interviewed, there were eighteen women who did not construct heroic narratives. They attributed quite different meanings to war work. For them, the conventional roles of young single women in the family, in education, or in women's work or training, exerted a strong pull against the demands to become part of the wartime process of gender displacement.

One type of response was to take, or to continue within, a conventionally defined women's job, such as secretarial and clerical work. This could be the result of deliberate rejection of a more dangerous or masculine role, or the consequence of expectations (their own or their parents') that their contribution to the war effort would be within the sphere of 'women's work'.

For some women this involved an explicit rejection of the heroism of wartime rhetoric, and the choice of an option that caused the least disruption to their feminine identities. For example Evelyn Mills (whose sheltering parents we met in the previous chapter) would have preferred to remain throughout the war with the firm of builders and estate agents on whose accounts she worked from 1938 to 1942. The work was close to home and she was treated well: 'I was very sorry to have to leave there when I was called up'.[62] At her call-up interview she was faced with a choice between a munitions factory, and clerical work at the Admiralty. She described nervously taking a typing test (which she failed) at the Admiralty: 'they offered me a duplicating job which I had to accept, otherwise it was to go in the munitions factory and I didn't want that because it would be being sent away from home'.[63] It would also have involved a level of personal risk that was abhorrent to her, as we shall see later. The duplicating work, which she did for two years, was messy and monotonous: 'you slipped the stencil on and then put the catch over it, and that was your job really. I suppose in a way it was boring', but at least it 'counted' as war work. Although proud of her ability to duplicate neatly and quickly, Evelyn was relieved to return to the builders and estate agents in 1944.[64]

Others did not feel that they had resisted the new wartime norm, but rather emphasised their occupational continuity. Unlike the clerks and secretaries reviewed earlier, such as Ann Tomlinson and Gladys French, who insisted on escaping from their peacetime work identities, these women did what was expected of them, given their work skills. Family pressures had prevented some of them following an urge to join the women's auxiliary forces, but although this was a disappointment they did not articulate (as Marion Paul did) a desire for any specific alternative, or tell a story of being denied such an option. They were either resigned to doing 'women's work' in wartime, or it coincided with what they wanted for themselves.

For example, Joan Stanton, whose parents had prevented her joining the Services, and for whom the Cheltenham Employment Exchange found a succession of wartime civilian clerical jobs, did not recall her war work positively. It was not a new opportunity in terms of either her occupational identity, or indeed her identification with the nation. She described her war jobs as uniformly 'dead boring', exemplifying her statement thus: 'you can't get terribly excited about hydraulic tipping gear and the correspondence thereby entailed'[65] (in contrast to the enthusiasm which the more heroic Pamela Wootton expressed for the hydraulic wing systems on which she worked as an aircraft rigger). Joan, like other 'stoics', did not suggest that she was 'doing her bit'. On the contrary, she positioned herself rather regretfully outside the heroic construction of women's part in the war, saying 'I don't think I contributed all that much to the war really ... not like other people who were welders and things like that'.[66] She drew on a formulation which was widely used to indicate resignation both to an unheroic role in the war effort, and to coping with adverse circumstances imposed by the war which did not conform to the woman's own preferences: 'we had a job to do and we didn't sort of moan and gripe ... we just got on with it'.[67]

Dorothy Rose talked in a similar way. Her supportive parents encouraged her to take the clerical job she wanted, issuing ration books in the Ministry of Food, when she left school at 14 in 1941. She regarded the job as an opportunity created by the war, but her sights were set on obtaining office work, rather than contributing to the war effort, about which she spoke with resignation. Conditions at work were not good but 'people just got on with it' in a situation in which they were more than usually controlled by their employer. For example, there were regular training courses: 'you had no option of going, you had to go, it wasn't from choice I went, it was just that I was sent'. Dorothy connected this capacity for endurance with national identity: 'We just plodded on. That's the old British thing'.[68]

In contrast another lifelong clerical worker, Yvette Baynes, whose experiences in the Home Guard we have already reviewed, was keener to position herself on the heroic side of the war work boundary than Evelyn Mills, Joan Stanton or Dorothy Rose. She had no desire to join the Forces, and was not called up, but found her own civilian secretarial jobs with firms which she regarded as involved in the war effort, such as D. F. Taylor, Birmingham wire manufacturers, and Westmed Transporters, a haulage company. Looking for ways of emphasising that this work was worthwhile in war terms, in the interview she described a course she took to learn to use adding machines. These were skills usually taught to young men. Did the instructors think women could acquire them? 'Oh yes, I think so. Most people did in those days, because you had to work anyway, you had to do men's jobs'. Yvette identified her secretarial work with war work, explaining that as far as invoicing and taking telephone orders was concerned: 'you had to be accurate with those orders because of course it was munitions a lot of it, and the wire was required for munition work, and you had to get it right'.[69] In spite of her expression of this sense of compulsion, Yvette left the haulage company in 1944 to become secretary to the managing director of Gwenda Products, a firm making gifts rather than munitions, without, apparently, any opposition from the Ministry of Labour even though she was 19, and thus within the age range targetted for war work. Perhaps because she was aware that her account of taking this job, in which 'I was very spoiled' by the boss and his wife, suggested that she had ducked the rigours of war work, Yvette's response to a question about how she rated her response to the war effort stressed her voluntary work as one of the few women members of the Home Guard and the weekend work she did in a factory canteen rather than her paid work.[70]

Women like Evelyn, Joan, Dorothy and Yvette, who did not move into military service, or indeed alter their occupations during the war, are perhaps the least remembered of all wartime workers. They used the interviews as opportunities to work out, and justify, their relationships with the dominant wartime construction of the role of the young single woman. They were interviewed as a result of their responses to our notice which (unusually in media items concerning the war effort) specified interest in women's wartime non-manual, civilian work, as well as other kinds of war jobs. In spite of our attempt to break the silence surrounding this type of wartime work, the interviews are likely to have put them on the defensive, because of the project's apparent (if unintended) place in the commemoration of wartime heroism. Thus although the work was boring they stressed that it was regarded as a contribution by the authorities, about which they had no choice, or else they asserted its value by emphasising the competence with which they did it, and by stressing any points of contact with 'men's work' that they felt they had, whether on the job (for example using adding machines) or in voluntary activities outside work (such as the Home Guard). Whatever the case 'you just got on with it', while worrying retrospectively that other women, 'welders and things like that', might be regarded as playing a worthier part in the war effort.

Some women who remembered no wish for change, on the other hand, were directed by the state into new wartime occupations which women did not usually do. In contrast to the women who struggled to be allowed across the gender boundary, these women regarded these relatively unfeminine jobs with hesitation if not with dread. Their experiences and attitudes echo those recorded by M-O in its studies of young women conscripts in industry, such as *People in Production* and *War Factory*, although the interviewees did not evince the same degree of alienation from the work and the

war effort that observers thought they detected in the factories studied in 1942 and 1943. On the contrary, some of those who 'just got
on with it' were converted to their war jobs, as for example welders,
aircraft assemblers, bench fitters or lathe operators, and became
proud of their competence. They used our interviews as opportunities both to emphasise the contribution they felt they made to the
war effort, and to examine the changes that they went through in
overcoming their reluctance and redefining themselves in unantici-
pated ways.

For example, Ethel Singleton was loath to leave her job as a
grocer's shop assistant in Manchester, where her sheltering parents
thought she would be exempt from call-up. However, the hand of
the state sought her out in 1941 and sent her to A.V. Roe's Engineering where she was trained to weld. She depicted herself and the
other conscripts as helpless victims: 'You were just thrust in! We
were like sheep, you know, just a crowd of new recruits, you know,
just thrust in.'[71] Ethel continued to emphasise how she was forced
by the state across the gender boundary into welding, and made to
stay there. 'They'd had men doing these jobs before, well they were
taking the men that were eligible into the Forces so we were taking
on the men's jobs really ... You couldn't pack it in and say well I've
had enough, I've finished. I mean you were forced to carry on. You
daren't have given your – well you couldn't give your notice in, you
were conscripted into that job you see, like being in the Forces'.[72]
Nevertheless Ethel became a proud welder, learning alloy as well as
steel welding and working on aircraft fuel tanks. She summed up
her feelings about the job: 'I think afterwards it made us feel good
you know, that we'd actually done a job that was worthwhile'.[73]

A similar account was given by Helena Balfour. She depicted herself as a free agent in relation to her family at the age of 21 in 1941,
having been sent into domestic service by her father at 14. But she
did not welcome the intrusion of the wartime state into her life. She
would have preferred, at the time, to remain in service than to go
into an aircraft factory. Her account of becoming a wartime factory
worker at the Windsor Engineering Company near Glasgow, which
made aircraft wings, was resigned. 'It was just something that had
to be done', 'You were given this job to do, I mean you just had to
get on with it'.[74] But Helena, like Ethel, nevertheless developed
pride in her skills, particularly in the ability which she and other
women developed to assemble ailerons, part of the aircraft wing.

She described becoming a dedicated and perfectionist worker, learning her favourite expression 'if it's not bad, it'll not do' from one of the men with whom she worked, and implicitly contrasting her dedication to the attitude of the 'silly wee lasses' who 'treated everything as a huge joke'.[75] Helena's self-portrait fits the characterisation of one of M-O's diarists, a labour manager, who said 'Scotch servant-girls we found good hard workers'. The 'silly wee lasses' of her account sound like the time-wasters and tool-breakers of M-O's *War Factory*.[76]

Ethel Singleton, Helena Balfour and several of the other reluctant conscripts who 'just got on with' their wartime men's work became, as we have seen, enthusiastic war workers, proud of their skills and their contribution to the war effort.[77] But the record which these women made of their wartime experiences contrasted with that of the first group of women we discussed, the 'heroes', whose accounts were a celebration of their wartime identities. This second group emphasised their stoicism in accepting the imposition of war jobs, their capacity to endure them and their pride in the skills they acquired. Among the 'stoics', however, were a few who entered war work unwillingly, and evinced continuing detachment, or even resistance, towards the construction of young women in wartime. Their consistent refusal of the role related in part to gender, and in part to other aspects of identity, such as the training and work aims they had been pursuing prior to call-up, in relation to which they felt the war was a rude interruption. Some also expressed a nascent pacifism, involving dissociation from the waging of war in itself.

Hester Hamilton's call-up was particularly inauspicious. She was the daughter of fishmongers in Port Seton near Edinburgh, who were in agreement with her that continuing her studies at college was more important than taking part in the war effort. However, Hester was made to leave by the college authorities after failing her second year examinations, and she thus became eligible for conscription, something about which her protective parents could do nothing and a bitter blow since she wanted to become a teacher.[78] In her clouded account the arbitrary hand of the state then descended in the form of 'a telegram out of the blue saying "Report!"' to an aircraft factory at Leven in Fife where she was told she would work as a progress planner, a job of which she knew nothing and for which she was given no training. The only instructions offered to Hester and her young woman colleague were to follow a piece of metal round the factory and read some books. She believed the job was created because 'the government at that time must have made some rule that all factories had to have a planning office and we were it'.[79] However, the two young women took it seriously and worked out their own successful system of monitoring the use of materials and of timing the ordering of supplies so as to maximise the continuity of production. Summing up her war work Hester called upon the concept of 'doing your bit', much used in the more heroic accounts, but she distanced herself from the patriotic involvement the phrase usually implied. Her job (rather than she herself) was part of the policy of increasing the efficiency of the war effort: 'I suppose it did its bit'.[80] But this was followed by a definitely anti-war statement. Whatever the benefits to the individual of the experience of war work (and she referred to several), she disapproved of the war effort itself: 'I think we felt the war really was a waste of a lot of lives and a lot of time. No I don't think war was a good thing at all'.[81] Ultimately, then, the successful progress planning was for no good purpose.

A parallel case is that of Barbara Wilson, whose college career was also interrupted by the call-up, and who likewise detached herself from a heroic wartime identity. As we saw in the previous chapter, Barbara spoke of deciding to join the WRNS independently of her comfortable middle-class family. In contrast to accounts of other ex-Wrens, hers did not subscribe to the patriotic construction of war participation. 'I think one was probably pretty numb about it ... you didn't question it', 'one was living at that particular time and that's what one did ... I wasn't feeling heroic about it or anything like that'.[82] The language she used, in particular the impersonal 'one' and her spontaneous dismissal of the relevance of heroism, charted the distance she felt from an identity which, as we have seen, was popular with other women. She described being 'just allocated' to the job of electrical mechanic in the WRNS, in sharp contrast to the epic narratives of WRNS and WAAF air mechanics in which this job was attained only after a process of struggle and self-assertion. These accounts, for instance those of Felicity Snow, Pamela Wootton and Ann Tomlinson, radiated the desirability of the position of air mechanic, derived from the glamour of close association with military activity and with servicemen. Barbara drew on the phrase 'doing your bit' to describe her participation in war work across the gender boundary, but like Hester Hamilton, she displaced it, so that her usage did not convey pride or confidence in women's capacities. The men she worked with were tolerant: 'they all respected us I think, you know, that we were doing our bit as best we could and probably a bit stupid anyway'.[83] She was not outraged by this male view of the limited competence of women war workers, but subscribed to it herself, in sharp contrast to women with a stronger sense of heroism, as we shall see in the next chapter. Barbara used diminutives to describe herself as an air mechanic. She was 'the lowest on the rung of authority' doing 'modest jobs' and 'didn't feel I would be very competent perhaps if there was an emergency'.[84]

The war upset the progress through life of women like Hester and Barbara, in ways they did not want retrospectively to eulogise, even though, by responding to the piece in *Women's Weekly* and agreeing to be interviewed, they demonstrated that they did want to contribute these experiences to the historical record. Their wartime work profiles bore similarities to those of many of the women who told tales of triumph over the obstacles of prejudice obstructing women's glorious participation in the war effort. But their accounts were not epics. They were the products of scepticism, resignation and orientation to personal rather than national goals.

The 'stoics' were not sharply differentiated socially from the 'heroes'. There was a higher concentration of women from working-class families among them, than among those who gave heroic accounts: ten out of seventeen of the 'stoics' (59 per cent) were working class, compared with eight out of twenty-five of the 'heroes' (32 per cent). The concentration is apparent confirmation of a view of working-class mentality as relatively passive and fatalistic, forever 'putting up with things'.[85] But the distribution of views across even the small number of women in this sample, indicates that this construction fits only some members of the group to which it is applied. The other seven stoics were almost equally split between the middle and the lower middle class, while there was a greater concentration of the other heroes in the lower middle class.[86] Most of the 'stoics' described their parents as either authoritarian, or as offering them welcome protection from the intrusion of the wartime state into their lives.

Memories of danger

The main way in which women characterised themselves as heroes and stoics was, as we have seen, through their reconstructions of call-up and war work. A theme within these accounts, the treatment of which confirmed the differentiation, concerned a central feature of war work and of the war more generally, that is the danger to which it exposed those involved. Danger was part of the experience of 'total war', its omnipresence indicative of the artificiality of the distinction between combatants and non-combatants. Women within as well as outside military organisations might not be equipped with weapons, but they were nevertheless at risk from enemy attack and from the production, maintenance, storage and supply of the materials of war within Britain. This reality contradicted the construction of wartime military masculinity, in which men's purpose was to defend helpless women and children who passively watched their departure for combat and awaited their return. As we have seen in the case of the Home Guard, the conventional gendering of warfare was sustained throughout the Second World War, in spite of all the evidence against it, in terms of both numbers of women involved in the war effort, and the manifold dangers of the 'Home Front'.[87]

The responses to wartime danger remembered by the women interviewed, paralleled the polarisation of their identification with the war effort. At one extreme women drew satisfaction from the wartime dangers to which they were exposed. These perils represented evidence of the job's value and the woman's proximity to the battlefront. For example, Moira Underwood, who volunteered for work in a filling factory as soon as war was declared, said: 'there was an element of danger which was, made it quite exciting'.[88] She gave a detailed description of that 'element of danger'. Everyone in the factory had to walk slowly 'because you might meet people carrying gun powder which was highly explosive ... the slightest flash might send it off'; 'if anyone made a mistake or we'd got something, powder that wasn't working properly, could cause an explosion, you know'; even a cap falling off someone's head could set off an explosion. Moira told a horrifying story of an accident caused by 'drumming', drying out detonators in drums which were turned by hand, and then had to be opened and emptied: 'One girl lost her arm and that was terrible. She was a lovely girl. There were four sisters worked together and their father. And I always wondered why he let them work there, but he knew how dangerous it was. And this particular time, she came running out of this room, with her hand blown off and she said "Daddy, daddy, daddy, daddy". Oh you know, it was awful. Tears, crying for her father you know.'[89] Moira's comment about the father letting his daughter do this job and the daughter's desperate, belated quest for his protection, emphasised the unfeminine danger of the work and the patriotic sacrifice made by a supportive father and his daughter. It also served as a reminder in the narrative that Moira had no father to oversee her, inside or outside the factory: unlike the girl in the accident she confronted wartime dangers alone, which accentuated her heroism. Although appalled by this event, Moira relished the danger in the factory, minimising its horrors by saying 'we only had three deaths whilst I was there, so in that respect we were lucky, you know'. She responded to the question 'you liked it dangerous?' by declaring: 'Yes, I quite liked it, it added a bit of excitment to life'.[90]

At the other extreme, women described shrinking from the dangers of war work, and invested their accounts of them with horror and fear. Evelyn Mills was, as we have seen, reluctantly conscripted to the Admiralty as a duplicator operator. Evelyn's strong aversion to the horrors of dangerous war work was diametrically opposite to Moira Underwood's proclivity towards such work. A story of an accident in a munitions factory featured in Evelyn's account of her call-up and war work, as it did in Moira's, but for Evelyn its meaning was inverted. 'I think I was pretty lucky because I'd got a cousin, she was called up and had no choice, she had to go in a munition factory, and she only used to come home weekends. I think it was at Stoke. And there was a particular weekend she came home and she said she was dreading going back on the Monday because there was a job there that nobody would volunteer for, so they picked somebody out each week, and it was her turn. It was something to do with bullets, you had to put your hands in this – whatever. And she was dead unlucky, she had the accident and her arm blown off to there. Honestly. And she was due to get married within a few weeks … Terrible. And she's two years older than me. So I reckon I was lucky in going to the Admiralty really!'.[91] Evelyn's reference point was not the bravery and self-sacrifice of the girl 'doing her bit' in this dangerous work, but its potential to ruin her cousin's 'normal' feminine aims in life.

Evelyn's evaluation of the relationship between her own duplicating job, which she did for two years, and the war effort, was informed by the fact that even though it did not involve (to her relief) the dangers of work in a war factory, it qualified as 'doing your bit': 'It made you feel as if you'd done your bit towards the war, even if it was not fighting anybody or not being right in the front line, but at least you were doing something, doing your best or what you were called up to do ... Oh, it might not have seemed a glamorous job, but it was better than some people had to do. It was quite a relief to know that at least you weren't going to come out with an illness'.[92] Ironically in view of this comment, Evelyn later described the toll on her health taken by shift work and constant standing at the duplicator, and of obtaining her discharge on medical grounds. In spite of the unheroic safety, which she stressed, of a clerical job in the basement of the Admiralty, she herself did eventually 'come out with an illness'.

By contrasting her work with that of her cousin, Evelyn placed her own contribution to the war effort well away from the battlefront (even though the papers she was duplicating were urgent reports of naval action for high-ranking service personnel). By implication, in her account, the dangers involved in other kinds of women's war work positioned it closer to 'the front line'. Some of the women's accounts of accidents celebrated this location. For example, Caroline Woodward, initially a reluctant recruit to a Scottish engineering company and later an enthusiastic welder, described falling off a platform when welding a pontoon and seriously injuring her head. 'My war wound', she said, smiling and fingering the scar.[93] Her wry use of terminology usually reserved for men on the battlefield elided her war work and herself as a woman, with danger and heroism.

In contrast a stress on women's vulnerability in the face of the dangers of war work was characteristic of the accounts of the women reluctantly conscripted, who 'just got on with it'. Sadie Bartlett was one of these. She drifted into the Timber Corps of the Women's Land Army from casual work on the land, after unsuccessfully trying to persuade her asthmatic mother to exempt her from call-up by claiming that she needed her at home.[94] Sadie emphasised the fearsome aspects of cutting down trees. Felling in a high wind could be lethal, she explained, describing in detail an occasion on which a tree that was blown askew as a man felled it 'sort of went on his head evidently ... he was absolutely sort of splattered'.[95] The axes which the women as well as the men had to use, could 'jump and cut your leg off'.[96] These frightening descriptions substantiated Sadie's claim that this was men's work, which she should not have been doing because it was fundamentally unsuitable for women.[97] Stories of women in war factories being scalped by getting their hair caught in drills, or being dragged bodily into machinery or menaced by enormous guillotines, had similar meanings in other 'stoic' accounts.[98] In spite of such horrors, however, these women 'just got on with it'.[99]

The women who, in contrast to the stoics, 'clamoured' for work across the gender boundary, were more inclined to recall an insouciance about dangers to themselves in wartime, than to speak with dread of the horrible things they witnessed. An important part of the heroic identity was not to think of the personal suffering that the quest entailed. For example Gladys French, a wireless mechanic in the Fleet Air Arm, was dismissive about the time 'I fell over a propeller shaft and cut my leg ... we didn't think about safety, we didn't think about things in those days'.[100] Amy O'Connor was cool about working next to an ammunition dump near Bath: 'Never frightened, never thought about it. Alright it was an ammunition dump, they'd got to store it somewhere. Just didn't occur to us it could have gone off. We'd have gone up with it'.[101] The staccato sentences with which she spoke of this threat were military, and masculine. Denial of pain was also a (supposed) heroic (and masculine) attribute. More than one 'hero' recalled how, when in pain, 'you just didn't think anything about it really', but kept on with the job.[102]

'Heroic' women spoke about the dangers of their work with an excited awe, commenting that they would never have done such things later in life. The dangers and their tolerance of them belonged to a special period when they were behaving in exceptional ways. They bore pain 'manfully', they biked to work in air raids,[103] they subscribed to official versions of morale, asserting for example that 'People still came in when their house had been blitzed the night before ... there was no sort of slacking, it was unheard of'[104] and 'I don't know a single woman during the war who panicked or screamed or behaved irrationally'.[105] At least one of the 'heroes', Beryl Bramley, recounted how she still (in 1992) relished the sight of military aircraft, such as 'the ones that flew in the Gulf, the black ones – they go "tchew!" – and oh they're wonderful'.[106] In reconstructing herself as the girl who 'served with the men who fly', the woman of the heroic narrative demonstrated her own appropriation of the qualities apparently possessed by those men. She, like him, was a hero, coping calmly, working efficiently, controlling emotion, the woman with the stiff upper lip.

In contrast, those who did not make the heroic wartime discourse their own recalled their sensitivities to the horrors of war. They confessed their fear of bombing, they spoke of the times they went home, rather than going to work in a raid. Evelyn Mills explained that she did so often: 'I was always frightened that if I got caught out in an air raid, where was I going to run to ... I just got a nervous wreck with thinking that the sirens were going off and I was going to be in the street with the bombs coming down'.[107] In contrast to the stiff upper lips of the heroes, Yvette Baynes recalled her trembling legs at the advent of a raid. 'I really was terrified', she said, especially by the prospect of 'being burned to death' as she lay in the family Morrison shelter. In contrast to Beryl Bramley, she harboured an enduring loathing of low flying aircraft.[108]

We have reviewed in this chapter the range of ways in which women remembered themselves as war workers. At one end of the spectrum they reworked the official construction of the young woman in wartime, identifying themselves with the characteristics of the (masculine) war hero. At the other end, they cast themselves in roles in which such heroism was not required, and endowed themselves with identities from which 'feminine' attributes were not removed. These subject positions were not rigidly maintained by all the women. We have observed, for example, how Yvette Baynes recalled on the one hand wanting to learn to use a rifle in the Home Guard, a relatively heroic desire, and on the other hand her unheroic choice of a series of 'safe' clerical jobs and her terror of air raids. We have seen how some of the reluctant subjects of the wartime conscription of women who stoically endured the war jobs into which they were thrust became proud of their contribution to the war effort. On the other hand, some enthusiastic recruits, who longed for heroic roles, such as Edith Dixon, described becoming disillusioned and bearing stoically, for no longer than was required, the wartime service to which they had committed themselves.[109] If the discourse of the heroic woman war worker is muted in today's society, that of the woman who did not really want a role in war at all, but was made to have one, is doubly so. It was remarkable that women in the latter category wanted to participate in our project at all. Our implied aims may have led them, when composing their wartime selves for the particular audience which we constituted, to position themselves closer to the heroic model than they would have done for a different audience. Women who were even more detached from, or alienated by, the contradictory discourse of wartime feminine identity were unlikely, regrettably, to offer their memories of the Second World War for public consumption.[110]

Women reinvented themselves in the interviews in relation to living others, as well as to those represented in recruitment literature and advertisements. We have seen them doing so *vis à vis* their parents and their brothers. They also reconstructed their own identities in relation to the men and women with whom they worked. It is to their memories of these others, first the men and then the women, that we turn in the next two chapters.

Notes

1 J. D. Cantwell, *Images of War: British Posters 1939–45* (London, HMSO, 1989), plates 21, 10, 45.

2 J. Derracott and B. Loftus, *Second World War Posters* (London, Imperial War Museum, 1972), p. 65. Controversy over the depiction of women in recruitment posters hinged on the type of femininity represented. A 1941 poster by Abram Games using a painting of an ATS member, was withdrawn after complaints that it was too glamorous, and replaced by a poster which used a photograph of a real ATS private. As Derracott and Loftus comment, 'Photos were felt to be simultaneously more realistic and more idealistic'. The search for photographs of suitably idealistic women for use in recruitment posters was evidently considerable!

3 See, for example, J. Purvis 'The Prison Experiences of the Suffragettes in Edwardian Britain', *Women's History Review*, 4, 1 (1995), pp. 103–33 and the bibliography in note 1 of this article.

4 Illustrated in J. Waller and M. Vaughan-Rees *Women in Wartime. The Role of Women's Magazines 1939–1945* (London, Macdonald Optima, 1987), p. 108. They date the advertisement January 1943. A similar advertisement was placed in *Woman's Friend*, 15 January 1943.

5 L. C. Noakes 'Gender and British National Identity in Wartime: A Study of the Links Between Gender and National Identity in Britain in the Second World War, the Falklands War and the Gulf War', unpublished D.Phil. thesis, University of Sussex, 1996. Noakes argues that the presence of women in the field in the Gulf War was destabilising to such images, but that newspaper articles and parliamentary

comment reasserted the masculinity of war as the norm, by problematising or demonising women's presence at the front: they were there either as sexual playthings for soldiers, or because feminism had gone too far; either way their place in combat was unnatural. See pp. 205–12.

6 See chapter 1, note 89. A lively interchange within a US e-mail discussion network (H-Women, 8–12 June 1994) was stimulated by the absence of images of women in the 1994 fifty-year commemorations of D-Day (6 June 1944). The opening comment was: 'During the many D-Day shows with actual veterans on them I saw one FEMALE veteran who landed during the first day under gunfire. She was ... a nurse'. The correspondents agreed that more women were involved than the commemorative coverage revealed. I am grateful to Lynn Abrams for saving me this material.

7 See for example, the *Independent*, 26 April 1995. Breaking into a stream of features about men's war roles, in the run-up to the fiftieth anniversary of VE Day (8 May 1945) was a feature entitled 'But what did women do in the War? It wasn't all waiting at home for the men'. Thanks to Alan Scott for clipping this piece.

8 For example Moira Underwood, who worked at Risley ROF wrote 'I have always thought that the work done there by both men and women was not publicised enough after the war' (M. Underwood, letter to Nicole Crockett, 16 August 1991).

9 V. Brittain, *England's Hour: An Autobiography 1939–1941* London, Futura, 1981; 1st pub. 1941), p. 137.

10 M. R. Higonnet and J. Jenson *et al.*, *Behind the Lines. Gender and the Two World Wars* (New Haven, Yale University Press, 1987), p. 35. The Higonnets characterise this construction of wartime gender relations as a 'double helix', a structure with two strands that are intertwined but never meet. During war, men and definitions of masculinity move along the male strand of the helix towards the military front. Women and femininity shift along the female strand into previously male domains but remain subordinate to the position on the male strand (pp. 6, 34).

11 J. D. Cantwell, *Images of War*, p. 10; Derracott and Loftus, *Second World War Posters*, p. 54.

12 *Ibid.*, p. 27

13 *Ibid.* The authors state that 'the quotations are from Foss's letters to the Imperial War Museum, 1971'.

14 *Woman*, 12 June 1943.

15 Pat Kirkham, 'Fashioning the Feminine: Dress, Appearance and Femininity In Wartime Britain', in C. Gledhill and G. Swanson, *Nationalising Femininity. Culture, Sexuality and British Cinema in the Second*

World War (Manchester, Manchester University Press, 1996), pp. 152–74.

16 J. B. Priestley, *British Women Go To War* (London, Collins, 1943), p. 55.

17 P. Scott, *They Made Invasion Possible* (London, Hutchinson, 1944) pp. 7–8. See also P. Scott, *British Women in War* (London, Hutchinson, 1940).

18 This phrase was also widely used in recruitment campaigns of the First World War, for example in the poster 'These women are doing their bit. Learn to make munitions'. See A. Woollacott, *On Her Their Lives Depend, Munitions Workers in the Great War* (Berkeley, University of California Press, 1994), illustration 3, between pp. 112 and 113.

19 Moira Underwood (155).

20 Moira Underwood (163). She liked the 'element of danger' which placed her close to the front line (504).

21 Moira Underwood (532).

22 For parallel accounts of brothers as wartime role models see A. Woollacott, 'Sisters and Brothers in Arms: Family, Class and Gendering in World War I Britain', in M. Cooke and A. Woollacott, *Gendering War Talk* (Princeton, Princeton University Press, 1993), pp. 128–47.

23 Felicity Snow (19, 21).

24 Felicity Snow (27).

25 Pam Wootton (165, 169).

26 Pam Wootton (256, 282).

27 Gladys French spoke knowingly of this process. She joined the WRNS, determined to be 'in the thick of it' but described how 'they say to you, you'll be a cook or a steward, you know. You say, *no I won't*, you know!': Gladys French (86), emphasis in original. Gladys insisted on training as a radio mechanic, and found the job, which involved hard manual work 'carrying these heavy transmitters and things', satisfying: 'it is terribly important. You sort of think, well, in a way, it makes lives at risk if you do it wrong' (326).

28 Ann Tomlinson (59).

29 Ann Tomlinson (72).

30 Ann Tomlinson (99).

31 Ann Tomlinson (101).

32 Ann Tomlinson (101, 108).

33 Ann Tomlinson (159).

34 Ann Tomlinson (106).

35 See, for example, C. Cockburn 'The Gendering of Jobs: Workplace Relations and Reproduction of Sex Segregation', in S. Walby (ed.), *Gender Segregation at Work* (Milton Keynes, Open University Press, 1988), p. 40, where she discusses as a reason for young women's pref-

erence to conform to gender stereotypes in their choices of training and jobs, the 'high social costs that we all pay if we disobey gender rules'. See also S.Heath, 'Whatever Happened to T.V.E.I.'s Equal Opportunities Policy', *British Journal of Educational Policy*, 11, 5 (1996), pp. 543–60.

36 The Census did not record clerical workers as a separate category until 1921. L. Holcombe estimates that there were 279 women clerks in 1861 (0.3 per cent of all clerks), compared with 124,843 in 1911 (18.1 per cent): L. Holcombe, *Victorian Ladies at Work, Middle-Class Working Women in England and Wales 1850–1914* (Newton Abbot, David and Charles, 1974), p. 210. In 1921 the figure was 492,000 (46%) and in 1951 1,409,000 (60%): B. R. Mitchell and P. Dean, *Abstract of British Historical Statistics* (Cambridge, Cambridge University Press, 1962), p. 61.

37 Margaret Gray (6, 188, 218, 306, 557, 604). She was modest about the contribution her work made to the war effort: 'It was just a job to be got on with. You felt in a tiny tiny way you were contributing to a certain extent to the war effort' (612); 'I was a really small cog in the wheel, very small indeed. But nevertheless, it was a contribution' (614).

38 Kate Lomax (730). .

39 Kate Lomax (730). Another defiant ex-clerical worker was Janice Brunton, whom we met in the last chapter trying to obtain her choice of war job in the face of parental opposition. Janice Brunton volunteered for the WAAF and agreed to continue to work as a clerk, but she was particular about the type of clerical work she was prepared to do. The job for which she volunteered, Clerk, Special Duties, was not ordinary filing or typing. Without knowing what it involved, she insisted on doing it: 'when I had my interview they said "well why do you want to do that if you've been a clerk before. Wouldn't it be better to do something that you know about?", so I said, "well no, that's the very reason why I don't want to do it, I want to do this clerk SD" and they said "oh, well, they didn't know if there were any vacancies", and they were obviously short of ordinary clerks, so I said, "well you know, as I'm volunteering" – I think that was the first time I ever got my dander up in my life – I said "If you don't let me do what I want, I won't volunteer, I'll go home". So they said "all right"' (164). Janice was trained to plot aircraft in response to radio messages, and felt that she was making an important contribution in a similar way to other women with more obviously gender transgressive jobs: 'I liked the involvement of knowing I was doing something useful. Obviously it was such a dangerous time for pilots that any information on their whereabouts was useful. You felt as if you were really doing a helpful

job' (397). She was aware that 'if you didn't do it properly somebody would perhaps suffer' (548).

40 Marion Paul (191).

41 Marion Paul (514).

42 Wartime Social Survey, 'An Investigation of the Attitudes of Women, the General Public and A.T.S. Personnel to the Auxiliary Territorial Service' (October 1941); D. Parkin, 'Women in the armed services 1940–45', in R. Samuel (ed.), *Patriotism: The Making and Unmaking of British National Identity*, vol.II (London, Routledge, 1989), pp. 158–70.

43 There were complaints, for example, that young women were being moved from the East End of London to Birmingham, while northerners were being sent to take their places. See Mass-Observation, *People in Production. An Inquiry into British War Production* (London, John Murray, 1942), pp. 165–6.

44 Ann Tomlinson (106).

45 Parkin, 'Women in the Armed Services 1940–45', p. 168.

46 *Ibid.*, p. 169; J.Rosenzweig, 'The Construction of Policy for Women in the British Armed Forces 1938–1945', unpublished M.Litt. dissertation, University of Oxford, 1993, pp. 131–4.

47 Greta Lewis (128).

48 Heather McLaren (281). Vee Robinson, *Sisters in Arms* (London, Harper Collins, 1996), pp. 77–8 describes her experience of the requirement that ATS patrol the perimeter of their Anti-Aircraft Gun Sites at night, a duty known as 'Prowler Guard': 'The ATS did all the Prowler Guard duties on F site armed only with a pickaxe handle and a whistle. We did two-hour shifts in pairs. The whistle for emergency, we hoped, would be heard by the sentry on the main gate; the men were armed with rifles and there were four of them. Understandably, we were a little uneasy when on this duty ...'

49 Amy O'Connor (773).

50 Amy O'Connor (789).

51 Yvette Baynes (356).

52 Yvette Baynes (342, 344).

53 Parliamentary Debates (Hansard) vol. 388, col. 1532, Oral Answers, 20 April 1943.

54 *The Times*, 12 November 1941.

55 Parliamentary Debates (Hansard) vol. 388, col. 1532, Oral Answers, 20 April 1943. See also N. Longmate, *The Real Dad's Army. The Story of the Home Guard* (London, Arrow Books, 1974), pp. 115, 122–5, for an account very much within the discourse of male exclusiveness. He writes, for example, that women 'clamoured to be enrolled', but a 'supporting army of cooks, drivers and telephonists' (neatly pigeon-

holing the role of the women's auxiliary forces) was not needed, and in any case women had 'ample opportunities to help the war effort ... in organizations like the Women's Voluntary Services' (p. 115).

56 For a fuller treatment of these issues see P. Summerfield, '"My Dress for an Army Uniform!": Gender Instabilities in the Two World Wars', Lancaster University *Inaugural Lecture Series*, 1997.

57 Pamela Wootton (133); Gladys French (86); Ann Tomlinson (106); Kate Lomax (730).

58 Gladys French (90, 94); Ann Tomlinson (130, 132).

59 See P. Scott, *They Made Invasion Possible* (London, Hutchinson, 1944), p. 7, where she discusses 'The "Woman in Slacks" doing a "Man's Job"'.

60 Amy O'Connor (328). See Waller and Vaughan-Rees, *Women in Wartime*, p. 82, for the reproduction of a wartime magazine feature on 'The Liberty Cut' by Mary Embery.

61 Accounts of enthusiastically contributing to the war effort in ways which were exceptional for women characterised most of those who felt they had made their decisions about joining up independently of their parents, or who recalled parental support. Among those with authoritarian parents, the occurrence of such heroic narratives depended on whether these women felt they had slipped the parental net, and obtained the type of war work they desired.

62 Evelyn Mills (33).

63 Evelyn Mills (40).

64 Evelyn Mills (77, 299).

65 Joan Stanton (164, 249).

66 Joan Stanton (375).

67 Joan Stanton (300, 301).

68 Dorothy Rose (488, 536, 289). Dorothy's narrative revealed how steeped in the new wartime norm a young girl like herself, leaving school in 1941, could be: 'I didn't feel that I was something special because I was doing war work, because everybody was doing war work. My sister was on munitions, she'd been a garment worker and then she had to go on munitions during the war. My father was a bus driver, but he was doing war work in so much as he was a warden ... My mother was knitting like mad, you know for the forces and what have you. So everybody was doing war work, you weren't special doing war work – it was just what type of war work you were doing, you know everybody had to do it' (532). The fact that the 'type of war work' she did was office work was, in her account, the result of a combination of preference and inevitability.

69 Yvette Baynes (259, 281).

70 Yvette Baynes (648, 650, 688).

71 Ethel Singleton (78).
72 Ethel Singleton (176).
73 Ethel Singleton (84, 113, 180).
74 Helena Balfour (281, 315).
75 Helena Balfour (400, 376).
76 Mass-Observation, *War Factory* (London, Victor Gollancz, 1943), pp. 42–9. See also M-O, *People in Production*, pp. 163–6. M-O said that the management view of the young women drafted into factory work was as follows: 'A minority of the conscripts were satisfactory and took to the job. A majority were less satisfactory, some definitely disgruntled, difficult to deal with, constantly absent from work, late or slack' (p. 164).
77 Those who gave stoic accounts of joining the war effort, but who looked back proudly on their contribution, were Helena Balfour, who moved from domestic service to aircraft assembly; Jean Grant, who moved from shopwork to riveting; Wilma Harrison, an upholsterer sent to work on a centre lathe in an engineering factory; Ethel Singleton, who left shopwork for welding; Nora Vickers, who went from bank work to a Royal Ordnance Factory and Caroline Woodward, who left waitressing for welding. Some of the 'stoics' were uncertain about the value of their war work. They included Sadie Bartlett, who left hairdressing and became a member of the Timber Corps of the Women's Land Army, and who spoke of being unnerved by stories that the pit props she was providing were 'no good' (260). Those who had a low opinion of their war work included Barbara Wilson, ex-interior design student and wartime aircraft fitter in WRNS; Hester Hamilton, ex-university student and wartime progress chaser; Elizabeth Little, former grocery shop worker and wartime bench-fitter and gauge-setter.
78 Hester Hamilton (16, 20).
79 Hester Hamilton (29, 43).
80 Hester Hamilton (250).
81 Hester Hamilton (257).
82 Barbara Wilson (82, 84).
83 Barbara Wilson (209).
84 Barbara Wilson (217, 219, 165).
85 R. Hoggart, *The Uses of Literacy* (Harmondsworth, Penguin Books, 1958), pp. 91–3: 'T. S. Eliot says somewhere that stoicism can be a kind of arrogance, a refusal to be humble before God: working-class stoicism is rather a self-defence, against being altogether humbled before men. There may be little you can do about life; there is at any rate something you can be'. Hoggart links such stoicism with an absence of idealism.

86 *Social Class of 'Heroes' and 'Stoics', by Parental Occupation: Heroes* (total number 25) – working class: 32 per cent (n = 8), lower middle class: 44 per cent (n = 11), middle class: 24 per cent (n = 6), *Stoics* (total number 17) – working class: 59 per cent (n = 10), lower middle class: 18 per cent (n = 3), middle class: 23 per cent (n = 4).

87 Thus it was anticipated that servicemen would oppose the conscription of women because they did not want their wives and sweethearts placed in danger: PRO Cab 65/20, 121st Cabinet conclusions, 28 November 1941. At the end of the war it was argued that women had been leading anxious, 'empty' lives throughout the war as they waited for their heroic menfolk to return. Parliamentary Debates (Hansard), 404 *HC* DEB 5s, 15 November 1944, Debate on Manpower (Release from Forces), cols 2033–4.

88 Moira Underwood (496).

89 Moira Underwood (496).

90 Moira Underwood (167, 504). Some of the women in the Forces used the same kind of language. Greta Lewis, working on anti-aircraft guns, echoed Moira Underwood when she answered a question about what she liked about her job: 'a bit of excitement, weren't there, you know, when there were an air-raid. I know it weren't very nice, but you got that bit of excitement ... they used to let you know from headquarters how many had been shot down that night' (323, 331).

91 Evelyn Mills (257).

92 Evelyn Mills (257).

93 Caroline Woodward (251).

94 In this case an authoritarian mother acted as an agent of the state, insisting that Sadie should do her bit, rather than either trying to prevent her doing so, like other authoritarian parents, or seeking to protect her from it, like the sheltering parents.

95 Sadie Bartlett (116).

96 Sadie Bartlett (130).

97 Sadie Bartlett (202).

98 Helena Balfour (480); Elizabeth Little (542); Nora Vickers (546, 417, 512–21).

99 Sadie Bartlett (246, 254).

100 Gladys French (310). The work culture in the sections of the Forces which women mechanics joined may have encouraged such attitudes. For example May Richards, an ATS radar mechanic, remembered a huge notice in the army workshops which said, 'Dead radar mechanics can be replaced. Equipment cannot' (151).

101 Amy O'Connor (548).

102 Janice Brunton (586).

103 Moira Wraith (93).

104 Emily Porter (128, 130).
105 Beryl Bramley (655).
106 Beryl Bramley (474).
107 Evelyn Mills (125).
108 Yvette Baynes (809, 813, 815).
109 For example, Edith Dixon was keen to join the WRNS against her parents' wishes, but hated service life, felt that her job contributed little to the war effort, and left as soon as she could. Fiona Thomas on the other hand put up with a job in an aircraft factory after her authoritarian mother stopped her joining the Forces, but became enthusiastic about doing her bit as a bus conductress, after defying her mother by taking this job.
110 A. Thomson makes a similar point about the absence of alienated Anzacs from his oral history project: A. Thomson, *Anzac Memories. Living with the Legend* (Oxford, Oxford University Press Australia, 1994), p. 231.

'The Attack Begins in the Factory' by Oliphant, c.1944

Chapter 4

Wartime masculinities and gender relations

The new Airborne Army is now in action in Europe—equipped by British factories.

THE ATTACK
BEGINS IN THE FACTORY

In the last chapter we looked at the ways in which women constructed their participation in the war effort in the interviews. Heroic accounts of overcoming gendered barriers to 'do your bit' in work which women did not usually do were characteristic of women who volunteered for the women's auxiliary forces or sought out demanding 'masculine' civilian jobs. Accounts of stoically 'getting on with' wartime work were offered by women who were directed by the state into war work or remained within their peacetime occupations, usually in civilian settings. The polarisation was marked, although even in this small sample there were heroes among the industrial conscripts and stoics among the service volunteers, and some slippage between the two identities over time.[1] But in general the 'heroes' were acutely conscious of their position in the process of wartime gender displacement. They wanted to take a man's place at work, or at least to work in a masculine environment. The 'stoics' were not motivated in the same way, but nevertheless some of them found themselves placed in 'men's jobs'. In this chapter we shall explore their memories of the men with whom they worked, focusing specifically on their constructions of wartime masculinities, to discover what war work meant, subjectively, for gender equality and difference. In their discussion of these issues, interviewees drew on the discursive accounts of wartime masculine identities popularly available during the war and afterwards. We shall start by examining some of these cultural representations of men and war.

Roper and Tosh write 'masculinity is always bound up with negotiations about power, and is therefore often experienced as tenuous'.[2] Historians have suggested that masculinity was particularly 'tenuous' following the First World War because trench warfare (futile, squalid, the opposite of honest combat) undermined the strong, unreflective masculinity which had been the ideal before the war.[3] After the First World War the reconstruction of masculinity as dominant and assertive in part involved antagonism towards women, especially in view of the apparent increase in women's power during and after the war. A substantial part of the female population was enfranchised in 1918, and some of the reforms which women's organisations and trade unions were now demanding (including the admittance of women to the professions, the removal of the marriage bar, and the introduction of equal pay) would further change formal relationships between the sexes.[4] Women in paid work, symbolic of the apparent redistribution of power between the sexes, were special targets of male aggression. The explicit misogyny of men's professional organisations such as the National Association of Schoolmasters, was matched by more general hostility to women in the workplace, intensified by rising levels of unemployment between the wars.[5]

This was the context within which women crossed gender boundaries at work in the Second World War, a period when masculinity was again under pressure and received special attention. Attempts were now made to dispel the shadow cast on manhood by the First World War by representing military masculinity in a dynamic way linked with technology. In contrast to the stagnation of the trench warfare of the First World War, this was to be a war of movement and speed, symbolised by the use of high powered tanks, planes and ships.[6] The motivation of men was important and the cause was a vitalising one. Not only was the war about men's virility as fighters and protectors of women, home and nation. It was also a moral war, about liberty from tyranny. Victory was vital for the future of democracy and citizenship, and could be achieved only by the compulsory mass mobilisation of men from across the social spectrum.

The rehabilitation of military masculinity in the Second World War by government policy-makers and propagandists emphasised the young fit male. He was the target of conscription to the Armed Forces. To be eligible for service a man had to be relatively young, aged 18 to 41, extended in December 1941 to 51, and physically fit. A medical examination weeded out those with 'marked physical disabilities or evidence of past disease' and those suffering from 'progressive organic disease', although such men might still be capable of working in industry.[7] By implication the man who was not a soldier in the Second World War was either too young, or too old, or unfit.

At the height of wartime mobilisation, in 1944, there were 4.5 million servicemen. There were also 10.3 million men in civilian employment not all of whom were under 18 or over 50.[8] This was the measure of the divide between the fighting forces of healthy young men destined for the front line, and the men who were apparently classified as inadequate to serve in the Armed Forces.

However, this polarisation of the fit and the unfit male obscured a further sifting process, more complex and subtle than selection

based on age and fitness, which separated some men from involvement in the military effort. Men who were both within the call-up
age range and in perfect health were exempt from military service
as a result of the Schedule of Reserved Occupations, first issued in
1939. The Schedule, constantly revised during the war, was a key
part of the Ministry of Labour's attempt to balance fluctuating
requirements for trades and skills in civilian employment against the
demands of the Armed Forces.[9] But although done in the name of
the national war effort, the process of 'reservation' was relatively
obscure to those affected, as well as to the public generally. The categories of work and the age groups exempted from call-up changed
in the course of the war, and individual firms could obtain the
exemption of particular employees whose counterparts in other
firms might not be 'reserved'.[10] Compared with these complexities,
the criteria of age and fitness in the call-up of men were much more
obvious, and as we shall see, more memorable.

Women's allocation to war work was linked to the process of the
reservation and conscription of men. The removal of men was the
condition for 'dilution' by women workers to occur.[11] Women's participation in war work followed the adjustments in the supply of
male labour. Culturally, reservation and conscription contributed to
constructions of masculinity which interacted uneasily with men's
subjective responses to wartime work possibilities and the identities
they endowed. Men who wanted to join the Forces, to become military heroes, to do their bit, might be made to stay in civilian work
on the grounds of their skill categorisation or by very specific local
labour demands. On the other hand, men who did not fall into these
categories had no choice but to leave civilian work and join up.
There is evidence of men who were enthusiastic and hard to restrain
from joining up voluntarily.[12] At the other extreme there were men
who were very reluctant to join up because, for example, they could
earn more in civilian work, they preferred to stay at home, they had
no desire to fight, or they felt dissociated from the entire project of
war. But unless those lacking enthusiasm wished to argue their pacifist case as Conscientious Objectors before a Tribunal, they were
compelled to serve.[13]

There were, then, frustrated heroes among civilian men, as well
as reluctant ones among servicemen. Women dilutees met both
sorts, as well as civilians and servicemen who were glad to be where
they were. Women also encountered public verbal and visual repre-

sentations of soldiers and civilian men. Soldiers were depicted as fit young men who assumed the identity of the soldier wholeheartedly. But if wartime heroism and masculinity were embodied in the military man, where did that leave the civilian male worker? Was there a problem about convincing him and the rest of society that he was a necessary part of the war effort and a real man? It seems that little was done to counter the implication that civilian men must be old and unfit in spite of the 'legitimate' presence in wartime civilian life of men who were both young and fit.

J. B. Priestley's 'Postscripts' provide a window on the construction of wartime masculinities. 'Postscripts' were chatty, informal commentaries on civilian life in wartime, which Priestley, the author of fiction and documentary writing, gave as ten-minute weekly radio broadcasts from June to October 1940. Priestley portrayed the war as a struggle for the defence of democracy, deliberately exposing as he did so the limitations of the achievements of pre-war British democracy. He claimed to voice 'the growing hope in decent folk everywhere' that the war would lead to the more complete fulfilment of the principles of a civilised society, namely 'a reasonable liberty along with a reasonable security'.[14] For this degree of radicalism 'Postscripts' were taken off the BBC Home Service, having achieved enormous popularity.

Priestley's society of 'decent people' was one of women and men united in support of those defending them, who were fit young soldiers, especially airmen. Priestley celebrated civilian contributions to the war effort, but left no doubt who the real heroes were:

> It's possible that distant generations will find inspiration, when their time of trouble comes, in the report in their history books of our conduct at this hour; just as it is certain that our airmen have already found a shining place for ever in the world's imagination, becoming one of those bands of young heroes, creating a saga, that men can never forget.[15]

The pilot, 'a figure from some epic – a cheerful young giant'[16] was a recurrent motif in Priestley's broadcasts. In contrast to him, civilian men were on the sidelines of bravery and heroism. They were assumed to have 'done their bit' in the previous war, like J. B. Priestley himself, and hence to have earned their 'pipe and slippers' and exemption from combat. While the soldier was serious, a hero, the civilian man was comical.[17] Young fit civilian men, who might have been exempt from military service under the Schedule of Reserved Occupations, were missing from his accounts. In contrast to both the likeable young men who became soldiers and the women participating in the war as iconic wives-and-mothers or factory and office 'girls', they were a blank in Priestley's word pictures. The male civilian void was filled in his broadcasts only by the comic figure of the old man in his slippers.

Some iconographic attempts were made to bridge the gap between notions of desirable manhood, conditioned by the demand for men on the battlefront, and the experience (common to the majority) of being required to remain outside the military. Various poster campaigns endeavoured to emphasise the importance to the war effort of men on the home front. One, announcing to male workers 'Combined Operations Include You', depicted a male factory worker using a piece of machinery, beneath a picture of a soldier firing a machine-gun in exactly the same posture. Both men had the same rippling wrist muscles and intent expressions on their faces. In the background were female 'dilutees', diminutive figures in white caps, contained and relatively inert, lacking colour and muscle compared with the men.[18] But even this representation of the civilian male worker, his masculinity enhanced both by the parallel with the soldier and the contrast with the woman workers, seems to have been exceptional. Most posters designed to raise the morale of civilian workers by linking their efforts to those of the military did not depict the industrial worker explicitly. Two poster series were produced to accompany the military campaign in North Africa in 1943 and the invasion of Europe following D-Day in 1944–45, using the captions 'The Attack Begins in the Factory' and 'Back Them Up'. As well as showing ships, tanks and bombers in action, these posters depicted soldiers in the thick of battle jumping from aircraft, firing guns and sinking ships, their lifelikeness enhanced by details such as their clothing, sometimes in tatters which revealed muscular bodies, and their resolute facial expressions. Those initiating the attack in the factories, and doing the backing up, to whom the posters were addressed, were in contrast completely invisible.[19] Posters in which civilian men became visible depicted them, like Priestley, as comic figures: little old men staggering under the weight of giant vegetables in the 'Dig for Victory' series; ageing 'gents' lounging in clubs or phone boxes in 'Careless Talk Costs Lives'; self-absorbed swells hovering in front of booking offices or working-class types furiously stuck in railway carriages surrounded by freight in 'Is That Journey Really Necessary?'[20] Post-war filmic representations of Britain at war carried on the polarisation. Men in war were soldier heroes in films such as *The Cruel Sea* (1953), *The Dam Busters* (1954), *The Colditz Story* (1954) or *The Great Escape* (1963).[21] Alternatively they were comic civilians playing at soldiering in 'Dad's Army', the much-loved gentle satire of the Home Guard, first shown on British television from 1968 to 1977.[22]

The impaired man and the superior woman

The recollections of the women interviewed in the 1990s of the men with whom they worked in the 1940s followed the polarisation between the young fit soldier and the old or unfit civilian remarkably closely, with scant references to the practice of 'reserving' fit young men in civilian employment. This was so whether the women's accounts were 'stoic' or 'heroic' although, as we shall see, there were differences between the two groups in the meanings for them of the presence of men at work.

Among the 'stoics' doing manual work in civilian industry there was a consensus that any men in civilian work 'weren't fit for the forces'.[23] Fiona Thomas produced a representative account which at the same time described the selective recruitment of men to the Forces and indicated her endorsement of the wartime evaluation of masculinity: the only 'real' men were servicemen. She was working on aircraft wings, at Vickers Armstrong's Squires Gate factory in Blackpool.

> There was no men. The men were all away, and, like I say 18 to 45 was the call-up age and that. Most of them were older men, over 45, or some who perhaps, something, they hadn't passed the medical for the Forces ... the youngest men we ever saw was some from the RAF that used to have a base at the top end of our factory.[24]

Similar contradictory constructions characterised the accounts of women stoically doing non-manual civilian work. As a secretary Yvette Baynes worked in the offices of various Birmingham factories during the war. On the question of men in these workplaces she, like Fiona, emphasised the absence of 'real' men: 'There were no men because they'd all gone to the war, there were just boys' and 'the men had all gone to war, so the elderly men had to just knuckle under'.[25] References to the system of reservations were rare. Ethel Singleton, a Manchester welder, acknowledged it after asserting, like the others, that the men she worked with 'might not have been, what shall I say, one hundred per cent healthy'. She added as an afterthought 'they couldn't send everybody and just fill it with women could they? So there had to be men that knew the job and understood it so they could teach the girls'.[26]

The answers given by those who constructed stoical accounts of doing war work to questions about the number and type of men at work, consisted of observations on the particular type of men to be found in the background in wartime. In contrast, the composition of the male workforce was a more significant reference point in 'heroic' accounts. The system of reservations might put in jeopardy a woman's chances of getting the war job she wanted; comparison of women's performance with that of male colleagues doing the same job gauged women's success in their war roles.

Marianne Lloyd became an engineering draughtswoman against opposition, but she found that the demand for women in this job was limited, even in wartime, because the sexual division of labour had been rigidified by the reservation of male draughtsmen. 'I was very rarely in a large office ... I didn't seem to have the opportunity somehow because most of the men who had been reserved in those years, you see, they were already in their jobs, and others were sort of regarded as juniors.'[27] Instead she worked in small offices, always under a male boss and with no peers of either sex, but in such offices she did not get the detail work she wanted and for which she had been trained.[28] Marianne's account suggested that the Schedule of Reserved Occupations deprived her, as a woman, of opportunities which would have been open to men.

Women in the Armed Forces worked with men who were designated sufficiently young and fit to be soldiers. But servicewomen who gave heroic accounts of their experiences made a further differentiation, between soldiers at 'the front line' who conformed to the archetype, and soldiers who worked with women in jobs that were, by definition, non-combatant. The women themselves, as we have seen, were well aware that although they might be as close to the front line as it was possible for a woman to get they were nevertheless in non-combatant, supporting roles. Servicemen working alongside them were also at a distance from actual fighting. Two constructions of these servicemen recurred in these women's narratives. They were either on their way to the battlefront, 'overseas', 'abroad' or 'on aircraft carriers' depending on the Service and job concerned. Or else they, like civilian men, were in some way impaired, and by wartime standards emasculated – they might be soldiers but they were not heroes.

Janice Brunton, a 'Clerk SD' in the WAAF whose job was to plot the position of aircraft on a huge map, reconstructed the different implications for men's and women's identities of the same military job. Selection for the secret work of 'plotting' was one of the pinnacles of WAAF achievements: only the most intelligent, fit and trustworthy woman was selected to become a 'Clerk SD'. In contrast, the men who were allocated to the plotting rooms were on their way down the military hierarchy. They 'didn't cope as well as the ladies … Mostly they were flying types who had either crashed or become unsuitable mentally and they were sent to us. They were extremely nervous'. She described how during emergencies the men would 'come out in perspiration, it'd be coming down their face'.[29] Janice emphasised her steadiness and competence in this 'stressful job' with a story contrasting her own and a male colleague's reactions to an accident which she suffered. During a 'two minute relief' to go to the lavatory she crushed a thumbnail in a door. She coolly cycled to the sick bay where the RAF medical orderly and his WAAF assistant covered her with a plastic sheet, and, reading instructions out of a book, gassed her prior to removing the thumbnail. She then returned to the telling room to carry on with her work. A Squadron Leader given to dramatic entrances and other attention-getting actions, saw her bandaged hand and asked, '"Oh woman, what have you done?" And I said, "oh I've taken my nail off sir". He fainted, and I went on telling the tracks!'.[30]

Such stories were ways of indicating that these women felt that they were not only better at their war jobs, but more heroic war workers than the men with whom they worked. Janice Brunton said that the question of whether women were superior plotters was never discussed with the men, 'but it was always privately agreed by the women that we were better'.[31] This was a common construction among 'heroic' women in the Forces, whether they were doing non-manual or manual work. Ivy Jones voiced it when comparing WAAF weather observers like herself with the young male observers en route for RAF meteorological offices abroad who came through her

office towards the end of the war. Ivy regarded the men as lazy and
believed that the women were simply better at the job.[32] Felicity
Snow, in the WAAF, likewise believed that women were superior
aircraft fitters to men: 'A lot of the men were – some of them were
lazy. Like you get in all jobs. Some didn't pull their weight, but the
women nearly always pulled their weight.'[33] Pamela Wootton, a
Wren aircraft rigger, enlarged on the same point: 'we were very conscientious … we didn't do things we shouldn't do. Men tended to
think, they were a little slap happy. There weren't as careful as we
were. We remembered our training. We remembered that we
shouldn't mix certain metals together, and we would be careful not
to. But the men tended to pick up whatever they could find on the
hangar floor and use it, you know.' Pamela's explanation of the
gender difference was based on the relationship of male aircraft fitters to the front line:

> A lot of them had chips on their shoulders, a lot of them had become
> mechanics, maybe, who wanted to be pilots, but just hadn't made the
> grade, this sort of thing … we knew what we were there for, but the
> men sometimes felt, perhaps some of them wanted to go sea-going,
> wanted to go on carriers and had been put on a shore base, and per-
> haps they didn't like it – that sort of attitude, you see.[34]

Pamela's statement 'we knew what we were there for' indicated
that, like Janice Brunton, her position as a Wren aircraft rigger was
at the summit of a woman's wartime ambition, as near to the front
line as she could get. In contrast, a man might not 'know what he
was there for' because he was pining for a war job which would
bring him closer to the wartime masculine ideal.

A common theme in these accounts was that women's greater
conscientiousness led to their exploitation. Felicity Snow explained
'Sometimes they'd have a job come up and the men would sort of
walk away and they would just call out one of the women to do it.
I think it was because mainly we were keen and we'd do it, really,
you see. Because we had to keep our image up you see!'[35] 'Keeping
up our image' was part of 'knowing why we were there'. In short,
memories of the (lazy, slapdash, inadequate, resentful and exploitative) men with whom they worked, featured in the accounts of these
women as reference points from which to reconstruct themselves in
wartime as proud and patriotic workers, more than capable of
doing a man's job.[36]

Women in civilian work also emphasised the advantages that men took of their conscientiousness. In heroic accounts these narratives worked in a similar way to those of the servicewomen we have just reviewed. For example, Moira Underwood, working with twelve men as a storekeeper at Risley ROF, remembered with a smile how she kept acquiring extra work, as the management decided that more checking of stocks was necessary: 'I was the only reliable one of the group, apparently, you know'.[37] She did not protest. Suggestions of exploitation in stoic accounts were more resentfully constructed. Sadie Bartlett, a tree feller in the Timber Corps, remembered angrily that 'they always seemed to give us the hardest work, the men the easiest'.[38] Helena Balfour, making aircraft wings at Hillington in Scotland, recalled protesting against the tendency of the tradesmen to give the women 'little fiddly jobs that they didn't like' such as putting perspex covers on the hinges of the aileron. She 'got very annoyed' with her foreman one night 'because, for several shifts, I had been sent down to the paint shop to put these covers on and I said to him one night, I said, "I really think, you've got, you've taken a dislike to me". I said, "this is maybe the third or fourth time, you know, that I've been sent to do this job". "Not at all, there's nothing to it", he says, "you just do it so well". Talk about flannel. And I said to him, "that's all very well, but it's time some of the rest of them took their turn. It's a horrible job and I hate being way down there on your own in the middle of the night", you know. I just thought I was being put upon.'[39] This reconstruction of complaining about 'being put upon' was quite different from that of heroically accepting extra work in order to 'keep up our image'. In stoic narratives women put up with being pushed around (by their parents, the state, their employers and their fellow workers), but only up to a point. They were doing their war job on sufferance and (even if they took pleasure in the memory of their skills and endurance) there were limits to the extent to which they would 'just get on with it'.

As we have seen, the idea of a masculine 'self in deficit' characterised servicewomen's accounts of inefficient men. In contrast, the explanations which women working in civilian industry offered for gender differences in productivity were more materially based. Men might take advantage of women's willingness to work hard, but they also disapproved of it because of its implications for industrial relations. Civilian factories were a site in which women might detect the tensions between the rhetoric of the war effort and the discourse of the long-running struggle between the collective interests of labour and those of capital. Nora Vickers, a former bank clerk who worked in wartime on a centre lathe in a Royal Ordnance Factory in Bury, for example, discovered that the shopfloor restraint on high productivity was not simply a product of laziness:

> People worked quite hard, but you'd not got to absolutely rush, which I found strange at first. You see, in wartime, people risking their lives – you do as much as possible – ... no, you see, 'cause lots of these people had worked in the cotton mills probably at the time of great exploitation and very low wages, and they'd worked in factories. And they'd seen that if you rushed you got your prices knocked.[40]

Wilma Harrison, also working on a centre lathe, in her case at an engineering factory in South London, added a gender difference in attitudes to unemployment into the picture. Men were disinclined to speed up because of their anxieties about being put out of work: 'when you think of how there's four million unemployed before the War, which my dad had been one of them, it could be a real fear ... I think the Guv'nors did tend, if they wanted a job really done on time, they gave it to the women, because they knew that we weren't worried about tomorrow.'[41] Women's sense of superiority over the men with whom they worked was legitimised rhetorically in speeches directed at women's morale, such as Bevin's 1943 announcement that the government had expected that three women would be required to replace two men, but that in fact the ratio worked the other way.[42] But both women's consciousness of superiority and Bevin's praise were also contradicted by institutional indicators of women's inferior status, notably pay differentials. (Wilma Harrison's 'Guv'nors' did not reward the women's reliability with equal pay.) Servicewomen received two-thirds of the pay of men. Women in industry were supposed to get equal pay if they were directly replacing a man and received 'no additional supervision or assistance', but rarely in practice received the same pay as men.[43] In 1942 about 75 per cent of women working in engineering had no chance of equal pay with men, because they were doing jobs classified as 'women's work', and even women who were doing 'men's work' were not likely to get equal pay because employers exploited the clauses in the agreements concerning 'assistance'. Not surprisingly, in view of this, women's average industrial earnings were only 53 per cent of those of men in 1945.[44]

The interviews were conducted in the early 1990s. In the twenty years since the Equal Pay Act of 1970 the principle (if by no means always the practice) of equal pay had been widely publicised in Europe and the United States, particularly through struggles to implement the legislation. For us as interviewers an obvious question was whether the wartime contradiction outlined above, between women war workers' conscious superiority and their institutionalised inferiority, had produced an awareness of gender inequality. But in reflecting in the 1990s on the discrimination of the 1940s, these women referred to a private sense of injustice and to an absence of a public language and culture in which any feelings of injustice they might have had could have been expressed. For example, Ann Tomlinson, the Wren aircraft fitter, was annoyed by the official replacement ratio on which the differential was based:

We were supposed to replace boys. They went onto aircraft carriers. The more Wrens who came, the more boys would be released to go into the war itself. But scandalously it was sort of three Wrens to release two boys ... I thought the Wrens did as good job as the boys as air mechanics. I really did, and we all thought that, but I don't remember that we ever felt militant. We used to laugh about it and look at the boys and think you know 'Three of us, lovely us, to replace only two of them, it's ridiculous'. And we laughed about it but we never made an issue of it or a fuss. No. It was so much taken for granted that women earned less, that women were considered in some ways inferior. It's strange now, the change is so great isn't it?[45]

Ann registered inter-subjectively that the interviewer might have been wondering why she and the other Wrens were not 'militant' about their sense of injustice. But such a reaction would have involved making 'an issue of it or a fuss'. Ann's choice of words indicated that such a step would have been unacceptable to her at the time. (It would also have been regarded as mutinous in the Armed Forces.) Ann's formulation also hinted at her disapproval of present-day feminism's 'issues' and 'fusses'. At the same time she acknowledged the marked difference in attitudes (produced by repeated challenges to the notion of women's inferiority) between the 1940s and 1990s: 'the change is so great'.

Ivy Jones, WAAF meteorologist, and May Richards, ATS radar mechanic, recalled their irritation about the gender-based pay differential in the Forces in similar terms. It was unjust and it 'niggled' but there was nothing to be done about it, apart from having jokey arguments with the men.[46] Action went no further than teasing, a relatively ineffectual way of registering a grievance.[47] May Richards explained that 'women's equality hadn't been thought of then'.[48] The contemporary wartime efforts of women MPs to obtain equal pay for women dilutees and teachers, and the success in 1943 of their campaign for equal compensation for war injuries,[49] were evidently not part of popular consciousness at the time, just as they have not been given a place in popular memory since the war.

The women heroically doing 'men's jobs' in civilian industry told the same story. Some of them emphasised that their reference points when thinking about pay were not necessarily what men earned, but how far the wage stretched, and how it related to a woman's previous earnings. Moira Underwood, storekeeping at Risley ROF, was not concerned about the gender differential, but was insistent on her rights to travel concessions, so that her wage would stretch over her own and her mother's needs.[50] Emily Porter had struggled to find employment before the war because of a disability. Getting a wartime civil service job with relatively good pay was far more important to her (and to her supportive lone mother) than the question of whether she received equal pay with her male colleagues.[51] Our questions about pay differentials put interviewees on the defensive. Marianne Lloyd, the engineering draughtswoman, asserted that there were gender issues other than unequal remuneration at stake: 'the fact that we were actually out there working, you know, was an achievement in itself'. In any case there was no channel through which women like her could have expressed a sense of injustice, in contrast to women today: 'we hadn't any Women's Lib in those days'.[52]

'Stoics' who had gone reluctantly into civilian war work voiced the same resignation about unequal pay with less defensiveness. For example, Sadie Bartlett, the Timber Corps tree feller, dismissed the question by saying 'It wasn't like that in those days. You know, men earned their money, and you were lucky if you had any.'[53] 'We had to be satisfied with it', said Fiona Thomas, an aircraft fitter at a firm in Blackpool.[54] Caroline Woodward, a welder, earning a relatively large amount for the first time in her life, spoke for many when she said simply, 'we never bothered' about the pay differential with men.[55]

Views such as 'men earned their money and you were lucky if you had any', were those of 'stoics' who went into war jobs reluctantly at the behest of the state. They were consistent with a general resignation towards war work. But for some of these women the experience of doing a man's job in industry stimulated an awareness of the gendered meanings of pay inequality which meant that they did 'bother' about it. The process paralleled the way in which, as we have seen, the same women's insights into the different meanings of productivity for workers and bosses enlarged their understandings of industrial relations.

The role of the trade unions in protecting the pay levels of their male members in wartime featured in all these accounts. Wilma Harrison, working on a centre lathe at Bamber Engineering in South London, spoke of her awareness of the pay differential. It explained the men's strategy of recruiting women to the union. The men wanted to unionise women because they were paid less than them, and they wanted to be sure that the women 'wouldn't be taking their jobs away from them', in other words that employers would not keep on women at the expense of men.[56] Wilma wondered whether the employers would 'have paid us equal pay' if the women had not joined, and had not been subject to union negotiations about their temporary status.

Two other women who, like Wilma, had not wished to enter the masculine sphere of engineering work in wartime, described the development of a forthright consciousness of their rights to equal pay with men during the war. Helena Balfour started her pay story by saying 'you never felt that you got enough' at Windsor Engineering, at Hillington near Glasgow, and continued with an account of objecting to unequal pay with men, 'once we had got smart enough to realise the wages that they were going out with and what we had'.[57] However, she presented the women as being in a no-win situation, making no reference to the contemporary equal pay strike at the Rolls Royce factory at Hillington in 1943.[58] Women were 'only, you know – I don't know what they called you, dilutees I think it was, so therefore they could pay you anything they liked more or less ... we did object. It never got us anywhere. There was no way, no.'[59] Helena took her objections to the Amalgamated Engineering Union, which admitted women for the first time in its his-

tory in 1943. But she echoed Wilma in believing that the men
wanted the women in the union to protect their own position,
rather than to promote gender equality. She reconstructed her marginality to the union in a vignette of an encounter with its alien pub-
based culture. 'I'd never been in a pub in my life, and I remember
going to a pub, because I was the only woman and I had to meet
three of the men' to hand over the subscriptions. Although Helena
'just wasn't a drinker' the men bought her her first gin and lime, but
after this there was no discussion of the women's cause. Helena
doubted whether her union activism made any difference to the
women's pay: 'I don't know that it ever helped us in any way'.[60]

The relationship with the union to which both Wilma and Helena
referred needs contextualising. As other accounts have shown,
under the Extended Employment of Women Agreements made
between unions and employers in 1940, if women war workers
were classified as 'dilutees' men were safe from displacement: the
women earned a proportion of the male rate, moving to the full rate
if they were direct substitutes doing the work without special supervision or assistance, and were regarded as temporary wartime workers who would be the first to be laid off. While it was to the union's
advantage to recruit them as members (for their dues and to subject
them to union discipline), there was no particular need to push for
equal pay, which was unpopular with some men since it challenged
their superiority. The unions' main objective was to protect their
members from permanent displacement, which could occur if
women were not classified as dilutees but as women doing 'women's
work' which did not come under the dilution agreements specifying
women's temporary status.[61] In some factories (such as Rolls Royce,
Hillington) women, with the support of trade union men, fought
against the 'women's work' classification, and for the higher pay
they should receive as dilutees.

Helena's reconstruction of union politics and the issue of pay
placed her closer to activism than the resignation to inequality or
lack of awareness of it described by other women. But even women
who were (unlike Ann Tomlinson) militant about pay, did not necessarily subscribe to other aspects of gender equality. Ethel Singleton is a case in point. She remembered attempting to take action to
obtain equal pay, and yet she explicitly rejected the idea of the
equality of the sexes. Ethel reluctantly went to work at A.V. Roe's
engineering company, welding aircraft fuel tanks, in 1941.

> The job we were on, we could have had equality with men, because it was a skilled job we were doing you see, we'd had to have training and we'd had to – we were doing a skilled – we were doing a man's job, and we did say one night that we thought we should have equal pay with the men you see. Why should they get more pay than us for us doing their job? And anyway we did kick against it but unfortunately nothing ever came of it.[62]

She followed this by saying that after the war, when she was an office worker at A.V. Roe's, she made a startling discovery. The General Manager, reminiscing with her about 'the night that you all suggested that you should have had equal pay' told her that the women welders were entitled to their demand, 'you really had a case, you had a cause', but that they did not get anywhere with it because they were not members of the union.[63] Wilma, as we have seen, thought on the contrary that the women's membership of the union at Bamber Engineering stood in the way of them getting equal pay and Helena believed that it had not helped. Both explanations have validity. Without union membership women had no basis from which to negotiate for the enforcement of the Extended Employment of Women Agreements with employers. With union membership they were dependent on trade union men to negotiate for them.

Ethel recognised that the manager might have been right, that she and the other 'lady welders' could have joined the union to further the cause of equal pay, but 'it never entered our heads to join a union'.[64] In any case she rejected the strategy, because it connected with options which women in the 1990s appeared to be taking (and which the interviewer, Nicole, pressing her on the issue of equality, might have represented), from which she wanted to distance herself:

> Now it's different, women want equality don't they? But 50 years ago it wasn't heard of. You wouldn't have gone into things like that. I mean we were quite happy to do the job, we were green really weren't we? But on the other hand I think we had a better frame of mind and a more happier and more serene frame of mind than you get a lot of women now, wanting top jobs and aggression ... I believe in a woman's place being in the home. I must be old fashioned mustn't I?[65]

One woman's union did negotiate for equal pay for her, but her satisfaction with the outcome was mixed. Elizabeth Little, another reluctant recruit to engineering, made no attempt herself to obtain equal pay. She subscribed to the view that the man with whom she worked at Reyrolles in Pelaw, County Durham, should receive more than her: 'he'd been apprenticed and served his time and done everything, so, well, I mean, he knew more about it than I did'.[66] However, the union took up her case on her behalf (and without giving her any choice in the matter). This action achieved equal pay for her, but (in conformity with the Extended Employment of Women Agreement) at the cost of her job at the end of the war.

> I was made redundant at the end of the war. Because while I was work-ing in there, a shop steward said 'I'm going to have to do something about your wages'. So I said, 'oh, why's that?' He said, 'you're not get-ting as much wage as the men' and he said, 'if they come back from the forces, you'll probably get the job and all sorts, so we'll have to do something about getting the girls' wages up' which he did. So that was all right. But then at the end of the war, I was made redundant.[67]

In contrast Elizabeth Little's friend Kitty was working in the trans-former room at Reyrolles, 'winding armatures and things', work evidently classified as women's work. No shop steward took action to raise her pay and 'she was kept on after the war' when Elizabeth was dismissed.[68]

Male aggression and the 'honorary man'

Women's reconstructions of the men with whom they worked in wartime were not, on the whole, very flattering. Men were old or unfit, and frequently less competent or less conscientious than women. They exploited women and neglected their interests. It would be consistent with this poor report for women to have recalled negative or hostile reactions to them on the part of the men they worked with. There was in fact a marked difference between the stories about men at work told by the 'heroes', who were keen to cross gender boundaries and do men's work in wartime, and those told by the 'stoics', who were reluctant conscripts and tolerated their mobilisation by the state for war work with little enthusiasm.

'Heroes' who were in the classic position of dilutees had vivid memories of men's hostility towards them.[69] They reconstructed the various ways in which men made women aware that they were entering a man's world on sufferance. Their narratives conformed to a pattern. Men cast doubt on women's competence and directly or indirectly tested them, but women consistently triumphed, proving the men's doubts unfounded.

Women mechanics in the Armed Forces had in common particularly vivid memories of encountering suspicion and antipathy in their war jobs. Felicity Snow's account is representative. She was an aircraft mechanic in the WAAF.

> Some didn't really like women coming into it, so you'd feel a natural resentment of – because in those days women didn't do jobs like that, and if anything went wrong, oh it used to be one of the WAAFs that had done it, you know, it always used to be the women. But you got used to it. But others were extremely helpful, you know, if you didn't understand it, they'd repeat it again. But some would repeat it again, there'd be lots of sniggers and 'oh wells, women are stupid' that sort of thing.[70]

The numerous 'buts' in this part of Felicity's account ('but you got used ... but others .. but some') suggest that she was wrestling with memories of the interaction of negative and positive experiences in her quest for the war job of her choice. More specific types of testing were remembered by other women. There were stories of screwdrivers left in aircraft engines to catch out the unobservant woman air mechanic, and of radar mechanics being called out in the middle of a foul night to mend a fault on a transmitter.[71] The most extreme 'test' was described by Pamela Wootton, Wren airframe rigger in the Fleet Air Arm. Pamela recalled making herself ill by picking up the gauntlet flung at her by a hostile lieutenant in charge of her hangar.

> He didn't like Wrens ... women doing a man's job ... He thought he'd give us a challenge, and he said, 'you see that frame over there?' 'yes sir' 'That's a Swordfish frame. Build it!' So I went back to my crew, to the girls, and I said 'five of us have gotta build that Swordfish'. Which is a joke, but we set to. We had one Leading Hand to help us, and we set to. It took us weeks, months, but we got it, from scratch. From just the fuselage frame ... I took over the job of splicing steel cable for the flying wires and control wires. And oh, my fingers were sore, they bled, but we were going to show this Lieutenant what we could do ... It took us months, but we did it and it flew. Put me in sick-bay mind you ... I was in sick-bay for a fortnight, I had a – exhaust – nervous breakdown. But it was very satisfying. It was very very satisfying, to know that it flew.[72]

The pilots who had to fly the aircraft the women had repaired were particularly sceptical about the women's abilities. Felicity recapitulated their suspicions:

> Once we'd proved ourselves, they were quite happy, but to start with, they'd never seen women working on aircraft and when they knew that a woman was going to look after their aircraft, they sort of – you saw a few raised eyebrows from the pilots because they hadn't worked with us before you see. It was very new to them. But once they got to know us and realise that we really meant – and could do what we were doing, they were, had confidence.[73]

Pilots nevertheless continued to put the women under pressure. Heather McLaren, another WAAF air mechanic, remembered that pilots sometimes 'showed off' to the women in ways that were highly dangerous, for example coming up at them fast, propellors whirling, when the women were signalling them in at night.[74]

Some women remembered that men expressed their doubts about women's presence as slurs on women's morality. For example, Katharine Hughes' experience of joining a naval Signals Office was that, initially, the male signallers 'didn't think the girls could do it, but they came unstuck'.[75] However, proof of women's competence provoked hostility from Army Signallers with whom they later worked and whose skills, she believed, were inferior to those of the Wrens. Katharine remembered that the hostility was expressed in the common allegation that the role of women in the Forces was to provide sexual partners for men. She said:

> They weren't up to scratch, no. But I mean you'd never get a man admit that, you know. Some of them used to say things like the women were officers' groundsheets and things like that you know. You'd have some nasty things but they were like water off a duck's back. We knew what we were doing. We knew we could do it, and it was just a case of jealousy more or less.[76]

She was convinced that women proved themselves, saying that she was proud to do the job 'to prove that women weren't stupid', and, in an interesting shift from rebuttal of the sexual slur on women in the military, to rejection of a feminine reproductive image, she went on 'they weren't the ones, just the hands that rocked the cradle kind of thing'.[77] In Katharine's account the implication that the role of servicewomen was primarily a sexual one could easily be ignored in the knowledge that on the contrary, women did a vital job better than the men they worked alongside.[78]

Several women recalled the situation as one in which there were no concessions to women's biology. 'Like monthly times, when women perhaps didn't feel too good, you still had to keep on, because you really had to pull your weight, because otherwise they would say, "oh look, women are no good. Look they flake out once a month" sort of thing.'[79] May Richards, an ATS radar mechanic, remembered the same pressure when she was in the early stages of pregnancy in 1944, feeling 'rotten, groggy' but 'you were given no leeway'.[80]

These accounts suggest that the women themselves had internalised the pressures they talked about. They were keen to do men's work in wartime, and so they imposed upon themselves an obligation to prove not only that they could do it, but that they were as good as, or better than, the men. Their self-image as heroic war workers did not permit them to, as it were, walk away from the Swordfish fuselage or retreat to the sick-bay with their period pains. Felicity made explicit the response of all these women to the experience of male hostility. It was worth stoically putting up with the adverse situation, in pursuit of the heroic role that the women wanted. 'You just had to battle through ... you just got on with it', even though the quest involved superhuman effort: 'you really knew that you'd have to work – we had to work harder to prove ourselves than the men did'.[81]

Women doing 'men's work' in civilian industry reported that their superhuman efforts isolated them. There was no happy reconciliation with their male colleagues in their narratives. For example, even when Marianne Lloyd had proved her competence as a draughtswoman in the small drawing offices where she was the only woman, relations with the draughtsmen for whom she worked remained strained. 'I think two or three of the superiors, I was a bit edgy with. I didn't take to being dictated to very easily. And I think they were a little dogmatic at times, possibly because I was a girl, and I did have little arguments'.[82] Beryl Bramley, working for the Aeronautical Inspection Directorate (AID), made explicit the isolation which Marianne implied. The resistance of the men whose work she was inspecting declined, but she was not accepted: 'after a while I didn't have much trouble, but I was very lonely'.[83] The year spent in the AID was a 'lonely dodgy bit' of the war for her, and in

spite of her enjoyment of the work itself, the tense relationship with
her male colleagues prompted her to volunteer for the Air Transport
Auxiliary (ATA).[84] The masculine industrial culture within which
both these women worked, as relatively skilled workers, could not,
apparently, accommodate them. Their male colleagues kept them at
a distance which they, from their side, maintained.[85]

In the narratives of 'heroes' doing men's work in the Forces, on
the other hand, there was always a moment when the women were
accepted and assimilated, a satisfactory resolution of the setbacks
previously encountered. May said that once she had successfully
repaired the radar transmitter at midnight, 'I was accepted then'.[86]
Felicity summed up what acceptance meant: 'we just literally
worked together ... We were all just friends, all mates together.
They treated us as men really'.[87] This was reiterated by numerous
'heroes'. Eventually the men treated Heather McLaren 'Just like
themselves. We were just like one of them'.[88] Pamela Wootton spoke
of being similarly accepted, after surviving the trials placed before
her: 'we were treated like men, we were treated like men ... we just
joined in and we were part of the crew'.[89] Gladys French, a Wren
radio mechanic, said 'you were just one of the boys so to speak ...
you weren't treated specially as a woman'.[90] Yvette Baynes, a
civilian secretary during the war, used the same words about her
testing experiences across the gender boundary in the Home Guard.
'We weren't treated any differently to the men. We had to do
exactly the same as they did', she said. Once the women had shown
they could manage 'We were treated as though we were just one of
the boys'.[91]

What did being treated as 'one of the boys' mean? Paula
Schwartz's discussion of gender relations in the French Resistance is
illuminating. Schwartz suggests that women in men's roles (including, for a very small number of Resistance women, leadership and
combatant ones) acquired an androgynous status. They 'were
divested of their sexuality by the men with or over whom they were
working'.[92] This was in part a military strategy. 'Gender scrambling',
in which men and women adopted noms de guerre of the opposite
sex, concealed their identities and enabled them to perform acts of
resistance undetected. But women's androgynous status also served
other purposes, with equivalents in the context of the non-clandes-
tine British war effort in which the women we interviewed were
working. It promoted solidarity in the group, because desexed

women were no longer defined in terms of conventional gendered roles (such as wife, girlfriend, lover) which, by attaching women to particular men would have divided the men's loyalties. As 'honorary men' women were defined only in terms of their membership of the group, and gender was not divisive. The repeated references of the British women to being 'just one of the boys' suggested the same degendered sense of belonging.

Women's androgynous status was not, however, a stable one. Markers of difference remained. The price of integration for women was adherence to a male super-norm, rather than to the standards of male proficiency that the women observed around them, which, as we have seen, these women thought were rather low. They set themselves targets based on idealised masculine work performance, at the same time as feeling that they had to deny any 'feminine weaknesses' in themselves. In trying to become one of the boys, the women in fact marked themselves as different.

As far as the men were concerned, degendering the women with whom they worked may have promoted group solidarity, but it also meant that men lost in these 'honorary men' the markers of feminine otherness which normally worked to establish masculinity. These trouser-clad androgynes destabilised the polarisation upon which gendered identity normally rested. Men attempted to salvage it in a variety of ways. One was to resurrect a few vestiges of the chivalry which was now irrelevant, so, for example, swearing in front of the women workers was commonly outlawed.[93] The men were not behaving quite as they would if the women had not been present, or if assimilation had been complete and each woman had really become 'one of the boys'.

Another male strategy for maintaining gender difference was quite the opposite, involving 'after hours' sexual attention. Gladys French, WRNS radio mechanic, said that as far as work was concerned 'romance didn't often enter into it. It really was that you really all worked together'.[94] But off duty, gender lines could be redrawn: 'there were some that obviously wanted you to go to bed with them. There were people like that, people that were cheeky and you just laughed at them and said not on your nelly, you know. There were people like that in those days, of course, they thought the Wrens were fair game, but of course it wasn't true, not to a great extent'.[95] The idea that servicewomen were 'fair game' belonged with the allegation referred to by Katharine Hughes, that they were

'officers' groundsheets'. They had stepped out of women's protected sphere in wartime, and their public appearance could be
interpreted to mean that they had made themselves sexually available. Their gender transgressiveness could also be regarded as a
provocation to men; the 'masculine' response was to remind
women where power really lay.[96]

Several of the women remembered occasions on which they
repelled unwanted attention. It was, after all, coming from men
whose competence and conscientiousness they did not rate highly,
and who did not possess the more glamorous wartime identity of
the soldier hero at the front who figured in numerous 'heroic'
accounts as an object of desire.[97] For example, Gladys French said,
'I remember once having to walk home when I went out with a
fellow that I met in the hangar, and I did walk home. You did walk
home in those days, you said, you know, no, I'm not having any'.[98]
While the women telling these stories recalled their anger in the
interviews, they also stressed their assertiveness. Part of their
wartime identity involved being able to tell men who tried to take
advantage of them that they 'were not having any'. However, colleagues' sexually predatory behaviour off duty, like their restraint
on swearing when working with women, operated against the
degendered condition of being 'just one of the boys'.

Manly men, womanly women and 'pleasant camaraderie'

Women who constructed themselves as stoic recruits to the war
effort told very different stories of gender relations at work. For
'stoics' there was less pride tied up in battling for the right to do
their war job, and less internalised pressure to do it better than the
men around them than there was for the 'heroes'. Stoic narratives
emphasised the ways in which men indicated to women doing men's
work that they were different from men, in spite of their involvement in masculine jobs. They also reconstructed the part which
women themselves played in the everyday, usually benign, reitera-
tion of gender differences. Theirs were not narratives of assimilation, but of the construction of differentiated gender identities in
situations in which distinctions might become blurred.

In contrast to the epic stories told by the heroes, of being resisted,
tested and assimilated, while in subtle ways being reminded of their
difference, stoics produced matter-of-fact accounts of mutual toler-

ance. The war meant that men had no choice but to accept women working alongside them, in the same way that women had to put up with war work which was not of their own choosing and 'just get on with it'. This was the case for 'stoics' in the Forces as well as in civilian industry. For example, Barbara Wilson reluctantly mending planes in the WRNS recalled 'some of the men didn't like it and some did', but 'we were just necessary at the camp ... we were just part of the whole set up'.[99] Caroline Woodward said that the men 'just had to accept us' because 'there wasn't any men left' and, similarly, Helena Balfour said that the men in the factory 'hadn't any option, they had to tolerate you'.[100] Several of these women in fact (like the heroes) recalled intolerant men, such as critical trainers and fault-finding foremen who 'didn't like the idea of having women in factories'.[101] But even if a preference for an all-male working environment was a general attitude among the men in the factory, gender tension of the sort that the 'heroes' described was not the outcome. The comments of Jean Grant, a wartime riveter, suggest that this can be explained by the symmetry in the attitudes of the men and the women: 'I think, just, they thought that women shouldn't be doing that kind of thing. But then we thought the same but we just had to do it'.[102]

Some stoics suggested that men played a more positive part in their working relationships than mere tolerance. Wilma Harrison and Elizabeth Little recalled kindly foremen deciding what type of work they should do, within the context of the shifting wartime sexual division of labour. Both were moved from rough to more precise work, in Wilma's case on centre lathes, and in Elizabeth's from bench fitting to setting the gauges used in precision work by toolmakers. They did not suggest that they particularly wanted, or had to struggle to get, such jobs. Power lay with the men in charge of them, who made the decisions about their allocation to work, their removal from it and their remuneration.

Physical and verbal teasing were common features of these memories. Elizabeth Little recalled a male trainee who teased the girls with pranks like pulling their chairs away as they were about to sit down.[103] Wilma remembered that in general women put up with or even enjoyed such antics. Helena Balfour described such games and the verbal interchanges which accompanied them as 'pleasant camaraderie'.[104] Only when Wilma thought the men were doing it at inappropriate moments did she retaliate: 'sometimes you had to be firm with the men, because they did like to muck about a bit. And that's alright if you're not working, but if you're working, and if someone comes up and sort of digs you in – oh, I used to just turn round and swipe them one, because it's dangerous'.[105]

Verbal teasing had a sexual slant. Examples at Windsor Engineering included the treatment of Helena Balfour's friend, a young woman member of the Salvation Army, who sometimes came to work in her uniform: 'she'd come in and walk through the factory, she got a lot of wolf whistles and calls, you know when she came in, and she was teased a lot about that … and of course they tried, sometimes they tried to, you know they would tell sort of suggestive jokes to try and get you to blush or, you know, these kind of things, but you just got that you took it all in your stride, or you ignored it'.[106] Similarly Caroline Woodward said cheerfully that the men at Scottish Motor Transport (SMT) where she was a welder, 'tormented' the women workers, a word also used by Jean Grant, but they were 'never nasty or dirty spoken'.[107] Caroline was teased about whether she had a boyfriend: 'You know, are you going out with anyone, you know, have you not got a boyfriend yet? You know. I bet you have. I'm going to see your mother, tell your mother you're going with a boy, you know, and all this'.[108] As a 17 or 18 year old she did not know how to respond except to 'go purple like a beetroot, be embarassed', but she remembered that an older married woman, who 'mothered' her, 'used to shout at them, you know, give them back'. Caroline's evocation of this banter was by no means critical or bitter: 'it was just all good clean fun'.[109] There was one exception in her account concerning her older woman friend. This story revealed differentiation, based on race and cultural difference, in Caroline's perceptions of heterosexual teasing. A Black man from British Honduras 'was always throwing pieces of paper at her, you know, letters and that, and she was a married woman, her man was out fighting in the war and that. She had to report him. Apart from that they never bothered us … they respected us and we respected them'.[110] The Honduran evidently did not understand the unwritten rules of 'pleasant camaraderie', notably what women meant when they 'gave as good as they got' and when men should desist. His persistent targetting of a particular woman who was not only married, but married to a soldier, remained a remembered offence in Caroline's mind.

Some of the 'stoics' remembered occasions when they 'gave as good as they got', discomfiting their male colleagues. Fiona Thomas, assembling aircraft wings at Vickers Armstrong in Blackpool, said the men 'teased us rotten, but we didn't take any notice of it, we just teased them back again'.[111] Her memories conjure up the pleasure she took in repartee. A story she told twice was about a guard on the factory gate who insisted on searching her gas mask case:

> He said, 'I'm sure you haven't got your gas mask in that case'. I said, 'Well why bother then if you know I haven't got it?' He said, 'Where is it?' I said, 'Well if it's not in there it must be at home' ... He said 'I'm going to have to search it' and he tipped it out and I had two sanitary towels in. I said 'I told you, didn't I?' His face was like a beetroot.[112]

She also loved mimicking her foreman. 'We used to take the mickey out of him something rotten. He'd been a carpet salesman before he had to join up and he used to walk around there as though he was somebody, you know. We used to walk behind him like this, pretending that we had a roll of lino on our shoulder'. She summed up her youthful delight in cheeking the opposite sex with 'in them days it was deadly to dare'.[113]

Ethel Singleton's account highlights the contrasting features of the stoical and the heroic accounts of relations with men at work. Ethel, the reluctant welder at A.V. Roe's in Manchester, remembered working with both skilled fitters and unskilled labourers, all but one of whom were men.[114] There were some tensions between the men and women at first. Some of them were 'not so polite with us' because 'we were women weren't we, you know I suppose to them' and 'they resented the women working in the factories'. Men's resentment took the form of teasing: 'they would say things and joke and you know, make fun of you and things like that' and some of them swore.[115]

These problems disappeared over time as in other accounts, but Ethel's explanation of the establishment of 'equality' between the men and women was strikingly different from the accounts of the 'heroes'. Ethel explained that the women's task was to 'tame them', which meant curbing the negative features of men's behaviour and making them 'respect' the women as women. She described how they emphasised to the men that they were welding only because the state had sent them to weld, and that their purpose was simply to do the job, and not to prove that women were as good as or better at it than men. 'We knew we *had* to do a job and we *weren't* there to prove we could do it, and once we got over that they accepted us then as equal more or less, you know, and we had lots of fun with them'.[116] 'Equal more or less' referred to equality based on difference, not the equality achieved by defeminising women and turning them into 'honorary men'. Ethel's subsequent elaboration of the relationship between the 'lady welders', as she and her friends called themselves, and their male colleagues made this clear. The principal manifestation of this type of equality was being 'respected' by the men, something to which, as we have seen, other women such as Caroline Woodward referred. 'I wanted to be treated like a woman, and I think that's why we got respect from the men.'[117] This was achieved by the women emphasising their gender in various ways. They did so verbally, 'if you spoke right to them, they would treat you right',[118] through their behaviour, 'we didn't drink, we didn't smoke, we didn't – you know – do the things that a lot of them [women] wanted to do to be equal to men',[119] and visually, by not wearing trousers to work. Ethel and her friend always dressed in frocks over which they wore their welding aprons. To Ethel, wearing trousers, smoking, drinking and swearing were markers of a gender transgression which she did not want to commit:

> Some girls wore trousers if they preferred to wear them, but I never liked them. I didn't want to lose my identity and it was the same with the girl who was my mate as you call, my friend. We never lost our identity as being girls on the job or women. I think the war made a lot of women masculine you see, and they thought that to wear a pair of trousers and to smoke a cigarette and be brash, that they were only equal to men. Well I didn't want to be like that. I didn't want to lose being a woman, female.[120]

Ethel made it clear that she had no desire to become 'just one of the boys'.

The assimilation which Ethel achieved through her 'taming' strategy was marked and maintained by heterosexual game-playing between the two groups, at work and after work. In contrast to the 'heroic' repudiation of such sport, Ethel welcomed and enjoyed the game, which emphasised the gender difference which she prized. Power was by no means concentrated on the men's side. There were flirtations between the welders and the fitters: 'we had some boyfriends amongst them let's say! Some of them used to sing to us and take us out you know, we had dates with them'.[121] But 'taming' also involved keeping men's advances under control. Married men were 'taboo' and Ethel described the 'system' by which the 'lady welders' decided if a man who wanted a date was to be accepted or not. Since a common prelude to seduction on a date was 'my wife doesn't understand me', the girls got together to 'find out if his wife understands him' by discovering who was married and who single.

> We had cards that we used to clock on and off the time, you know, when we went in the morning, when we left in the evening, we had these clocking cards, so we used to go and find out his name and what code number he had on it and if he said he was single, and he'd got B, C or D on it, well we knew he was a married man with one or two or three or four children![122]

Commenting on this wily scheme, Ethel said with great zest, 'Those were things you learned on your own, they weren't taught with the welding! Oh it was a great life, it was grand, I enjoyed it. I had lots of fun.'[123]

Gender relations in women's work

The context of the degendered relations with male colleagues described by 'heroes' and the engendering dynamics described by 'stoics', was 'men's work', in either the Forces or industry. Women who, in contrast, did 'women's work' in either setting, reconstructed their relationships with men at work differently again. The classification of their wartime work disqualified them from becoming 'one of the boys'. Their work was feminine and so were they. Thus marked as 'others', they served to maintain rather than to threaten gender identities.

A woman who moved from a masculine to a feminine job during the war reconstructed men's responses to women in the two different work situations as strikingly different. We have already reviewed Pamela Wootton's recollections of the tests set by a hostile lieutenant for women aircraft riggers. In her impassioned account she had to succeed in the impossible task of rebuilding a Swordfish aircraft from the frame, even though it 'put me in sick-bay'.[124] She was subsequently sent for officer training. However, there were no postings for a Naval Engineer Officer's Assistant, the job for which she qualified, and she did not want to take on different work. She therefore returned to the airfield where she had previously been a mechanic. However, she was not sent back to the hangar, but became secretary to the Commander of the station, when her pre-war clerical experience was revealed.[125] At first this step back from the 'heroic' work she had wanted upset her, but she reconciled her-self, constructing the relationship with her new boss in terms of rec-iprocal (if hierarchical) affection: 'he was such a dear, oh he was a darling'.[126] In sharp contrast to her life as a mechanic, she felt that she was pampered in her new role, not only by her boss but also by the naval personnel affected by her work. She was responsible for making out the duties of the men: 'That was a really good job because I was showered with chocolate, showered, "Don't put me on on Thursday, I'm taking a girlfriend out" ... it was wonderful, yes, and I made the most of it'.[127]

Marion Paul spoke in similar terms about her male colleagues' response to her. As we saw in chapter 3 she would have liked to have been an ATS driver, but as a pre-war clerical worker she was made to become a Regimental Clerk. She was one of five 'girls' working with 120 men of the Royal Electrical and Mechanical Engi-neers (REME) at an isolated base in the Yorkshire Wolds.[128] She was the only ATS clerk, at the bottom of a small masculine hierarchy in the Regimental Office where the establishment for each workshop, postings, promotions, leave, and catering requirements were worked out. In spite of her disappointment about driving, she took to the job 'like a duck to water'.[129] It was not dissimilar to her cler-ical job in the colliery office, but she greatly preferred it, both because she was no longer tyrannised by an oppressive boss and because she felt well treated by the REME soldiers. Her description of them as the 'tradesmen of the army' expressed the respect she felt for them. They were not 'impaired' in her account. Her memories were of unadulterated masculine chivalry:

> Really, we were cared for, we were pampered, we were looked after, all the men were so kind to us, you know, there was no nastiness at all, they were so kind to us; they were protective towards us and all this. And at the ATS Headquarters at Bedbury ... they thought 'those poor girls out in the wild' you know, 'life is hard for them', whereas we were having a whale of a time because although we worked quite hard, as I say, we had such lovely friendships with people there and they were so kind to us, and it was really very nice.[130]

The experience of chivalrous treatment as one of a minority of women was repeated when Marion was later posted to Italy with a REME regiment: 'You were dined and wined ... there were so few ATS, so few women with all those men, and they never took advantage of you. They were always kind and brotherly'.[131] Even though Gladys French working as a WRNS radio mechanic on Orkney was also one of a group of women heavily outnumbered by men, as were the women working on airfields as mechanics, they did not describe the men with whom they worked as 'kind and brotherly'. In these accounts male colleagues were testing them out or treating them like men on duty, or alternatively trying to 'take advantage' of them off duty.

The 'pampering' of personal secretaries by their bosses was a compensatory feature for dull clerical jobs in the narratives of some stoics, as well as in these 'heroic' accounts. Yvette Baynes reconstructed the special treatment she received from a succession of bosses as the reward for her dedication as a secretary. 'I was very spoiled ... I liked being spoiled'.[132] 'Spoiling' by 'lovable' bosses, was flattering. It meant that she was trusted, given time off, presented with gifts and cakes, and incorporated into the boss's family. It made her feel special.[133] Joan Stanton, who described her clerical jobs as 'uniformly boring', gave a similar account. She illustrated it with a story of one of her bosses entrusting her with the task of spending black market clothing coupons on fancy underwear for his mistress. She found these shopping expeditions much more interesting than typing correspondence concerning hydraulic tipping gear.[134]

The special treatment which women such as Pamela Wootton, Marion Paul, Yvette Baynes and Joan Stanton remember receiving in their 'women's work', was the product of a relationship in which the roles of each of the participants were polarised by gender. The 'pampering' and chivalry they recalled were summed up in the words of Peggy Peters, civilian secretary at a naval base, who said 'They seemed to treat us with kid gloves'.[135]

However, while chivalrous treatment was one way of marking the female 'other', sexual exploitation was another. Marion Paul's repetition of the fact that the men she worked with 'never took advantage of you' suggests that this was surprising, and the possibility of a sexual threat lurked in the accounts of a number of those who had done women's work.[136] One of the women in 'women's work' who did remember being 'taken advantage' of when on duty was Estelle Armitage, a Black woman who had volunteered for the ATS in Jamaica and came to Britain in 1944. She worked as a clerk at an army headquarters in Central London. Her duties included typing letters and taking them to the offices for signature.

> Once when the Commanding Officer sent me in, this old man, this old Colonel, came to – I said, 'is that all right sir?', you know, and gave him – and was going out – and he came to the door and wanted to kiss me! I said, 'do you mind!'. So I reported him to the officer, I was so mad. This old bloke! I suppose they were trying it on, you know that it happens, if you were that type of person you would just, 'oh yeh' you know. But we were brought up differently.[137]

Estelle's account is interesting on several levels. It is a story of what was probably routine low-level sexual harassment in office work before, during and after the war. It also had a racial dimension. A 'Colonel', occupant of a position redolent of British imperialism, was attempting to exact, in addition to Estelle's typing, a small sexual favour, from a colleague whose status as a Private, a woman and a 'coloured person', was low relative to his own. Estelle's reconstruction of her robust refusal of his demand, stemming from her clarity about the proper way to behave, referred explicitly to her own strict Christian and middle-class upbringing in Jamaica, and implicitly to the rejection of a subjugated, colonial status by the Jamaicans before the war. Furthermore, Estelle's disgust at 'this old bloke … trying it on' speaks of her perception of the undesirable masculinity of soldiers left at home, working in offices because they were too old for active service, another expression of the almost universal construction which we reviewed earlier in this chapter.

She was not the only woman doing 'women's work' in the Forces who recalled demands for sexual favours from the men she worked for. Waitresses, like secretaries, could be the targets of such expectations. Mary Mackenzie worked as a WAAF waitress in a sergeants' mess. She recalled frequent sexual invitations from the 'groundcrew' at the airbase. She made it clear that the groundcrew did not possess the romantic status of aircrew, but they were Mary's superiors in rank. Their suggestions that she and other waitresses might obtain advantages (including promotion) by having sex with them were given added force by their positions of authority. Mary reconstructed her rebuttal of their invitations both as 'cheekiness' by which she meant insubordination, reflecting her position in the power hierarchy, and as 'primness', that is moral superiority, on her part:

> These were the groundcrew men I'm talking about. You know, 'Come and sleep with me and you'll get this and you'll get that' sort of thing ... Well that was something I was very very much against. I suppose I was a Miss Prim in my way, but I can't help that, and I'd be cheeky to them then, and I'd say, 'Right you report me' – one of them said he would report me, he'd put me on a charge for being insubordinate. I said, 'You do that and I'll tell them why I was insubordinate. I'll tell my officer why' ... One of them suggested that I'd get my promotion if I'd spend the night with him. I said, 'Supposing I never get promotion, I will not get it that way'.[138]

This kind of interaction, like the colonel's treatment of Estelle, was not regarded as 'pampering'.

The gender dynamics of pampering and what we would now call harassment operated on the same trajectory. In both relationships women were treated as feminised 'others'. The definitions which the women themselves gave to these types of behaviour were informed in part by their moral values. They were also informed by the way they positioned themselves in relation to the consciousness of 'harassment' to which the feminism of the last twenty years has given rise. As in the discussion of equal pay in the interviews, which we reviewed earlier in this chapter, our understandings and awareness of sexual harassment put our interviewees under pressure to accept or reject such a description. For example Janice Brunton (who during the war was a filter plotter in the WAAF) recalled with disgust the 'wandering hand' of the boss's son in the job she did as a 16 year old before joining the WAAF. He used to keep her behind at the office until her bus had gone, and then took the opportunity to drive her home and to give rein to his hand. She felt powerless: 'it was just something you thought you had to put up with'.[139] On the other hand, Pamela Wootton remembered cheerfully that, when she worked at her local town hall before leaving to become an aircraft rigger in the WRNS, the Assistant Treasurer's Secretary 'used to chase me round the desk, you know. But in those days it was a bit of fun, you know. I didn't get uptight because he used to chase me around the desk ... it was light relief really when you think about the war and the bombs and everything that was going on ... it was all done in fun, you know, it was just a little bit of light relief, a change from taking down shorthand notes'.[140] Whereas Janice Brunton thought that 'these days' her whole approach to the attention of the boss's son would be different, Pamela Wootton was dismissive, asserting 'if everyone just treated it as [fun] there wouldn't be half all this trouble about sex equality and sexual harassment and – it's a load of nonsense'.[141]

Women's views of wolf whistling were similarly polarised between seeing it as offensive and as 'harmless fun'. Yvette Baynes disliked crossing a bridge over the furnaces of one of the wartime factories at which she worked, because 'the men could see up, you see they would look up and of course they would wolf-whistle, they could see your legs'. She went a long way round to avoid this bridge, in spite of the loss of time.[142] In contrast Myrna Wraith, also working in the offices of a factory, remembered sometimes having to go on the factory floor to take messages:

> All these men thought it was, you know, fantastic having a 16 year old … and you know, there were lots of whistles … these days, you know when there's this thing about sexual harassment and all that, well I can't understand you know why women can't … I didn't find it a problem at all. I suppose in one way I was quite flattered … you know, giving anybody a wolf whistle, I can't really think that's anything to get upset about.[143]

In these subjective reconstructions similar male behaviour could be laudatory or exploitative, and could augment or diminish a woman's sense of self. Whether these women in 'women's work' felt that their unequal and sexualised working relationships with men produced 'pampering' or 'harassment' depended on their memories of how the special attention which marked their feminine identities made them feel, as women and as people.

All the women discussed above had memories of working relationships with men in wartime. They reconstructed them in terms of both the wartime ideal of masculinity, and their own sense of themselves as wartime women workers. As we have seen, those who depicted themselves as heroically taking on men's jobs saw the masculinity of the men with whom they worked as impaired. They remember working to prove to the men that they were their equals (at least) and resisting male sexual strategies for maintaining and reinforcing gender differences. 'Heroic' women welcomed assimilation to the ranks of their male colleagues, although this was more commonly achieved in military jobs than in civilian industrial ones.

Women who stoically put up with 'men's' work across the gender boundary also remembered the masculinity of their male colleagues as 'in deficit'. But their accounts of gender relations at work were quite different. They might have perceived their male colleagues as old and unfit, but they were still men, in relation to whom women could define themselves as different, feminine. Women who were performing work understood to belong in the classification 'women's work', on the other hand, were, by definition, not in a position to claim equality with the men among whom they worked. Whether they undertook such work as a contribution to the war effort which they took up proudly, or as a dull chore, their memories of the treatment they received from the men around them indicated that the women represented to the men (and to themselves) the feminine 'other'. This was the case whether they understood that treatment in terms of today's feminist constructions as 'harassment' or in terms of longer-standing cultural constructions, as 'pampering' and 'harmless fun'.

For some women, however, questions about how they got on with the men at work were meaningless because they came into contact with so few. For Dorothy Rose, a clerical worker at the Ministry of Food in Manchester, and Evelyn Mills, operating a duplicator at the Admiralty in London, the working environment was 'all ladies', it was 'a women's world'.[144] The salient social relationships at work for these women were with other women. Even among civilians who did work with men, only a few were the sole woman in their work setting. On the whole, a gendered division of labour persisted, such that most women, whether mending aeroplanes in the Forces or operating centre lathes in engineering factories, worked principally with women. Whereas this chapter has been devoted to women's reconstructions of men and masculinities, the next will examine their accounts of the women with whom they worked in wartime.

Notes

1 For example, Edith Dixon was an enthusiastic recruit but was discouraged by the conditions in the WRNS and the feeling that her job

was unimportant. Fiona Thomas was a reluctant (and possibly unreliable) worker in an aircraft factory, but a later job on the buses appealed to her, and in this context she constructed a portrait of herself as a committed war worker.

2 M. Roper and J. Tosh, 'Introduction: Historians and the Politics of Masculinity', in M. Roper and J. Tosh (eds) *Manful Assertions: Masculinities in Britain Since 1800* (London, Routledge 1991), p. 18.

3 On the idea that Edwardian manhood failed the test of trench warfare, see E. Showalter, 'Rivers and Sassoon: The Inscription of Male Gender Anxieties', in M. R. Higonnet, J. Jenson *et al.*, *Behind the Lines. Gender and the Two World Wars* (New Haven, Yale University Press, 1987) pp. 61–9. On inter-war changes in the construction of masculinity, see K. Boyd, 'Knowing your Place: The Tensions of Manliness in Boys' Story Papers 1918–1939', in Roper and Tosh, *Manful Assertions*, pp. 145–67. For an account of the (sometimes violent) reassertion of masculinity in the post-war years, see S. K. Kent, *Making Peace. The Reconstruction of Gender in Interwar Britain* (Princeton, Princeton University Press, 1993), ch. 5, pp. 97–113.

4 H. L. Smith, 'British Feminism in the 1920s', in H. Smith (ed.) *British Feminism in the Twentieth Century* (Aldershot, Edward Elgar, 1990).

5 On the intensification of anxieties about masculinity as a result of the First World War among male teachers, see A. Oram, *Women Teachers and Feminist Politics 1900–1939* (Manchester, Manchester University Press, 1996), pp. 74–9. For hostility towards women at work more generally, see D. Beddoe, *Back to Home and Duty. Women Between the Wars 1918–1939* (London, Pandora, 1989) pp. 52–3, 60–1.

6 See, for example, Lyddel Hart, *Dynamic Defence* (London, Faber and Faber, 1940); T. Wintringham, *New Ways of War* (Harmondsworth, Penguin, 1940).

7 H. M. D. Parker, *Manpower. A Study of War-time Policy and Administration* (London, HMSO, 1957), pp. 163, 494. The Ministry of Labour explicitly stated the differences in the quality of men required by the military and by civilian industry. A condition, such as 'a non-disabling physical deformity' which made a man unfit to be a 'fighting unit' might not 'detract from his efficiency as an industrial unit': p. 493.

8 Central Statistical Office, *Fighting with Figures. A Statistical Digest of the Second World War* (London, HMSO, 1995), Table 3.3.

9 The Ministry of Labour and National Service (MOLNS) tried to use the Schedule both to restrain men from entering the Armed Forces, and to make them do so, in relation to the numbers needed to satisfy industrial and military requirements for a supply of technical skills. The Ministry also used the Schedule to move skilled men round the

country so that enough tradesmen were allocated to various different branches of war industry, e.g. aircraft factories and Royal Ordnance Factories. Different government departments, firms and factories competed with each other and with the Armed Forces for supplies of skilled labour, and resisted the withdrawal of skilled men, to varying extents. See P. Inman, *Labour in the Munitions Industries* (London, HMSO, 1957), pp. 35, 52, 67, 135; Parker, *Manpower*, pp. 158–60.

10 *Ibid.*, p. 158.

11 Inman, *Labour in the Munitions Industries*, p. 135.

12 *Ibid.*, p. 34

13 Parker, *Manpower*, pp. 155–7; Dennis Hayes, *Challenge of Conscience: The Story of the Conscientious Objectors of 1939–1949* (London, George Allen and Unwin, 1949).

14 J. B. Priestley, *Postscripts* (London, William Heinemann, 1940), p. 100. The kinds of 'radical' statement that Priestley made were as follows: 'we're fighting not merely to keep the German jackboot off our necks but also to put an end once and for all to that world, and to bring into existence an order of society in which nobody will have far too many rooms in a house and nobody have far too few' (p.80), and 'democracy is not an experiment that was tried and that failed, but a great creative force that must now be released again' (p. 100).

15 *Ibid.*, p. 69.

16 *Ibid.*, p. 41.

17 See for example Priestley's portrait of himself as 'short and plump', 'a bleating old sheep' and 'a pipe and slippers man': *ibid.*, pp. 66, 67; his description of road menders discussing when to 'leg it' to the nearest air raid shelter (p. 69), and his account of the Bradford shopkeeper who safely nursed his chief advertising attraction, a giant perpetually-steaming pie, through the bombing of his shop (pp. 81–5).

18 J. D. Cantwell, *Images of War: British Posters 1939–45* (London, HMSO, 1989) plate 44.

19 *Ibid.*, plates 47–9 and 52–7.

20 *Ibid.*, plate 9; J. Derracott and B. Loftus, *Second World War Posters* (London, Imperial War Museum, 1972), p. 71; *Ibid.*, pp. 32 and 55.

21 N. Pronay 'The British Post-Bellum Cinema: A Survey of the Films Relating to World War II made in Britain between 1945 and 1960', *Historical Journal of Film, Radio and Television*, 8, 1 (1988), pp. 45–6. I am grateful to Jeffrey Richards for this reference and for correspondence about post-war films.

22 Jeffrey Richards, 'The Way We Were', *Guardian*, Friday 15 August 1997.

23 Wilma Harrison (294). Ethel Singleton, welding fuel tanks at A. V. Roe's engineering company in Manchester, thought the men she

worked with were mostly older: 'because most of the youth had had to go into the Services hadn't they? It was only if there was something that was keeping them back, they might not have been, what shall I say, one hundred per cent healthy' (216). Jean Grant, riveting aircraft wings at SMT in Edinburgh explained 'about a quarter were women and about three quarters were men, and they would be men you see that couldn't get into the Forces and things like that' (210). She illustrated her point with a portrait of 'two boys who were deaf and dumb' working on the next wing tip to her (221). Elizabeth Little, bench fitting at Reyrolles engineering factory in Pelaw, County Durham reflected that the men she trained with 'must have have been people who, you know, weren't fit enough to go into the forces', and among the men she worked with in engineering 'There was quite a lot of older men there, you know. The younger ones, as I say, I think there must have been some reason why they didn't pass their medicals or something' (298).

24 Fiona Thomas (204).
25 Yvette Baynes (253, 492).
26 Ethel Singleton (216).
27 Marianne Lloyd (122).
28 Marianne Lloyd (321). She explained this in part in relation to changes in the draughting process. She was trained as a detailer in a system in which the draughtsman did a general outline, the detailer produced separate drawings of each part, and the tracer traced these and printed 'blue prints'. But during the war 'they were drifting into the era where it was much more casual and quicker. They didn't have the time for that any more, and they were almost skipping the detail stage'. The work went straight from the draughtsman to the toolroom workers (219).
29 Janice Brunton (196, 210).
30 Janice Brunton (270).
31 Janice Brunton (208).
32 Ivy Jones (272). Katharine Hughes' job of Wireless/Telegraph (W/T) operator in the WRNS was also a desk job that was unusual for a woman, and like both Ivy Jones and Janice Brunton she believed that women were better than men at the job. Her description of becoming a W/T operator set the tone of her account. She was initially working as a WRNS steward, looking after naval officers in Anglesey. One of them agreed to teach her and a friend Morse code, and 'told the captain that he'd found that the women were far better, quicker at picking things up than the men' (86). He trained them to a certain point, then they went to London to be brought up to 'Post Office standard'. To illustrate the women's superiority, Katharine told of being sent on

Army manoeuvres as a WRNS W/T, 'to intercept all the messages because the men they had, didn't have the standard of receiving and sending that we had' (86).

33 Felicity Snow (110). Ann Tomlinson, who left school after matriculating, formed an impression when training to be an aircraft mechanic that the superiority of the women could be explained by social and educational differences between the 'boys' and the 'girls'. 'I think perhaps the girls may have had the advantage in a sense because the girls had all reached the School Certificate standard, whereas many of the boys you see had left school before this and hadn't had an opportunity to do the School Certificate ... many of the girls did better on the course' (142). Furthermore, 'secretly' she thought the girls were more efficient: 'at the time I used to think that the girls were perhaps inclined to be more thorough than some of the boys and never take anything for granted ... the boys liked to appear more casual' (191). On the other hand May Richards (who had also had a secondary education, although at a convent school) thought that the scientific and technical education of the male radar mechanics with whom she worked meant that they 'had the edge' on the women (225). As we shall see (note 46 below), she nevertheless deplored the gendered pay differential.

34 Pamela Wootton (31, 318).

35 Felicity Snow (181).

36 Similarly Heather McLaren, another WAAF aircraft mechanic, felt the women on the aircraft base were made to work harder than the men: 'There was more men than women but we used to notice that our names were up on the board more than the RAF were. A lot of them had been in Canada and came back and I think they thought they were having a holiday when they came back' (484). Amy O'Connor, an ATS Signalwoman, remembered that when American GIs arrived on the switchboard they resisted the high levels of productivity that the ATS women had been prepared to achieve. 'When the men took over at Cheltenham they thought we were working wrong because we'd, we thought nothing of working the three positions on the switchboard and they said one was enough for anybody' (484).

37 Moira Underwood (191).

38 Sadie Bartlett (202). She continued, 'you might not believe this, but that was quite true. If they were picking up nine by nines and three by threes, they'd give it to the men and we'd be landed with the nine by nines. I mean some of the time I couldn't pick 'em up! We used to get one hand and shove it up and over, and it'd sort of bounce, and go a bit further'.

39 Helena Balfour (384).

40 Nora Vickers (533).

41 Wilma Harrison (356).

42 Ernest Bevin, addressing the Diamond Jubilee Congress of the Co-operative Women's Guild in June 1943, said: 'I had calculated that it would take three women dilutees to two men in building up our labour power; but the number of women who have entered industry is 30 per cent higher than I originally calculated. The output of the women, instead of being that of three women to two men, was slightly the other way, compared with production in 1939. The result is that, with the increase in the number of women workers who have come forward and the increase in production over 1939 standards, the total production now is nearly double what I had estimated it would be in 1940': quoted in V. Douie, *Daughters of Britain. An Account of the Work of British Women During the Second World War* (London, Women's Service Library, 1949), pp. 19–20.

43 See Inman, *Labour in the Munitions Industries*, Appendix (iii), pp. 441–2: 'Memorandum of Agreement between Engineering and Allied Employers' National Federation and Amalgamated Engineering Union, to provide for the Temporary Relaxation of Existing Customs so as to Permit, for the Period of the War, the Extended Employment of Women in the Engineering Industry'. Similar agreements were made by employers' organisations and trade unions in other industries.

44 *Ibid.*, pp. 374. See also P. Summerfield, *Women Workers in the Second World War* (London, Routledge, 1989), ch. 7.

45 Ann Tomlinson (193, 195).

46 Ivy Jones said of male weather observers' higher pay: 'we got a bit niggled at that time ... it was pretty light-hearted but I suppose it was an injustice in a way. Well it was always considered that men had responsibilities you see and the women didn't, ha ha' (272). May Richards, a radar mechanic in the ATS experienced the same irritation: 'we were always resentful that we only ever got two thirds of the man's pay, even though we were doing the same work' (379). She described having 'dreadful arguments' with the men. 'Their come-back was, "oh well, we're liable to be posted overseas and you're not." ... So we used to say, "Well in that case, you should still get, you should get the same while you're here and then you could get extra if you were posted overseas."' (383–5). May was emphatic that as far as pay was concerned women did exactly the same job as the men, and should not have been paid less 'simply because you were a woman'(390).

47 For example, Felicity Snow: 'we didn't think about it ... we just thought that men always got more than women ... we used to pull their legs about it, "you've got more money than we have"' (228,

230). Joyce Greaves' comment, 'It never entered our heads that we should query it' (275) stands for the responses of many working-class as well as middle-class servicemen, including those like Mary Mackenzie and Kate Lomax who were supporting their parents from their service pay. See Mary Mackenzie (199), Kate Lomax (659).

48 May Richards (385).

49 A. Oram '"Bombs don't Discriminate!" Women's Political Activism in the Second World War', in C. Gledhill and G. Swanson, *Nationalising Femininity. Culture, Sexuality and British Cinema in the Second World War* (Manchester, Manchester University Press, 1996), pp. 53–69.

50 Moira Underwood (326).

51 Emily Porter: 'We were paid three pounds two shillings and six pence [£3 12.5p] ... which was awfully good pay, because in those days, a man doing a quite a, like a minor engineering job would only get that much. It was very good, oh that was fine' (82). As for equal pay, 'it never seemed to be discussed' (155).

52 Marianne Lloyd (217). The response which Beryl Bramley, the AID inspector, made to a question about pay, suggested that she had objected to inequality at the time, but she rapidly modified this. The sense of injustice had come later (with the change in popular thinking about gender to which Marianne referred). Women inspectors did not get the same pay as the men: 'I can't remember what it was but I know we were all insensed that we didn't' (583). This was followed by Beryl repositioning the idea that she was 'insensed' from wartime to the more recent past: 'Well, I mean, you know of course it was all right for them. I didn't know what they were talking about half the time. But as I say I hadn't been out of the cocoon all that long, as it were. I wasn't into this men versus women stuff at all. Now, I feel very strongly about it, and I felt very strongly about it working in some positions [later on]' (587).

53 Sadie Bartlett (240).

54 Fiona Thomas (226).

55 Caroline Woodward (356).

56 Wilma Harrison (388).

57 Helena Balfour (516, 524).

58 Women at the Rolls Royce factory at Hillington went out on strike in 1943 for equal pay. This strike, illegal in wartime under Order 1305, became a *cause célèbre*, provoking a Court of Enquiry and a ruling which placed machines in a gender-related grading system, rather than simply attributing wages to the sex of the worker. There are several accounts of the strike. See for example G. Braybon and P. Summerfield, *Out of the Cage. Women's Experiences in Two World Wars*

(London, Pandora, 1987) pp. 176–7.

59 Helena Balfour (524).

60 Helena Balfour (528, 532).

61 Summerfield, *Women Workers in the Second World War*, ch. 7; R. Croucher, *Engineers at War* (London, Merline, 1982), ch. 5.

62 Ethel Singleton (252).

63 Ethel Singleton (252).

64 Ethel singleton (272).

65 Ethel Singleton (268).

66 Elizabeth Little (594).

67 Elizabeth Little (322).

68 Elizabeth Little (322).

69 That is to say, women who were substituting for men in either the Armed Forces or in industry, in technical or mechanical jobs that women did not normally do in peacetime.

70 Felicity Snow (104).

71 Such stories included those of Heather McLaren and May Richards. Heather trained as an aircraft engine mechanic in 1942. At the end of her training she remembered being subject to a test designed to catch her out: 'They put a screwdriver in the engine, this was to see if I'd pick it up because if the aircraft had gone into flight with that it could have caused a lot of bother. That was the sort of thing you were up against': Heather McLaren (419). May Richards trained to become a qualified radar mechanic. After the first phase of training she was 'only given the sort of little scrag ends of jobs to do. I don't suppose anyone thought we were capable of much else'. Then she was sent to her first posting. She described being greeted by a sceptical Scots corporal: 'He said "Well I've hearrrd of ATS radar mechanics, but I've never seen one before!" and I thought, "oh heck" … I had to prove my worth':' May Richards (192, 231, 233).

72 Pamela Wootton (327, 329, 330).

73 Felicity Snow (112).

74 Heather McLaren (616): 'You had to signal the planes in with two torches and some of the younger officers, you know when you were trying to slow them down, they'd come up at you. Well in these days it was props, you know, a propeller in the plane, well this was what you'd to watch for, that you didn't come in contact with the plane, with the prop.'

75 Katharine Hughes (242).

76 Katharine Hughes (340).

77 Katharine Hughes (330).

78 The men with whom she worked closely came to recognise this, expressing their affection towards her and the other WRNS wire-

less/telegraphists by writing a cheerful (though somewhat derogatory) poem about them, addressed to the men at the next naval base to receive them: Katharine Hughes (240–2).

79 Felicity Snow (110).

80 May Richards (471).

81 Felicity Snow (104, 110).

82 Marianne Lloyd (263).

83 Beryl Bramley (225).

84 Beryl Bramley (183, 186).

85 Moira Underwood, storekeeper at a ROF, in charge of twelve ex-miners who did the manual work linked to storekeeping, did not describe lonely isolation, but she was not assimilated either. The ex-miners treated her with exaggerated gallantry, for example sawing off the legs of her chair the moment she said it was too high (246) and making her a cushion when she said it was too hard (250). They also teased her. She gave the example of how they put her on a box with rollers to weigh her every week, and made a public announcement of her steady increase (254).

86 May Richards (233).

87 Felicity Snow (191, 193).

88 Heather McLaren (498).

89 Pamela Wootton (322).

90 Gladys French (237, 241). Relationships were harmonious and fun: 'We were all very friendly, we all went out together, and towards the end of the war, when people would start being demobbed, well then of course you went out drinking together on wild parties' (French, 193).

91 Yvette Baynes (324, 322).

92 P. Schwartz, 'Partisanes and Gender Politics in Vichy France', French Historical Studies, 16, 1 (1989), p.138. Schwartz writes of women's participation in the Resistance: 'the gender of the person did not redefine a 'male' task; rather the gender tag of the task redefined the person. Tasks were not so much gender-integrated, or open to women, as they appear. Rather, the woman herself was considered a sort of 'honorary man' at least for the duration' (pp. 137–8).

93 Several of the women who talked of becoming 'one of the boys' referred to this, relating it to the 'respect' shown to women in the 1940s (explicitly or by implication, in contrast to the 1990s). Ann Tomlinson said, 'I never remember that they ever swore in front of us at all ... things were a bit different then, you know, ladies were ladies kind of thing, weren't they?' (187). Gladys French repeated that men were 'almost too polite ... They always used to guard their conversation when the women were around, but we didn't mind that, it was

rather expected in those days you see' (221). Margaret Gray, an ATS driver, said 'although we were working alongside these quite rough men often, I never heard them swear, in all my Army career. I came out still not knowing the Army swear words which I thought was very considerate' (348). Their comments suggest that, from the woman's point of view, unbridled swearing would have been difficult to respond to, or embarrassing.

94 Gladys French (241).

95 Gladys French (257).

96 P. Summerfield and N. Crockett '"You Weren't Taught That With the Welding": Lessons in Sexuality in the Second World War', *Women's History Review*, 1, 3 (1992), pp. 435–54.

97 Some of the women made it clear that they were not sexually attracted to the men they worked with because these men were (like them) not on active service. Amy O'Connor was one of many young ATS women working in the Signal Corps as a telephonist. Men and women on Army switchboards were normally segregated, because, Amy thought, if men and women had worked together 'they might have got, you know, crafty with each other – dear dear'. But she made it clear that when segregation was lifted so that American GIs could gradually take over the women's positions at a Cheltenham army base where she worked, the possibilities that these men might 'get crafty' were of no interest to her. She did this by drawing a distinction between servicemen who stayed in Britain and 'real soldiers' who went abroad, which she constructed also as a division between American and British Signalmen. The men who worked on the switchboard in Britain were 'the ones that weren't fit to go abroad, you know. Because our Signalmen went out with the Eighth Army, out in the desert with Monty, you know'. Amy claimed considerable heroic status for them: they laid telephone lines in the desert, but were given no guns to protect themselves. She was full of admiration for their bravery. 'They were marvellous': Amy O'Connor (280, 492).

98 Gladys French (257). Off tape Ann Tomlinson told a story of a naval officer trying to go further than she wanted after a date, as a result of which she found herself in a physical struggle with him and lost a silver brooch bearing the Wren insignia, which a former fiancé had given her.

99 Barbara Wilson (201, 221, 223).

100 Caroline Woodward (247); Helena Balfour (376). Jean Grant said that men accepted women because it was wartime (250); Fiona Thomas said men accepted women 'because there was no men. The men were all away' (204).

101 Elizabeth Little (202, 514).

102 Jean Grant (280).
103 Elizabeth Little (294).
104 Helena Balfour (476).
105 Wilma Harrison (416).
106 Helena Balfour (468).
107 Jean Grant (265); Caroline Woodward (308).
108 Caroline Woodward (308).
109 Caroline Woodward (310, 311).
110 Caroline Woodward (243).
111 Fiona Thomas (144).
112 Fiona Thomas (176, 178).
113 Fiona Thomas (186, 169).
114 Ethel Singleton (127).
115 Ethel Singleton (210, 212, 214, 218).
116 Ethel Singleton (my emphasis, 220).
117 Ethel Singleton (248).
118 Ethel Singleton (212).
119 Ethel Singleton (248).
120 Ethel Singleton (248). Ethel was emphatic that the strategy worked. The men 'got to know us and they were marvellous, they treated us wonderful you know. They were never awkward with us' (210).
121 Ethel Singleton (133).
122 Ethel Singleton (228).
123 Ethel Singleton (232, 234).
124 Pamela Wootton (330).
125 Pamela Wootton (387).
126 Pamela Wootton (387).
127 Pamela Wootton (391).
128 Marion Paul (201).
129 Marion Paul (254, 266).
130 Marion Paul (245).
131 Marion Paul (510).
132 Yvette Baynes (632, 648, 650).
133 Yvette Baynes (496, 658).
134 Joan Stanton (281).
135 Peggy Peters (125).
136 It was expressed in comments about the authorities' provision for the protection of women. For example, Edith Dixon related the require-ment that girls worked in pairs at night on a Naval switchboard to their need for protection from all the male ratings sleeping in the building where they worked (137, 320). Amy O'Connor, who also worked on a switchboard, described the sex segregation of work teams, and how her sleeping quarters were barricaded so that no one

could get in or out when American GIs started arriving at her base in Cheltenham (280, 348).

137 Estelle Armitage (150).
138 Mary Mackenzie (175).
139 Janice Brunton (99).
140 Pamela Wootton (111).
141 Janice Brunton (99); Pamela Wootton (111).
142 Yvette Baynes (446).
143 Myrna Wraith (59, 61, 63).
144 Evelyn Mills (193); Dorothy Rose (604).

West Indian recruits to the Auxiliary Territorial Service, 1944

Chapter 5

Feminine bonding and the maintenance of difference

The last chapter traced the differentiating force of gender. Women who aspired to 'heroic' wartime roles reconstructed their assault upon gender difference and inequality, at the same time as emphasising that they lacked, in the 1940s, a feminist vocabulary in which to express and understand what they were doing. Those who participated reluctantly in masculine war work, or who were doing jobs defined as 'women's work', recalled their involvement in the reproduction of gender differences, sometimes with delight, occasionally with disgust. Gender evidently cut through the idea of the unity of a people at war. National unity was not, as we saw in the previous chapter, a construction upon which the women interviewed drew in discussing their relationships with their male colleagues. The concept was, however, more conspicuous in women's accounts of their relations with other women at work, the subject of this chapter.

The wartime discourse of national unity, although pervasive, was not unified. We shall start with a brief discussion of the main understandings of wartime national unity and women's position within it, before exploring the deployment of these ideas by the women interviewed, in their reconstructions of other women. There was wide consensus during the war that the war effort, involving collective work and mutual dependence, would heal the sores of social divisions which, in the 1920s and 1930s, had been potentially destabilising. Understandings of the sources of unity were different on the left and the right. As Morgan and Evans point out in *The Battle for Britain*, Churchill's enormously successful calls for national unity were based on an understanding of a democratic British heritage in no need of change.[1] This approach is represented by the well-known iconic poster of the massive figure of Churchill superimposed on British tanks and planes moving through a bucolic British countryside over the caption 'Let us go forward together'.[2] But Churchill also viewed the Empire as an integral part of the nation. National defence involved defence of the Empire; should the nation be unable to defend itself against invasion, the Empire would come to its aid.[3] Other posters hammered home this message, which had been promoted in popular culture since the jingoistic music-hall songs of the 1880s.[4] An example is 'Together', in which soldiers from the white dominions march beneath the Union Flag, at the head of a column at the back of which are Black soldiers from the

British colonies of India and Africa.[5]

In contrast to the conservatism and imperialism of Churchill's vision of national unity, the idea stimulated a popular movement for social reform among those further left. In this version, 'national unity' represented a moral economy based on hard work. The consequences of the victory to which it would lead would be rewards for the British workers upon whom the war effort depended, in the form of post-war reconstruction which, through welfare reforms and guarantees of full employment, would deliver social justice to all.[6] If the left-wing account referred to the Empire at all, it was to suggest that the reward for imperial participation in the war should be dissolution: self-determination and independence were the proper goals for the colonies. Many authors writing within the broad framework of wartime radicalism believed that the experience of 'all pulling together' could be a force for the dissolution of social divisions among all those involved, women as well as men.[7] The key effect of mass mobilisation to factories and the Forces, according to popular writers like J. B. Priestley, was that those mobilised were 'meeting all kinds of people, both in the workshops and the canteens, and discovering a different and larger and friendlier Britain'. As a result women as well as men would 'soon find themselves asking for a bigger share of a better Britain'.[8]

Churchill's version of national unity assumed willing co-operation with a benevolent leadership; anything less was treachery. The radical variant identified more specific obstacles to the achievement of wartime togetherness and to its desired consequences. In most accounts these obstacles lay in the perpetuation of self-interest and individualism within particular segments of society whose members were not fully participating in the war effort. Women, particularly wealthy women, were a focus of criticism. For example, in his popular broadcasts of 1940, J. B. Priestley identified 'middle-class women' as 'gaps in the roll of honour' in wartime. He argued, for example, that well-off women who refused to take in evacuees from the East End of London shared the 'cold narrow minds, greed, privilege and love of power' which had contributed to the outbreak of war. Such women also stood in the way of the social transformation that should follow the war. Priestley contrasted 'ladies doing nothing in inland resorts where their energy is all turned inward instead of outward' with ordinary women, busily contributing to the war effort.[9] 'Good women' in wartime worked hard, in contrast to the demonised women of the middle classes. They were working 'girls' who turned up to work after nights of bombing, and women of all ages who were 'nursing under fire, or looking after evacuated babies'.[10]

Priestley's was one of the most direct and graphic depictions of the evils of the idle rich woman and it contributed to his hostile postbag and the BBC's termination of his broadcasts. But there were many other critical representations of non-participant women. One who did not expect 'to do a day's work' but who discovered both that she could, and that she became a better person as a result, was 'Jennifer Knowles' (played by Ann Crawford) in the film *Millions Like Us* (1943). She first appeared in the film arriving as a conscripted woman worker at a factory hostel, with a gigantic wardrobe and a huge hat. The snobbish Jennifer was appalled by the manners and mores of the working-class girl with whom she had to share a room, and expected special treatment in the allocation of work. When she did not get it she responded by being a lazy and careless worker, subverting the war effort through her selfishness.[11] She was, however, transformed by the development of a love-hate relationship with her foreman, which paralleled her growing understanding both of the importance of wartime co-operation and of the need for the creation of a new world afterwards. The message of the film with respect to national unity was that the war effort depended on women's stamina, courage, common sense and ability to work hard. Working-class women already possessed these attributes. Wealthy women could acquire them through emulation.

The levelling process resulting from 'social mixing' was, however, also a source of anxiety. The reputation of the women's services, particularly the ATS, for sexual promiscuity, and of the war factories for low moral standards, caused the government considerable concern. The official reaction was to initiate enquiries and hold discussions, which in itself gave the rumours some legitimacy.[12] The government was concerned above all to counter the harmful effect on recruitment of the belief that mass mobilisation meant that women of 'low morals' were included in the mix. Even though its enquiries rejected the view that some members of the ATS were influencing other women to follow their example of 'sexual impropriety', the discussion placed the onus on the Services to impose discipline on their members which would check social pollution and ensure that if any levelling took place it was in an upward direction.

The differences between the idle rich woman and the hard-working 'ordinary woman' on the one hand, and between the respectable ordinary woman and the slut on the other, were not the only differences that were popularly depicted. Another was of the contrast between women in positions of authority, and the women over whom they exercised power. Educated middle-class women were portrayed, notably by feminists, as supplying the moral guidance and control that young and particularly working-class women needed. The feminist writer Elaine Burton led criticism of the government's handling of the war effort on the grounds that it had allowed such educated women to become unemployed early in the war, because it did not appreciate their value to the war effort.[13] The British Federation of Business and Professional Women took up the cause, lobbying MPs and Treasury officials in 1940-41 to 'ask for women to be given posts carrying greater responsibility'.[14] Jobs did become available for educated women in civilian managerial work and, in particular, as officers in the women's auxiliary forces.[15] Much of the popular writing celebrating the wartime contribution of all women, like Peggy Scott's *British Women in War* and *They Made Invasion Possible*, applauded their efforts and was written from their perspective. *British Women in War* projected the viewpoint of 'the woman in charge' in its portrayal of a succession of women in authority. The tone, although kindly, was patronising. For example, the commander of a Women's Land Army Camp said of her 'girls' that once they had realised 'that a forest is not usually in the middle of a town ... most of them settle down and are as happy as sand-boys'; a WAAF officer in charge of a balloon site who 'had been a headmistress and school inspector ... was used to handling young people'; the Director of the WRNS defined discipline as coming 'from the heart. It is co-operation between individuals and those in command'.[16] *They Made Invasion Possible* dwelt on the 'uphill work' of a welfare supervisor in a Birmingham factory to persuade her women workers to wear their safety caps over their coiffures: 'they have so many curls and they spend such a lot of money on them that they do not want to hide them'.[17] In each of these cases, the woman in charge demonstrated her understanding of the youthful, irresponsible and probably socially inferior women she was managing, and her capacity to 'handle' them.[18]

The 'woman in charge' was the antidote to the 'idle rich woman'. She shared her social-class position but used it in wartime to better effect. The special responsibility of the woman in charge was to oversee the surrendering of individualism to a group life patriotically devoted to national service, in which assimilation to group norms was vital. This was indicated by the comments of the women quoted above, about recruits who did not conform. For example the Land Army commandant said, 'the girls who do not fit into the surroundings or make friends ... simply fade away' and the Director of the WRNS stated 'if they do not want to come into line for love of the Service, the Director does not mind if they leave the ship'.[19] Conformity to group norms was an essential part of being 'all in it together'.

These positive representations of the woman in charge insisted that co-operation across the supervisory boundary was being achieved. Class differences might remain but, under the guidance of such women, the work of all women was harnessed to the promotion of the war effort. These middle-class women facilitated rather than impeded national unity. For example in an account of women in the Armed Forces Priestley said, 'Most of their officers are seen by them not as mysterious beings who enjoy giving strange orders, but simply as more experienced and capable members of the same unit'.[20]

However, accounts of women supervisors, managers and officers were not uniformly sympathetic. A popular construction of relationships between women in employment, which Scott defensively tried to dismiss, was that 'women cannot work together'.[21] Other writers, including M-O and, more surprisingly, the doughty feminist Vera Douie, expressed a view of women in authority which was prevalent in the inter-war years, when they wrote that women in minor supervisory positions were frequently 'of the bossy, schoolmistressy type and unpopular with the girls whose labour they direct'.[22] Just as the idle rich woman was demonised, so was the 'bossy schoolmistressy type' of woman in authority, even though there were few other models for women in charge to follow. At the same time that the war presented opportunities for women to occupy such positions, it was also the occasion for renewed doubts to be expressed about the possibilities of women co-operating across boundaries drawn by power differentials.

National unity in the Second World War, then, meant unity of the entire British nation and the Empire in fighting the war. In its radical form, the discourse emphasised the crucial position of working-class men and women in total war, and the social rewards due to them for their contribution. But within this construction, specific groups of women were identified as potentially disruptive. Idle rich women, immoral lower-class women and bossy authoritarian women could destabilise national unity and with it the prospects of achieving victory.

This gendered discourse of national unity informed the interviewees' accounts of their relationships with other women in wartime in a variety of ways. The concept of 'togetherness' appeared in all accounts, but there were differences with respect to this, as to other aspects of wartime experience, between stoics and heroes. To break the pattern of the last two chapters (and to disrupt the possible creation within this book of a 'norm' of heroism in contrast to 'deviant' stoicism, by the ordering of the analysis), we shall start by considering the 'stoic' accounts.

Happy families, good friends and the woman in charge

Women who had civilian industrial or clerical jobs were, as we have seen, only exceptionally working with men. Indeed those such as Beryl Bramley, Marianne Lloyd and Moira Underwood, who had 'heroically' and unusually for women obtained relatively skilled jobs in civilian industry, constituted the minority who worked mainly with men. Most civilian women described stoically entering war work, and being teamed with other women, commonly under the authority of men (whom, as we saw in chapter 4, they remembered as old and unfit). A metaphor used by several of these women to describe social relations at work was of the workplace as a 'family'. Yvette Baynes, for example, secretary in a wire rolling mill in Birmingham, described relationships in the factory as 'exceptionally good ... you were just one big family, all together'.[23] Elizabeth Little, testing gauges in an engineering factory in the north-east, described the workers at Reyrolles as 'quite a nice crowd' and the boss was 'a nice old man. He used to talk to everyone. You know, you felt you were part of a family, you weren't bossed around or anything'.[24] Ethel Singleton evoked a similar atmosphere at a small factory in Manchester where she was a welder: 'we were all like one big happy family'. She expanded on the idea in a classic rendering of 'togetherness': 'everybody, even from the police on the door, right down to the firemen and the labourers and the girls that did the washing, we were all just one big family. It was a lovely atmosphere in that factory'.[25] Ethel's details of the composition of the factory suggest that the family metaphor referred both to the gender mix and to its relationship to a hierarchical structure. Men were in charge as bosses and policemen (father figures) and other men (uncles and brothers) occupied lowlier positions as firemen and labourers. Women were 'girls' (sisters) in the office or on the shopfloor, to whom a good boss would talk in kindly ways. Elsewhere, as we saw in chapter 4, these same women described problematic aspects of their relationships with men at work.[26] But when asked to evoke relationships in general they recalled harmonious hierarchical 'family' dynamics.

Civilian women's reconstructions of relationships specifically with other women were rather different. The organisation of the work was a crucial factor underpinning the formation of relationships with other women. The phrase 'we were all in it together' was used by members of this group to mean that the women depended on each other in order to perform work which most of them had not chosen to do. It applied to work in offices as well as in factories. For example, Evelyn Mills, a reluctant conscript working entirely with other women at a row of duplicating machines in the basement of the Admiralty, remembered how the women took it in turns (determined usually by who needed a rest) to sit in a 'cubby hole' and divide the incoming work fairly amongst the others. They had in common their subjection to compulsion and to the unpleasant hours and conditions of work, and all got on well.

> We were all friendly with one another. We had to be really, you know.
> We were all quite – we'd all been called up really, we were all about
> the same age, because in that sort of job, I mean you wouldn't get a
> volunteer really, would you. It was a case of having to do these jobs'.[27]

The labour process dominated memories of relationships within factories even more firmly. Jean Grant, riveting aircraft wings at a Scottish factory, explained that riveting required co-operation and trust between pairs of workers, one of whom would fire the rivet at the sheets of metal to be joined, and the other place a piece of metal behind them to fasten the rivet at the back. Jean spoke of the special bonding between herself and the woman with whom she worked: 'Most of those that were in the twos, they were quite friendly and kept together. And as I say I've kept that friendship up all this time'.[28] She summed up relationships between women in the factory in the language of wartime unity: 'we all mixed together because you were all in it together and you were sort of thrown into it weren't you, because it was wartime'.[29] Similiar relationships, forged by the labour process, were described by Caroline Woodward, who was a welder. Six or more women would work together on one pontoon, 'all doing the same job. As I say one couldn't slack because it wouldn't have been fair to the other person'. Caroline's memory of the friendship stimulated by this collective effort was ecstatic: 'we were all a happy crowd, oh it was great, I loved working with them all'.[30]

Caroline remembered pleasure in each other's company spilling into free time after work: 'the atmosphere and the company was great. Used to go to their houses, if we were day-shift, maybe for the night, and they would come to mine, you know', 'we were all good friends'.[31] These women welders created for themselves, then, on a temporary basis and as their own chosen way of enjoying leisure, experiences of the communal living which, as we shall see shortly, were characteristic of women in the Armed Forces.[32] This conviviality had no flaws in Caroline's account. Even a woman marked by difference because she came from a wealthier background than the others and had not done paid work previously (one of the 'idle rich'), was easily absorbed into the 'happy crowd': 'there was a girl from – that lived opposite the Ramsay Tech, in a bought house, I'm talking about – in the war, and she had never worked. She had watched [cared for] her mum. It was a big shock to her. She did the same as me, she volunteered to go in there, because well she would have been put away in the Forces, and – well nobody would have watched her mum, you know. It was a big shock to her, you know, but she loved it. And she was nice. She was with, from monied people, but right nice she was. Got a right dapper house as well, it's nice'.[33]

Women described sharing not only pleasures but also griefs and anxieties. Nearly half of all women in civilian work in wartime were married, a much higher figure than in peacetime.[34] The young women in the sample remembered supportive talk in breaktimes about families. Dorothy Rose, working as a clerk for the Ministry of Food said:

> You knew all about their families, they talked about their families and one thing and another, and it was quite interesting you know. In a

morning we used to have a ten minute tea break ... we used to sit
round in a little group and have a gossip, you know ... everybody
knew everybody else kind of thing. Knew when their husbands were
coming home on leave and one thing and another.[35]

Helena Balfour, assembling aircraft in a factory, amplified the story:

> You had people who had sons and brothers in the forces. That Salva-
> tion Army girl that I was talking about had a boyfriend who was killed.
> And the lady ... whose son was in the forces, he went missing. Now
> that was very hard for those people to continue working, never know-
> ing where they were and what was happening ... You'd get ten min-
> utes in the morning and afternoon and then your half hour break, so
> the conversation was all about if somebody had a letter, and where
> were they, you know and what was happening.[36]

In these constructions, the personal and particular family of each
worker was given discursive space within the larger 'family' constituted by the workers in the factory or office. A caring and mutually
supportive wartime unity was the remembered outcome of the
interaction, conducted through 'gossip' between these families.[37]

But the cosy togetherness of convivial breaktimes was not the
only story of civilian women's wartime relationships. Women in big
factories emphasised the unity of the team. Such memories were
more divisive, since the qualities of the team were reconstructed in
comparison with rival teams, the negative reference groups of the
narratives. Nora Vickers was impressed by the solidarity amongst
the women she worked with in a vast Royal Ordnance Factory in
Bury, especially in comparison to relations in the bank where she
had previously been employed. 'I felt a greater sense of loyalty in
the Factory, a greater sense that if anybody wronged you, we would
really stick up for you ... And the sharing of course, which perhaps
was a bit more evident in wartime anyway, I think that general sort
of feeling of sharing'.[38] But she made it clear that this solidarity
operated only within workgroups: 'You sort of tended to go with
your section ... a cigarette was shared amongst six people if necessary; part of an apple because, you know, it was very rare to get
fruit'. However, Nora remembered animosity towards women outside the workteam, who were excluded from the division of spoils.
'If anything was wrong, it was the other shift, who no doubt said it
about us. The other shift was not nice, we were nice, but they
weren't'.[39]

After working for some time in a team of six women, fitting bay-
onets, Nora and one other member of the group were moved to the
other, disliked, shift. The move was deeply resented, both because
of the group loyalty which the women had built up, and because the
team had developed a way of working that speeded up the process
considerably, enabling the women (who were on piecework) to earn
more. The others in the shift 'didn't want us to go, because they
were sort of splitting us up'. To indicate their sense of solidarity the
members of Nora's old team left 'presents' on a shelf under the
bench at the end of their shift: 'there was half a cigarette ... part of
an apple there, or maybe one sweet, or even half a biscuit, were put
there for the two of us, because they'd share it with us, you know
... A terrific sense of comradeship there'.[40] Furthermore the old shift
ensured that they were reunited. Nora discovered that in their
absence 'the four that were left had really gone to town on the foreman and so we just did a couple of nights on this hated other shift.
Not as nice as our shift!'.[41]

Some of the women who worked in office jobs in wartime factories indicated that they were aware that they could be the targets of
hostile constructions as 'others'. They were not only working in
offices rather than on the shopfloor, but were usually working alone
or in pairs rather than in teams of five or six. They were marked out
as different types of worker with different hours and conditions of
work. The comments of Joan Stanton reveal the polarisation which
several clerical workers remembered finding threatening.[42] Joan,
secretary at a factory making hydraulic machinery, said 'there was a
great animosity between the shopfloor workers and the clerical
staff, but I had to go onto the shopfloor many times during the day
with memos and so on and so forth, so knowing that there was this
animosity I went out of my way to make quite sure that I was liked.
But we used to have separate cloakrooms so I always used to use –
deliberately go on to the shopfloor because I thought it was very, I
didn't think there should be this division'. Questioned as to the
gender content of the problem she confirmed that she was talking
about tensions between women: 'oh it was the females, the males
were alright'.[43]

These memories reconstructed the long-standing cultural and
class tensions of British society, tapping into the other side of the
story of the factory family, in which the hierarchy was not a harmonious unity but was riven with tensions and jealousies. Office

workers like Joan Stanton could easily be subsumed within the identity of women in positions of authority. The deployment of the negative construction of the 'woman in charge' was common in the narratives of factory workers. Elizabeth Little, gauge setter, singled out a woman supervisor called Alice as an exception to the pleasant 'family' atmosphere of her engineering factory. 'She used to you know take care of everything really. Go round the factory and make sure that everyone was doing their job right, and wearing their hats right, and wearing proper shoes and things ... and if you had any problems you went to her ... She was a bit bitchy, but she'd worked in Reyrolles for years and years, and I think she, she thought, you know, we were a load of no-hopers'.[44] If Reyrolles was a family, Alice was the spiteful aunt or the wicked stepmother.

Women supervisors who interpreted their role as supporting rather than criticising the women under their control were, on the other hand, remembered as likeable. Sadie Bartlett, chopping down trees in the Timber Corps of the Women's Land Army (WLA), compared forewomen favourably with men in the allocation of the trees to be cut down. The foremen (for misogynist reasons) would give difficult work to the women whereas 'if the girl put it out, she used to give us all the easiest ones'.[45] Sadie had particularly fond memories of a motherly supervisor, an ex-governess, who was definitely 'on the women's side'. On one occasion the Land Girls were given some particularly difficult trees to cut down, 'I mean you'd put your axe there and your axe'd just jump off, the wood was so hard, it was terrible. And it snowed and she used to treat us like children really. We all liked her, she used to say "Come along girls, we'll have a snowball match before we start work! Let's all get warm".'[46]

Ellizabeth Little's 'Alice' and Sadie's ex-governess were in the position of the forewomen and supervisors whose identities oscillated in popular representations between the petty tyranny criticised by Priestley and the understanding control depicted by, for example, Scott. Their function was mainly a 'welfare' one, uneasily poised between support for and surveillance of the women for whom they had responsibility. Those who were perceived as sympathetic were better liked than those regarded as more authoritarian. But whichever way they geared their performances, the power of these women differentiated them from other women, yet did not make them equals of men.

Women who were themselves in charge of other women had

chillier memories of colleagues than those we have discussed so far. Peggy Peters was a civilian secretary at a naval base from 1939. Towards the end of the war she was in charge of newcomers who were older women: 'I'm afraid I was very very picky. I'd never send anything out that wasn't perfect and a lot of them absolutely hated it. When you're doing something that is so important, it's got to be perfect hasn't it? But a lot of them, you know they did object, I used to send things back to be corrected and they didn't like it'.[47] In sharp contrast to the accounts of women in clerical as well as manual work, of warm and supportive wartime friendships, Peggy Peters answered a question about whether she made friends at work by saying, 'I don't think so really. I think we were all just too busy'.[48]

Women who told 'heroic' stories about joining the civilian war work of their choice, evoked similarly uncomfortable dynamics. Moira Underwood, who became a storekeeper at a Royal Ordnance Factory, described being apprehensive about her relationships with the women on the shopfloor. Her reconstruction recapitulated the popular image of women factory workers as low class and immoral. She said 'I made up my mind when I went ... that I wasn't going to be afraid of them; I wasn't going to be standoffish. I thought, I'm going to look at them and see the good part in them, because there's good in everybody, you know, even some of the ones who told smutty stories, which I didn't like, and some of them used terrible language, which I didn't like.' For the sake of the war effort Moira was (heroically) determined to make herself accept these women, whom she regarded as beneath her socially and morally. She concluded her reflections, with some lack of self-awareness, 'The idea got around about me, that I was a clergyman's daughter. I don't know why'.[49]

Other women in positions of relative authority in civilian war work, who like Moira gave 'heroic' accounts of joining up, tapped into the tensions between women provoked by their status when they asserted that they 'could not work with women', or that they preferred to work alone or with men. Beryl Bramley illustrated the first statement with a story about refusing a job in charge of six women in an office, after the war, because women are 'incredibly unkind'.[50] Fiona Thomas explained that one reason that she prized her job in the male world of the buses was that she 'prefer[red] to work with men than women' because 'women are catty'.[51] Marianne

Lloyd, engineering draughtswoman, said simply that working on her own, without female company, 'suited me, I didn't mind'.[52]

Inclusion, exclusion and the body in the Armed Forces

Most of the ex-servicewomen responded to questions about their relationships with other women at work in the war, in the first instance, in the language of wartime togetherness whatever their job had been. For example, Katharine Hughes, a wireless/telegraphist in the WRNS said, 'We all used to mix in with each other ... we were all in it together ... We worked together, we played together, we lived together and everybody was happy'. Pamela Wootton, aircraft fitter in the Fleet Air Arm, said, 'We all got on with one another. We had a whale of a time.' Mary Mackenzie, WAAF waitress, explained, 'they were a very friendly bunch. I think everybody seemed to be, you know, we were at war and everybody was trying to help everybody'. Greta Lewis, working on anti-aircraft guns, expressed her regrets about leaving the ATS due to her pregnancy in terms of togetherness: 'I didn't want to go because I were going to lose all my friends. We stayed together all the time you see. And they were nice friends.'[53]

Further discussion of friendships and group dynamics brought memories of disharmony to the surface. But the language in which women recalled it, denoted the importance of wartime togetherness as a cultural construct within which to frame experiences of wartime relationships. For example Janice Brunton, filter plotter in the WAAFs (plotting the movements of aircraft on huge maps in response to coded messages), followed the statement 'There was a great friendship' by saying: 'There was always the odd person that was a little bit disruptive but ... it was more comfortable to all work together, pull together, otherwise – because it only needed one person to be awkward, it spoilt it for everybody.'[54] Janice's testimony, and that of other women in the Forces, indicated that togetherness was achieved as a result of a process of establishing group norms of co-operation and congruence. These women had memories not only of the difficulties of assimilating to male work groups (which we discussed in chapter 4), but of having to work at becoming 'one of the girls', too. The process focused on the erosion of indicators of difference. One of these related to evidence of social class and regional differences expressed in speech and education.

The other, intensively discussed in the interviews, related to differences in the body.

Janice Brunton evoked a sharp sense of cultural exclusion from the other WAAF plotters with whom she worked. She had a strong sense of her own difference from them, due to her lower-class background and her limited education. She explained how she felt:

> We were in bunk beds. Those around me had all been to university so at night I used to switch off and pretend I was asleep. I was terrified of taking part in the conversation. They were all saying which university they'd been at and all about their exams, languages – I couldn't even speak English! Well that part frightened me more than anything else.[55]

The turning-point in her narrative, marking her integration, was coming top in the examination at the end of the training course. 'It really did more for my ego, that, and especially having been so afraid of – you know, lack of education, you know, it gave me a bit of confidence.'[56] Part of her coping strategy had evidently been to work very hard to acquire the skills specific to the job, to compensate for her (as she saw it) inadequate cultural capital.

The second marker of difference in the interviews was the body. The process of achieving congruence between women's bodies was given a great deal of emphasis by women who had been in the Forces. Women described various ways in which their bodies and appearances were brought into line. For example, Marion Paul, an ATS clerk from a mining family in a small village near Doncaster, who described her background as 'sheltered', remembered how during her training at Leicester, 'one of the girls said, "your eyebrows are too bushy, I'll pluck them for you" and got, three of them got me down on the bed and she plucked my eyebrows, and I had a skinny thin line across my brow'.[57] Marion was happy to undergo such treatment to aid her assimilation (although to others it might have been traumatic). She described how as well as her appearance, her understanding of sex and the body was 'improved'. 'I'd led a very sheltered life', she reiterated, but her room mate was 'a woman of the world' who always attracted a crowd of recruits: 'I used to sit on my bed and my ears were like tureens, listening to all this conversation, half of which I didn't understand, and half of which I never knew. I mean I thought you could get a baby from a lavatory seat, but you know, I had all this information fed into me and – it was quite a hectic time.'[58] In contrast to Janice's problem with the cultured talk around her, Marion also enjoyed the lower-class language used by 'two cockney girls' at her first base. Marion remembered that the sense of belonging, of unity, was established by the sharing of norms of appearance, understandings of sexual relations, use of risqué language, and also by the suspension of judgements about other women, especially moral judgements. In a striking celebration of wartime levelling, which also came close to accepting wartime constructions of the ATS as immoral, she said:

> Nobody bothered about who you were or what you were. You were taken on face value. There was no question of you come from this position or that position or, you're a prostitute or you're this or that, or religion – nothing like this came into it at all. It was simply a rapport between people. And you never bothered about what they were doing, ok if she was married and she went out with this soldier, so ... that was her business, it wasn't yours, and you never even thought that it was yours. You just met people as they were, and took them at face value and made friends very quickly.[59]

Other women in the Forces described a more proactive involvement in the levelling process, focused on bringing deviant members of their groups up to standards of behaviour which they felt that they themselves embodied. These stories described stemming a tide of pollution, literally, with soap and scrubbing brushes, in acts which were also ritualised and symbolic.

For example Mary Mackenzie, a waitress in the WAAF, recalled a 'cheeky' girl in the WAAF who was slatternly in contrast to the clean, smart uniformed appearance of Mary and her friends.

> We had a lovely billet, the girls were all nice, they were a nice – we weren't goody-goodies, but we had a nice clean billet and we looked after it and you know we were all friendly and it was very nice, but she was a cheeky wee thing, and she would never change her collar, and we were all proud, you know, we used to see who could have the shiniest shoes and the shiniest buttons, just to be nice, and she would never – and she had holes in her stockings and things like that. So they said 'let's get her ... how about giving her a bath?' ... so you see I was left in the bathrooms there and they got this girl, gave her a call and they said to her, 'What are you going to do?' She said, 'I'm just going off'. So they said, 'You're wanted along there. There's somebody wants to see you.' There were two of us and when she got along there we dumped her in the bath, clothes and all! So we sorted her out, told her that would teach her to be clean.[60]

Variations of the same story recurred (independently and without the interviewers prompting them) in other narratives. For example a shorter version was told by Amy O'Connor, ex-domestic servant and wartime Signals Operator in the ATS. 'Most of the girls that I met in the ATS were pretty – from just ordinary decent homes, but you got the odd one that wasn't. I only met one dirty girl and the girls scrubbed her, they got scrubbing brushes and scrubbed her. They told her she'd keep herself like that, or she'd get another bath'.[61]

The scrubbing stories were about bringing individuals whose manners, morals and behaviour deviated into conformity with group norms. They focused symbolically and materially on bodily hygiene and manners, matters of immediate and daily concern to women living together in close proximity in the Forces. But they also drew on an older discourse linking human filth with immorality and cleanliness with propriety. While these ideas were distinctively Victorian, popular culture in the twentieth century reinforced and gendered them. Magazines for girls and women in the 1920s and 1930s, and during the war itself, gave enormous emphasis to bodily purity for women.[62] The removal of body hair with depilatory creams such as 'New Veet', and the achievement, for example, of odourlessness by washing with Lifebuoy soap and applying O'Do Ro No deodorant, of oral hygiene by the use of Kolynos dental cream, and of inner cleanliness by daily doses of Eno's Fruit Salts, were the woman consumer's path to social acceptability.[63] The magazines presented them as no less than vital for the performance of a woman's feminine identity. Although the products have changed, there has been little reduction of the pressure since. The interviewees' scrubbing stories, and others relating to cleanliness which we shall review shortly, deployed these associations in the reconstruction of the achievement of wartime bonding between women, inextricably linked in their accounts with the larger national unity vital to winning the war.

Women in the Forces, then, described a process of forming relationships with other women based on close bodily proximity as well as on strong bonds of loyalty and affection. The reference points in such accounts were to shared experiences of dressing, sleeping, eating and washing as well as working. For example Greta Lewis, gunner in the ATS, expressed the pleasures of friendship in a description of the bodily comforts of lying in bed eating sausage sandwiches sneaked for her and a friend from the canteen by other friends.[64] She also spoke of bathing in pairs, and of sharing beds when it was cold. The sensual intimacy of these accounts was suggestive of homo-eroticism, but Greta could not recount such incidents without recalling also the prohibitions surrounding them at the time and since. She said of communal bathing:

> The bathroom was a big bathroom with two baths in you see, so two of you went together, so you picked your own friend to go with like. I mean there was some funny women you know that you didn't like, because one used to always be saying 'I'd love to go for a bath with Curly'. 'Oh', I used to say, 'never put me down with her because I'll never go for a bath if you do'.[65]

Greta was even more explicit about the possibilities of lesbian contact, now emphasising the formal penalties it occurred, in the case of bed-sharing. She said:

> Sometimes you'd creep into your friend's bed if you were both frozen and then you'd get put on a charge because that were a crime, to be caught in somebody else's bed. I mean you weren't doing anything wrong. Well we weren't, I don't know about anybody else. You weren't doing anything wrong. It were just because you were both frozen, you couldn't get warm. You used to just snuggle up.[66]

As (heterosexual) interviewers we were unable to use such opportunities to talk with our interviewees about lesbianism even though, as feminists, we wanted to hear about love between women. Looking back now, I would like to have asked whether women expressing same-sex affection were identified as 'lesbians' by their peers in an era when popular discussion of homosexuality was not only limited but also unremittingly hostile.[67] Were such women defined as deviant and in need of collective discipline, like the women singled out as 'dirty'? Greta's own account contains the possibility that, on the contrary, a woman who climbed into bed with another woman was not regarded as unusual. Her statement '[we] weren't doing anything wrong ... I don't know about anybody else' implied tolerance. Greta indicated that she did not think it was appropriate for her to enquire into what others were doing in bed, just as Marion Paul, as we saw above, remarked of a fellow servicewoman committing adultery, 'that was her business, it wasn't yours, and you never even thought that it was yours'.[68] Furthermore, the way that Greta told these stories suggested that women sharing beds, like women eating sausage sandwiches in bed, were practices which ATS Privates collectively concealed from the prying eyes of the military hierarchy. However, inter-subjectively, the taboos of the 1940s which Greta reconstructed ('you'd get put on a charge ... that were a crime') interacted with the homophobia of the 1990s ('there was some funny women') to render us as interviewers too confused and embarrassed to pursue the discussion of lesbianism in the Army.[69]

Women in the Armed Forces appear to have worked harder than civilian women to establish unity by bringing women who they did define as deviant into line. As far as the 'heroes' were concerned it was an important part of the construction of their individual and collective identities. Felicity Snow emphasised the comradeship among the WAAF aircraft mechanics, who, as we have seen in the last chapter, she rated more highly than the men. But she revealed that standards were maintained among the women by group action: 'Some of the men were ... careless, some of them were lazy. But not many women were. Occasionally were, but we used to weed them out ourselves. Because we couldn't let them let us down'.[70]

Such group bonding led to the demarcation of an interviewee's own unit from others. The same servicewoman who said 'we were all in it together' also said 'we didn't mix with them at all' when referring to other teams of women workers.[71] This was similar to the process we have observed among women in civilian work, but had its own peculiarities arising from its place within military organisation and the gendering of work in the Forces. Tense relations between servicewomen who were doing 'secret work' or 'men's work' and those, like cooks and stewards, doing 'women's work' were frequently recalled. Katharine Hughes was one of many who depicted her particular work group, in her case WRNS wireless/telegraphists, as 'a special crowd' marked out by the confidential status of the work from the other ranks, who sometimes expressed hostility towards them.[72] Gladys French, in the 'masculine' job of WRNS wireless mechanic, remembered 'that the cooks and stewards would be a bit off with us, thinking we were, had a bit of airs'.[73] The most extreme example was that of May Richards, woman radar mechanic. Although herself in the ATS she worked with the REME, always as the only woman mechanic among them. The other ATS at her army base (doing a variety of other jobs) 'were never very friendly'. May thought they were jealous 'because I was doing something that little bit different' as a result of which 'there was a

bit of resentment sometimes'. Far from developing a sense of solidarity with the other ATS, May favoured her status as one of the
boys: 'I preferred to be with the men to be quite honest'.[74] Such
accounts demonstrated the specificity of the construction of
wartime unity as feminine solidarity. Katharine Hughes' comment,
quoted earlier, 'we worked together, we played together, we lived
together and everybody was happy. There wasn't any bad feeling at
all'[75] applied to the women working at the task of wartime telegra-
phy. It did not embrace the WRNS as a whole, let alone all women
in British society.

For one woman, Janice Brunton, recall of this solidarity brought
with it an anxious memory of the accompanying pressure imposed
by the requirement to conform. After talking about sharing the
harshness of WAAF life, and the collective dodges such as smuggling
in irons 'to make life more comfortable' in which she and the other
women in her billet engaged, Janice started to talk about a 'worrying time' when 'we had one girl who made us steal, and I mean
made us steal'.[76] Janice could justify the stealing on the grounds of
the poor quality and quantity of the food, but nevertheless reconstructed feelings of fear and discomfort about what they were
doing:

> When the food was exceptionally bad in the mess, she would say, 'it's
> your turn for a loaf'. I used to nearly die! And I used to have to steal
> this loaf, I mean it was our food, I know, but it was stealing and she
> had such a hold on us, she made us do it. And then she'd say to
> another one, 'Butter!' and they would have to get the butter and per-
> haps some jam and we'd go back to the mess and eat this, and I know
> it was the fault of the authorities because the food was so bad, but it
> was still stealing, and well I used to die a thousand deaths, some of us.
> Some of them did it very easily but I didn't and I really used to worry
> about that. And always half afraid of this particular girl.[77]

Different types of work organisation, and particularly different
time schedules within a residential context reinforced social divisions and were productive of tensions between different work
groups. The reconstruction of such disunity in the Forces once again
hinged on cleanliness, but referred this time to collective rather than
individual purity. Ann Tomlinson, air mechanic in the Fleet Air
Arm, described sharing a billet with Wrens working in other trades,
such as radar mechanics and secretaries. The air mechanics had

longer shifts than the others and did not want to spend their limited free time cleaning and polishing the billet:

> It was a long, long day. And I think most of us felt that perhaps we ought to have some small privileges to make up for that. Now there were inspections every week, our bedrooms were inspected, and we used to polish the floor, and the only way you could polish your floor was by using black boot polish, your own black boot polish. There were no materials provided. But everybody seemed, the norm seemed to be to make your quarters look very clean, very nice. And we tended not to want to do this, and were quite happy to let other people do this. And the others got quite cross about this and thought we ought to do it, take our place with the rest, which was quite right, we should. And we did it, we did it frequently, but not as often as it should have been done. Really because of the lateness of our return and the fact that it meant spending the whole evening before the inspection doing it, when we were tired. But the fact that we did all this outdoor work, long hours, didn't really wash with the other people at all.[78]

On the one hand Ann described this tension over participating in the cleaning ritual. On the other hand, as the privately-educated daughter of a comfortably-off bank manager, she depicted a discovery in keeping with the discourse of wartime unity, namely that women from social backgrounds less privileged than her own were her equals: 'I learned how to like and respect other people who were not of backgrounds like mine'.[79] The attitude towards a woman like Ann of the working-class women whom she learned to respect might, however, have been different. Her disinclination towards polishing the floor could have been interpreted as a sign that she was, in spite of her war work, one of the idle rich. Amy O'Connor, ex-domestic servant from a poor home run by a widowed mother, who became a wartime ATS signalwoman, told a floor polishing story which stands as a counterpoint to Ann's. She described how the ATS (like the WRNS) had to polish their own corridors:

> You had to do from your door to the next one, so I got it done, polished it all and put the things away – we had our own polish me and me mate actually, shared a room, we bought some polish and used our own cloths you know. Officer came and said 'Oh what a nice job you've made of it'. I said, 'Thank you'. She said, 'Where are you going now?' I said, 'I'm just going –' 'Would you do this piece for her, this other girl?' I said, 'Why?' 'Well she doesn't know how to do it'. So I said to her, 'Well, get the polish on that cloth', I said, 'get another

cloth and rub it off'. She said, 'will you do it for us?' I said, 'No. No
better time to learn than to get down on her hands and knees and do
it'. I said, 'I think she ought to'. And she did. I said, 'I'll stand here and
watch her do it if you like and show her – tell her how to do it', but
I said, 'I'm not doing it for her', I said, 'I don't do anybody's work for
them'.[80]

Amy, who had escaped domestic service for a less arduous and
higher status job in the ATS, was not going to be put in the position
of doing other people's domestic work again, especially in the
middle of a 'people's war' when idle rich women should be learning to admire and emulate working-class women like herself. However, class relations outlived wartime radicalism and were against
her. She went straight on in the interview, without prompting, to
talk of how she had 'never got on, never got made anything' (such
as a non-commissioned officer) in the ATS, implying that this was
the consequence of both her lowly class position and her habit of
defiance. Ann, in contrast, became a fully commissioned officer. The
two stories, Ann's and Amy's, are suggestive of the contradictions
of the discourse of wartime unity, which provided a framework
within which to understand (and reconstruct) the dissolution of
class divisions, but were not accompanied by the material changes
which would have removed them permanently.

Unity and 'colour'

The importance of matters of appearance and manners in the construction of differences between women, raises the question of relationships with women who looked distinctively different from the
white British women who formed the majority of the members of
the Armed Forces. According to Ben Bousquet and Colin Douglas,
in their book *West Indian Women at War*, about six hundred Black
West Indian women were recruited from the Caribbean to serve in
the ATS in Britain, following the collapse of the War Office's pro-
longed resistance, in the autumn of 1943.[81] I interviewed two of
them. Their memories of their wartime experiences in Britain did
not suggest that they felt as though they were constructed negatively
as 'others' by the women with whom they worked. Both told stories, on the contrary, of being made to feel warmly welcome during
the war. Estelle Armitage, who became a clerk in the ATS,
explained:

> I can't say that I had much prejudice during the war, all English people
> were very good inviting you – especially in Edinburgh we went to tea
> – went on holiday to the Isle of Man – and people invited us to tea you
> know. We were accepted you know, we were helping with the war, it
> was after the war that you sort of – well after I did my training –[82]

Estelle's voice trailed off and she did not utter the words (which
would have distanced her from her white interviewer) 'met prejudice' or 'encountered racism'. Her reflections on the attitudes of the
population of Britain towards her as a Black colonial are suggestive
of the way in which such colonials were popularly represented
during the war. As the poster 'Together' which we discussed earlier
emphasised, and as others proclaimed, 'Allied, Dominion and Colonial troops' were vital to the war effort. There were just under 1.5
million of them in Britain in 1944.[83] Churchill, as we saw earlier,
repeatedly evoked the loyalty of the colonies and emphasised in his
Augustan speeches that the Empire (together with the United States)
would support and if necessary save Britain. British policy towards
Black American soldiers indicates that racism, with roots in nineteenth-century imperialist constructions of the subordinate Black
native and the civilising effects of white supremacy, continued
throughout the war.[84] But the popular cultural construction of Black
as well as white people from the British colonies, specific to the
Second World War, was that they were in Britain to help. A patriotic and appropriately grateful gesture, therefore, was to invite
them to tea! In the changed understandings of the presence of Black
people in Britain in the 1950s, to which Estelle referred, however,
this was the very last thing that these same people would have
done.[85]

Nadia Beale, also a clerk in the ATS, gave both a more detailed
and in some ways a more guarded account of her reception in
Britain. Unlike Estelle she did not represent herself as *ever* having
encountered prejudice in Britain, either during the war or after her
return in 1954. Perhaps this made her wary of questions which
seemed to be fishing for experiences of racism. The self-esteem
which radiated from her heroic account of coming from British
Honduras to Britain to help the war effort as a member of the ATS
would have been diminished by such admissions. In her account
interactions between Black and white people in Britain were in
equilibrium. Thus the curiosity of the ATS women about the West

Indians at her first camp was equalled by the interest of the West
Indians in the British: 'wonderful reception, curious again, you
know where we came from, and why we were all different shades of
people, and wanted to know the mixture and so on. But very exciting, and also we wanted to know why did they speak, why Glasgow
speak like that, why Yorkshire speak like that, you know, so we had
lots to share with each other'.[86] But when asked a question about
whether the ATS women with whom she mixed had ever met
coloured people before, she gave a brief terse answer: 'I never got
that impression'.[87] The interviewer (embarrassed) simply repeated
her words to her, 'You didn't get that impression?' and Nadia
relaxed a little and reflected on the reasons for the warm response,
ultimately resolving it in terms of the unity of all women in the ATS.
She said,

> No, personally, it is just like you walking into a house and meeting a
> crowd of people, you get jabbering about you know, the questions
> they were asking us, we were asking them. So no I – that didn't come
> over then, at that time – I think mostly one would get that out in the
> community, you know, out in the streets. But we didn't get it at the
> camp. Whether they were coached to say that we were coming – but
> I don't think so, no it was – it was like when you are in the services,
> we are all there to do a job, and nobody has time to pick. You know,
> we just got on with it.[88]

She constructed herself thereafter as the exotic object of friendly
interest. The ATS girls at her first posting to Preston, Lancashire, in
the winter of 1944, had made a fire in the hut to welcome her, without knowing she was West Indian: 'so they said to me, my goodness
it is just as well we put on the fire – you come from the tropics ...
and we made friends'.[89] She described some of these wartime friendships, sudden and intense, in some detail. For example, at Nadia's
next posting, a Scottish ATS corporal insisted on sight that she
should join her company and share her billet, and her commanding
officer took special care of her, sending her to stay with her own
parents (her father owned a tea-importing business) in Dulwich in
London for Christmas and other periods of leave.[90]

Social distinctions of any kind, based on 'race' or any other
marker of difference, did not hinder the sense of belonging within
a united war effort in Nadia's account. Estelle, on the other hand,
not only emphasised that 'race' was a divider after, although not

during, the war, but spoke of her own constructions of difference based on social class. She came from a well-off, entrepreneurial family, who employed servants in Kingston, Jamaica. She looked down on working-class Britons when she arrived and remembered that people said to her, 'you are a bit of a snob you know'.[91] But she remembered changing during the course of the war. Her account of personal change hinged on a floor-scrubbing story. She was required to scrub a floor by an ATS officer, as a punishment for walking down the street without wearing her cap. The interviewer might have been expecting this to be a story about either racial victimisation, or the tyrannical figure of the woman in charge. But Estelle did not use either of these tropes. In her narrative the event revealed the consequences of her class origins to her, and began the process of levelling which brought her down from her position of relative privilege:

> You were disciplined, you had to go before the commanding officer and say why you were doing this, and then you were given a punishment. The first punishment I had was to scrub – they had stone floors in the kitchen, and coming from the family I came from I couldn't even boil an egg. I didn't do anything at home, we had servants to do cleaning and everything else. So this English girl, I said to her, how do I do it? So they gave me a bucket and a big brush and a big bar of soap, some cloth, I guess. I said what do I do with it? I was pleased to learn what to do with it![92]

One wonders whether Amy O'Connor was there to show her! as Estelle did not construct herself as the Black Other in the ATS, but as one of the idle rich learning to be useful to the war effort.

Officers and gentlewomen

The female hierarchy was institutionalised in the Armed Forces in the divisions between privates, non-commissioned officers and commissioned officers.[93] Questions about relationships with women officers provoked similar reconstructions of the division between ordinary women and the woman in charge, to those evoked by civilian women remembering their supervisors. There were numerous accounts of the snobbishness of officers. For example, Kate Lomax, WAAF photographer, who herself became a sergeant and whose account we shall review in greater depth shortly, described two

WAAF officers stopping when she was hitch-hiking. She thought
they were going to pick her up, but to her lasting fury all they did
was to say, 'Put your hat on straight, you're on view' and drive
away.[94] Amy O'Connor made it clear that only the exceptional ATS
officer was worthy of respect. The example she gave was of a
'smashing' woman, whose qualities appear to have been that she
was prepared to engage in the democracy of feminine nakedness in
the ablutions: when her sink blocked up she would 'just come in and
strip off and get washed with us, you know. Nobody sort of stared
at her, and that was what she was like'. Nevertheless Amy etched
her distance from this woman into the account: 'we didn't overstep
the mark with her ... she was some sort of top woman'. Echoing
some of the negative popular constructions of the woman in charge
reviewed earlier, she said of women officers in general that many
were petty and snobbish: 'Some of the women officers were good
and some weren't. I think they were always frightened of losing
their dignity, the women officers. They daren't ... it always seemed
to me as if they daren't let go'.[95]

How did women officers represent themselves and their relationships with other women? Ann Tomlinson became a fully commissioned officer in the WRNS in the last year of the war. However, she
was never put in charge of other women, so her testimony does not
bear on the difficulty of the relationship directly. Nevertheless, her
description of her training underscores the inculcation of the cultural differences between women, which was evidently thought by
the authorities to be a necessary part of women assuming positions
of authority over other women. Ann was sent to an Officer Cadet
Training Unit at the Naval College at Greenwich. She recalled meal-
times there:

> I remember sitting at one of those long tables, being very much aware
> of the high table which was raised on steps at the far end of the room
> under this magnificent arch, where the senior members of staff of the
> College sat, and we all knew – how we knew, I do not know, but we
> did know, all of us – that we were being watched throughout every
> meal, and that our manners were being taken note of. The way we
> conversed with people and the way we behaved ourselves, our whole
> demeanour was being watched and noted. And we would say to each
> other, 'Now that is not becoming to an officer and a gentlewoman'.[96]

The course focused on naval lore and procedures and current

affairs. The women trainees had to give speeches, learn how to drill a squad ('and not march them into a wall') and also pass a final examination. They were instructed by senior Wren officers, whom Ann described in the following terms: 'They were a bit like perhaps the most popular and the nicest gym mistresses. Always very good-looking people and rather upright and splendid and great disciplinarians I suppose'.[97] However, they did not teach the cadets all aspects of the job. Ann said in response to a question informed by the prevalence of management training in the 1990s, 'I don't remember ever getting anything about how to manage people at all'.[98] Women officers, then, were taught to be ladies, but not how to conduct the relationship between themselves and those in their charge. The other interviewee who was sent to prepare for a commission, Pamela Wootton, said no more about the experience than that 'It was an officers' training course. How to be a lady'.[99] By means of emulation and osmosis, officer cadets learned the culture, the tone of command and the physical presentation of the self which constituted the performance required of them. In the woman officer the social superiority of 'the lady' was harnessed precariously to the demands of the democratic war effort.

The difficulties inherent in this position, in the context of the hostile constructions of 'the woman in charge' which we reviewed earlier, may help to explain both women's uncomfortable memories of officers and supervisors which we have already reviewed, and the negative feelings of those 'in charge' about the women for whom they were responsible. The testimony of Kate Lomax, who became a sergeant in a WAAF photography unit, stands out as unsympathetic or even inimical towards the women with whom she worked, many of whom she described as stupid, lazy and incompetent. Kate was responsible for allocating other WAAFs to work and seeing that they did it properly, as well as maintaining their discipline more generally. She gave a critical (rather than humorous) account of WAAF 'dodges', for example of women who tried to obtain their release from the WAAF on the grounds of fictitious pregnancies, by borrowing urine samples from genuinely pregnant women. She spoke from the perspective of someone who was supposed to prevent such dodges, rather than of someone sharing in the fun of devising them.[100] Kate's critical accounts of women getting themselves stuck when loading cameras into aircraft, riding bicycles down runways when aircraft were trying to land, and knitting in the darkroom when they were supposed to be developing photographs, were similarly told from the point of view of the woman in charge.[101]

Kate's severity towards women was mirrored by sympathy towards men. The photography unit was mixed, so Kate had to team women with men, and her perceptions of the women she controlled were more closely aligned to a male than a female perspective. For example she recalled having to protect men from women who teased them. 'There was another woman who, we used to call her "Twitch" and she used to go up to the men and bang them on the head and say "you weren't expecting that" you see, and these men used to come to me and say "for god's sake don't put me on with her".' She emphasised that she herself was careful with the men, reiterating in more general terms her story of protecting them: 'I never upset a man, in duty, I mean they were quite happy to work with me.'[102] Yet in spite of Kate's confidence about the men's trust in her, she thought that her relatively senior position meant that she was not 'one of them', either.[103] Being a WAAF sergeant in a more senior position than many of the RAF men in the mixed unit upset the gender hierarchy in Kate's eyes. It displaced her from the camaraderie with other women in her unit which many respondents celebrated, and yet did not make her 'one of the boys'. Kate repeatedly referred back to the issue of whether men and women could really be considered equal, bouncing the question off her interviewer, Nicole, who evidently appeared to Kate to hold the view that they were. This was an aspect of Kate's life review about which she had not yet made up her mind: 'I think it's a very difficult subject and I want real proof'.[104] Just as in civilian war work, as we saw, women in charge of other women remembered tensions rather than togetherness with other women at work, so in the Forces a woman with officer status could feel relatively isolated from, as well as critical of, the women in her charge. In both cases the woman in charge was also distanced from the men around her.

Bodies, appearance, locution, manners, it seems, were vital markers of women's social position in the wartime Armed Forces. Conducting the body in the wrong way, with insufficient attention to cleanliness, for example, was likely to be seen as an indicator of major social transgression and to provoke group correction. Having a different notion of the relationship between the effort to be expended on the job, and the effort to be expended on keeping a billet clean and tidy, could mark women out from each other. It could inspire expressions of class tension between women, remembered within the frame but against the grain of wartime unity. Only by conducting herself in a way that conformed to unwritten standards of 'ladylike' behaviour could a woman hope to become an officer, but if she did so she was given little protection against the construction of the woman in charge as petty and tyrannous.

The theme of this chapter has been that, although women couched their accounts of their wartime relationships with other women in the language of national unity, the phrase 'we were all in it together' had very specific meanings for them. It related above all to the group of women with whom they worked. Women who told stoic stories of their wartime experiences in industry focused on their workteams' collective enjoyment of bodily comforts such as food and cigarettes, and of each other's companionship in and out of work. These joys were not available to the relatively few women who told 'heroic' stories of their civilian war service. By virtue of their special efforts to obtain work which was more skilled than that which women usually did, these women were relatively isolated from female companionship. Furthermore their positions endowed them with authority over other women, confirming that isolation. Likewise, provided that they were not 'in charge', or working solely with men, women in the Armed Forces recalled delight in the company of other women. But servicewomen's accounts differed from those of women in industry, in their emphasis on their shared pleasure in the collective performance of 'men's' work, in their smart appearance in uniform, and in the proximity of their (clean) bodies. While women in industry recalled a bonding process based on the projection of imagined identities on to other groups, group solidarity for military women was forged through bringing deviants into line by collective acts of discipline or exclusion, focused upon the cleansing of actual bodies or of the spaces which bodies inhabited.

Many women, civilian and military, 'heroic' and 'stoic', referred to the lifelong friendships they made in war work. The war, as we have seen, was the occasion for a special stress on such bonding, which, in these cases, was not undone at its end. War work, on the other hand, did, for many women, cease with the 'ending of hostilities'. In the next chapter we shall examine the position which war work occupied within the personal work histories reconstructed by these women.

Notes

1 D. Morgan and M. Evans, *The Battle for Britain. Citizenship and Ideology in the Second World War* (London, Routledge, 1993), p. 24.

2 This poster has been reproduced by many authors. See, for example J. Derracott and B. Loftus, *Second World War Posters* (London, Imperial War Museum, 1972), p. 70.

3 For example, in his famous speech to the House of Commons following the evacuation of Dunkirk in May/June 1940, Churchill said, '…we shall never surrender, and even if, which I do not for a moment believe, this island or a large part of it were subjugated and starving, then our empire beyond the seas, armed and guarded by the British fleet would carry on the struggle' (quoted in A. Calder, *The People's War. Britain 1939–1945* (London, Panther, 1971), p. 127).

4 See P. Summerfield, 'Patriotism and Empire: Music-Hall Entertainment, 1870–1914', in J. M. Mackenzie (ed.), *Imperialism and Popular Culture* (Manchester, Manchester University Press, 1986), pp. 17–48.

5 This, and other posters featuring 'Our Allies the Colonies', is reproduced in J. D. Cantwell, *Images of War. British Posters 1939–45* (London, HMSO, 1989), plates 37–41.

6 S. Andrzejewski and R. M. Titmuss both argued in socio-political terms that such rewards followed total war. See S. Andrzejewski, *Military Organisation and Society* (London, Routledge, 1954) and R. M. Titmuss 'War and Social Policy', in R. M. Titmuss, *Essays on 'the Welfare State'* (London, George Allen and Unwin, 1958).

7 See, for example, Stephen Spender, *Citizens in War – And After* (London, George G. Harrap & Co Ltd, 1945). In this book about Civil Defence (CD), Spender argues that the war presented an opportunity 'to create a kind of society in which people can be individuals, but in which they are neither surrounded by hedges of class, nor victims of an automatic self interest': p. 17.

8 J. B. Priestley, *British Women Go to War* (London, Collins, 1943), p. 41.

9 J. B. Priestley, *Postscripts* (London, Heinemann, 1941), pp. 88–9.

10 *Ibid.*, pp. 78–9.

11 For a discussion of women as wartime subversives in filmic representations and propaganda, see Antonia Lant's discussion of the 'Careless Talk Costs Lives' and 'Prevent VD' poster series, and of such films as 'Next of Kin' (1942): A. Lant, *Blackout: Reinventing Women for*

Wartime British Cinema (Princeton, Princeton University Press, 1991), pp. 75–9.

12 See, for example, Central Office of Information, Wartime Social Survey, *An Investigation of the Attitudes of Women, the General Public and ATS Personnel to the Auxiliary Territorial Service*, New Series Number 5, October 1941. This survey recorded problems of recruitment to the ATS caused by its 'immoral' image. See also, PRO Lab 26/63 Women's Services (Welfare and Amenities) Committee. Minutes of Evidence, 19 May 1942. This committee discussed the possibility that prostitutes had joined the ATS at this meeting.

13 E. Burton, *What of the Women? A Study of Women in Wartime* (London, Frederick Muller, 1941), especially pp. 15–35.

14 V. Douie, *Daughters of Britain: An Account of the Work of British Women during the Second World War* (London, Women's Service Library, 1949), p. 9.

15 See, for example, 64th Report of the Select Committee on National Expenditure, quoted by V. Douie, *The Lesser Half: A Survey of the Laws, Regulations and Practices Introduced during the Present War, Which Embody Discrimination Against Women* (London, Women's Publicity Planning Association, 1943), p. 58.

16 P. Scott, *British Women in War* (London, Hutchinson, 1940), pp. 117, 57, 17.

17 P. Scott, *They Made Invasion Possible* (London, Hutchinson, 1944), p. 100.

18 On the theme of the interplay of class superiority with the ethos of maternal care and the pursuit of a professional identity among women industrial welfare supervisors, although in the First rather than the Second World War, see A. Woollacott, 'Maternalism, Professionalism and Industrial Welfare Supervisors in World War I Britain', *Women's History Review*, 3, 1 (1994), 29–56.

19 Scott, *British Women in War*, pp. 118, 17.

20 Priestley, *British Women Go to War*, p. 30.

21 Scott, *British Women in War*, p. 78.

22 Douie, *The Lesser Half*, p. 58. See also M-O, *People in Production. An Enquiry into British War Production* (London, John Murray, 1942), pp. 129–30, which reports women workers' resentment of 'the almost maternalistic attitude of the forewomen' and 'the tendency to choose teachers and others with that sort of background as people particularly likely to make forewomen'. For the difficulties experienced by women schoolteachers trying to devise socially acceptable identities within positions of authority, see Alison Oram, *Women Teachers and Feminist Politics 1900–1939* (Manchester, Manchester University Press, 1996), pp. 72–88.

23 Yvette Baynes (297, 299).
24 Elizabeth Little (470).
25 Ethel Singleton (238, 240).
26 Yvette Baynes spoke of being harassed by the boss's son and by men on the shopfloor; Elizabeth Little described becoming the centre of her shop steward's demand for equal pay as a protection for men's wage rates; Ethel Singleton described the women's playful solidarity in response to amorous male attention in the larger factory where she worked.
27 Evelyn Mills (195).
28 Jean Grant (293).
29 Jean Grant (291).
30 Caroline Woodward (298, 259).
31 Caroline Woodward (261, 294).
32 The point is strongly borne out in the wartime letters of a group of women welders from Huddersfield. See M. Jolly, 'Dear Laughing Motorbike': Letters from Women Welders of the Second World War (London, Scarlet Press, 1997).
33 Caroline Woodward (271).
34 Central Office of Information, Wartime Social Survey, Women at Work: The Attitudes of Woking Women Towards Post-War Employment and Some Related Problems. An Inquiry Made for the Office of the Minister of Reconstruction by Geoffrey Thomas, June 1944, p. 1. Thomas estimated that 43 per cent of women in civilian work in 1943 were married. This compares with a Population Census figure of 16 per cent in 1931.
35 Dorothy Rose (392).
36 Helena Balfour (488).
37 For a discussion of women's gossip as a key constituent of supportive social networks, see M. Tebbut, Women's Talk? A Social History Of 'Gossip' in Working-class Neighbourhoods 1880–1960 (Aldershot, Scolar Press, 1995).
38 Nora Vickers (955).
39 Nora Vickers (615).
40 Nora Vickers (615).
41 Nora Vickers (623).
42 Hester Hamilton, for example, who was a progress chaser at an aircraft factory in Leven, Fife, remembered the animosity of the women on the shopfloor, who disliked the fact that office staff like herself had shorter working hours than they did, even though the shopfloor workers took home more pay (150, 152).
43 Joan Stanton (80, 84).
44 Elizabeth Little (490, 474). The Huddersfield women welders drew

similar portraits of their supervisor, Miss Marflett, in their letters. See Jolly, *'Dear Laughing Motorbike'*.

45 Sadie Bartlett (208).

46 Sadie Bartlett (218).

47 Peggy Peters (113).

48 Peggy Peters (131).

49 Moira Underwood (264).

50 Beryl Bramley (264). In her account, as we saw in chapter 4, the men with whom she worked were not very 'kind' to her either, making her feel extremely isolated.

51 Fiona Thomas (264).

52 Marianne Lloyd (389).

53 Katherine Hughes (248, 252, 326); Pamela Wootton (440); Mary Mackenzie (163); Greta Lewis (201).

54 Janice Brunton (461).

55 Janice Brunton (514).

56 Janice Brunton (514).

57 Marion Paul (195).

58 Marion Paul (187).

59 Marion Paul (209).

60 Mary Mackenzie (183).

61 Amy O'Connor (693). Kate Lomax, WAAF photographer, spoke in similar terms of group pressure to keep the billet tidy: 'You had to keep your place tidy, and if you had one girl that didn't, you'd get the slovenly one, well, you got rid of her. Or if you didn't get rid of her you made her tidy' (694). On the other hand, in her autobiographical account, *All the Brave Promises*, Mary Lee Settle, a volunteer WAAF from the United States, describes being punished by other WAAF recruits for the difference between her and them. She was grabbed and thrown into a muddy puddle on her return to barracks one afternoon. The pretext was her thorough and meticulous approach to bodily hygiene, which involved stripping naked to wash twice a day, compared to their greater prudishness and (in her eyes) lower standards of cleanliness. See M. L. Settle, *All the Brave Promises. Memories of Aircraft Woman 2nd Class 2146391* (London, Pandora Press, 1984), pp. 33–8.

62 On the nineteenth century, see A. McClintock, *Imperial Leather. Race, Gender and Sexuality in the Colonial Context* (London, Routledge, 1995), especially ch. 5. On magazine instruction on bodily hygiene and appearance in the twentieth century, see P. Tinkler, *Constructing Girlhood, Popular Magazines for Girls Growing Up in England 1920–1950* (London, Taylor and Francis, 1995), ch. 6 and especially p. 162. On 'beauty as a duty' during the Second World War,

see Pat Kirkham, 'Fashioning the Feminine: Dress, Appearance and Femininity in Wartime Britain', in C. Gledhill and G. Swanson, *Nationalising Femininity. Culture, Sexuality and British Cinema in the Second World War* (Manchester, Manchester University Press 1996), pp. 154–6 and Penny Summerfield, '"The Girl that Makes the Thing that Drills the Hole that Holds the Spring ...": Discourses of Women and Work in the Second World War', in Gledhill and Swanson, *Nationalising Femininity*, pp. 41–2.

63 Advertisements for these products were published frequently throughout the war. A cursory survey suggests that they were particularly targeted at servicewomen. Examples include 'New Veet' depilatory, *Peg's Paper*, 22 April 1940 (thanks to Penny Tinkler for this reference); Lifebuoy toilet soap, which was advertised under the heading 'What they do and what they wear ... Women's Auxiliary Air Force', followed by a brief history of the WAAF, and then the statement 'Jobs in or out of uniform make us value the healthy freshness that enables us to do them well and enjoy our leisure too! Happily we can all renew that splendid feeling of Personal Freshness daily by using Lifebuoy Toilet Soap'. For Lifebuoy see J. Waller and M. Vaughan-Rees, *Women in Wartime. The Role of Women's Magazines 1939–1945* (London, Macdonald Optima, 1987), p. 80; O'Do Ro No: *Woman*, 12 June 1943 ('However hard you work, however thick your uniform, O'Do Ro No will give you complete protection'); Kolynos ('Spotlight on Service' illuminating a WAAF, 'Kolynos, the password to whiter and brighter teeth, renders a service to the Services – and to you too!'), *Picture Post*, 11 October 1941; Eno's Fruit Salts' advertisement features an ATS private sandwiched by the text 'When change of air and food upset you ... take Eno's Fruit Salt first thing every morning'. For Eno's see Waller and Vaughan-Rees, *Women in Wartime*, p. 100. They date this advertisement December 1940.

64 Greta Lewis (283–7).

65 Greta Lewis (215).

66 Greta Lewis (261).

67 Sheila Jeffreys, *The Spinster and Her Enemies. Feminism and Sexuality 1880–1930* (London, Pandora, 1985), pp. 113–27, on discursive constructions of lesbianism in the 1920s and 1930s. Sheila Jeffreys, *Anticlimax. A Feminist Perspective on the Sexual Revolution* (London, The Women's Press, 1990), pp. 50–7, on anti-lesbianism in the 1940s and 1950s. Jeffreys states, 'Literature on lesbians before the birth of lesbian feminism [in the 1970s] has been very scarce' (p. 52).

68 See footnote 59 above.

69 See Hall Carpenter Archive, Lesbian Oral History Group, *Inventing Ourselves, Lesbian Life Stories* (London, Routledge, 1989) for a col-

lection of life history interviews conducted by and with lesbians. The oldest interviewee was born in 1921 and was involved in the peace movement during the Second World War.

70 Felicity Snow (114).

71 Edith Dixon (298).

72 Katharine Hughes said, 'I mean I think people – they didn't know what we were doing and a lot of it was sheer ignorance you know. "Look at her, a chief Petty Officer, what's she done to deserve it". You know, and all that kind of thing': Hughes (342). Similar comments were made by other women including Edith Dixon who said of the 'cooks, stewards, maids, cinema operators' on her naval base, 'we didn't mix with them at all': Dixon (298).

73 Gladys French (261). Amy O'Connor, ATS Signals Operator, remembered that the waitresses in the NAAFI discriminated against servicewomen in general in favour of soldiers: 'Who's going to be bothered serving an ATS girl when there's a hunking great Grenadier stood behind her?': O'Connor (632).

74 May Richards (299, 305, 339, 430).

75 Katharine Hughes (326).

76 Janice Brunton (457, 465).

77 Janice Brunton (465).

78 Ann Tomlinson (202).

79 Ann Tomlinson (218, 220).

80 Amy O'Connor (697).

81 Ben Bousquet and Colin Douglas, *West Indian Women at War. British Racism in World War II* (London, Lawrence and Wishart, 1991), pp. 107, 126. I am extremely grateful to Colin Douglas for putting me in touch with some of the West Indian women whom he interviewed for his book. In this case my use of pseudonyms is particularly strained, since both the women whose testimony is used here appear under their real names in the book by Bousquet and Douglas cited above, and in a video recording, *Caribbean Women in World War II* produced by the Video and AV Unit, London Borough of Hammersmith and Fulham.

82 Estelle Armitage (144).

83 A. Calder, *The People's War. Britain 1939–45* (London, Fontana, 1971), p. 355.

84 On this theme see Sonya Rose, 'Girls and GIs: Race, Sex and Diplomacy in Second World War Britain', *The International History Review*, 19, 1 (1997) pp. 146–60.

85 Estelle Armitage (240). See B. Bryan, S. Dadzie and S. Scafe, *The Heart of the Race – Black Women's Lives in Britain* (London, Virago, 1985) for discussion of the racism directed against Black women,

particularly in the 1950s and 1960s.

86 Nadia Beale (81).
87 Nadia Beale (83).
88 Nadia Beale (85).
89 Nadia Beale (99).
90 Nadia Beale (111, 113).
91 Estelle Armitage (68).
92 Estelle Armitage (132)
93 Non-commissioned officers were called Sergeants and Corporals in the ATS and the WAAF, Petty Officers and Chief Petty Officers in the WRNS. Commissioned officers were Subalterns and Commandants in the ATS, Section, Flight, Squadron, Wing and Group Officers and Commandants in the WAAF, and First, Second, Third and Chief Officers, Superintendents and Commandants in the WRNS. See M. Brayley and R. Ingram, *World War II British Women's Uniforms* (London, Windrow and Greene, 1995).
94 Kate Lomax (750).
95 Kate Lomax (532, 741).
96 Ann Tomlinson (240).
97 Ann Tomlinson (260). Ann presented a vignette of how the officers had to be treated by the cadets: 'Well when the Chief Wren Officer visited us, we all played ping-pong with her and we were advised – you know, the underground told us, that the great thing was to let her win and then it would be all right you see. She did like to win. Whether this was true or not I don't know, but we did let her win' (258).
98 Ann Tomlinson (246).
99 Pamela Wootton (383).
100 Kate Lomax (623).
101 Kate Lomax (503, 365, 603).
102 Kate Lomax (623, 676).
103 'I felt I hadn't been in longer than some of the men that were coming from overseas. Yes, I did feel – some of these men you see that came over as LACs, that's Leading Aircraftsman, you see, some of those that came over, they hadn't had promotion, and you felt they should have': Kate Lomax (686).
104 Kate Lomax (659, 663, 672, 676).

'A Bus Conductress ... At Home with her Baby' 1943, from J. B. Priestley, *British Women Go To War*

Chapter 6

Demobilisation and discourses of women's work

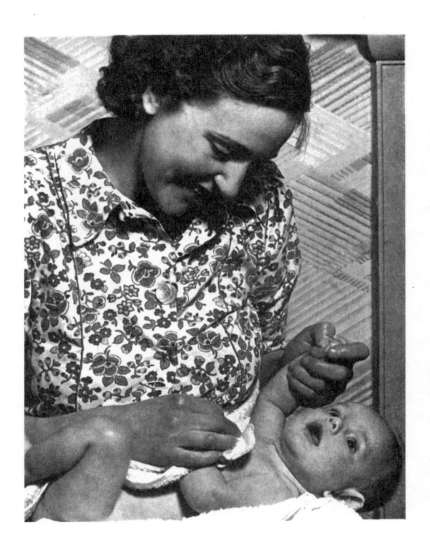

'Demobilisation' was a term used to refer to the reduction of the numbers of men and women in the Armed Forces and industrial war work, as the war effort was scaled down. The word evokes reverse movement and the breaking up of groups formed for the purpose of waging war. It encourages a view of the end of the war as a period of disruption and transition. The demobilisation of women has been the focus of special attention, because of assumptions that war work, whether civilian or military, was exceptional for women. Historians have argued about whether women 'willingly' quit their wartime jobs, or went reluctantly, whether they wanted to 'return home' or were keen to pursue their war work further.[1] The issue of what women wanted at the end of the war was one of the specific questions which, as we saw in chapter 1, Denise Riley decided was unanswerable. To recapitulate, she wrote in the early 1980s that she did not think that 'considering the expression of wants is pointless'. But 'the difficulty is that needs and wants are never pure and undetermined in such a way that they could be fully revealed, to shine out with an absolute clarity, by stripping away a patina of historical postscripts and rewriting'.[2]

In this chapter we shall not try to answer the question of what women wanted in 1945, directly. As in earlier chapters, we shall explore instead the historical 'patina' itself and its relationship to memory. We shall discuss the discourses of women and work to which the women interviewed were exposed during their lives and the use they made of them in giving an account of their place in the labour market at the end of the war and in the post-war years. There were four major formulations of the relationship between women and work from the First World War to the 1990s. One powerful representation was of the marginality of women to paid work. Another emphasised opportunities for women in work. Both of these representations span the entire period of my interviewees' lives. A third, which emerged in the 1950s, conceptualised women's relationship to paid work and to the home as the 'dual role'. Fourth, from the 1970s to the 1990s, popular feminist analysis challenged, and yet in various ways drew upon, all three.

The discourse of marginality

In the period from the 1920s to the 1970s women were persistently represented as marginal to the workforce in documents directly concerned with employment. Government reports, as well as more popular writing, repeatedly declared that 'women's work' did not demand skill or strength, but required the exercise of 'feminine' characteristics such as dexterity or maternal qualities, and was located in 'woman-employing' niches in industries, services or professions. The explanation of the association between women and such work lay in what were usually referred to as 'natural and conventional' factors. These were the temporary place of paid work in a woman's life cycle, and its unimportance to a woman relative to domestic concerns because of her prior orientation to marriage and motherhood which biologically, socially and morally dominated her life. Married women who added paid work to their domestic responsibilities committed themselves, according to this account, to irksome toil. They were, according to the trade unionist Mary Agnes Hamilton in 1941, 'doing double employment, paid and unpaid: running a home in the hours left over from factory or domestic or casual employment'.[3] The objective of women in the labour movement, such as Hamilton, was to relieve married women of the necessity of doing paid work, and to raise their status as housewives and mothers in the home.

The demand for labour in the Second World War caused a temporary shift in representations of women and work. As we saw in chapter 2, wartime recruitment campaigns proclaimed that women's patriotic duty was to release men from industry and from military offices and workshops in order to fight. From 1941, the Ministries of Labour and Information orchestrated the official campaign to compel women, including married women, to move into the so-called 'essential industries', those seen as vital to the production of the means to fight the war. The popular construction of women's war work was that it was men's work, temporarily taken on by women to help in an emergency.[4]

This wartime disruption was not accompanied by any striking alteration to the marginalising discourse of women and work, in whatever source one seeks it, including those from which one might have expected a challenge. For example in 1945 Gertrude Williams, an economics lecturer at Bedford College, London University, published a book called *Women and Work* in a series aimed to stimulate popular discussion of important issues. Her arguments were remarkably conventional, recapping the accounts of the inter-war years in a discursive summary for a popular market. She made four main points. First, the war had changed women's working lives temporarily, but most women would want to withdraw 'when the men were free to take up their usual occupations again', as Williams believed women had done in 1918.[5] Second, she represented the sexual division of labour as the natural order. Women did different work from men because they were made differently. The captions to two pairs of photographs illustrating her book read, 'Men have muscular strength', and on the opposite page, '- but women have the deft touch'; and, over the page, 'the man applies the skill' and '- the woman runs the machine'. The other reason for the sexual division of labour was that men's and women's primary bio-social functions were different. Women's was to bear and rear children: 'for women, the bearing and rearing of children and the maintenance of a home ... is the primary task, and all her other activities are inevitably shaped and coloured by this fact. For man, the home is not a daily, constant, tie'.[6]

Third, women necessarily occupied a marginal position to the labour market, working in undemanding jobs while unmarried because they would withdraw or work only temporarily or on a part-time basis after marriage. Training, the acquisition of skill, and the assumption of managerial responsibilities were irrelevant to them. 'Marriage and the expectation of marriage, are the dominant factors in moulding the pattern of a woman's life', she reiterated.[7] Her account glowed with the influence of the contemporary concern to increase the birth-rate, known as pronatalism. She echoed its more conservative proponents' arguments for home-based childcare by the full-time mother. While more 'progressive' pronatalists advocated nurseries to supplement maternal care and offer respite to mothers of large families, others were implacably opposed to institutional care for young children.[8] In 1945, when Gertrude Williams was writing, it might appear that the war had demonstrated that nurseries were a benign alternative to full-time maternal care, which made it possible for mothers to combine paid work and childrearing. But Williams asserted that 'as a substitute for the home the nursery school leaves ... much to be desired', capping these comments as an economist by arguing that nurseries were in any case not cost-effective.[9] Apparent exceptions to the argument that motherhood and paid work were incompatible were swept away. A 'small handful of professional women' working from interest rather than necessity might carry on after having children, but marriage and motherhood undermined even their effectiveness: 'the majority of women find that, despite domestic assistance in housework, their capacities can no longer be so narrowly canalised when they have children and that much of the vitality and strength that a man can put into his work necessarily goes into the unique relationship with the growing family'.[10] This text was positioned beneath an appealing picture of two babies in high chairs, chewing rusks.

Williams' fourth point represented a new development which still marginalised women. While she was adamant that married women should stay at home and rear children while young, Williams also argued that confinement in the home was bad, psychologically and in terms of citizenship, for older women. When a woman's children were grown up, and no longer required all her 'skill, interest and energy', she should work part-time. The home bereft of children suddenly became not the joyous focus of a woman's life's work, but a 'prolific breeding-ground of neurasthenic unhappiness'.[11] Herein lay the post-war future for women: as mothers they must devote themselves to their children, but as older women they should return to paid work in unskilled jobs with little responsibility.

The discourse of opportunity

Williams' views of women's present and future prospects in 1945 were part of a powerful set of messages popularly communicated from many media at the end of the war and after.[12] There was, however, an alternative story to this strong representation of the marginality of women to paid work. Throughout the period 1920 to 1970 educational and training literature, and popular versions of it, referred to the opportunities available to girls and women at work as a result of investment in education. Contrary to the monolithic story of the marginality of women to paid work, which applied to all women whatever their social class or education, in this account the female sector of employment was highly differentiated and offered a range of opportunities.

Official literature concerning the education of girls in the inter-war period was, as Felicity Hunt has argued, two-faced. On the one hand it advocated the domestic norm, for which training at school in domestic skills was surely the logical preparation. On the other there were several reasons to stress the benefits of either a more intellectual education or specific types of vocational training, even if girls had 'deficits' caused by biology and social function, which meant that identical provision to that of boys would never be appropriate.[13] These reasons included both the cultural advantages to husbands and children of educated wives and mothers, and the idea of education and training for girls as an insurance against spinsterhood, widowhood or a husband's failure to fulfil the role of breadwinner.

Such views were popularised in magazines targetted at schoolgirls and young women workers in the period 1920–50. Penny Tinkler analyses the magazines' involvement in the construction of a range of opportunities. She stresses the highly differentiated approach of the magazines. Their messages to girls were determined by editors' assessments of the intersecting effects of social class, educational or work situation and life stage on a girl's interests, and hence on the scope of the magazine's appeal. Papers aimed at elementary schoolgirls (assumed to be working class) omitted the future working lives of their readers, because, Tinkler argues, such girls were expected to take routine unskilled 'meantime' jobs. Such prospects (central to the discourse of marginality) did not offer the magazines possibilities for presenting girls with an 'attractive identity'.[14] But magazines addressed to working-class girls actually at work constructed a more positive version of their readers' situation. These magazines offered young women guidance on how to survive in an uncertain labour market and communicated a strong work ethic, praising girls for training and taking work seriously. They addressed girls who might have taken vocational courses at school or after, in skilled trades such as millinery, upholstery, dressmaking, office work and catering. Nevertheless, Tinkler writes, papers in this group, like *Pam's Paper*, tended to portray work, particularly through fiction, 'as a means to find a husband or develop skills useful to the potential wife and mother'.[15] The magazines presented marriage, followed by motherhood, as the point in working-class girls' lives at which they would become marginal from the labour market, after brief careers in which there were opportunities for those prepared to work for them.

In contrast, magazines for secondary schoolgirls such as *Girls' Own Paper* and *Miss Modern* constructed a positive picture of the relationship between education and employment for middle-class

girls. Their message was consistent with the approach of the headmistresses of girls' secondary schools from the 1920s to the 1970s,
in whose philosophy marriage was a legitimate and normal objective for girls, but whose prior goal was that 'women should develop
their skills and utilise these and their talents in the service of the
community'.[16] These magazines presented their readers with a range
of possible careers, in professional and skilled occupations. Above
all, teaching was consistently presented to girls as an opportunity
for a satisfying and worthwhile career.[17]

Tinkler argues that magazine accounts qualified the advocacy of
women's work opportunities in two ways. First, they emphasised
the compatibility of the careers they advocated with femininity.
Thus women's essential combination of maternalism and dexterity
specially equipped them, according to these magazines, for the
branches of professions like teaching, dentistry and veterinary med-
icine which dealt with young children and small pets. Second, at the
same time as offering serious careers advice, at least one magazine
(*Miss Modern*) consistently cautioned girls against revelling too
much in the independence that training and work would give them.
The price they would pay would be unmarriageability and loneliness.[18]

The idea that the fulfilment of women's biological and social
functions was not compatible with paid work was not challenged by
the discourse of opportunity in the period before the Second World
War. This idea was institutionalised between the wars in the marriage bar, under which women in white collar and professional
work were required to resign from their jobs on marriage.[19] The discourse confirmed gender difference by defining the sector of
employment offering opportunities for women as naturally suitable
because of its special requirements for feminine attributes.[20] However, in the discourse of opportunity of the 1920s and 1930s,
women's universal marital destiny was seen as a postponed moment
of closure for the girl seeking education and training, rather than as
removing opportunity from work at the start. And at the end of the
Second World War, in some renderings of this version of women
and careers, marriage was not seen as a necessary closure at all. In
tension with the requirement of full-time maternal care, which, as
we have seen, was central to the account of marginality in 1945,
were the dictates of new ways of conceptualising the post-war
labour market. The official removal of marriage bars from teaching

in 1944 and the civil service in 1946, for example, prepared for a post-war labour shortage in some professions and industries, which would necessitate a continuation of the wartime participation of married women.[21] A contributor to *Girls' Own Paper* introduced this approach to the discourse of opportunity, in November 1945:

> I would like to see almost every girl married. Even more fervently I would like to see her equipped for a career. Both offer different ways of enriching and fulfilling her individuality. Marriage and motherhood can, of course, be a whole-time-job, and the most selfless career in the world. But motherhood should be regarded as a temporary one, for the sake of the children as well as the parents.[22]

This writer could, like Williams, have been referring to views derived from post-war psychiatry about the benefits to a woman and her family of her working outside the home in middle age, rather than becoming a smothering mother prey to 'neurasthenic unhappiness'. But the statement said more than this. It argued that careers had a vital part to play in the individual fulfilment of 'every girl', in contrast to the idea that part-time jobs might be psychologically beneficial to middle-aged women. Most importantly, this writer advocated the dual pursuit of motherhood and a career, rather than presenting motherhood as a woman's main goal, and a job as a therapeutic supplement.

The discourse of the 'dual role'

The idea that married women, including mothers of young children, could and should participate in the labour market gained momentum in the 1950s but was controversial, because it was in tension with the account of women's bio-social priorities in the discourse of marginality. The book written by Alva Myrdal and Viola Klein and published in 1956, *Women's Two Roles*, endeavoured to settle the controversy at the same time as telling a story of women's paid work in terms of opportunity. The discourse of the dual role to which they contributed accepted the married woman worker as someone who had a permanent place in the labour market. Her 'dual role' was not the irksome and ill-advised toil envisaged in the discourse of marginality. Their arguments were based on the idea of the importance of participation in both domesticity and paid work, for women and for society.[23] The idea of the dual role was underpinned by conviction that women's relationship to work in the home had been altered by the effects of domestic technology and by the advent of companionate marriage. This style of marriage was widely discussed in the 1940s and 1950s, both positively for the advantages which would accrue to women from marriages conceived of as teamwork and partnership, and negatively for the destabilisation of marriage threatened by such a reorienting of the marital hierarchy and apparently evident in rising rates of divorce.[24]

Myrdal and Klein had in mind women who would choose and train for 'vocations' rather than those who would take unskilled jobs. Women were advised to choose 'occupations which they will be able to continue after marriage or resume after an interval of a few years', and this meant the feminine jobs of the discourse of opportunity, such as teaching, clerical work, nursing and social work.[25] Above all teaching jobs were advocated, because they were, according to Myrdal and Klein, 'so easy to combine with marriage and motherhood that, metaphorically speaking, a woman can practise them almost with one hand at the cradle'.[26] From the 1950s to the 1970s this approach was emphasised in educational documents such as the Crowther Report of 1959 and the Newsom Report of 1963. Their official recommendations differentiated between relatively academically successful girls who could qualify for the 'women's professions' and most women who would occupy a marginal position in the labour force. Those pursuing such opportunities as teaching were not, in the late 1950s and the 1960s, represented as the abnormal career women of Williams' account. They were heading for destinations which, in the post-war situation of a shortage of this kind of professional labour, had been redefined as not only natural to premarital women, but also compatible with women's primary bio-social functions of marriage and motherhood.[27]

The feminist challenge

A more radical challenge to the assumption that women's social functions as wives and mothers must dominate their lives was made in the 1970s by the women's liberation movement. All three of the discourses outlined above were criticised in publications of the 1970s, including the magazine *Spare Rib*.[28] Scepticism was expressed about the extent of opportunities for women. The prized 'feminine' careers of teaching, nursing, social work and clerical work were re-evaluated as a limited range of options which exploited the caring qualities associated with femininity, and within which women were relatively disadvantaged.[29] The language of equal opportunities was rewritten: prejudice became discrimination, inequality became subordination. The exclusion of women from areas of work deemed unsuitable (because the work was, for example, heavy, skilled or responsible) was challenged, and the barriers to women's chances of promotion (named in the 1980s as 'the glass ceiling') were explored and their causes debated. The dual role was seen as intolerable and was reconceptualised as the double burden, as it was in the discourse of marginality. But rather than being seen as an unfortunate by-product of flouting the natural order, it was depicted as a consequence of dual oppression, at work and at home. The origins of the double burden were traced to male exploitation within marriage, and the implications of this for women's labour market position were spelt out. The concepts of masculinity which were inexplicit within and yet central to the discourse of women's marginality to work were exposed.

The feminist discourse of the 1970s and 1980s, although not as unified as this brief summary implies, nevertheless offered an analysis of women as oppressed whatever their education, training and work: all women were marginalised. But it also presented a programme of challenge, resistance and aspiration. Why should men not take responsibility for housework and childcare? Why should it be assumed that women had to do so, and that this debarred them from more skilled and responsible types of work? Why should women not receive equal pay? Why should women put up with all the daily reminders, from wolf whistles to washing up, that they were subordinate to men?[30]

Women interviewed in the 1990s about their wartime lives and the 'choices' they made about training, work, marriage and childbearing in the later 1940s were remembering events which took place in the context of the discourses described here. At the end of the war the idea of women's marginality to the workforce was loudly proclaimed. It was evoked in Parliament and the press as central to post-war reconstruction, and hence as the route to social stability and harmony.[31] But the discourse of opportunity was by no means dead. It was stressed by women educationalists and by organisations of professional and business women, and was a sub-theme in the debates of women trade unionists about post-war reconstruction. 'Resettlement' opportunities for servicewomen may have been restricted, but government-funded education and training for the women's trades and professions were available.[32] Respondents were also recalling their work histories within a time-frame in which the idea of women's dual role moved from a peripheral to a central position in the construction of the identity of the woman worker. Accompanied by a huge increase in the availability of part-time work, the dual role became the dominant model for the modern woman's resolution of the home-work dilemma between the 1950s and the 1990s.[33] However, all these ways of understanding women's relationships to the labour market were under pressure from the feminist understandings of women and work developed in the 1970s and 1980s. We shall now explore the take-up of these various discourses by the women interviewed. How did they use them in rendering accounts both of their place in the labour market at the end of the war and of their lifelong work histories?

The regretful return to marginality

It would not have been surprising if women who told 'heroic' stories of insisting on 'masculine' war work as close to the 'front line' as they could get had remembered regretting demobilisation, if it marked the end of their special status in the workforce. Among the 'heroes' there were indeed a group of women who constructed such accounts. They had in common an understanding of their earlier and subsequent work histories as frustrating experiences of marginalisation, from which war work was a short-lived escape.

A strongly told account of this sort came from Felicity Snow, a wartime air mechanic in the WAAF. Her account of her (limited) education as the daughter of hard-working parents who ran a café, of leaving school at 14 and being channelled by parents and teachers into office work, speaks of the marginal woman worker, with no special interest in her low status occupation or in training or education which would improve her position in the labour market. The war temporarily transformed her work history, however. Felicity volunteered for the WAAF as soon as she was old enough and sought a mechanical, military, man's job, as an air mechanic. Giving up this hard but, to her, deeply satisfying skilled job at the end of the war was the cause of passionately remembered sorrow: 'You were demobbed and you came out back into civilian life and found it very hard to start with, because you missed the comradeship, and you missed the freedom'.[34] She applied with a WAAF friend to join the Police Force but the friend was not accepted, so the two of them found jobs as telephonists at the General Post Office. Felicity thus drifted back into clerical work. She vividly reconstructed the loss of freedom in her new job, describing how she resented being confined to a chair in an office, 'plugged into the telephone operator's position'.[35] But she described making herself adjust out of a sense of 'reality': 'there was no openings for flight mechanics, not in that way, not in those days, 1946 … they didn't want women back in that job'.[36]

Reflecting on this loss of a valued opportunity, Felicity commented on what she might have done had she had her life over again. 'These days I probably would have gone into engineering as a career, but in those days there was nothing whatever in that way, no openings for women in those days at all.'[37] These comments, based on her perceptions of the changed possibilities for women in the labour market by the early 1990s, constitute tokens of earnest placed within her testimony to give it the conviction she wanted it to carry. Felicity's reflections drew upon and projected the discourse of feminine opportunity, which by the 1990s had claimed engineering as a suitable career for women, even though, in practice, women still had an uncertain place in such work.[38]

In contrast to her wartime work narrative, Felicity told her immediate post-war work history in terms of marginalisation. She left her routine clerical work on marriage in the early 1950s, and stayed outside the paid labour force, caring for her ageing parents-in-law and young children. But her account shifted back into the language of opportunity (and with it the crossing of gender boundaries) in the early 1960s, when she trained and qualified as a driving instructor in order to work in her husband's family firm. This, like her war work, she said, was 'very unusual for a woman to do … it's a woman into a man's world'.[39] She depicted it as only possible because her transgression was neutralised by the demands of the family business.

Felicity remembered her wartime work as a welcome interlude in a career which, until the 1960s, followed a marginalised pattern. The wartime opportunity was impossible to retain because of the inevitable regendering of the labour market at the end of the war: 'they didn't want women back in that job'.[40] Felicity was unusual in later finding a new career in 'a man's world', but among the forty-two women interviewed there were no fewer than twelve who constructed stories which were in other respects similar to Felicity's. They all told heroic tales of joining up, followed by dismay at having to quit their jobs at the end of the war, and of a life thereafter in which for most of them paid work was no more than a humdrum necessity subordinate to family concerns.[41] Their accounts of satisfying war work, and deep regrets about giving it up, throw into sharp relief their constructions of otherwise marginal working lives.[42]

Among these work histories there were several in which it was not the end of the war in itself but pregnancy which ended the woman's war work. As we have seen in the discussion of Gertrude Williams' 1945 account of women and work, the construction of women as marginal to the workforce was given a special gloss by the contemporary emphasis on the need to increase the birth-rate. Motherhood, undertaken full-time and not combined with paid work, was the socially acclaimed role for women in the 1940s' discourse of pronatalism. But in the accounts of women who regretted the end of their heroic wartime role, its advent was at best remembered with ambivalence and at worst distinctly unwelcome. Beryl Bramley's story is a good example. Beryl told a pre-war work history of drifting into hairdressing after failing the exams for her preferred career of librarianship. The war offered her a new chance, and her account shifted gear as she outlined her progress within the new set of opportunities. She moved from riveting in an aircraft factory to training and working as a member of the AID, and had plans to join the ATA. But the account came to an abrupt end with a bitter story about giving up war work. It was 1944 and Beryl was about to leave her AID job at the Preston New Road components factory to train to be a pilot in the ATA:

> I was just going into that, and found out that I was pregnant. So after I'd been sick on the trains several times and wandered along the Promenade also being sick and utterly wretched, I went and told the chief inspector, and he said, 'Oh well never mind', he said, 'you go and have the baby', he said, 'and then after six weeks your mother can have it and you can come back'. I said, 'You don't know my mother!' I could just imagine my mother's face when I told her, 'Would you mind looking after this while I go back to work?' So that was the end of it, that's why I say it's rather boring because the rest of the war there was just –

horrible really because I couldn't do anything obviously because I had the baby, and I must admit that I was always a bit resentful.[43]

Beryl could not find anything to salvage from the wreck of her plans in rearing a family. This form of feminine fulfilment was not satisfying to her, but she did not feel that she could defy the conventions surrounding motherhood for someone from her social milieu in order to pursue her ambitions across the gender boundary. She focused on motherhood, rather than the removal of women from wartime men's work as the barrier to her occupational progress. Such progress remained alive in her account, as a foregone possibility: 'I sometimes think that I would have had a very rewarding career, if I hadn't had any children'.[44] She did return to paid work after the war, but it was subordinated to family. She described meandering in and out of a number of welfare and retailing jobs. Even if she enjoyed some of them, her account did not communicate the satisfaction with which she spoke of her war work.

These were the demobilisation stories of 'heroes'. It was not, however, only the women who constructed accounts of enthusiastically entering war work who emphasised their regrets on leaving. A number of the reluctant recruits who became proud and dedicated war workers indicated that they resented their removal from war work as much as they disliked being forced into it in the first place. Sadie Bartlett represented this feeling of being subjected to labour market pressures beyond her control at both the beginning and the end of the war, particularly graphically. Sadie became a shop assistant on leaving school in rural Norfolk at the age of 15 in 1937, started a hairdressing apprenticeship in 1939, and then did jobs on the land. After trying to avoid the call-up she joined the Timber Corps, a branch of the WLA, in 1942 and became a committed worker. In 1946 she left the Corps. She described accepting that opportunities for women tree fellers were now at an end, but remembered acute distress about having to return to work indoors:

We never had any ideas of going for it after. Actually I would have liked to have gone on in it – it was terrible when I came out of it – work and … Oh it was really terrible … everything was sort of chaos, you came out, you got a job and they asked me if I wanted to go back to hairdressing and I said yes, and they said yes, I could have a grant … And while I was waiting for the grant they said would I like to go and be a telephonist, so I said, 'Oh yes, I don't mind what I do' …

actually I liked the work but I hated being indoors. If I could have sat outside and done it that would have been all right. It seemed to be terrible to me, when it was a nice day and you were shut up, you know, it was more or less like a gaol to me.[45]

Like Felicity, although more vividly, Sadie reconstructed the confusing post-war labour market ('everything was sort of chaos'). There were plenty of jobs for women within stereotypically feminine sectors, but this meant exchanging the freedom that women like Felicity and Sadie had enjoyed in heavy, outdoor 'men's work' for the stasis and confinement of women's work, 'plugged into the telephone operator's position' in Felicity's words. Sadie left her job as a telephonist seven years later, after marriage, to have a child. She depicted the marriage as one of separate spheres rather than teamwork. To help make ends meet she later took up charring and then, in a deliberate effort to obtain a better (although still marginal) position in the labour market in the 1960s, she became a part-time clerical worker.

Another 'stoic' who expressed regrets about leaving war work was Caroline Woodward. Pushed by her mother, Caroline had become a welder at Scottish Motor Transport in Edinburgh, but after a reluctant start developed a real love of the work for itself, and for the socialised labour process involved. She reiterated that she was deeply sorry when the job came to an end: 'I just loved the job, and I loved the company really. I really liked that job. It doesn't mean I was sorry the war ended, but I wished it had went on, you know, as a job'.[46] Like several other women who gave stoic accounts of joining the war effort, Caroline described surprised satisfaction in discovering that such 'masculine' war work as welding was an occupation which suited her, but like Felicity and Sadie she regretted her impotence in the face of regulations which said that women did such work only temporarily. Welding was a man's job, and at the end of the war women welders were forced to look for other work. Caroline married and meandered through a variety of cleaning and catering jobs.

These accounts of a regretful return after the war to a marginal position in the labour market, in which family responsibilities were combined with what the women themselves saw as rather insignificant jobs, are the ones celebrated in popular feminist representations of women's participation in the war effort. The American film

Rosie the Riveter, released in 1982, epitomised this version of the impact of the war on women's work histories.[47] The film told a story of women in the United States enthusiastically taking up war work across the gender boundary. They found that they were good at such skilled work as riveting and welding, enjoyed the high wages, and would have liked to have stayed in it after the war. But with the armistice came their dismissal notices and they found that they were required to 'return home', much against their will.

The welcome return to marginality

This was not, of course, the only story. Several alternative versions were told by the women we interviewed. In one, characteristically stoic, an understanding of the self as a marginalised woman worker made sense, and found expression in an account of wanting to return to 'meantime' women's work, if to any work at all. Such work was described as intrinsically unimportant and subordinate to the prospect of matrimony and motherhood. Demobilisation, in these accounts, was represented as a let-out, an end to a period of enforced war work, possibly in a masculine environment, which the woman had tolerated on sufferance. In 1946, Margaret Goldsmith claimed to know that 'Many women, possibly the majority of married women, have not enjoyed this new independence; they have been made miserable by the war-time interruption of family life. As a result many married women, again possibly the majority, fervently wish themselves back into their pre-war home routine.'[48] The end of the war for these women was both an opportunity to return to women's work, and above all a chance to fulfil feminine expectations within marriage by having a family. This interpretation of the meaning of the end of the war for women was the standard one in the 1940s, projected by a great deal of mid-1940s film, literature and commentary.[49]

Evelyn Mills remained in the same occupation, clerical work, throughout her working life, but, as we saw in chapter 2, she was required to move to 'essential work' during the war. Her complete work history conformed to the model of the marginal woman worker. She spoke of disliking school, of leaving as soon as she could at the age of 14, and of taking up, under her father's watchful eye, whatever paid work was available locally. After working in a laundry she moved to a building contractor's office where she collected rents and did some bookkeeping. She was called up by the state in 1942, and went to work reluctantly as a duplicator operator at the Admiralty. She spoke with relief about obtaining a discharge from this job on grounds of ill health after two years, and returning to her old job at the builder's. Marriage was now a high priority for her. She married in 1946, and although she did not stop doing paid work, she constructed herself as developing a different relationship to the labour market. She took part-time and temporary jobs as a married woman, and also, at times, worked from home. Evelyn expressed the relationship between herself as a wife and as a worker in terms which are almost precisely those which Gertrude Williams used when arguing in 1945 that 'the majority of women' were not able to pursue skilled or responsible job options, because once they had become wives and mothers they found that 'their capacities can no longer be so narrowly canalised'.[50] Evelyn said, 'I didn't want a job with any responsibility, you know, like a wages clerk or a bookkeeper or anything like that. Once I was married. Those sort of jobs, if they're short of staff or if you've got a day's holiday, you've still got to make up and do your work, and I thought, I can't work in that way so much now I'm married, because you've got other ties'.[51]

Even a return to 'masculine' wartime work could be cast as an account of marginality. Elizabeth Little's narrative of her working life emphasised a combination of episodic women's work with prioritisation of the family. Her wartime venture into the male sphere of work could have been no more than a brief interlude, undertaken reluctantly, in a work history which otherwise conformed to the norms of feminine marginality. However, the dynamics of gender in the workplace disrupted this narrative, without displacing the marginal place of paid work in Elizabeth's life. Before the war she was a grocery shop assistant. Wartime call-up led to her training for work as a bench fitter and then a gauge setter for Reyrolles, an engineering company in north-east England. Her job as a dilutee was classified as 'men's work' and, as we saw in chapter 4, her shop steward insisted that she should receive equal pay, which also meant that, under the 'Extended Employment of Women Agreements', she was made redundant at the end of the war. Although she said, 'I was sorry really when I finished there',[52] Elizabeth was far from outraged by the fact that 'they didn't want women back in that job'. She spoke of quietly accepting it: 'you just took it in your stride, you knew it was going to happen sort of once the war finished, yes, and you expected just to go back to your normal work'.[53] In the event, however, she could not 'go back to her normal work' because she could not get a job as a grocery assistant in the Tyneside area. Instead she was sent by her family to help in an uncle's betting shop in London. At this point her career sounded like the meandering one of the marginalised woman worker.

However, on her return to South Shields in 1946, Elizabeth became a beneficiary of the gender restructuring of engineering, in which the sectors labelled women's work were expanding. One of the male toolmakers from Reyrolles sought her out and asked her to work with him at Reyrolles' Hebburn factory, in a storeroom.[54] She fell in with this, and later moved into work similar to her wartime work in the gauge room, with a woman friend from the war. Elizabeth thus re-entered her wartime firm and resumed a job similar to her war work, although she did not now receive equal pay with men. Her return was not prompted by enthusiasm for the opportunities opened up by the war. She was not heroically seeking to pursue a job unusual for a woman. On the contrary, she emphasised that the new work at Reyrolles was specially designed for women and this was why she was comfortable about doing it: 'the department that I was looking after the store for, that was all women'.[55] 'I knew what was going on in there, I quite liked it.'[56] She maintained her career in engineering for five years from 1947 to 1952, when her family sent her to look after a widowed cousin's children. She subsequently married the cousin. Elizabeth did not return to the gauge room after this, in spite of the fact that 'I just seemed to enjoy it all'.[57] Marriage and motherhood deflected her from her war-initiated career, although they did not end her participation in paid work. Her subsequent employment fitted around the family. In the 1960s she ran a pub with her husband, and in the 1970s she worked once more in a grocer's shop. Elizabeth's account was of a life within which work was marginal to her central role in the family. Family demands, intersected in wartime by those of the state and after the war by those of the changing local labour market, determined the course of her work history.

Although such accounts were characteristically stoic, there were women who entered war work heroically who indicated that they were pleased to leave it when they could, and that they welcomed the subsequent marginalisation of paid work in their lives. May

Richards became a radar mechanic in the ATS against the odds, after a period of clerical work which she regarded as boring and petty. She was one of those who remembered arguing with male colleagues in the Army that unequal pay was unfair, and she described enjoying her position as 'one of the boys'. But although she was, in these ways, conscious and proud of her wartime journey across the gender boundary, she said of leaving the ATS in 1945 'I was glad to get out'. She had married a soldier and was pregnant. She expressed herself in terms of the conventional understanding of the meaning of post-war reconstruction: 'I was looking forward to married life and having a home of my own'.[58] In the event she had to wait four years for this dream to be fulfilled because of the housing shortage, but she had a family of four. Her account of her later labour market participation suggested that she deliberately marginalised paid work so that she could concentrate on family commitments: 'I did some part-time jobs. Nothing until the three eldest were all well established at school, and I did some market research work for the BBC and one, Mass Observation, it was called. But they were assignments I could take or leave, you know, I fitted them in.'[59]

The women who regarded their roles as wives and mothers as preferable to anything more than a tangential involvement in paid work, were mobilising in their narratives the post-war view of women's role in the family as an important and worthwhile one, a welcome opportunity. They were also defying the various discourses of work, including the 1970s feminist one, which defined women in such roles not only as 'marginal' but also as 'oppressed'. They turned this meaning round to indicate that it was they themselves who had, by choice, marginalised paid work in their lives becaue they had other priorities which they did not regard as oppressive.

Opportunities for progress up the clerical ladder

The research project for which the interviews under discussion in this book were undertaken revealed, as we saw in chapter 1, that wartime training and work led directly to an improved position in the labour market for only one group of women. These were clerical workers. While some, like Evelyn Mills, saw their jobs as marginal to their lives, several emphasised the wartime enhancement of their careers, framing their accounts in terms of the discourse of opportunity. For example, Dorothy Rose recalled her feelings about starting work at the Ministry of Food in 1942: 'I thought, "well yes, there's more chance of promotion here than there is anywhere else" because it was all on grades and when you'd been on one grade for so long, if you'd qualified on that grade, you moved up to the next grade'. She celebrated her step by step progress up the pay scale and achievement of 'established' status in 1946 in the interview.[60] Myrna Wraith told a similar story of wartime opportunities enhancing her clerical career. She spoke of the new skills which she learned in the WAAF, specifically in teleprinting, which she found highly marketable when she left in 1947. 'I liked teleprinting. I mean I liked that better than I did shorthand. And I mean it was well paid then you see compared. I think I got about £4.75 a week which was quite good then really'.[61] Myrna found jobs as a teleprinter operator easily, first in the General Post Office and then for the Distillers Company.

The most positively told of these accounts of the wartime augmentation of clerical careers, was that of Emily Porter. Her story was of nothing less than being rescued from unemployability by the opportunities for new types of clerical work created by the war. Emily had suffered from bovine tuberculosis as a child, resulting in a handicap which affected her spine and thus both her deportment and her ability to carry anything. Her mother, who had been deserted by Emily's father since her birth, apart from a brief period when he returned to them as a dying man, worked as an embroiderer and low paid clerical worker to give Emily opportunities at school and art college. However, when Emily was 16 they were shattered to discover that her disability debarred her from almost every type of employment. Emily found a low paid teaching job in a private school. She described her employment, by a headmistress whose own brother had suffered from the same complaint as Emily, as close to charity. But the war marked a turning-point in this story of Emily's marginalisation as a disabled (if well-qualified) woman. During 1940 Emily and her mother noticed that the Civil Service was recruiting clerks for postal censorship, and Emily proudly passed the examinations and was accepted.[62] She progressed to the post of supervisor earning 'the astonishing sum of £400 a year' during the war.[63] But the censorship of letters was ended in August 1945, and Emily's anxiety about her job prospects returned. However, she managed to transfer to a succession of other Civil Service

departments, including Pensions, Post Office Savings and National
Assistance. She was aware that opportunities were now open to her
which she could not take, because they would have required either
mobility which would have meant leaving her mother, or greater
stamina than she felt she possessed, especially after a serious illness
in the late 1940s. In 1950 she applied to become an established civil
servant. She passed the examination, but confronted other hurdles.
She explained the special importance to herself and her mother of
her eventual success:

> That again was a bit of a triumph, for me personally, because I thought
> I would – you had to pass a medical and I thought, 'I won't get it'. But
> I was lucky, I had a special medical because they sent me to an
> orthopaedic consultant because of my disability and he said, 'There's
> no reason at all why you shouldn't be a permanent Civil Servant'. So
> it was a great day for us that, because my mother – I was what, in my
> 30s then – my mother thought, 'Oh my daughter's' – you know – 'set-
> tled'.[64]

Emily was evidently deeply satisfied with the opportunities which
the war opened to her, remaining a civil servant until her retirement
in the 1970s. Marriage and motherhood did not intrude on her
career.[65] For other ambitious clerical workers, however, they did.
Both Dorothy Rose and Myrna Wraith emphasised that their career
progress was interrupted by statutory regulations rather than as a
result of their own choice following marriage. Dorothy's status was
lowered from established to temporary civil servant when she married in 1953, and Myrna was expected to leave the General Post
Office (GPO) on her marriage in 1952 (regardless of the official
abolition of the marriage bar). Both women were paid 'marriage
gratuities'. Dorothy carried on in the civil service for four years, in
spite of her loss of promotion prospects, but left on the birth of her
first child in 1957, later finding a new career as a nursery assistant
in a hospital school. Myrna found another job as a teleprinter operator in a private company as soon as she left the GPO, but quit on
the birth of her first child in 1955. After a long family break, she
successfully pursued a new opportunity within the Citizen's Advice
Bureau.

Opportunities for new departures

Clerical workers aside, most of the women who framed their work histories in the discourse of opportunity relegated war work to an eccentric position. For these women the war marked an interruption to a career cast in terms of opportunity, and they had no expectation of continuing with war work afterwards. For them the disruption at the end of the war represented a chance to resume or improve upon an old career direction, or to take a new one, in most cases unconnected with their war work. There were both 'heroes' and 'stoics' among the tellers of such work histories. The heroes described the wartime interruption as an interesting and not unwelcome diversion. The stoics, in contrast, represented it as an irritating intrusion on their personal plans. Women in both groups deployed the discourse of the dual role in speaking of later negotiations between marriage, motherhood and these opportunities.

Striking stories of wartime interruptions which, indirectly, considerably augmented the pursuit of fulfilling careers, were told by the two Black women interviewed. Nadia Beale was in the process of qualifying as a teacher in British Honduras in 1943, when she patriotically signed up for the ATS. Although this act fractured a promising career, it ultimately paid off handsomely. Nadia's account as a whole was a story of achieved self-esteem, rather than the troubled life review visible in some other accounts. Its central theme was that Nadia was a 'coloured' colonial entering a welcoming and tolerant 'mother country' in which she could realise her childhood dreams. Nadia vividly reconstructed the excitement she felt about the 'big experience' of leaving the West Indies to join the war effort in Britain. She thoroughly enjoyed life as a clerical worker in the ATS, and stressed what it did for her in terms of expanding her horizons and providing a stepping-stone to other things, rather than emphasising what she was doing for the war as some other 'heroes' did.[66] When she was demobilised in 1947 she obtained a place at St Hilde's College, Durham, to acquire a British teacher's certificate.[67] She went back to British Honduras as a qualified teacher in 1949, but was struck by how small the country now seemed, culturally and in terms of professional opportunities, and became determined to leave again: 'I thought, mm, no way am I going to stay here'.[68] Her opportunity came through marriage. She told a romantic story of a relationship with a Welshman which developed from a single meeting when he was visiting the Caribbean with the Royal Navy in 1950. They corresponded for three years, 'then he asked me if I might get married' and sent for her to join him in Ceylon, where he was posted.[69] They returned to Britain as a married couple in 1955.

At this point Nadia's view of the relationship between paid work and marriage was cast in terms of the widely legitimated feminine career fracture, which heralded withdrawal from the labour market in the pre-war versions of the discourses of both opportunity and marginalisation. Life as a married woman was preferable to life as a working wife: 'I wasn't going to work any more, he was going to look after me, you know, I thought no way now, I was, have finished with teaching, forget it'.[70]

However, in the early 1960s, after the birth of their three children, her husband left the Navy, money was short and Nadia was ready for a change. She said that although she liked being a housewife, she also 'had itchy feet ... I began to move out, you know, from domesticity then'.[71] She was recruited to a local primary school suffering a shortage of teachers when it was discovered that she was qualified. Problems about the care of her under-school-age daughter were swept away. The school head teacher suggested that Nadia should send her to a nursery half-time and bring her with her to the primary school for the other half of the day. Nadia had already put her daughter's name on a nursery waiting list, and went to see the nursery head when offered the teaching job: 'She said, "well why didn't you tell me you were a teacher ... I would have taken her from then" ... And I used to take her to the nursery on my way to school, because the nursery wasn't very far, and then my husband would pick her up at lunchtime for me if it was necessary, but I used to be able to walk down and bring her back with me to school. And that's why I came back into teaching'. It felt, said Nadia, 'like I had never left'.[72]

Nadia's story was one of assuming a 'dual role' unproblematically. Social attitudes were not against her as a woman, an immigrant or a Black person. Her pursuit of a professional role had the support on the one hand of the teaching and caring professions, and on the other of her husband, within an evidently companionate marriage. Nadia's description of her return to teaching belonged within the frame established by Myrdal and Klein, of doing the job 'almost with one hand at the cradle'.[73] This was a story of the combined pursuit of opportunity, and fulfilment of the feminine familial role. Nadia described taking further training in the 1960s, and pursuing a highly successful career, to which her husband adapted his own work plans. She became a primary school head teacher before her retirement in 1985.

Estelle Armitage described an even more strategic use of the opportunities opened up by recruitment to the ATS in the West Indies. Estelle emphasised that on leaving school in Jamaica in 1937 she had wanted to train as a midwife and her family had been ready to send her abroad for training, but the death of her father and the onset of the war denied her this chance. Instead she did a secretarial course. In 1943 she joined the ATS in Kingston, Jamaica, as a wages clerk, and then volunteered to serve in Britain in 1944. She spoke of her motives as both patriotic and opportunistic: 'they sort of asked who would like to go abroad, and of course I said could I – you know, England – and I could do my nursing after'.[74] Estelle reflected that her job in the ATS was important but temporary, and felt that in some ways the whole thing was 'just a holiday'. She had no regrets when the end of the war came in sight. On the contrary, this gave her the opportunity to fulfil her long-term career ambitions. 'They sent out these things asking us do you want to go home, or was there anything you wanted to do, training, you wanted to do, before you were sent home? So naturally I had always wanted ... to do nursing, so I applied you see, and they got me into Hammersmith Hospital'.[75] During her training as a midwife Estelle was still a member of the ATS. When she had completed the qualification in 1951, she was officially demobilised and repatriated to Jamaica.

The part of Estelle's narrative concerning her return to the West Indies conjured up closure and dismay, just as Nadia's did, in contrast to the optimism and sense of new openings that accompanied her story of the end of the war. She recalled a New Year party: 'we joined hands to sing Auld Lang Syne, and the tears were running ... I said I am not staying here, because I haven't got any friends here, they are all in London, I am going back'.[76] She returned to London in 1952, to a midwifery job at Lewisham Hospital, married her husband, an immigrant from British Guyana, in that year, and continued with a lifelong career in nursing. But in contrast to the benign and supportive attitudes to her dual role which Nadia recalled, Estelle told some harrowing stories of the difficulties thrown up by racist attitudes and practices. For example, in contrast to Nadia's

memory of obtaining a nursery place for her young child with ease,
Estelle remembered humiliating experiences when seeking childcare. A childminder was recommended to her by the local authority
when she wished to return to work as a midwife after the birth of
her son in 1953. Estelle went to see her:

> I said, 'My name is Mrs [Armitage], and this is my baby [John] 4
> months old, and the council sent me this letter this morning to say I
> should bring him' and so she said – 'AH' – she went like this [putting
> her hands to her face]. I said, 'whatever is the matter?' She said, 'I told
> them I didn't want any coloured children' ... I just looked at her and
> said, 'Well my dear you are quite entitled to your opinion, good morn-
> ing' and walked away.[77]

Estelle maintained her dignity, in this story, through her ironic
riposte. But the exasperation beneath the controlled exterior burst
out in her next statement, 'I only went round there to find out if it
was a clean house!'[78]

Estelle's account of struggling to make appropriate childcare
arrangements and carry on working was couched in terms of a combination of necessity (the explanation of married women's work
offered by the discourse of marginalisation) and of desire to fulfil
her professional potential (the dominant motif of the discourse of
opportunity). She located her account within the frame of the style
of marriage most compatible with the pursuit of opportunity, the
companionate marriage. Estelle's skills as a midwife were both
socially valued and superior to those of her husband. He found it
impossible to realise his ambition to become an accountant in
Britain and found that, as a Black immigrant, only routine factory
work was available to him. Estelle's account was of sharing a 'dual
role' with him, rather than developing a specifically feminine one
with his support. She described an intensely egalitarian approach to
childcare and home-making, as she and her husband struggled to
make ends meet and to bring up their two sons in London in the
1950s and 1960s. Estelle's husband, Clive, was present at the interview and started to contribute his own additions to her narrative
when she was talking about the 1950s, which had the effect of
vividly demonstrating to the interviewer the egalitarian style of
companionate marriage which Estelle was describing. For example,
Clive broke into Estelle's account of their lives as young parents,
saying 'there was no way you could exist without sharing'. He

referred to doing washing, childcare and cooking, and described proudly the three-course breakfasts he regularly made for his sons. 'You should have seen the size of the boys when they were little!' quipped Estelle, at once confirming Clive's account and teasing him about his proficiency.[79]

As in Nadia's case, war work in itself did not give Estelle's career its post-war direction. But the opportunity arising from her wartime 'mobilisation' enabled her to embark on the new career of her choice. In the context of the racist discrimination of the 1950s, within which Black people of both sexes were particularly disadvantaged in the labour market, the material consequences of her marriage to a Black man (in contrast to Nadia's marriage to a white man) were that she could not afford to become even temporarily marginal to the workforce. In any case, Estelle constructed herself as someone set on realising her career objectives. Even if it was hard to combine work as a midwife with caring for two young children, she did not suggest that she had ever wanted to withdraw from the workforce.

The accounts of these two women from the colonies necessarily introduced the discourse of racial discrimination to the life stories under construction, introducing a special tension to the inter-subjective exchanges within these interviews. The presence in Britain in the 1950s and 1960s of racist discourse was inexplicit in Nadia's account. But although she banished it as irrelevant, it hovered unspoken between narrator and interviewer as a set of negative possibilities. It was admitted in Estelle's narrative, and significantly shaped her story as it entered the 1950s when that discourse was strong. But she and her husband handled their understanding of experiences of 'racist discrimination' with a humour and irony which eased the interchange between Black narrator and white interviewer. Estelle's construction both emphasised her own pride and self-confidence, and put the interviewer at ease, enabling her to laugh at the gross injustices perpetrated by white people (like herself) forty years previously. Indeed, Clive specifically rejected the more oppositional understandings of what it meant to be Black, available in the 1990s: 'coloured people, Black as they call it now ... they look for trouble themselves ... if you look for it, you are going to get it. So I'm not getting involved'.[80]

Racist discourse did not become a recognisable part of any of the other interviews. But the depiction of war work as an interruption which constituted an opportunity for a career resumption or reorientation, was characteristic of two other types of account. On the one hand there were narratives of obtaining and excelling in a 'man's job' in wartime, told in the heroic language of aspiration and achievement, in which the renunciation of that desired job at the end of the war was described as painless. On the other hand there were stories in which war work was entered with trepidation and stoically endured, but became a welcome stepping-stone to new career possibilities. One example of each type of account gives us scope to explore the resolutions of these seeming contradictions, as well as to investigate the complex inter-subjective dynamics of this part of the interviews.

Ann Tomlinson had left school in 1939 with qualifications for university entrance, but because of the outbreak of war she did not go, and instead trained and worked as a secretary. In 1943 she joined the WRNS. However, in spite of her epic story of battling to become an aircraft mechanic, and her pride and enthusiasm about the job, which we reviewed in chapter 3, she was neutral rather than sad about giving up the job at the end of the war. She referred, when asked, to the idea of continuing to work as a mechanic after the war as a 'romantic notion', explaining:

> We loved the work, enjoyed the life, and we all had romantic notions about going on … And we did make tentative enquiries about the possibilities and met with very negative responses to that. The whole argument seemed to be that there would be so many men being released from the Forces who would need jobs that there wouldn't really be much hope of women getting jobs other than being pump attendants in a garage.[81]

Ann's message was that 'they didn't want women back in that job'. But rather than depicting the post-war prospects for women in engineering as unwelcome marginalisation, as Felicity Snow did, Ann constructed an account of a choice of alternative opportunities. She took what seemed to her a less 'romantic' option than pursuing engineering, which was to obtain a university place at the London School of Economics to read economics, sociology and psychology.[82] It may have been a more realistic strategy, in her view, but it was not without its difficulties and was still a relatively unusual step for a woman to take.[83] First, she had to work hard to obtain a Further Education and Training Grant from the Admiralty, having arrived in London in early 1946 with nothing but thirty shillings (£1.50p) remaining from her naval pay.[84] Then she had to prepare in six months for the first year examinations, which most students took after twelve months. Immediately after the exams, in June 1946, she married a man she had met as a naval officer, and who was now also a student, and found to her horror that, as a married woman, the grant for which she had fought so hard was 'severely cut'. In keeping with her presentation of herself as a person of determination, she appealed to the Ministry of Education and managed to get a supplement.[85] Ann completed her degree successfully and embarked on postgraduate training in psychology. However, she then became pregnant and could not finish the course.

In Ann's narrative pregnancy was not the disaster it was for other women with ambitions, like Beryl Bramley. Ann did not present her withdrawal from training and employment while her children were small as a problem. She drew on the language of post-war psychology about the salience of the mother to her young children's wellbeing to indicate her personal investment in the role: 'I wanted to look after them. I wanted positively to be there to feel responsible perhaps for them in a way that I wouldn't have been happy to delegate to anybody else … I just felt a tremendous motivation to be the one who was looking after them, to be there, perhaps influencing their development'.[86] But she also kept alive her plans to resume her preparations for the career to which her qualification gave access. When both children were at school in the late 1950s she 'knew that that was all right … I could go off and teach which was a preparation for the future work I was going to do'. She arranged her work around her children's school hours and what she perceived as their needs from her as a mother. 'I didn't feel that I was going to use a lot of emotional energy in what I was doing at work, which would deprive me of emotional energy to look after the children.'[87] Furthermore her husband, as well as welcoming the extra salary, was prepared to give some help. He 'was always willing to do the taking to school and that kind of thing, so that I could go off in order to be at the school I was teaching in at the right time'.[88] In the context of this companionate marriage, the dual role was manageable.

In the mid-1960s Ann completed the course which had been interrupted by the birth of her first child, and worked as an educational and later a clinical psychologist until her retirement in 1985. Her work history was told unequivocally in terms of opportunity, in pursuit of which acknowledged obstacles could be overcome. Thus the theory of maternal deprivation figured in her narrative, but as a negotiable rather than an absolute truth. She devoted herself to childrearing until the younger child had reached the age at which Ann believed full-time maternal availability was no longer necessary, and she not only made practical arrangements with her companionate husband, but also managed her emotional economy to accommodate both mothering and professional work. She referred obliquely to the difficulties of the dual role, in talking about her salary. It was 'a tremendous help. An incentive to go on of course, not just give up. Not that I wanted to give up. I wanted to work and do what I had set out to do'.[89]

But although Ann's testimony about the post-war years was cast in the same mould of heroic pursuit of a worthy goal as the story of her wartime experiences, the tone was less assured than that of the earlier stories. Her account shifted from one of maintained self-esteem to a more anxious review of this part of her life. The inter-subjective processes at work throughout all the interviews, developed in particularly complex ways as Ann composed this part of her life story. First, she was visibly reconstructing her subject position as a mother in relation to the subject 'mother' in the 1950s discourse of maternal deprivation. This was apparent both in her 'take-up' of that discourse (her account of her commitment to mothering) and her partial rejection of it (her justification of her return to work in 1959). Second, she was, it must now be acknowledged, being interviewed by her own daughter, the younger child of the narrative. Ann's account of her practice as a mother, and her daughter's assessment of Ann's mothering (which she did not voice in the interview) might have been at odds. Furthermore that daughter had chosen not to take a career break while her own children were small, but had 'delegated the responsibility' of their care to others. The interviewer might have been both defensive about her contrasting interpretation of the maternal role, and challenging to her mother's, in that her own maternal practice was based on the post-1970s critique of the theory of full-time maternal care. Ann's account became particularly questioning as she reflected on her feelings about mothering in the 1950s:

> I was also very very happy looking after the children, very, exceptionally happy I think. I never felt bored. I loved reading to them, I loved

playing with them, I loved taking them out. I hope that I did let them be, and wasn't a smothering mother. I liked knitting and sewing and that kind of thing, and I think that when they were playing very often on their own, I maybe sat and knitted and sewed and read and that kind of thing, and was just there, but didn't perhaps overdo the mothering. I hope not, but one can't really be very objective about things like that. I do remember feeling a great love for them and wanting to be with them and look after them as long as I felt they needed to be looked after, with my presence there all the time.[90]

In composing this part of her story Ann was confronting the validity of her life as the mother of young children, possibly seeking to integrate it for the first time with stories of her earlier life, in which, in contrast, her worth and value as a war worker were well established.

The narratives of women who relinquished heroically won wartime jobs without regret when demobilised, welcoming the chance to pursue other lines of opportunity, were told by those who came from middle-class backgrounds or who were upwardly mobile.[91] But at least one woman from a working-class background who was a reluctant recruit to war work gave an account of her working life in similar terms of opportunity, even though at face value her work history sounded like one of the most meandering and marginal careers in the sample. Ethel Singleton described doing clerical training for a year after leaving school at 14 in 1935, but her first jobs were as a sewing machinist and then a shop assistant, before she was called up for war work in 1941. She worked as a welder at A.V. Roe's in Manchester from 1941 to 1945 and, like many wartime conscripts, after a cautious start became a committed worker. However, she never considered carrying on with welding after the end of the war: 'we were only just taken on for the war period'.[92] Asked how she felt about giving it up, Ethel evoked the closure of this opportunity to do 'men's' work with great finality: 'You didn't think about it, it just happened, you were just finished you know. You never thought about it. It was a job that was finished … that was finished, that life'.[93]

However, although the job of welding was now closed to her, Ethel found another opportunity with the same firm, this time in the office. It was a job she could take because of her earlier office training and because she was already working for the firm, albeit on the shopfloor. She turned her back on the grocer's shop job from which she had been called up, and which had been held open for her, because the hours in the office were shorter and conditions better. Ethel worked in the office of A. V. Roe's for seven years: 'And I thoroughly enjoyed it'.[94] She left when she married in 1952 and became a housewife and mother, but she indicated that she did not expect this to be a permanent withdrawal from the labour market. In the mid-1960s she and her husband opened a grocer's shop which she ran for fifteen years.[95]

Far from thinking of this as a meandering work history, a 'shapeless drift', along the margins of the labour market,[96] Ethel saw her career explicitly in terms of a discourse of opportunity which her father had instilled into her. It involved the acquisition of a range of skills and work experiences which she put to good use. The exception was the enforced wartime spell in welding, which was not a skill she listed among those which she later deployed. But her wartime work in engineering nevertheless served a purpose in enabling her to find an office job and escape the long hours of the grocer's shop. She rejected the notion of a single-skill career, without the 1990s concept of multiple careers based on the acquisition of a portfolio of skills being put to her in the interview: 'those things I did in them days put me in good stead for later in life ... machining for instance, I made practically all my own clothes afterwards ... also the shop training I had there put us in good stead, because one day my husband said to me, "Would you like a shop?" and I said, "Oh yes I'd love one" ... so all those things I did in them days have helped, which as my father said "learn what you can". And I always think about those words, because to stay in one job all your life, you're in a groove aren't you?'.[97]

Wartime opportunities renounced

Among the women interviewed there were three who constructed their work histories as stories of opportunity rather than marginality, but who actually *rejected* opportunities to continue with their wartime occupations. In all three cases these were types of work which were (in peacetime) unusual for women. As we have just seen, Ann Tomlinson dismissed as 'romantic' ideas of extending into peacetime her wartime venture across the gender boundary, while Felicity Snow and Beryl Bramley, quoted earlier, reconstructed pasts which, if lived over again, would have embraced a continuation of the kinds of work they had done in the war. But the three women whose work histories we shall now discuss, had precisely that chance – and turned it down. One was offered a continuation of her job on a centre lathe in an engineering works, another was offered funding to go to university and train as a personnel manager by the company which had employed her during the war as a progress chaser, and the third was offered work on aircraft design and construction with a private company (de Havillands) after working as an aircraft rigger in the WRNS. For this group of women it was not the case that 'they didn't want women back in that job' and yet they all renounced offers.

Wilma Harrison described her early work history in terms of opportunity and progress. She had trained enthusiastically at a trade school as an upholsteress and embroiderer before the war, and worked for Eventide Bedding Company from 1937 to 1942. After going into engineering cautiously when called up, she took great pride and interest in the work of cutting and grinding metal to precision measurements, and spoke of the trust her bosses had in her. Nevertheless, at the end of the war she chose to return to the bedding company, a decision which involved her turning down an offer of continued employment from her wartime boss at a South London engineering firm. She described herself as 'a bit depressed' by the work at the end of the war, the ostensible reason for which was that she believed that people doing the same work for other engineering companies were earning far more than her.[98] Reading from some notes, she said, 'I wanted out of there as quick as possible. Not that the work was not interesting, but low pay and long hours. I was released at the beginning of 1946'.[99] She presented her return to Eventide Bedding Company as 'a challenge', rather than as being consigned to marginality. She was given work on internally sprung mattresses by a trusting boss who wanted her to find 'a quicker way of doing it'. Accomplishing this, she taught other workers her method, moved on to the cutting side of the business and became a chargehand.[100]

Wilma's story was of having a strong preference for the upholstery work for which she had been trained before the war, and which still offered opportunities. However she interpolated into her post-war work history a startlingly romantic, if brief, vignette of her courtship. It was worthy of the magazine accounts reviewed earlier, in which work in itself mattered to young women, but was even more importantly a means to attract Mr Right. Wilma's future husband worked in a cardboard firm next door to Eventide. He 'used to go up and down in the lift and he used to see me cutting, and he fell in love with me in me white overall'.[101] They married in May 1947 and their daughter was born in January 1948.

Yet the reason Wilma gave for preferring the bedding to the engineering company did not seem totally satisfying to her. The fact that she read out the statement about leaving engineering from some notes she had made before the interview, the only point at which she did this, suggests that she was taking refuge in the authority of the written word to protect herself from challenging enquiry. After all, she had the chance to pursue opportunities which had been denied to 'Rosie the Riveter', a denial which 1980s feminists had publicly deplored.

Later Wilma wrestled with how she felt about the relationship between paid work and marriage and motherhood, as if she was using the opportunity of the interview (like Ann Tomlinson) to try to assess the validity of the course she had pursued in the 1950s and 1960s. Wilma described her mixed feelings about moving in and out of paid work as a wife and mother, and emphasised the difficulties of managing the two roles. Rather than the equilibrium model of Myrdal and Klein, she evoked in this reassessment the double burden and the advantages of being supported by a man's wage, both of them central to the discourse of marginality. 'Women do put themselves – too much on themselves, make life much harder for themselves, than they need to ... I have had to go out to work, and I've had to keep a family, and I think, you know, you realise that when you can sit back, it's nice.'[102]

Even though she gave an account of shared decision-making with her husband (who became a lorry driver after leaving the cardboard factory), Wilma put forward a view of the propriety of masculine precedence at work and at home. 'I've always been of a mind that women should give way to the men. I think men do need work outside ... perhaps women do an' all ... I like to see men being the breadwinner myself.'[103] Enlarging on this, she explained that she felt she could fulfil her role at home better when her husband was supporting her financially and she was not doing paid work. Inexplicitly using Ann Tomlinson's concept of emotional economy, she explained that it meant that she could rest in the afternoon and be fresh when her daughters and husband came in: 'you can listen to all their problems and things, it makes life much easier'.[104] And yet her uncertainties about her assertion that men had a special need to go out to work ('perhaps women do an all'), suggest that she was uncomfortable with the transition in her telling of her work history, from an account couched in the discourse of opportunity, to one of marginality. It was as if the latter did not completely suit the identity she wanted to construct in reviewing her life with, in her case, an unmarried, childless interviewer aged about 30 and in full-time work.

Another woman who told of rejecting an offer for continuation of her wartime employment came from a more privileged place than Wilma in the class and educational structure. Like Wilma, Hester Hamilton told her work history in terms of opportunities, but as far as she was concerned, wartime conscription by the state represented an unwelcome interruption to her planned migration along what she understood as a feminine route within the labour market. As we saw in chapter 3, Hester Hamilton was made to leave university and work as a progress chaser at an aircraft firm in Fife in 1942. At the end of the war, she was glad to give up the work that had been imposed upon her, and resume the career she had intended for herself on the female side of the gender divide. Hester Hamilton's decision to leave her war work (like Wilma Harrison's) involved definite rejection of an opportunity to become more firmly established within the managerial hierarchy of the masculine world of engineering. Hester obtained an early release from the Leven firm in 1944, so that she could go to Moray House to pursue the educational qualifications she needed for entry to the feminised profession of infant teaching. In doing so she *rejected* an offer from the Leven firm to pay for her to go back to university (which she had been forced to leave to enter the firm, in 1942), this time to take a degree in personnel management. She said, 'I wasn't interested in it at all', in spite of the fact that such an offer was both unusual for a woman, and enormously valuable in financial terms.[105]

Hester taught from 1946, then voluntarily 'gave up' teaching when she married a dance band leader in 1948. However, Hester's expectations of a typically 'feminine' career, ended by marriage, were not fulfilled. She found herself propelled back into work by necessity. Hester's story was that she went back to teaching after a few months because television was already beginning to compete with dancing and her husband and his dance band were not getting enough work. Following the 1944 Education Act, the East Lothian local education authority did not operate a marriage bar, but it did require married women teachers to be 'temporary'. Hester was given the temporary job of 'infant mistress relief teacher': 'I had 4 different schools, one day each to allow the mistress to do her clerical work'. Far from seeing herself as exploited in such a role, Hester said 'I found that a very interesting job'.[106] She worked as a 'temporary' for eight years, by which time her husband had qualified as a music teacher and was working in a secondary school. When Hester's son was born in 1953 she left, again assuming this would be the end of her career.

Hester's story of her return to teaching after childbirth implied that she would have been perfectly content to be a full-time mother, but that, once again, external pressures forced her back into the labour market. This time the proactive role was taken by the education authorities as it was in Nadia Beale's similar account of returning to teaching: 'They came for me when he was four and a half, and I said, "I'm not going back until he goes to school". So they said, "Well bring him with you". So I took him with me'.[107] Hester's use of the phrase 'they came for me' expresses her sense of compulsion. She continued, nevertheless, to have temporary status until 1960, when she moved to Musselburgh. Here she obtained what she represented as a plum job, but she described this in non-ambitious, almost self-deprecating terms: 'There'd been a big turn around, and I got one of – I was one of the first people to get a big school as head teacher. It was quite surprising. I think I was there at the right time. Where they were saying, "the women aren't getting any of the big jobs" and I got this big school.'[108] Hester's tone was that, like her return to teaching after the birth of her son, this opportunity was almost forced upon her as a social duty. Hester's account of the relationship between this job and her home life was that 'it fitted in very well, because I had a woman who did my work. She came in every day, and it was fine, worked great. No problems'.[109] Her use of the words 'my work' to describe housework, childcare and cooking, and her confidence in the arrangement, speak of her understanding of what she was doing as a feminine 'dual role' for which she took full responsibility. Her husband featured as a supportive but shadowy figure in her account of managing her domestic and professional lives.

The rejection by both Wilma Harrison and Hester Hamilton of

opportunities to continue in their war work after the war, may be surprising in view of their commitment to the pursuit of opportunity, but it is consistent with their reluctance to enter war work in the first place. The refusal of such an invitation by one of the most enthusiastic 'heroes' is much more remarkable. Pamela Wootton was a clerical worker in a town hall before she volunteered with alacrity to become an aircraft rigger in the WRNS in 1942. She was intensely proud of her skills as an aircraft rigger and, as we saw in chapter 4, of rising to challenges placed before her. Astonishingly, unlike the other aircraft mechanics, such as Felicity Snow, who hankered after continuing with the work but saw no openings, Pamela was offered an opportunity to work as a civilian engineer when her demobilisation came up in 1946, but she turned it down. Her account of this decision bristled with ambivalence:

> I wished I'd gone back to it after the war. I had the opportunity, because with my mother and father knowing Geoffrey de Havilland, he said, did I want to go and work in de Havilland's as an engineer after the war – and I should have taken it. Yes, I had regrets then, I wished I'd gone back to it. But the call of London and the highlights, and having been in Scotland all that time, no I had to go and work in London. Ah, London was the place for me. Got a good job – got a good job – the Film Producer's Guild. Yes, I'm not sorry about that, but yes.[110]

She continued working there as a public relations secretary from 1946 to the birth of her second child in 1960. Later she worked briefly as a teacher in a private school, and then resumed her clerical career, now as a school secretary.

Finally, there was among those interviewed just one woman who did continue with her 'masculine' war work after the war. Marianne Lloyd told her wartime work history in terms of opportunity, but, like Ann Tomlinson and Wilma Harrison, although for different reasons, she became less confident about the discourse within which to frame her post-war experiences of work and marriage.

Marianne Lloyd emphasised her determination to acquire secretarial skills at commercial school on leaving her elementary school in Birmingham in 1937, rather than getting one of the 'menial jobs' typical of girls from her background. She became a bookkeeper for a large company.[111] She perceived the war, however, as offering better opportunities for self-improvement, and jumped at the chance to train as a draughtswoman. She described, as we saw in chapter 3, overcoming barriers of prejudice to get access to training and to obtain work as a draughtswoman in engineering and chemical firms during the war. Furthermore, in spite of the specifically wartime context in which she acquired these skills and her isolation as a woman in the drawing offices in which she worked, she presented her wartime decisions as part of a long-term strategy. She said that she did not look on her war work as temporary: 'being a drawing office, it would carry on after the war, you see, wouldn't it?'.[112]

Nevertheless she represented the end of the war as a difficult time for her in terms of finding work. The years 1945–49, during which she continued to work, were a period in which opportunities were 'tailing down'. She reflected on four reasons for this, three to do with the work itself, and the fourth to do with marriage. First, changes in the draughtsmanship labour process during the war cut out much of the detail drawing for which she had been trained: 'They were drifting into the era where it was much more casual, and quicker. They ... were almost skipping the detail stage'.[113] Second, in 1945 she moved to a chemical company where the atmosphere was deeply unpleasant: 'the drawing office extrusion fan didn't work, so you can imagine how the actual smell invaded us, and the windows were so opaque with the chemicals, you just couldn't see through them, so it was like being enclosed'.[114] Third, although she considered returning to college and improving her qualifications she felt uninterested in the post-war direction of draughtsmanship: 'if I'd stayed at college and taken a Higher National I might have opened up some more opportunities, but they were going to go on to more automobile engineering in that year, and quite honestly I wasn't really interested in motor cars. I was more interested in the general engineering, factories and machines and tool machines'.[115] Above all, marriage in 1945 altered her orientation. She reiterated several times 'I wasn't a career woman'. Echoing the 'what might have been' comments of Felicity and Beryl, with more substance since her wartime occupation (unlike theirs) did survive the end of the war, she said: 'I actually think I could have gone further with engineering looking back on it, but I don't know, I think the fact that I knew my future husband before I went into it, and we were together all through the war, and I knew I was going to get married, that sort of coloured my outline, I wasn't a career woman. If I had have been, I think I could have been much harder and pushed harder'.[116] Later, reflecting on leaving her last job when she was pregnant in 1949, she said that she might have gone on 'if I'd been a really career person'. 'I think I did miss some opportunities, looking back on life, you know, you can always think if I'd done so and so, perhaps!'.[117] But she ended her career as a draughtswoman on the birth of her first child, and never returned to the paid labour market.

Marianne brought up the subject again later in the interview, when discussing other women's attitudes to working as mothers, as if worried by the fact that she had never returned. 'I would have gone back myself after I was married and had my children, but again, no [childcare] facilities and I didn't want to start travelling into Birmingham every day, and there were no part-time jobs at all in drawing offices you see. If I'd been living in the middle of Birmingham and perhaps been able to have found a small job in a factory of some description I might have done, but there was never the real necessity, so I didn't'.[118] Even though she represented her marriage as teamwork, there was a clear division of labour. Her husband, an industrial chemist, would not have helped with childcare: 'that age group, they didn't expect to do anything with children themselves!', and her parents lived too far away to have minded the children.[119] Returning yet again to the theme of the relationship between being a mother and doing paid work in the 1950s, Marianne evinced more anxiety about her position of complete marginality to the paid labour market: 'I did get quite restless when they were school age. I would have liked to have gone back into a drawing office ... I suppose if you like to think about it, it was professional pride, I didn't really need the money'.[120] As if to salvage her 'pride' from these worrying memories of passing up opportunities, she now emphasised the considerable unpaid contribution that she made to the family, by making children's clothes and soft furnishings, and by drawing up designs (using her skills as a draughtswoman) for the numerous extensions and garages that her husband built on to the various houses they owned.

Why was Marianne uncertain and uncomfortable about how to represent her work history in the post-war years? She had drawn upon the discourse of opportunity to explain the path she took before and during the war. It offered a construction which could override the end-of-war constructions of women's marginality to the labour force and centrality to the home, and hence could explain and justify Marianne's (exceptional) continuation in her war job after the war was over, and after her marriage. But having presented her career in these terms, Marianne did not have to hand a construction with which to explain, not why she left work when expecting her first child (which was a normal development within the discourse of opportunity), but why she never returned to this or any other type of paid work, in spite of her periodic desires to do so. The discourse of opportunity, as it developed after the war, could have led to such a return, possibly after further training, as Marianne acknowledged. The 1950s and 1960s discourse of the dual role would have justified the combination of such professional work with running a home. And the feminist discourse of the 1970s and 1980s would have expected it, while at the same time anticipating for Marianne experiences of the contradictions of the double burden and the frustrations of the glass ceiling. The discourse available to Marianne, on which she did not choose to draw in the construction of her work history, was the discourse of women's marginality to the workforce, in which marriage and particularly childbirth were end-points for paid work. But even this story did not necessarily provide a comfortable version for someone like Marianne. As we have seen, in post-war renderings of this version of a woman's life, part-time work when children had grown up featured as both a civic duty and the only way to avoid neurosis.

Conclusion

The personal accounts on which this chapter has drawn have exemplified the difficulties for women of achieving subjective composure. The multiple discourses of women's relationship to the labour market, available from the 1920s to the 1990s, offered women contradictory identities as workers. In the mid-1940s when these interviewees were experiencing 'demobilisation' the possibilities for reorientation were particularly confusing. There was heavy official investment in a feminine identity centred on the home, on marriage and on motherhood, to all of which paid work was firmly subordinated. We have observed the take-up of this construction both by women who were reluctant recruits, and by some of those who had enthusiastically committed themselves to war work across the gender boundary. We have also noted the frustration with it expressed by numerous women who would have liked to have retained the more exciting and rewarding job opportunities which war made available, but who found themselves instead consigned to a post-war identity with which, at least in retrospect, they felt dissatisfied. The discontent which they voiced might well have been stimulated by the contradiction between the idea of contented marginality and the possibilities proffered by the coexisting discourse of opportunity. It might have been further exacerbated by feminist discourse of the period since 1970, which criticised the wartime demobilisation process for depriving women of 'masculine' jobs in the reassertion of a gendered division of labour. This critique presented women who rejected such prized opportunities with particular difficulties for the achievement of narrative coherence and subjective composure in interviews in the 1990s.

The unsettling effects of these discourses, in tension with each other, extended across the social spectrum. Domestic marginality and career opportunity were not neatly separated by social class. Within the discourse of marginality, domesticity was an approved subject position for any woman and, as we have seen, it was taken up by women from both working-class and middle-class backgrounds. The meritocratic discourse of opportunity offered the able and hard-working woman from any social location an identity as a skilled and qualified member of a range of 'feminine' trades and professions. The feminist accounts of the 1970s were also relatively socially undifferentiated; the political imperative to establish a unified 'class' of women based on shared experience of exploitation and oppression encouraged reductionism, which only began to be reversed in the 1980s by the focus of Black and post-modernist feminisms on differences between women.

The changing place of marriage and motherhood in the public narratives of women and work was salient to those who married among the women interviewed. The possibility of combining a traditional feminine domestic role with paid work, couched discursively in the 1950s in the positive terms of the dual role rather than the negative ones of the double burden, was a reference point for all those who recalled their work histories in terms of opportunity. In constituting themselves as subjects fulfilling such a dual role, women emphasised the importance of associated practices etched in contingent discourses. Companionate marriage, whether it meant a husband's passive acceptance of a wife's dual role, or his active assistance in her achievement of the work-home balancing act, was crucial. In its absence, as in Marianne Lloyd's account, opportunities could not be realised.

Yet the dual role was itself unstable. As Wilma Harrison reflected, and as feminists of the 1970s declaimed, 'women put too much on themselves'.[121] By the 1990s, however, rejecting it meant, discursively, a retreat into an understanding of a woman's place not in a comfortable and fulfilling domestic niche on the margins of the labour market, but in a subordinate position within an oppressive institution. No wonder women like Wilma Harrison and Marianne Lloyd reflected with anxiety, in interviews with a young single woman in the early 1990s, on the validity of their lives in and out of the labour market in the period after the war.

Simliarly complicated negotiations were required of women who became mothers from the 1940s to the 1960s, with the discourse of mother-centred infant care. Theories of the 1950s, concerning the centrality of the mother to childrearing, paved the way for the withdrawal of mothers from the labour market. But these theories were in tension with the contemporary notion of the pursuit of opportunity by qualified women, not only before, but now also after marriage. In addition, those theories had, by the 1990s, been thoroughly criticised by the women's movement for underpinning women's subordination and oppression. These discursive shifts and tensions added to the inter-subjective complexities of women seeking to give meaning in the 1990s to experiences of the 1940s to the 1960s.

Academics, as we saw in chapter 1, have argued about whether the Second World War transformed women's position, or polarised gender relations, or did no more than ensure the continuity of both. Whatever the conclusion, the Second World War features in these academic accounts, as well as in popular ones, as a period of disruption to peacetime patterns, of abnormal stresses and strains, of sudden deaths and new lives. In the next and final chapter we shall explore, in relation to discursive constructions of the war as a harbinger of change, women's perceptions of its effects upon themselves.

Notes

1 See, for example, H. Smith, 'The Effect of the War on the Status of Women', in H. Smith (ed.), *War and Social Change: British society in*

the Second World War (Manchester, Manchester University Press, 1986) and the reply by P. Summerfield, 'Women, War and Social Change: Women in Britain in World War II', in A. Marwick (ed.), *Total War and Social Change* (London, Macmillan, 1988).

2 D. Riley, *War in the Nursery. Theories of the Child and Mother* (London, Virago, 1983), p. 191.

3 Mary Agnes Hamilton, *Women at Work: A Brief Introduction to Trade Unionism for Women* (London, George Routledge and Sons, 1941), p. 12. Hamilton was Labour MP for Blackburn from 1929 to 1931, and, from 1940, a civil servant working for the Ministry of Health. Other documents of the period 1918 to 1940 which depicted women as marginal to the workforce are as follows: Parliamentary Papers, *Report of the War Cabinet Committee on Women in Industry* Cmd 135 (London, HMSO, 1919); Parliamentary Papers, Home Office, *A Study of the Factors Which Have Operated in the Past and Those Which are Operating Now to Determine the Distribution of Women in Industry*, Cmd 3508 (London, HMSO, 1930); Parliamentary Papers 1930–31, xvii, *Royal Commission on Unemployment Insurance*, First Report, Cmd 3872; Pilgrim Trust, *Men without Work* (Cambridge, Cambridge University Press, 1938).

4 See, for example, J. B. Priestley, *British Women Go to War* (London, Collins, 1943); P. Scott, *British Women in War* (London, Hutchinson, 1940) and P. Scott, *They Made Invasion Possible* (London, Hutchinson, 1944).

5 G. Williams, *Women and Work* (London, Nicholson and Watson, 1945), p. 11. The frontispiece of the book explained the idea of the series: 'The New Democracy ... the essence of a democratic community is that its citizens should take an active part in its decisions; and this is more imperative than ever in an age in which the state is everywhere extending the range of its activity. Active citizenship is the indispensable condition of freedom in a planned society. But the citizen can only take an active part in the community if he (sic) is properly informed about the choices and possibilities before it. To contribute to this body of informed opinion, as a basis of social action, is the purpose of this series.'

6 *Ibid.*, p. 12.

7 *Ibid.*, p. 19.

8 Many medical doctors expressed views hostile to nurseries during and after the war. See P. Summerfield, *Women Workers in the Second World War. Production and Patriarchy in Conflict* (London, Routledge, 1989), ch. 4. Examples of women doctors writing against nursery care include Medical Women's Federation, 'The Health of Children in Wartime Day Nurseries', *British Medical Journal*, 17

August 1946 and Dr Hilda Menzies in *The Lancet*, 5 October 1946. The most well-known opponents among psychologists were Donald Winnicott and John Bowlby in the 1940s and 1950s. For a discussion of their analyses of the infant's need for a constant maternal presence in the early years of life, see Riley, *War in the Nursery*, ch. 4.

9 Williams, *Women and Work*, pp. 104–5

10 *Ibid.*, p. 118.

11 *Ibid.*, p. 127.

12 For similar post-war arguments, see Parliamentary Papers, 'Marriage Bar in the Civil Service' *Report of the Civil Service National Whitley Council Committee*, Cmd 6886 (1946); Parliamentary Papers, *Report of the Royal Commission on Equal Pay*, Cmd 6937 (London, HMSO, 1946), especially paras 343 to 366. Three women on the Royal Commission on Equal Pay wrote a Memorandum of Dissent. They argued that the reasons the majority gave for women's lower earnings, that is their lower efficiency due to physical weakness and the priority women gave to marriage and family, were rationalisations (para. 1). The real causes were women's exclusion from trades by trade union and legal restrictions, and lack of bargaining power, due to weak trade union organisation (para. 19). The 'dissenters' however, accepted key aspects of the dominant discourse, namely that 'the natural and traditional sphere of women's work' was 'housekeeping and the care of children' (para. 6), and that 'the majority of women workers stay in industry for a shorter time than the majority of men, and that most women are less eager than most men to acquire skill and to obtain promotion' (para. 7). The view that women were naturally marginal to the workforce was also emphasised in some educational literature of the post-war period, e.g. John Newsom, *The Education of Girls* (London, Faber, 1948); Ministry of Education, *Half Our Future. A Report of the Central Advisory Council for Education* (England) (London, HMSO, 1963).

13 F. Hunt, *Gender and Policy in English Education* (Brighton, Harvester, 1991), pp. 138–44.

14 P. Tinkler, *Constructing Girlhood. Popular Magazines for Girls Growing Up in England* (London, Taylor and Francis, 1995), p. 115.

15 *Ibid.*, p. 93.

16 *Ibid.*, p. 90.

17 A. Oram, *Women Teachers and Feminist Politics 1900–39* (Manchester, Manchester University Press, 1996), pp. 15–23.

18 Tinkler, *Constructing Girlhood*, pp. 94–100.

19 A. Oram, 'Serving Two Masters? The Introduction of a Marriage Bar in Teaching in the 1920s', in London Feminist History Group (eds), *The Sexual Dynamics of History* (London, Pluto Press, 1983)

pp. 134–53; M. Zimmeck, 'Strategies and Stratagems for the Employment of Women in the British Civil Service, 1919–1939', *The Historical Journal*, 27, 4 (1984), pp. 901–24; M. Zimmeck, 'Marry in Haste, Repent at Leisure: Women, Bureaucracy and the Post Office, 1870–1920', in M. Savage and A. Witz (eds), *Gender and Bureaucracy* (Oxford, Oxford University Press, 1992), pp. 65–93.

20 On the example of teaching, see Oram, *Women Teachers and Feminist Politics*, p. 21: 'As teachers, women were offered masculine privilege – scope for the intellect, material rewards, service to the state and access to citizenship – but without having to reject their femininity, their identity as women. On the contrary, teaching increasingly required this of them.'

21 Parliamentary Papers, *Economic Survey for 1947*, Cmd 7046 (London, HMSO, 1947), paras 30, 31, 32 and 118–26. See also newspaper coverage, for example, *The Times*, 2 June 1947, p. 8, column (a); Ministry of Education, *Report of the Working Party on the Supply of Women Teachers* (London, HMSO, 1949). The post-war employment campaigns did not take a radical stance on equality, or challenge the prevailing social construction of motherhood. Mothers of children under two were specifically discouraged from taking paid work, and married women teachers were encouraged to return to work because of the value of their experience of mothering, rather than because of the advantages to them of this professional opportunity. Nevertheless, the representation of paid work as an acceptable option for married women and mothers was quite distinct from its representation within the discourse of marginality.

22 *Girls' Own Paper*, November 1945, pp. 6–7, quoted by Tinkler, *Constructing Girlhood*, p. 114.

23 A. Myrdal and V. Klein, *Women's Two Roles. Home and Work* (London, Routledge and Kegan Paul, 1956; this edition 1968), p. xvi.

24 J. Finch and P. Summerfield, 'Social Reconstruction and the Emergence of Companionate Marriage, 1945–59', in D. Clark (ed.), *Marriage, Domestic Life and Social Change. Essays for Jacqueline Burgoyne* (London, Routledge, 1991), pp. 7–32.

25 Myrdal and Klein, *Women's Two Roles*, p. 155.

26 *Ibid.*, p. 157.

27 Ministry of Education, *15 – 18. A Report of the Central Advisory Council for Education* (The Crowther Report) (London, HMSO, 1959); Ministry of Education, *Half Our Future. A Report of the Central Advisory Council for Education (England)* (The Newsom Report) (London, HMSO, 1963).

28 See, for example, M. Wandor (ed.), *The Body Politic. Women's Liberation in Britain 1969–1972* (London, Stage One, 1972), especially

pp. 124–30; S. Rowbotham, *Woman's Consciousness, Man's World* (Harmondsworth, Penguin, 1973), especially ch. 6. *Spare Rib, a Women's Liberation Magazine* was published from 1972 to 1992.

29 See, for example, L. Mackie and P. Patullo, *Women at Work* (London, Tavistock, 1977), ch. 4.

30 Slogans of the 1970s included 'Don't whistle at me, I'm not your dog' and 'Y B A Wife?'. The Equal Pay Act of 1970 and the 1984 Equal Value Amendment to that Act making it apply to work of equal value, as well as the Sex Discrimination Act of 1975, were hailed by women's liberationists as positive steps towards equal rights, but they were also criticised as limited, both because the implementation of the Acts worked through individual tribunal cases, and because of the caution of the Equal Opportunities Commission. See, for example, J. Earle and J. Phillips, 'Equal Pay: Why the Acts Don't Work', *Spare Rib*, 86 (September 1979), pp. 22–3.

31 The demobilisation rules were that married women were to be released from war service before single women in order to prioritise the re-establishment of home and family: Ministry of Labour and National Service, *Report for the Years 1939–1946*, Cmd 7225 (1947), p.139. On the parliamentary demobilisation debate of November 1944, see Julia Swindells 'Coming Home to Heaven: Manpower and Myth in 1944 Britain', *Women's History Review*, 4, 2 (1995) pp. 223–34. The predictions of M-O and the Wartime Social Survey in 1944 were that, at the end of the war, 'women will want to go back home, or take up jobs which were usually considered suitable for women before the war, while awaiting marriage': M-O, *The Journey Home: A Mass-Observation Report on the Problems of Demobilisation* (London, John Murray, 1944), p. 66. For a discussion of the discrepancy between such statements and the data actually collected by these survey organisations, see P. Summerfield, '"The Girl That Makes the Thing That Drills the Hole That Holds the Spring ..." Discourses of Women and Work in the Second World War', in C. Gledhill and G. Swanson (eds), *Nationalising Femininity: Culture, Sexuality and the British Cinema in the Second World War* (Manchester, Manchester University Press, 1996), pp. 47–8. On women's dependence on a breadwinner in the post-war welfare state, see P. Allatt, 'Stereotyping: Familism in the Law', in B. Fryer, A. Hunt, D. McBarnet and B. Moorhouse (eds), *Law, State and Society* (London, Croom Helm, 1981), pp. 177–201.

32 See P. Summerfield, 'The Patriarchal Discourse of Human Capital: Women's Work and Training in the Second World War', *Journal of Gender Studies*, 2, 2 (1993), pp. 189–205.

33 B. Jane Eliott, 'Demographic Trends in Domestic Life', in Clark,

Marriage, Domestic Life and Social Change, especially pp. 101–4.
34 Felicity Snow (259).
35 Felicity Snow (259).
36 Felicity Snow (259, 263).
37 Felicity Snow (27).
38 S. Heath, *'Preparation for Life'? Vocationalism and the Equal Opportunities Challenge* (Aldershot, Ashgate, 1997), p. 159.
39 Felicity Snow (285).
40 Felicity Snow (263).
41 They include the following eleven women (the twelfth, Beryl Bramley, is described in the next paragraph). Janice Brunton was sent by her domineering father into a clerical job calculating purchase tax at Woolworth's on her demobilisation from the WAAFs. She left on her marriage in 1948 and did not return to paid work until 1961. Margaret Grey returned, when she was demobilised, to the GPO switchboard where she had worked before joining the ATS as a driver, then managed to get driving jobs. When these petered out she became an editor in a book club, a job about which she did speak in terms of opportunity. Joyce Greaves was released on health grounds from the WAAF in 1944, after being married and widowed within two years, and described a succession of dull clerical jobs followed by a stressful new marriage to a man who had cancer. Much later she took a part-time job as a shop assistant, but her depiction of this return to work was closer to the therapy model than to the discourse of opportunity. Katharine Hughes worked as a dental receptionist after demobilisation from the WRNS. She left to have children, and later returned to work as a waitress. Ivy Jackson returned from the WAAF to the library where she had worked before joining up, but was dismissed on marriage and then lost her husband two years later, just before the birth of their child. After a variety of part-time and temporary jobs and remarriage, she retrained as a teacher in the 1960s, a job she spoke of as a new opportunity after a period of marginalisation. Greta Lewis left the ATS in 1943 because she was pregnant, worked in a post office when her daughter was small and later ran a children's playgroup, but her involvement in paid work was slight after the 1960s. Mary Mackenzie was released from the WAAF in 1943 when she was pregnant. After a long interval at home with her children she became a civil servant in the 1960s. Heather McLaren was demobilised from the WAAF when she became pregnant in 1945. She withdrew from paid work, not returning until 1960 when she re-entered the labour market as a clerical worker because her husband was ill. Amy O'Connor combined a very wide range of jobs with two successive marriages after leaving the ATS switchboard in 1945. She was a laundry worker,

catalogue seller, television set adjuster, bread deliverer, bar maid, but spoke of these jobs as stopgaps rather than the opportunity she would have liked. Flora Thomas was made to leave her job as a bus conductress to make way for ex-servicemen at the end of the war, and like Amy O'Connor subsequently combined a wide range of jobs with marriage and motherhood. Moira Underwood left her storekeeping job in her 'exciting' munitions factory to return to hairdressing, which she did until the 1960s, when she left and found a low paid clerical job.

42 Work history research is on the whole conducted at an aggregate level to which it is difficult to relate the detailed work histories collected here. David Vincent's research is an exception. He proposes a typology of career pathways in the first half of the twentieth century. In his words, '"Gold watch" pathways are single-employer careers which last the greater part of a working life ... "Migration" pathways are those in which an individual's course through a sequence of jobs is shaped by the possession of a recognised skill or trade, however defined. The "meander" is the careerless career, the shapeless drift through a sequence of largely unrelated positions. Finally, the "fracture" is the career whose momentum is broken by choice or circumstance, and takes off on an entirely new course.' See D. Vincent, 'Mobility, Bureaucracy and Careers in Twentieth-Century Britain', in A. Miles and D. Vincent (eds), *Building European Society. Occupational Change and Social Mobility in Europe, 1840–1940* (Manchester, Manchester University Press, 1993), p. 225. Vincent's analysis showed that women entering the paid labour market before the First World War were concentrated in the meander and fracture categories. In his period once a woman's career had been fractured by marriage she did not pursue paid work again. The forty-two women in my sample, most of whom entered the paid labour market in the 1930s, had more complicated patterns, since most returned to some sort of paid work after a 'fracture' due to marriage or, more commonly in the post-war years, childbirth. Some of these returners could be described as migratory and some as meandering. However, not every meanderer *saw* her career as the 'shapeless drift' of Vincent's description. Those who were disappointed to have to give up war work with which they would have liked to continue, quoted above, tended to do so. But others, whose accounts we shall review shortly, saw their 'meanders' as patterns determined by their own deliberate choices. The effect of the war on the career patterns of the women in my sample was extremely complicated, as the rest of this chapter will indicate. Vincent states that for his sample the Second World War ended fractures or turned meanders into migrations: 'it was a matter of women who

had been out of the labour market for many years (some had never entered it), or who had been meandering through domestic labour, suddenly acquiring purposeful careers, which ... did not necessarily end with peace. Some discovered latent skills and ambitions and worked on until retirement in the 1950s and 1960s' (p. 229). Unfortunately Vincent does not quantify this statement. It does not apply to any of the women in my sample who did manual work in the war. It is more relevant to women who became clerical workers during the war than to any other group (though not consistently so). However, as we shall see, the group which most strongly *represented* their careers as 'purposeful' migrations, began those careers after doing some other type of war work. They perceived the Second World War itself as a fracture in their career paths, from which they had to recover afterwards. As discursive constructions of relationships to the labour market, Vincent's terms 'gold watch' and 'migration' belong to the discourse of opportunity, and 'meander' and 'fracture' to that of marginalisation.

43 Beryl Bramley (200).
44 Beryl Bramley (533).
45 Sadie Bartlett (264, 266).
46 Caroline Woodward (454).
47 Connie Field (Producer and Director), *The Life and Times of Rosie the Riveter* (Emeryville, CA, Clarity Educational Productions, 1982). Rosie the Riveter was the title of a patriotic song by Redd Evans and Joan Jacob Loeb released in the USA in February 1943, and the image of Rosie the Riveter, painted by Norman Rockwell, was published on the cover of the *Saturday Evening Post* on 29 May 1943. See P. Colman, *Rosie the Riveter. Women Working on the Home Front in World War II* (New York, Crown Publishers, 1995).
48 M. Goldsmith, *Women and the Future* (London, Lindsay Drummond, 1946), p. 15. Goldsmith argued that, nevertheless, women's wartime independence would produce changes, particularly in the institution of marriage, leading to greater equality between the sexes.
49 Such films as *Brief Encounter*, set in the winter of 1938–39 and released in December 1945, reinforced the moral standards of pre-war marital and maternal life through an exploration of the instabilities in the domestic idyll intensified by the war. See A. Lant, *Blackout. Reinventing Women for Wartime British Cinema* (Princeton, Princeton University Press, 1991), ch. 4, especially pp. 158–9. Alan Munton concludes his discussion of literary fiction about the war by arguing that it was essentially conservative as far as gender roles were concerned, citing work by, for example, Olivia Manning. See A. Munton, *English Fiction of the Second World War* (London, Faber and Faber, 1989).

50 Williams, *Women and Work*, p. 118

51 Evelyn Mills (292). Others who offered such accounts included Joan Stanton, who happily moved back to a secretarial job in London after her release from the clutches of the Cheltenham Employment Exchange in 1946, married her boss in 1948, and withdrew from paid work on the birth of her daughter in 1954. Peggy Peters moved to a better clerical job at the naval base where she worked during the war, then married, took a succession of part-time and temporary secretarial jobs while her children were small and then withdrew from the labour market in 1963. Yvette Baynes, who like Evelyn and Peggy was a clerical worker throughout the war, told a similar story. However, her account of her post-war work was coloured by economic pressure to continue in paid work when she was a wife and mother, because of the inadequacies of her husband who, she said, was constantly out of work because 'he couldn't get on with people' (765). This meant that Yvette was required to perform as a breadwinner, and hence welcomed more responsibility and evinced more ambition than Evelyn or Joan. Yvette drew on the language of the dual role to make it clear that her work 'always fitted in with my home' (749).

52 Elizabeth Little (738).

53 Elizabeth Little (790).

54 Elizabeth Little (738, 794).

55 Elizabeth Little (839).

56 Elizabeth Little (744).

57 Elizabeth Little (718).

58 May Richards (460).

59 May Richards (493). Edith Dixon was the other 'hero' who was pleased to leave her war job and immerse herself in domesticity. She described becoming disillusioned with life in the WRNS, and did not consider her job at a naval switchboard particularly demanding or interesting. She was glad to marry in 1943 and leave the Service, even though her circumstances were not ideal, in that her husband, a naval chaplain, was invalided out of war service because he contracted typhus from an inoculation. The couple thereafter produced five children, and Edith told a story of satisfaction with the demanding roles of clergyman's wife and mother of a large family. She did not re-enter the labour market at any point in her life. She explained: 'If I hadn't been married I would have worked outside the home, but I knew I wouldn't be doing that because I was taking on a large manse and the responsibilities of a minister's wife. At that time Church of Scotland ministers' wives all worked along with their husbands in the church and helped to run the church as well as running the house, so it was a busy life': Edith Dixon (430).

60 Dorothy Rose (408, 420). Dorothy remembered that she was paid nineteen shillings and then after the first six months over a pound 'and to have a pound in my hand, I thought it was great you know' (420). She reflected that the war had provided her with a 'back door' entry into the Civil Service, since by 1946 the Ministry of Food's workload was beginning to shrink (even though rationing went on until 1953), and no new juniors were taken on: Dorothy Rose (580).

61 Myrna Wraith 302.

62 Emily Porter 76. Emily expressed the enormous importance of this process in her precise recall of its timing, as in 'I had to go on 26 July 1940 which was a Thursday' (64).

63 Emily Porter (143).

64 Emily Porter (240).

65 Care of her mother, on the other hand, did.

66 Nadia Beale (31, 33).

67 Nadia Beale (129).

68 Nadia Beale (141).

69 Nadia Beale (151).

70 Nadia Beale (169).

71 Nadia Beale (221, 223).

72 Nadia Beale (175, 177).

73 Myrdal and Klein, *Women's Two Roles*, p. 157.

74 Estelle Armitage (17).

75 Estelle Armitage (170).

76 Estelle Armitage (212).

77 Estelle Armitage (240).

78 Estelle Armitage (240).

79 Estelle Armitage (276, 278).

80 Estelle Armitage (320).

81 Ann Tomlinson (353).

82 Ann Tomlinson (317).

83 C. Dyhouse, *No Distinction of Sex. Women in British Universities 1870–1939* (London, UCL Press, 1995), p. 17 gives a figure of 11,299 women enrolled in British universities in 1937–38, compared with 37,899 men. Women were therefore about one-quarter of the student population. This, however, represented a very small proportion of the population as a whole. Calculations by two sociologists in the 1960s suggest that only 1.5 per cent of all girls born between 1910 and 1929, and 4 per cent of the daughters of professional or managerial fathers in this age group, went to university: A. Little and J. Westergaard 'The Trend of Class Differentials in Educational Opportunity in England', *British Journal of Sociology*, 15, 4 (1964), Table 5, p. 129.

84 Ann Tomlinson (333).

85 Ann Tomlinson (345).
86 Ann Tomlinson (374).
87 Ann Tomlinson (374).
88 Ann Tomlinson (376).
89 Ann Tomlinson (382).
90 Ann Tomlinson (374).
91 Gladys French was a cost accountant for a railway company before
    the war, having obtained a place at university which she was unable to
    take up because her lower middle-class widowed father could not (or
    would not) afford it. She enthusiastically joined the WRNS in the war,
    becoming a radio mechanic. Although she was proud of her war work,
    her attitude to the end of the war and the end the job, like Ann Tom-
    linson's, was neutral. She said, 'we all knew that when the war ended,
    that women wouldn't be needed much. One of my friends stayed in
    ... but I couldn't see the point of it in peace time, so I wanted to
    resume – well, I wanted to start the career I'd always wanted to start,
    and become a teacher' (340). Before she left the Wrens she did a
    month's teacher training and then, in May 1946, she was discharged
    and after a couple of months duty service back in the railway offices,
    she embarked on a one year emergency teacher training course, which
    she supplemented immediately after she had completed it, with a two-
    year part-time course leading to a Froebel Certificate, which she took
    at the same time as working in her first teaching job (384). Gladys
    gave a strong, proud account of her experience and qualities as a
    teacher, explaining how she went to university later so that she could
    become a head teacher (401). Not every woman who reshaped a
    career after the war was a teacher or a nurse. Amabel Ingram in fact
    used the opportunity to leave nursing, which she had begun before
    she joined the WRNS as a decoder. At the end of the war she was not
    sorry to be demobilised. The secrecy of the work, and its relative
    monotony, had imposed terrific strain. Amabel regarded jobs as easy
    to come by in the second half of the 1940s: 'then, people were so
    short, so short that you could have worked as anything practically'
    (433). She described considering whether to take one of eight jobs
    which she was offered, and possibly to meander through marginal
    work until marriage, or whether to take the opportunity to train for
    a career. Her first choice of career was to become a minister of the
    Congregational Church, but the careers advisers to ex-service person-
    nel, whom she consulted, said, 'there's no way you're going to be a
    Congregational minister' because women did not do this job. How-
    ever, they suggested that she should take further training and become
    a speech therapist. Amabel recalled weighing up the opportunities
    before her. 'I was really having to toss up whether to try and study and

become a speech therapist or whether to take one of these jobs [which she had been offered] ... it was my brother actually ... he said, "I think I would go for the career" and that sort of tipped the balance' (433). Amabel made speech therapy the career which she pursued from 1949 until she retired in 1989, taking part-time work for short periods after the birth of her three children between 1955 and 1961 (449). Amabel had no sense of marginality to the paid labour force.

92 Ethel Singleton (286).
93 Ethel Singleton (292, 294).
94 Ethel Singleton (69).
95 Ethel Singleton (57).
96 See the discussion of this terminology in footnote 42. It is used by Vincent in his article, 'Mobility, Bureaucracy and Careers in Twentieth-Century Britain': see particularly p. 225.
97 Ethel Singleton (57).
98 Wilma Harrison (424).
99 Wilma Harrison (460).
100 Wilma Harrison (507).
101 Wilma Harrison (515).
102 Wilma Harrison (396).
103 Wilma Harrison (392, 396).
104 Wilma Harrison (396).
105 Hester Hamilton (233). See Dyhouse, *No Distinction of Sex*, pp. 27–33 on the extreme paucity of grants and scholarships for women students.
106 Hester Hamilton (284).
107 Hester Hamilton (313).
108 Hester Hamilton (293).
109 Hester Hamilton (309).
110 Pamela Wootton (540).
111 Marianne Lloyd (60).
112 Marianne Lloyd (349).
113 Marianne Lloyd (219).
114 Marianne Lloyd (219).
115 Marianne Lloyd (227).
116 Marianne Lloyd (219).
117 Marianne Lloyd (226, 227).
118 Marianne Lloyd (247).
119 Marianne Lloyd (309).
120 Marianne Lloyd (305).
121 Wilma Harrison (396).

'Country Landscape, March 1941' by Feliks Topolski

Chapter 7

The Second World War and narratives of personal change

This chapter draws on responses to one of the few direct questions of the interviews, 'Do you think that the war changed you?'.[1] The question needs to be contextualised. It was formulated in the light of the academic argument which we reviewed in chapter 1, about whether the Second World War produced social change, and in particular whether it altered women's position in society and hence gender relations. That historical debate presupposed the possibility of a unitary answer, indeed it was propelled by a succession of attempts to settle the matter – the transformation, continuity and polarisation theses. But, as we saw, each proposed resolution was revealed, by evidence of irresolvably disparate subjective experiences and understandings, to be a forced synthesis. The debate was inevitably inconclusive. It is not the intention here to construct yet another contribution to it, from new data. We shall, instead, first explore further the meaning of the question which we posed in the interviews, and then examine the relationship of available discourses of war and personal change to the stories which the women we interviewed composed.

The question 'Do you think that the war changed you?' was, I realise now, framed by the concept of a coherent self. It anticipated responses based on the capacity of interviewees to see into the inner processes of that self, specifically to perceive internal changes across time and attribute them to identifiable causes. As the feminist philosopher Jane Flax explains, such a notion is central to and taken-for-granted within Western rationalist thinking. 'Essential to all enlightenment beliefs is the existence of something called a "self", a stable, reliable, integrative entity that has access to our inner states and outer reality.'[2] Post-modernists have criticised this notion of the self and subjectivity as an 'Enlightenment metanarrative' based on the ideal of progress and the denial of ambivalence, division and discord. Feminist post-modernists have added that within the metanarrative one of the main denials has been of the social and historical processes by which gender divisions have been constructed. Gender has become not only 'a central constituting element in each person's sense of self and in a culture's idea of what it means to be a person' but also 'a differentiated and asymmetric division and attribution of human traits and capacities' and hence of power.[3]

The understanding of subjectivity used in this book is consistent with this critique. Oral history is a methodology which, like the literary genre autobiography, invites attempts to reconstruct the self as a coherent whole. In the foregoing chapters we have observed the difficulties for narrators of doing so, revealed by the inter-subjective processes of composure at work within interviews. We have viewed the subjects of the life histories discussed here as products and producers of the practices and discourses of culture. We have argued that the presence of multiple gendered and 'raced' discourses makes the achievement of a consistent and unfragmented self in the telling of such stories problematic. Indeed, the rationale for the book is that this interaction between culture and memory in the composition of oral histories is a serious and important site of historical study.

Answers to the question 'did the war change you?' will not, then, be read as essentialist expressions of individuals' unitary selves. Following the approach used in the other chapters of this book, they will be discussed as the products of interactions within the interviews between the narrative subject and the discursive subject and between the interviewee and the interviewer. Specifically, we shall explore women's accounts of how the war did or did not change them, as their selections from, and contributions to, the discursive constructions of war and personal change available in our culture.

Two versions of the effects of the Second World War on women have been in popular circulation since the 1940s. In one, the war hastened women towards modernity. In the other, it stimulated a return to traditional feminine lifestyles. These competing stories were current during the war, and one or other has been favoured within most popular and academic accounts since.[4]

War and the making of modern woman

Contemporary accounts of the modernising trends hastened by the war emphasised the desirability of women's emergence from domestic seclusion into public life. A recurrent motif in these accounts was of women enclosed within the home and literally liberated by war, and common metaphors were of the war lifting a curtain, opening a door or releasing women from a cage.[5] For example, writing in 1942 the Labour MP Edith Summerskill presented a brief history of women in the twentieth century, the theme of which was the vital role of both world wars in women's release from domestic bondage into citizenship. The First World War had offered 'four years of freedom to individuals who had hitherto led solitary, isolated lives, each securely shut up in her home'.[6] Both wars, especially the Second with its opportunities for military service, had produced a 'new woman' who had 'a mind of her own' which led her to desire participation in reconstruction and the promotion of peace, and therefore to want a voice in politics and the professions. Summerskill sketched a future in which, while women would not have lost the urge to be feminine (meaning to dress nicely and to marry and have children), they would demand egalitarian marriages in which they were not tied to the home, and had opportunities for paid or voluntary work and civic involvement. Wartime communal restaurants and nurseries had shown that full-time domesticity was not necessary. The traditional position of the housewife would 'not satisfy the post-war housewife who has tasted the joys of economic independence in the factories and the services'.[7]

Summerskill contributed, with no reservations, an image of the modern woman freed by war to discover her own value and her importance as a citizen. Other publicists, such as the novelist Phyllis Bentley, the public-opinion research organisation Mass Observation, and the popular writers Margaret Goldsmith and Peggy Scott, followed her lead. Bentley wrote in an Army Education pamphlet, 'Two wars in which women have been summoned into industry and the Forces to act as substitutes and aids for men, have broken down the conventions and taboos which kept them in the home, taught them that they can perform a vast range of jobs as well as men, and accustomed them to economic independence'.[8] In the same vein Goldsmith argued that 'in two or three years a measure of women's emancipation will have been achieved which would have taken at least a quarter of a century in peacetime. They have greater independence in a host of ways'.[9] The idea of release from domestic confinement was strong. M-O proclaimed that war work had provided the woman who had 'become a slave to the monotony of housework' with 'the first bit of variety and freedom she has known in her life'. It quoted two women who compared the experience to being let out of a cage.[10] Scott wrote that in the Second World War, 'thousands of girls have been forced to leave their homes and to find a wider life in industry or in the Services; thousands of housewives have had the curtain lifted which divided their own home from the troubles and trials of the nation.' She posed rhetorically the question 'Will they go back and shut the door again?'.[11] In all these accounts the war had breached the boundary between the home and the wider society, between the private and the public spheres.

This account of war and the making of modern woman intersected with the discourse of opportunities for women in the labour force and the concomitant post-war themes of companionate marriage and women's 'dual role', which we discussed in the last chapter. It added a more general notion of women's emancipation as citizens. The war figured within the story of modernisation as a major stimulus to the progress it depicted.

War and the traditional woman

A quite different version of war and social change was, however, available, in which the war was not represented as a period of freedom for women, but of constraint and instability, and in which its end signalled a welcome return to secure domesticity. Some of this literature was written in explicit opposition to feminist accounts like that of Summerskill.

In 1945, for example, Dorothy Paterson, founder of the Council of Seven Beliefs for the Guardianship of Family Life, published a book called *The Family Woman and the Feminist. A Challenge*, in which she explicitly rejected the construction of the home as a cage: 'Our friends the Feminists appear to think that the average home is built without doors or windows and that a woman in a home sits alone all day in a perpetual mental and social blackout!'.[12] In fact, Paterson argued, the domestic sphere was a 'natural outlet' for women, and the most important task in a woman's life was to build a home into 'a landmark of security' for herself and her husband and within it fulfil her destiny by creating a family.[13] The war, with its loss of life coming on top of the long-term decline in the birth-rate, gave special urgency to women's home-making and reproductive mission and placed it at the centre of post-war reconstruction.[14] For Paterson this matrimonial and maternal role, rather than economic participation, qualified women for citizenship. Women did not want to participate in public politics.[15] They did not need the continuation of wartime developments which replaced the family as the unit of social organisation with communal facilities, such as hostels, restaurants and nurseries. Such provisions undermined women's domestic role and lowered the housewife's status.[16] This

account meshed with the discourse of women's marginal relationship to the labour market, predicated upon the breadwinning male,
which we reviewed in the last chapter.

Paterson's text belonged in the context of the widespread production of ideas concerning the re-establishment of family life after
the stress and worry of wartime. The rebuilding of homes, physically and emotionally, and the birth of children within the security
of the familiar gender order, were presented as deeply comforting
and essential to post-war reconstruction. The reassurance derived
from such a view was in large part directed at male members of the
armed forces.[17] It was for their wives and sweethearts, their children
and their homes, that men were allegedly fighting. Hearth and
home, and the gendered social structure for which they were a
metaphor, were at the centre of national identity.[18]

A key site for the public generation and transmission of the discourse was the House of Commons, particularly as it turned its
attention to post-war reconstruction in the last two years of the war.
A debate on demobilisation from the Forces in November 1944, for
example, was preoccupied with the theme of men's return to welcoming homes. Lieutenant-Colonel John Profumo MP introduced
the dominant motif of the debate in his opening speech: 'The
nucleus around which we shall build all our future hopes and plans
for a happy nation must be the home, and the sooner we can unite
those whose intentions were thwarted by the outbreak of war, the
better'.[19] Major B. Nield (MP for Chester City) elaborated his point.
He evoked 'the long, weary years of separation from wife and
family' which servicemen had endured, and quoted a letter about
the proposals for demobilisation from a woman constituent: 'We
cannot think the scheme just which fails to take into account these
empty, wasted years, sacrificed in war: years deprived of husband,
often of home, and of the children we long to have'. Men must be
brought back home from overseas to the waiting arms of their wives
and families, as fast as possible.[20] There was virtual unanimity in the
parliamentary debate on the principle of the restoration of the
family. The idea that women were waiting anxiously for men to
return home was an unquestioned piece of common sense.

It was one which pervaded accounts of the effects of the war on
women. It characterised not only traditionalist accounts like Paterson's, which urged upon women the joys and fulfilment of family
life. It was also present in many of the modernising ones, like Scott's

although not Summerskill's, which suggested that the war had caused great changes. The compelling need to restore family life contradicted the message of women's liberation from the home, within the discourse of modernisation. At the same time as applauding new opportunities for women arising from the war, the authors quoted earlier, as well as that other voice of wartime 'progressivism', J. B. Priestley, expressed the view that women's response to peace would be an overwhelming desire to 'go home'. Scott, Goldsmith, M-O and Priestley differentiated the effects of the war on women by age, although they did not present a consistent picture of the ways in which the various groupings were affected. Priestley thought that older women would return permanently to their pre-war lifestyles, whereas younger women would soon discover that they wanted more than home life.[21] Goldsmith thought the same, arguing that older married women 'fervently wish themselves back into their pre-war home routine'.[22] Scott and M-O thought, on the other hand, that it was older women, who had experienced the isolation of home-life before the war, who would be readier than younger ones to welcome change.[23] In M-O's account, however, young servicewomen were an especially unsettled group.

The special case of the servicewoman

The women in whom these observers of social life variously believed they perceived signs of change included, of course, the wives to whom many servicemen would be returning. Traditionalists invested these women with a natural store of comfort, reassurance and stability which they believed vital to post-war life. But it was possible that the flow of this essential goodness had been jeopardised by the consequences of war for women proposed by the modernists. Writers like the 'medical psychologist', Kenneth Howard, who published *Sex Problems of the Returning Soldier* in 1945, counselled the serviceman on how 'to resume his rightful place as the breadwinner of the household', countering his wife's resentment of 'her loss of her newly-found prestige and power' in such a way as to re-establish happy and lasting marriages.[24]

It is striking that nowhere in his book did Howard conceptualise the 'returning soldier' as a woman, in spite of the 450,000 women serving in the Auxiliary Forces in 1945.[25] Any problems of readjustment which servicewomen might have had were rendered invisible in accounts like Howard's or Paterson's, and were marginalised in the parliamentary discussions of demobilisation in November 1944. In this debate the message concerning servicewomen was consistent with the return to gender norms expected of all women. It was encapsulated in Profumo's announcement of the government's proposal to give servicewomen a cash award for reclothing themselves rather than a 'demob suit' of the sort that would be issued to men when they relinquished their military uniforms. He stressed the importance of assisting women to become 'once again individually, adequately and gracefully dressed'.[26] Minority voices which suggested that servicewomen might be more concerned about their future job prospects than about how they looked were ignored.[27]

Peggy Scott, who otherwise portrayed the war as opening doors for women, followed the official line on servicewomen's feelings about demobilisation. 'The great desire among the girls in the Services is to have a home of their own, and it is the same with the girls in industry', she wrote in 1944.[28] M-O's reading of the situation was, however, that servicewomen constituted a particularly restless group. They had rejected the idea of settling down, they had a 'longing for adventure', and they desired change. 'Service women are, on the whole, much more interested in the future than their counterparts in factory and war-job'.[29] In M-O's account, it was within this group that the new feminine sense of citizenship was growing. 'These women have been taken from their homes, often for the first time in their lives, and for the first time are being forced to think for themselves instead of falling back on some opinion taken ready made from husband or father.'[30] This had led to political awareness, and, in M-O's view, to aspirations for 'equal competition between the sexes'.[31]

M-O was not alone in holding this view. Some wartime fiction which focused specifically on servicewomen embraced and advocated the idea that the war was facilitating women's entry into the world of work and social responsibility, and enhancing feminine citizenship. An example is a novel called *She Goes to War* by Edith Pargeter, published in 1942. Using the epistolary genre, it charted through letters written during the year 1940–41, the changes wrought in a young woman, Catherine Saxon, as a result of joining the WRNS. In brief, the plot is as follows. Inspired by a light-hearted patriotism, Catherine shrugs off parental control in order to do something more serious for the war effort than her job as a gossip columnist on a local paper. She works in the WRNS as a teleprinter operator in Liverpool, heroically carrying on through the Blitz, and becomes romantically involved with a serviceman, Tom Lyddon, veteran of the Spanish Civil War. Catherine and Tom have an affair and marry, without consulting her parents (he appears to have had none), and then she loses him to an overseas posting. The book closes with the high probability that he has died in action in Crete. In the course of these events, Catherine's patriotism deepens and becomes more complex, she moves towards socialism, develops an international perspective on peace and progress, and becomes determined to devote herself to a new kind of journalism after the war. The gossip column is behind her. Her writing will now be dedicated to the removal from the nation of 'all the inequalities and exploitations and snobberies and simonies and treacheries and embezzlements that enfeeble it'.[32] Catherine has undergone a personal transformation as a result of the war, from the frivolity and irresponsibility of a middle-class daughter to the independence, material and intellectual, of an emancipated woman.

To sum up, two narratives of women, war and change were popularly available during and after the war. They were apparently distinct and even opposed, but the discourse of modernisation was in fact riddled with traditionalism. Traditionalists regarded with suspicion the changes in women's identities which modernists suggested were consequent upon the war. The traditionalist emphasis was upon the vital role of women in reconstructing home life, in having children, and in re-establishing familial relationships within which male authority could be reasserted and accepted. Any other future would be socially unstable. In contrast, modernisers argued that the war had led to new openings for women as workers and citizens outside the home, which would make them discontented with a return to conventional roles. However, there was no unanimity amongst modernisers on the age and occupational groups of the women who would be the harbingers of change. Furthermore, few of them departed from the dominant, traditional view that women's main purpose at the end of the war was to 'return home' and recreate a domestic haven. The contradiction between this representation and the idea that the war had liberated women was resolved by the suggestion that, later in the post-war years, women would turn their backs on the domestic 'cage' and demand the freedoms made available by the war.

Servicewomen were a group with a particularly uncertain post-war identity. Within the traditionalist discourse they were assumed to be longing, like other women, for a return to conventional femininity, symbolised in their case by the exchange of the uniform for the pretty frock. Modernisers on the other hand looked upon servicewomen as a wild card, possibly longing to settle down in homes of their own, or alternatively ready to forge for women a new form of feminine citizenship.

The view that the war had produced a modern woman was restated by academics in the 1950s and 1960s, for example, by the sociologists Richard Titmus, Alva Myrdal and Viola Klein and by the historian Arthur Marwick as well as by numerous popularisers.[33] The traditionalist view was worked into opposing accounts within the historical debate, most notably that of Harold Smith.[34] The 1970s feminist rejection of the idea that the war had 'emancipated' women had a parallel effect to that which the feminist interpretation of women's subordinated position in the labour market had on the discourses of marginalisation and opportunity reviewed in chapter 6. The dominant interpretation of the Second World War by feminist historians in the 1980s was of the continuity of women's subordination across the period. In spite of an appearance of change due to labour shortages and state policies directed to the relief of domestic tasks, there was little change in the identification of women with domesticity and in women's subordinate position within paid work. The feminist story of war and the absence of change (to which my own books and articles contributed) obliterated the difference between the modernist and traditionalist accounts, treating them instead as a monolithic discourse supporting women's oppression.

Such a construction left little space for the idea of personal change for women occurring as a result of the war. The suspicions of feminists of the 1970s and 1980s, of claims that women had been emancipated by the war, suggested that any individual who believed this was true for her was likely to be deluded. There was, as a result, an unfortunate gulf (as I experienced at the adult education class in 1977[35]) between the feminist account of little or no change, and individual stories of the war as a special experience in a woman's life, which were necessarily drawing on other sources. The two narratives I have discussed were possibilities. Of special interest within them, as we have noted, was the position of servicewomen.

Servicewomen and the discourse of modernisation

Most of the ex-servicewomen interviewed took up enthusiastically the idea that their wartime experiences had changed them. All but two of them, as we have seen, told 'heroic' accounts of joining and contributing to the war effort. An epic narrative is structured by the idea of the tempering and refinement of the hero who conquers all difficulties in pursuit of the desired goal. A story of personal change was therefore to be expected from women who constructed heroic accounts of their wartime experiences. But their specific application of the available discourses of change, and particularly their negotiation of the contradictions within them, were by no means a foregone conclusion.

The change which was central to the discourse of modernisation was, as we have seen, the idea of the emergence of women from seclusion in the home: the lifting of a curtain, the opening of a door. Young women were supposed to have been permanently released from the protection and authority normally imposed by parents, and to have discovered what life was all about, that is the aspects of life from which they had formerly been sheltered. This kind of change was a logical extension of the representation of young women as free agents at the disposal of the state, in the wartime mobilisation policy and propaganda reviewed in chapter 2.

One of the ways such an experience was portrayed in personal terms was through a story of development from a shy and inarticulate personality to an outgoing one, as a result of experiences of meeting people within the Services. Such accounts came from across the social spectrum. Ivy Jones, for example, daughter of working-class parents in Cardiff, conjured up the sheltered, limited world which she left behind on entering the WAAF as a meteorologist. By the end of the war, she said,

> I suppose I must have had more confidence, I'd mixed more, I'd got used to dealing with men, because you see at home I had three sisters and I went to an all-girls school and in those days you weren't encouraged to mix ... yes, it brought me out, I was a different person at the end, and I felt differently ... I'm sure it did me a lot of good.[36]

In accounts like Ivy's, which tell a story of 'maturation' from timidity to extroversion, there was a strong view that experience in the Services had had a corrective effect on what were perceived (with

hindsight) as deficiencies in a woman's character caused by the sheltered lives imposed on her by her parents and schooling.[37] It was
summed up in the phrase used by Ivy and several others: 'it did me
a lot of good'. However, in an account which shifted from a heroic
to a stoic frame, this phrase took on a different meaning. Rather
than seeing her years in the WRNS as a liberation from protective
parents, Edith Dixon depicted them as re-educating her in the
virtues of a sheltered home life. Her response to the question, 'Did
the war change you?' was:

> I think it did me a lot of good because I tended to be an only daugh-
> ter, rather spoiled probably by my father and I felt that the conditions
> that I worked under, while we were happy, they weren't easy. And
> especially all the bad food and everything which I wasn't used to. It
> made me very very much more appreciative of my home afterwards.[38]

The public availability of the understanding that greater social
confidence was one of the effects of wartime service is suggested by
the response of one of the ex-servicewomen who told a heroic
account but felt that the war had *not* changed her. Myrna Wraith
replied negatively to the question, 'Do you think your wartime
experience changed you?', saying, 'No, I don't think so really'. She
then expanded her answer by referring spontaneously to a conviviality and sense of community which she felt she already possessed:
'I always liked people, you know what I mean, and I like talking if
I'm honest. You've probably noticed! So that meeting such a variety
of people, I always thought it's probably stood me in good stead.'[39]
Accounts of becoming personally more outgoing as a result of
leaving home for the Services were sometimes further embellished,
indeed embodied, in stories of not only rising to the challenge of
verbal self-expression and conviviality, but of freeing the body itself
from the confines of modesty and prudishness in the public world
of the Forces. Marion Paul was one of several women who commented on the enforced adjustment to exposing the body to the
public gaze in the Services. She vividly reconstructed her feelings
when, on first joining the ATS from a clerical job in a mines office,
she was told to change into her new uniform in a room full of other
women:

> This was very embarrassing, because I'd never changed, I'd never
> taken my clothes off in front of other people. And most of the others
> were the same, they – they were all very embarrassed, and we all sort

of got against walls and in corners, and turned our backs to the middle of the room and sort of gingerly took everything off and put all these other ones on.[40]

Usually such reflections related to learning to accept the personal and communal exposure of the feminine body in the company of other women.[41] Amy O'Connor, former domestic servant and wartime ATS Signals Operator indicated that this was, for her, a long-lasting change. She described the big huts for thirty women in the ATS,

> same as the ablutions, I mean a row of wash basins. You just stripped off and got a wash. They couldn't understand when I was in – when I'm in hospital, I don't give a hang. I just strip off and get a wash. A woman said to me, 'You weren't in the WAAFs by any chance were you?' when I was in hospital this last time. 'No', I said, 'I was in the Army, why?' She said, 'There's only us do this', she said, 'all the other women, they're doing this sort of thing' [covering her body]. She said, 'It doesn't bother me does it?'. I said, 'Well I don't care what you look like', I said, 'I don't suppose you care what I look like'.[42]

The process of shedding inhibition and arriving at improved understanding of self and society could also relate to women's growing knowledge of men's bodies. Ivy Jones, whose comments on the 'good' done to her by mixing with men as well as women as a WAAF we have already reviewed, referred specifically in this context to the benefits of an enlarged understanding of embodied masculinity. Between flights, RAF pilots slept on the airfield in the flying control building where Ivy worked as a meteorologist:

> They had these little cots and things and they relied on us to get them up in the morning at 6 o'clock, you see the Met. girl was the one who was awake. Because there was this room just full of – really smelly because everybody went to sleep in their clothes, you know. And you sort of got used to this sort of thing that you'd never been used to, and you'd sort of get on with men as people, yes it was a good thing. Didn't have any brothers! I think we learned a lot.[43]

Kate Lomax, WAAF photographer, implied that the specific awareness she gained was less of different types of body than of different types of sexual behaviour: 'I thought I knew – I went into the Service [at] say 21, and I thought I knew it all, and I learnt more about people and their way of life than I ever would have done in a private life. And there's all sorts – I met lesbians, and things like that. I met married women, married men ...'. Kate went on to reflect on the moral lesson she learned from these encounters: 'I made up my mind I would never encourage a married man'.[44] The inter-subjectivity in this interview, between Kate and her young single woman interviewer, enabled Kate to refer fleetingly to lesbianism, but she went straight on to reflect in greater depth on marriage. The interviewer, on the other hand, was evidently too inhibited by the taboos and homophobia prevalent in our culture, to backtrack. She did not take the opportunity to ask Kate what she felt she had learned from meeting lesbians during the war.

In other parts of the interviews, ex-servicewomen commented on the ways in which the women's military auxiliaries subjugated them physically (in parallel to the methods used in the men's forces): the 'square bashing' (military drill) which all women as well as men recruits had to do as part of initial training, the regulations relating to the components of uniform and how it should be worn, the strict timetables (watches, leaves, parades, fatigues) that had to be followed. Perhaps the warning remembered by numerous servicewomen, that the new lifestyle might disturb their menstrual periods but that this should not be a cause for alarm, was the most telling sign of the take-over of the rhythms of the feminine body by military routine. In contrast to accounts of this disciplining of the body, ex-servicewomen's stories of learning to cope with the exposure of their bodies to their fellow recruits were framed within the discourse of their emergence from domestic seclusion, and were constructed as relatively liberating.

Modernists believed, as we have seen, that a consequence of wartime release from the domestic cage was that women were becoming less bounded by their own individual concerns and more socially responsible. In these constructions the content of the new citizenship fostered by the war in servicewomen was vague. At its most precise it did not go beyond a sketchily defined concern with social justice and equality.[45]

The ex-servicewomen interviewed spoke in similarly general terms about the effects of their service on their social consciousness. They drew on the idea of the enlargement of social awareness to express how they felt the services had changed them. A prevalent theme was the idea of a growth in the personal capacity to feel a sense of commonality with other people. We have met this construction of social levelling in relation to workplace colleagues in chapters 4 and 5, where it referred to becoming 'just one of the boys' or being 'all in it together' with other women. Ex-servicewomen gave it more generalised expression in response to the question about how war changed them. It could involve levelling up or levelling down. For example, Katharine Hughes felt that the WRNS had taught her not to regard her working-class background as a social disadvantage: 'I think it made me more confident, myself, and I don't consider anyone better than I am. They might have a bit more money than I have but they're no better than me, because I've proved to myself that I can do these things and I can hold my own with people.'[46] Estelle Armitage, on the other hand, described the experience as one of 'levelling down'. The major change for her, as a result of joining the ATS in Jamaica and coming to Britain, was her re-evaluation of her relationship as a Black woman to the white people whom, as a middle-class Jamaican, she regarded as her social inferiors. Speaking of her upbringing in Jamaica, Estelle said, 'some white people, I wouldn't associate with some of them. I thought I was a better class than them'. Estelle explained that the ATS made a great difference to this: 'I ... learned to respect people that I thought were below me. Nobody is below you, people are what they are, and you accept them at face value.' Estelle was sure that this change in herself was beneficial: 'it made me a better person'.[47] Other women echoed her sentiments in statements such as 'I learned that to be rough isn't always to be bad ... you learned how to live with people, get on with people of all kinds, and who had come from all walks of life'.[48]

The only ex-servicewoman in the group of interviewees who gave a consistently stoic account of service, Barbara Wilson, provides an interesting counterpoint to this construction. Barbara was the privately-educated daughter of a relatively prosperous London businessman. She, like others, commented on the social education she received in the WRNS, but did not draw from it a 'levelling' conclusion. On the contrary, her account suggests an affirmation of her prior social position:

> You were all from very different stratas and areas of the country. I mean everybody had totally different backgrounds, you know, on the whole, say. One didn't really meet anyone perhaps that you felt was from the house-next-door from one at home. And that's not being snobbish in any way, it was just we were all different, and practically everybody one met came from the North of England or Yorkshire.

And my husband would say the same, and of course he was in the Air Force ... but everybody seemed to come from Yorkshire or Scotland, a few from Wales. It was very strange, you know, one came to the conclusion that where one came from was a very small part of England ... it was a very good education.[49]

In spite of this 'good education' in the characteristics of regional populations, Barbara sustained a sense of difference rather than commonality. It is expressed in her use of the impersonal and generalised 'one' which maintains the sense of self-as-norm in her statement. It belies her denial of 'being snobbish', which itself can be seen as a bid to enlist the support of her (equally well-spoken) interviewer in her expression of memories of personal differentiation which she knew conflicted with both the wartime and the 1990s rhetoric of social inclusiveness. The 'very small part of England' remains where 'one' would want to be, rather than in 'the North', 'Yorkshire', 'Scotland' or 'Wales'. This was not part of a story of an altered sense of self resulting from war service, but of a journey of social discovery, from which 'one' returned to 'one's' preferred lifestyle and social milieu.

Some of the 'heroes' extended their accounts of the inner changes produced by growing social awareness into discussions of other types of realignment of their social and political perceptions. Joyce Greaves was one of those who implied that they moved in a leftward direction:

It made me grow up. It made some of the things that you worried about when you were, you know, in those days, it made you realise how stupid it was, that life is for living and don't worry about the little things. It's the big things that you wanted to get sorted out in life really. You got an interest in various things, in politics and that, for a time, that we didn't have before.[50]

Speaking in the summer of 1992, the thirteenth year of Conservative governments consistently repressive of popular and participatory political culture, Joyce added, 'I've lost interest in that now'.[51] Others who did not refer to party politics indicated that the wartime process of maturation had involved a parallel growth in their sense of identification with the nation as a political entity.[52]

The theme of growing up was strong in the heroes' accounts. Stories of the development of new understandings of common humanity and the dawning of political awareness were often accompanied by the comment, 'I grew up'.[53] So, too, were descriptions of leaving a former state of uncertainty about personal competence and emotional and economic dependency. The changes accompanying wartime service were cast in terms of maturation, implying self-improvement, and manifest in feelings of greater confidence and self-sufficiency. These qualities were central to the masculine attainment of maturity in psychological theory.[54] Women's self-application of these concepts implied a changed gender identity of the sort that Priestley and M-O suggested. To some of the women interviewed this was the result of acquiring new skills and, more than this, of discovering a lifelong capacity to learn. For example, Katharine Hughes commented, 'I've proved to myself that I can do these things ... I mean I can adapt myself to anything'.[55] Gladys French reflected, 'It gave me a lot of confidence, I suppose, to think that we'd done all these different things and been all these different places. I suppose it did change my attitude, that I would tackle everything';[56] and Felicity Snow said, 'Made me more confident as a person, made you much more independent and whatever is thrown at you, you feel you can get on with it'.[57]

Sometimes the feeling of greater confidence was specifically linked to doing 'men's work' successfully. Ann Tomlinson said of the way the war changed her:

I felt that it had added a tremendous lot of experience to my life that I wouldn't have had, and may have made quite a difference to my feeling of myself as a woman ... It meant really that I felt capable of doing things that I would normally have expected just men to do. I could do it, and I had proven that I could do it, and I had achieved something in that world. And had to compete with men for further promotion and that sort of thing, had done it successfully ... It helped me to feel confident and very satisfied really.[58]

The currency of the idea that war service gave women a sense of equality with men, as writers like Scott and M-O suggested and those like Paterson feared, is indicated by negative testimony about change. We have seen that Myrna Wraith made a spontaneous reference to the social confidence she felt she possessed before she joined the Forces in explanation of her negative response to the question about wartime change. In a parallel way, Amy O'Connor responded to the question 'Did war service change the way you thought about yourself?' with an emphatic 'No' and went on to refer without prompting to a pre-existing sense of the injustice of the idea that women were the inferior sex. 'Just felt the same. I've always felt like that. Always thought women were more important than men.'[59]

Only one of the 'heroes' expressed scepticism about the inter-viewers' question itself, and hence about the discourse of war and change which the question bore inexplicitly on its back. Amabel Ingram, who had been brought up in an impoverished landed family and whose high-class education had been frequently interrupted on account of the family's financial predicament, suggested that the personal changes she remembered would have happened with or without service in the WRNS, war or no war.

> I don't know if it was the wartime experiences, because I was older, I was four years older when I came out, and I'd met a lot of people and lived with a lot of people, which is different from just living with a family, so I was fairly confident – more confident I think than when I went in. But I don't think I was ever lacking in confidence when I went in, poor education and all. I didn't particularly feel it. I don't think – other than just you know, sort of living with other people and I won't say learning to get on with people because I think I got on well with people anyway. But no, I don't think it changed me very much. I can't remember in what way it changed me at all, excepting I was obviously more confident because I was used to travelling ... and finding my way around and this sort of thing. But as I say I wouldn't put that down exactly to being in the Wrens, but simply to four years experience of living.[60]

In general, then, ex-servicewomen who gave 'heroic' accounts of their wartime service subscribed to the ideas concerning change ensconced in the discourse of war and modernity. They became better and more complete people, losing the inhibitions of a secluded existence, understanding their common social and physi-cal, spiritual and corporeal humanity with others, gaining a sense of identification with the nation and acquiring a new gender identity. If experiences in the women's forces produced none of these changes in a 'heroic' servicewoman, it was not because they did not occur, but because she already possessed these attributes. Stoic members of the Forces also regarded the experience as 'doing them good'. However, they meant that the war confirmed their tradi-tional views rather than transforming their outlook. Barbara Wilson was glad to get back to her 'very small part of England' having discovered 'how the rest of the world lived'. Edith Dixon was 'more appreciative of my home afterwards'.[61]

Civilian women's narratives of change

So far we have explored stories of personal change told by women in the Services. What about civilians? In some of the public accounts of women and wartime change no distinction was drawn between military and civilian women. It was suggested of all women that 'the curtain ... which divided [them] from the troubles and trials of the nation' had been lifted by the war, from which new feminine citizens would emerge.[62] The women who constructed heroic accounts of their civilian war work expressed themselves in similar terms to the ex-servicewomen. They spoke of gaining a deeper knowledge of humanity as a result of their war work, of developing a new sense of competence, and of release from restrictive homes.

The oldest among them, Moira Underwood, born in 1908 into a lower middle-class family, echoed the comments of servicewomen about gaining a deeper knowledge of humanity as a result of her war work. Moira became a storekeeper at a ROF in 1939, after working as a hairdresser for seventeen years. In spite of her long experience of work in contact with the public, she thought the war opened new doors for her:

> It did really, yes. I was much more outgoing, I think after the war ... I could get on with people easy. Although I'd been hairdressing all those years, you know, I had to sort – I found that – I thought I'd get on with any type at all after the war, when I met all the different kinds of people I'd met, you know. And I think I was more outgoing, more at ease with people really ... It was a worthwhile experience I think.[63]

Marianne Lloyd, who became an engineering draughtswoman after several years of clerical work, described a similar sense of personal development. She spoke of the broadening of her occupational horizons and the satisfaction she gained from her war work.[64] She emphasised her release from her restricted home and sense of growing up: 'I was very naive when war started. We were children in those days, literally children. And by the time it ended, you know, I was feeling far more mature ... it took me out into the world which I wouldn't have been out in before'.[65]

Beryl Bramley's account of becoming a member of the AID had

the same quality of release. Beryl (in contrast to Edith Dixon) celebrated the effect of the war in freeing her from what she described
as the 'spoiled life' of an overprotected daughter, who had not only
had little freedom but had 'not had to make any decisions about
anything at all'.[66] She linked this to a sense of confidence derived
from the competences she acquired during the war: 'I think that was
the breakthrough for me, because otherwise ... if it hadn't been for
the war, I don't know whether I would have had the courage to do
the things that I had done, or sort of the audacity to enter into
things that I hardly know anything about'.[67] She was referring to
pursuing a wide variety of jobs after the war in response to her sense
of frustration and boredom with home life as a wife and mother.
Her story drew upon the modernising narratives of Scott and M-
On. Young women war workers who had proved themselves during
the war would quickly recognise the limitations of domesticity and
family afterwards, and insist on a life outside the home.[68]

    Several of the themes of wartime transformation came together
in Emily Porter's account. As we saw in the last chapter, Emily's
story was of intense domestic and occupational confinement, from
birth into her twenties, exacerbated by her physical disability. All
this was changed by her war work in Postal Censorship, which she
described in terms not just of physical and social, but also of psychological, unshackling. 'It broadened my experience, because you
got into other people's minds really. And you learnt things you'd
never thought you'd learn, and of course also you learnt all the technical side. Oh yes it broadened my outlook. It made me really grow
up.'[69] Emily also emphasised the capacities to manage people (colleagues and clients) which war work developed in her: 'You had to
be able to criticise people, at the same time keeping their good will.
Well later on you see, I dealt with what I call the submerged tenth,
in the worst areas, murderers, prostitutes, all sorts of people, difficult people, very nice people a lot of them. So it was a help in my
later job. Oh definitely.'[70]

    Women who composed 'heroic' accounts of their wartime lives,
in civilian work as well as in the Forces, worked with the subject
position offered by the discourse of war and modernity. Their stories of personal purification were central to the construction of
'heroic' narratives. The hero was seeking a high standard of performance in pursuit of the honourable goal of war service, and the
dross of personal imperfections must be left behind. The discourse

of expanded horizons leading to improved social consciousness and a new sense of feminine citizenship, provided a framework within which to cast the account.

'Stoic' civilians and wartime change

A great deal more doubt about whether the war had changed their lives characterised the women who told stories of stoically putting up with civilian war work. Statements to the effect that war service had not changed the way that 'stoics' felt about themselves, either negatively or positively, were as pervasive as the confidence of the 'heroes' in the profoundly beneficial personal effects of war service, whether military or civilian. The short, terse comments of the stoics on the matter are striking.

For example, Evelyn Mills, pre-war clerk and wartime duplicator operator at the Admiralty, said in response to the question 'Did the war change you?', 'I don't think so, no'. Dorothy Rose, clerical worker in the Ministry of Food, said it was 'hard to say'. Hester Hamilton, who reluctantly left university to become a progress chaser in an aircraft factory, said, 'Not at all, I don't think so', as did Helena Balfour, pre-war domestic servant and wartime aircraft assembler: 'I don't think so, I don't think so really'. Similarly Wilma Harrison who moved from upholstery to engineering, said, 'I don't know, I can't think, just part of your life, isn't it?'. Elizabeth Little, who was sent from a grocer's shop to an engineering factory, said, 'I don't know that it changed me', and Edith Singleton, who also left shopwork, in her case for welding in an engineering works, said emphatically, 'No, it didn't change me at all'. Fiona Thomas, who moved from shopwork to an aircraft factory and eventually became a wartime bus conductress, was equally negative: 'No, not really, no I don't think so'. Reflecting on the question about personal turning-points, Fiona Thomas identified a much more recent shift in the way she felt herself to be socially defined and hence regarded herself. The main change in her life, she said, was not caused by the war but by becoming an old-age pensioner: 'I can't explain it, it's just a feeling that you're no longer wanted, you're on the scrap heap'.[71] Not even her dismissal from work as a bus conductress when the men came back (which she resented) compared with this transformation in her self-esteem.

Only two members of this group readily assented to the idea of personal change. However, the changes they described were not positively transformative ones. One was Yvette Baynes, whose testimony we shall review later in this chapter. The other was Sadie Bartlett, daughter of a working-class family in rural Norfolk. She had tried to avoid the call-up, but eventually moved from hairdressing into the Timber Corps of the Women's Land Army. Sadie's account drew both on the modernising account of women's emergence from blinkered seclusion due to the war, and on the language of feminist understandings of sexual politics of the 1970s and 1980s. Her response to the question about change was 'I think I grew up a lot, because after having been in a village, I think I was quite innocent when I went out into the world'.[72] She went on to explain that her wartime experiences replaced innocence about relations between the sexes with an understanding that they were prejudicial to women. Men had control at work, and used this to their own advantage; men also had sexual power over women. Sadie spoke of learning about sexual harassment in a number of contexts, at work in the woods where the 'countrymen' could 'be very brash and rough and hands up your skirts and whatnot',[73] and in one of her billets where the landlord was a peeping tom, who stood at the door of the wash house when she was bathing.[74] In her account she also learned an assertive way of coping, consistent with feminist recommendations of the 1970s about combating sexual harassment. She 'kicked' the countrymen and ran, or 'looked at them and said, "What the hell are you doing?"'; she and her fellow Land Girl engaged in 'battles' with their landlord, 'to keep that door shut'.[75]

Hitch-hiking in particular educated Sadie in the sexual threat present in adult life and the ways in which a young woman could cope. Sadie told a striking story of an attempted assault in a dark lane, and how her Land Army uniform and her own courage and assertiveness saved her. A man stopped and got out of a van telling Sadie that 'she knew what he wanted'. In her account she took him on, saying, '"Right mate! I'm stronger than you. You look a bit weedy! But one thing, you've got to get my trousers off first and that's rather difficult. You've got to undress me. I don't mind if you want to try, I'll come off best."' This assertive response disarmed the man, who drove away, only to come back later and meekly take her to her destination after promising that he was not going to 'start anything'.[76]

Learning the ways of the world, for Sadie, involved developing a particular kind of gender awareness. The war made no difference to the gender hierarchy, which was as it always had been, based on men's sexual, economic and political power, linked to their greater physical strength. War work revealed to the 'innocent' Sadie the implications of that hierarchy for her as a woman. But in her account the conditions of war itself produced the changes which enabled her to deal with her experiences of male sexual power. In the changed circumstances of the post-war world, and particularly of old age, she might not have been able to manage in the same way. Emerging from her vivid narration of the hitch-hiking story to reflect upon the wartime self she was describing, and its credibility to both her present-day self and her riveted interviewer, Sadie said: 'I wasn't worried or anything. I wasn't – you know, it don't seem possible, does it? I'd be scared stiff now if I was left on a country road!'.[77] When asked if war service changed her in any other ways she said, 'No, I think, really. I suppose in a way you knew that men were always going to be favoured against you'.[78] It was the opposite understanding to the message of equality and opportunity in the modernising discourse. It meshed with the 1970s feminist analysis of women's subordinate position at work and at home and echoed the 'continuity' thesis about the effects of the Second World War on gender relations. But Sadie distanced herself from the oppositional-ism of the feminism of the recent past. Referring to a recent charge of sexual harassment against a doctor for allegedly touching a woman patient's breasts, Sadie said, 'Sometimes when I think now how people demand this that and the other, and I think, "My god, what I've done in my time" you know, and I just have to laugh at them to be quite honest ... I mean as I say a man's only got to sort of brush past you and somebody's said they've been abused'.[79] Sadie's interpretation of the gender imbalance was resigned. She might have dealt on an individual basis with male power and other adversities, but in general 'you just accepted it, that was your life and that was it'.[80]

How do we understand the remarkably consistent negative replies about personal change of those who gave 'stoic' accounts of their war service? It is plausible to suggest that those who had not chosen war work, but regarded it as an unfortunate necessity, did not want or expect to change as a result of the war. Construction of a stoic identity in relation to wartime service involved distancing oneself from the idea that war work could have produced positive personal change. These women expected to maintain their existing sense of identity, which most of them, as we have seen in earlier chapters, constructed as conventionally feminine. They welded in skirts, enjoyed the 'harmless fun' of banter between the sexes and felt glad to swap war work for 'women's work' in 1945 or 1946. The story of the modernising effects of the war on women was not useful to these women as a language and set of concepts in which to frame their experiences. The war left intact the stoics' pre-war sense of themselves as women. Only in Sadie's account, informed by the concepts of 1970s feminism, did the war cause her to discover the negative side of what such an identity might mean in the 'real world' of unequal power relations between the sexes. But her stoicism led to resignation rather than to the collective agency advocated by recent feminism.

Part of the maintenance of a pre-war identity involved retaining a sense of social (as distinct from gender) position. We have already observed this in the case of the 'stoic' Wren, Barbara Wilson. Barbara was middle class, but such a view could be taken by working-class women too. Helena Balfour, pre-war domestic servant and wartime assembler in an aircraft factory, referred even more explicitly to the way in which her wartime education in social difference confirmed her own position rather than (as in heroic accounts) having a levelling effect. If she had not been sent by the state,

> no way would I have gone into factory work. Well when I saw some of the young people, and as I say there was nothing wrong with their character or anything, they were just a wee bit rough and ready in their speech, but I wouldn't have been happy mixing with them all the time on a conveyor belt or something like that.[81]

However, 'stoics' did not always produce clear-cut rejection or acceptance of the public account of the beneficial effects of wartime social mixing. For some women the growth in awareness of social difference was not easily resolved, either by an understanding of becoming more equal, or by a decision (whether conscious or not) to maintain difference. One woman in particular, ex-bank clerk and wartime lathe operator Nora Vickers, recalled the discomfort she felt in trying to live with the wartime disturbance to her social identity. She appreciated the 'education' in social difference which she acquired. She learned to value the 'rough and ready' factory women with whom she worked, who smoked and swore, and who were frank with each other about personal matters like sex and the body. However, by the end of the war she felt that she was still not really one of them, although by this time she did not fit in with her lower middle-class family either. In listing things she particularly disliked about war work she mentioned 'not seeing the friends that I had before' and then went on to explain:

> I also felt a bit of a division within myself because I was now, sort of – I mean in a slightly different world, of these sort of words that we wouldn't have used, your accent changes to a certain extent, probably becomes even more, you know – I know I've always had a, you know, a Lancashire accent, but probably becomes a bit more – a bit broader. Yeah, I think as I said before, I think sometimes, I was slightly hurt by the bluntness, but mainly I liked the people very much, and the sense of comradeship, and I liked the sort of openness and lack of formality. [But] I remember my mother saying to me once, my grandmother used to say 'don't stand like that – you look like a factory girl' ... And my mother once said to me, 'You know what Grandma Talbot would say, don't stand like that –!' and I said, 'But I am a factory girl!' ... So there was this slight difference which seemed awful and I didn't like that. I mean I like this business about if you like singing 'Roll Out The Barrel', then sing 'Roll Out The Barrel', and let's all be merry and gay, sort of thing ... But on the other hand it was – it was also something that people thought 'oh that's not done' sort of thing. So it was just this difference of the two worlds, you sort of felt isolated back from your own ... I can remember what I said to my sister was 'I sort of feel that I'm part of neither world', being in tears about that.[82]

Personal change and the horrors of war

As we saw in chapter 3, one of the characteristics of the stoics' accounts was reconstruction of their anxieties about the menace of war: about death and fear, loss and grief. Yvette Baynes was the other 'stoic' who, like Sadie Bartlett, did not emphatically deny change. Yvette's account, however, had a very different focus from Sadie's. Her answer to the question about whether the war changed her was, 'Oh I'm sure yes. They were very very happy days, apart from the fact that you had a lot of friends killed, and you never knew when you were going to be killed, and you never knew when you were going to wake up and find that your best friend had gone, as I did one day. You know, I think it changed everyone'.[83] Recall of such experiences in the context of 'personal change' gave a different meaning to the process of maturation from that which the 'heroes' gave it. Peggy Peters, secretary at a naval base, said that the proximity to death had an ageing effect: 'I think it makes you more grown up. The boy I was engaged to was killed ... I think it makes you older really before your time'.[84]

Rather than the war reducing anxiety by putting worries in perspective, as in the accounts of 'heroes' like Gladys French and Joyce Greaves, the war made 'stoics' more anxious. Evelyn Mills who, as we saw in chapter 3, repeatedly referred to her dread of war-factory accidents and bombing, qualified her denial that the war changed her in the following way: 'It might have helped you to grow up quicker. You know, where before you might have been more happy-go-lucky and not worry about a thing, I think after any experience of anything to do with wartime, I think it makes you realise a little bit of difference, you know'.[85]

It was not the case that those who told heroic stories of their wartime work were completely insouciant, or that they did not recall, like the 'stoics', experiences of anxiety and loss. Joyce Greaves was one of the 'heroes' who said that the war 'gave us freedom which we didn't have really before',[86] and that it helped her to put issues in political perspective. She suffered a devastating personal tragedy, but in contrast to the stoics, she related it to the positive version of the effects of the war on individuals:

> Oh it changed you, definitely. It must have done. You can't have all those experiences and particularly getting married and being widowed by the time you're 21 – it all has an effect on you. It's bound to do, isn't it? It either makes or mars you I think. I think I got quite a lot out of it really.[87]

It is characteristic of a heroic narrative to present setbacks and problems as trials which temper and refine the character, as Joyce did. Her construction 'It makes or mars you ... I got a lot out of it' is quite different in its optimism from Peggy Peters' view of wartime tragedy making you 'old before your time', or Yvette Baynes' lament for the almost unbearable loss of friends during the war.

Personal change and marriage

Marriage, as we have seen, was regarded as a vital, almost inevitable, part of a woman's life in both the modernising and the

traditional strands of the discourse of the effects of war. But the orientation to marriage within each was quite distinct. The modernising story gave it a less dominant position than the traditional
account: modern marriages were to be relatively equal and companionate; marriage and motherhood could be combined with outside activities. The traditional account explicitly rejected such a
prospect. Marriage and motherhood represented fulfilment for
women; a gendered hierarchy and a division of labour within marriage embodied happiness for men and women and stability for
society.

The salience of marriage in 1940s discourses of femininity makes
it unsurprising that marriage in itself was not a differentiating factor
between the two groups, the 'heroes' and the 'stoics'. All but four of
the forty-two women married. The representation of marriage as
essential and inevitable, however, and the concomitant negative
images of the 'frustrated and embittered' spinster,[88] left little cultural space for those who did not get married. These constructions
contributed to the notion that the life of an unmarried woman was
a life in deficit. The silence of the interviewers on the subject in the
case of the four spinsters in the sample was the product of embar-
rassment: how could the question 'why didn't you marry?' be asked
without evoking a sense of failure, given the discourse surrounding
marriage? One of the women did, however, use the invitation to add
anything she wanted at the end of the interview, to explain her
single status. Gladys French drew on the positive construction of
the 'career woman', who was throughout life a 'free agent', in order
to do so. She located her decision to stay single in the historical context of the marriage bar (even though by 1946 when she trained to
be a teacher the bar had been officially lifted under the 1944 Education Act), emphasising that the 'position for women is different
now'. She presented her single status as a choice based on her commitment to her post-war career as a teacher, while deftly dismissing
the idea that she might have been sexually or psychologically
repressed or frustrated.

> In our day, if you decided on this sort of career, you certainly
> remained a single woman, although you probably had your fun, but
> now you could do everything more. The position of women in my day,
> when, if you had a career, you had a career. In fact you got the sack if
> you got married. But I think that times are better now, when women
> can choose more, although I don't regret, because I've had a good life

anyway. I mean I went off to New Zealand for a year and things like that on an exchange and had a great time, so all these opportunities were open to us which wouldn't have been perhaps if you were married, so I don't regret one bit of it really.[89]

The other single women, although silent on the subject of marriage, like Gladys constructed positive accounts of the way that war had changed them. They all looked back on the war as a period of great personal significance. None of the stoics remained single.

Just as it is not possible to differentiate the 'stoics' and the 'heroes' in relation to the occurrence of marriage, so 'stoics' and 'heroes' among the thirty-eight who did marry did not behave differently in terms of their combination of marriage and paid work. Conforming to post-war trends all but two of those who married combined paid work, either part-time or full-time, with marriage at some point after the war.[90] But there was a contrast between stoics and heroes in the ways in which they spoke of marriage, in terms of who they married and how they felt about marriage, motherhood and home life.

Several women who gave heroic accounts referred to making very different marriages from those which had been expected of them. For example Katharine Hughes got married in 1943: 'I mean I was engaged to someone else when I was called up. I never married him. I married someone else. We met and married within about six weeks.'[91] She described a truly whirlwind romance. She went out for tea just once with the man she later married, thinking no more would come of it because he was 'just an ordinary private' in the Army, whereas she was a wireless/telegraphist in the WRNS, which meant that officially they should not have associated. What is more she was at the time dating his Captain. However, this man had made up his mind.

> My father and mother had a café, they had a business in Old Kent Road and he went to my father and just said to my father, 'I'm going to marry your daughter'. And when I came home on leave, my father said to me, 'I've had a fellow here. I think he's a bit nutty'. I said 'Why?' 'He said he's going to marry you!' So I just laughed.[92]

Within weeks they were indeed married. Katharine said proudly that the marriage lasted for forty-four years, until her husband's death in 1987. A similar sense of the fun of Forces courtships came through other accounts. Janice Brunton said that when she was stationed in Scotland, 'I was friendly with a Chief Petty Officer who had a motor bike and at the time when I was not supposed to be going out of the camp I would be on the pillion, and he would just sail through you see, and it was lovely because we used to go all round the lochs'.[93] Joyce Greaves, a WAAF radar operator, described getting married in 1943 after such a courtship. As in Katharine Hughes' case there was an imbalance in rank between her and her lover, though it was the other way round. 'I mean my first husband, he was a commissioned pilot you see, and we used to meet off the site. In fact he used to put on a sergeant's jacket and come to our dances, you know. Oh you did all kind of crazy things like that and got away with it'.[94] The excitement was enhanced by breaking disciplinary rules in order to pursue the romance, which was special in part because it was an independent liaison with someone from outside the family circle. Such stories of courtship and marriage were consistent with accounts of liberation from home and family, and of gaining a sense of freedom as a result of the war. Mary Mackenzie, one of those who met and married her husband while she was in the Forces, identified the man himself as part of the effect she felt that the war had on her: 'It gave me more confidence in myself, plus the husband that I've got, he has given me an awful lot of confidence'.[95]

Another characteristic of the accounts of the 'heroes' was ambivalence and restlessness about the experiences of marriage and motherhood at the end of the war. For example, Heather McLaren said that, on leaving the WAAF, she 'was quite excited about getting home to be with my husband and expecting my baby, that sort of helped a lot from leaving my job. But I'll say this much, when I came home I found it very difficult to settle. I felt I always had to be on the go. I missed all the company … civilian life seemed very humdrum after what we had had. And yet I mean I was happy, I was happily married. It was very difficult trying to settle.'[96] The change in subject position was what made it 'hard to settle'. The construction of the independent young woman doing a vital job in order to serve her country in wartime was at the opposite pole to the by no means exceptional identity of 'young wife and mother'. Women who, like Heather McLaren, reconstructed themselves as 'happily married' and glad to have children in the post-war years, could nevertheless recall the emotional discomfort of exchanging roles. Katharine Hughes, although keen to marry after her whirlwind romance, and proud of having two children close together in 1947 and 1948, spoke of feeling 'let down' as a new wife and mother. 'You just went in for a humdrum life back to the kitchen sink.'[97] Beryl Bramley described herself as resenting the effects of pregnancy and child-birth on her career, and set herself apart from the maternalism assumed of women in the traditional discourse: 'I can't actually truthfully say that I'm a motherly type ... I'm not one of those people who yearned for – some people yearned for children and all that.'[98]

The most ambivalent and unresolved account was that of Greta Lewis, an ex-weaver from Yorkshire. She married a soldier in 1941, while she was an anti-aircraft gun operator in the ATS, but her mar-riage meant that her desire for travel and adventure was thwarted: 'We volunteered all over. We volunteered to go to Africa. Well we couldn't go there because if you were married your husband's offi-cer had to sign the – so you couldn't forge his signature because they had to have the battery stamp and everything on it, so that had to go'.[99] She could possibly have been posted with her husband 'but I didn't want to go because I were going to lose all my friends. We stayed together all the time you see. And they were nice friends'.[100] Then she found she was pregnant. The authorities immediately laid her off work until the end of her third month, when she would be dismissed. During this idle time she became bored and frustrated and started to want to leave. She told a dramatic story of 'running away' one night.

> One night I got so fed up because my friend, she were pregnant and she'd been home ages so I thought, 'Oh I'm going'. And this, we were at Crewe. I went through the barbed wire, down the country lane, pitch dark. But you had to go through a cemetery. That were the only way you could get to where the trains was and that. You'd to go through this churchyard. Well as I got to the churchyard the clock started striking 12 and it were right frosty. I always remember it were right frosty. Well I daren't go no further. Oh I thought, 'Oh I'll have to go back'. I daren't go through this churchyard at 12 o'clock. And as I'm going back there's lights flashing all over the camp and they're all shouting 'Curly [Lewis], Curly [Lewis]'. But I never answered. And I went back through the barbed wire, crept up to my [hut]. 'Oh,' they said, 'Curly everybody's looking for you'. Anyway they got me a pot of cocoa and I had to go and see Ma'am next morning. She said, 'What would your husband have said if something had've happened to you?'

I thought, 'Well I don't know'. I didn't care, but I came home the week after. So I did something good.[101]

However, Greta proceeded to contradict this account of satisfaction with her own agency in obtaining her release ('I did something good'). She followed the fluently told, melodramatic story of her attempted flight through the churchyard by denying, in short, terse answers to questions, that she wanted to leave the ATS at all. There was a special inter-subjective stimulus to her memory, in that I, the interviewer, was, at eight months, conspicuously pregnant. My prompts to Greta to reflect on the causes and consequences of her own pregnancy apparently led her to voice feelings which had hitherto been unacknowledged, and remained almost unspeakable. The dialogue in the interview went as follows:

Q: You were pleased that the waiting around was over ...?
A: No, I didn't want to come home at all. I didn't want to be pregnant.
Q: Did you not? It was an accident?
A: Well, he wanted me out. It were him that wanted me to come out, you see.
Q: Did he want you at home?
A: Yes, he didn't want me in the Army.
Q: Why not?
A: I don't know.
Q: Too much freedom?
A: Happen so. Might have thought I'd got off with somebody else. I don't know, love.[102]

Earlier in the interview Greta had described her departure from the gunsite, emphasising in this first iteration the distress about leaving which she returned to after the story of trying to escape. 'The sergeant major called a parade up ... and they all came to the gate to me and they all sang "Will ye no' come back again" and I cried all the way to the bus station. Well I didn't want to go home. I think I didn't want to go and live with my mother'.[103] In this version of her departure it was her authoritarian mother who was the remembered cause of her tears. She and her husband had no house of their own (a common predicament in the 1940s) and spent the first years of their marriage after the war in Greta's parents' house. Greta regained her former fluency when the interviewer had ceased to probe her contradictory story of leaving the ATS. After the discussion quoted above, in which she cited her husband's role in forcing the pregnancy upon her as the cause of her distress, she spoke of the early years of motherhood. She remembered intense loneliness which her pleasure in having a child did not offset:

> I used to cry every morning at 10 o'clock when I used to imagine them all going in the NAAFI ... I used to just sit wondering what they were all doing you see. Of course you slept together like ... there were a lot of us in each Nissen hut ... So you missed all that because you were on your own when you came home weren't you?[104]

The phrase 'on your own' cannot be taken literally, since Greta was not on her own, but with her mother, her daughter and, when he was home on leave and then demobilised, her husband. It stood for swapping the conviviality and equality with other young women in the ATS, and their male Army colleagues, for the position of dependency upon, and subordination to, the authority of her mother and her husband. Greta found herself a part-time job in a post office, taking the baby to work with her, rather than continue to suffer domestic misery 'alone'.

The restlessness recalled by Heather McLaren, Katharine Hughes, Beryl Bramley, Mary Mackenzie and Greta Lewis was at the heart of the account of the modernising effects of war on women. No longer satisfied with the traditional role of wife and mother after the wartime discovery of their true identities, women, according to this story, found new ways of life subsequently. Their 'modern' feminine style, based on companionate marriages[105] and a combination of paid work and domesticity, was less secluded and confined than the traditional version. The curtain had been lifted on their lives, they had been let out of the cage.

Waiting and watching for the men to return

Those who told stoic stories did, on the whole, experience the war as 'long and weary years of separation', and they did welcome the restoration of home and family at its end. 'It was such a feeling of relief when the war was over,' said Yvette Baynes.[106] Evelyn Mills referred to the 'wonderful times during the war, when somebody was coming home on leave' and her feeling of joy when the man she was to marry returned from 'his Indian four years'.[107] Joan Stanton depicted in traditionalist terms the atmosphere in 1945, when she

obtained her release from her wartime secretarial job in Cheltenham and returned to her family home in London. 'It wasn't a
question of thinking how you could better yourself, you just had
to get the war over. Then of course I suppose a lot of them had
probably got – well loved ones to come home, and then of course
it was all a different life for everybody wasn't it?'. But as far as
Joan herself was concerned, 'I didn't have ever any problem adjusting'.[108]

The recollections of the stoics of courtship and marriage were of
more sedate affairs than those of the heroes, often with men they
had known for many years and who were already part of their home
lives. This could have been a simple consequence of working during
the war in offices or factories in their home towns, in contrast to the
servicewomen's greater mobility and opportunities for new social
contacts. But it applied as much to the 'mobile' Edith Dixon, whose
account of her experiences in the WRNS moved from heroic to
stoic, as to women in civilian work. She spoke of her relief in
obtaining her discharge to marry 'a Church of Scotland Minister
who had been our Minister in the Church at Prestwick where I
taught in the Sunday School and sang in the choir and my father was
the treasurer'.[109] Those who, like Edith, told stoic stories did, on the
whole, see themselves as the women who waited and watched for
men to return from war. In contrast to the intense regrets of some
of the heroes, such as Greta Lewis, about the loss of female conviviality marked by the end of the war, Dorothy Rose who had been
working almost entirely with women in the Manchester offices of
the Ministry of Food, said, 'You were pleased to see some of the
men coming back I think, you know, and mixing with them a little
bit. No, it was nice that it wasn't a woman's world any more, you
know, with getting back to normal'.[110]

The references which the stoics made to their marriages suggested that, even if there was a sense of inevitability about getting
married, that was what they wanted at the time. They were not
plagued by the uncertainties of the heroes, and whatever happened
to the marriage later did not affect their reconstruction of its auspi-
cious beginning. Perhaps because of these unproblematic memories,
few commented at any length on courtship and marriage, even
though all the stoics married. An interesting exception, however,
was Caroline Woodward. After a reluctant start in war work, as we
have seen, she eventually became enthusiastic about her wartime job

as a welder and regretted having to leave it at the end of the war. Reflecting on the subject of whether war work changed her, she said: 'Aye I wished it had ... Maybe I could have stood up for myself a wee bit better. But no, I just got married you see and that was that'.[111] Caroline Woodward constructed herself as an unconfident person, after the war as before it, in her marriage as well as in her life as the daughter of a mother who, as we saw in chapter 2, never allowed her a minute to herself. Her account contrasts both with the heroes' stories of personal development prompted by the war and with the stoics' accounts of contented acceptance of a return to a traditional feminine role. Caroline's comment placed her between the modernising and traditional narratives of war and social change. While acknowledging the personal change that might have happened as a result of war work, she communicated the idea that marriage as an end in itself was what she had expected and even wanted at the time. It was as if the interview caused her to review the life she understood within a traditionalist framework, from the vantage point of the modernising narrative, and to regret retrospectively the opportunities she felt she had denied herself in the past.

Conclusion

The women interviewed for this book were as polarised by the question 'Did the war change you?' as they were by their accounts of the meaning of call-up and participation in the war effort, and the polarisation went along the same lines. Those who saw the war effort as something to be endured, who 'just got on with it' until the welcome release of demobilisation, did not construct it as having changed them. If it taught them anything new, the lessons were negative. They were about coping individually and collectively with adversity, with tragedy and with fear, whether produced by military aggression, by perilous war work, or by the iniquities of the male sex. For these women, personal change of the sort posed by the discourse of modernity was not on the agenda. They did not expect the war to lift a curtain or open a door on their lives. They framed their wartime stories in terms of continuity with what women had always been: low paid workers, for whom the satisfactions of marriage, children, home-making and life (with all its variety and complications) in the bosom of the family were sufficient.

Women, on the other hand, who welcomed the war effort, who

strove to participate 'as close to the front line as a woman could get', constructed narratives structured by the concept of change. It began with the welcome upheaval of leaving one life for another, and continued with the story of learning and applying new skills and of mixing with unfamiliar social groups, both male and female. It ended with the experience, with demobilisation, of the abrupt end to war work which threatened to foreclose the changed identity. Whether they saw themselves with regrets, as subsequently marginalised by the traditional construction of femininity in relation to their former position of centrality to the war effort, or as making the further transition from wartime to peacetime opportunities, which modern versions of femininity invited and applauded, depended not on simple determinants like social class, age or education. It depended on how they 'took up as their own' the models of what it meant to be a woman, available to them during and after the war. It depended on their 'modes of female identification', that is 'the different ways in which women confront the institutions that reproduce and dictate social models of and for women'.[112] As we have seen, those models were confusing and contradictory. Even women who told confident stories conducive to the maintenance of their self-esteem about one part of their lives, became less secure in their narratives of other parts. 'Life is full of fork roads', said Kate Lomax when reflecting on her marriage and post-war life.[113] How did you choose which way to go, how did you know who to be? Recalling a life meant remembering the discourses in which that life could be explained.

If this book has argued anything at a general level, beyond insisting upon a relationship between the details of the fascinating and moving memories of individual women and larger cultural representations, it is this. The numerous public accounts of how women have been and should be do not now and have not in the past constituted a unified culture of femininity. The fragments, nevertheless, powerfully define, regulate and hence control the stories which it is possible to tell about oneself. The lines of fracture produced by the tensions between the different versions, reduce the possibility of subjective coherence. Recent feminism unsettles older stories of opportunities for women. Those accounts in turn negotiate space for themselves against the pressures of traditional stories of women's lives. The women who, in the foregoing pages, have deployed these accounts in reconstructing their own wartime lives, have by reiterating them anew also contributed to their public form, to their presence in popular memory.

This book is itself part of discourse. It belongs within the historical debate about the effects of the war on women's subjectivities. I have tried to reorient that debate towards the issue of what women were told its effects would be and how those ideas inform their own interpretations. The book also has a place within the autobiographical preoccupations of the 1990s: the concern to confess, understand and thus lay claim to a life, as well as to cope with its incoherence and confusions. I have learned from writing it why I was upset in 1977 by the two women at the adult education meeting, who told me that my story about the war was wrong. I did not have at my disposal at that time a way of understanding both our stories as 'right', theirs based (I would now argue) on a heroic representation of the woman war worker, mine informed by wartime representations of the marginal woman worker and by 1970s feminist analyses of women's oppression. To paraphrase Luisa Passerini, no one's story is wrong, but we need more than the story itself to understand what it may mean.

Notes

1 See chapter 1, 'Gender, Memory and the Second World War', pp. 21–6 for a discussion of our interviewing method.

2 J. Flax, *Thinking Fragments: Psychoanalysis, Feminism and Postmodernism in the Contemporary West* (Berkeley, University of California Press, 1990), p. 8.

3 *Ibid.*, pp. 23, 25.

4 As far as academic accounts are concerned, the traditional story is favoured by Harold L. Smith, 'The Effect of the War on the Status of Women' in H. L. Smith (ed.), *War and Social Change: British Society in the Second World War* (Manchester, Manchester University Press, 1986), pp. 208–29. The idea of progress to modernity is stressed by R. M. Titmuss, 'War and Social Policy' and 'The Position of Women. Some Vital Statistics' in R. M. Titmuss *Essays on 'The Welfare State'* (London, Allen and Unwin, 1958); also by Alva Myrdal and Viola Klein, *Women's Two Roles. Home and Work* (London, Routledge and Kegan Paul, 1956; 2nd ed. 1968); also by A. Marwick, *Britain in the Century of Total War. War, Peace and Social Change 1900–1967* (London, The Bodley Head, 1968) and *War and Social Change in the Twentieth Century* (London, Macmillan, 1974).

5 Carol Dyhouse's work on early twentieth-century feminist views of the family indicates the currency of the domestic 'cage' as a metaphor in feminist discourse in the period 1880–1939, and of the idea that women would obtain their release through the expansion of educational and employment opportunities. See C. Dyhouse, *Feminism and the Family in England 1880–1939* (Oxford, Basil Blackwell, 1989) ch. 1. The phrase it was 'like being let out of a cage' was also, of course, used about the effects of the First World War on women, and this and its echoes in the Second World War provided Gail Braybon and myself with the title of our joint book. See G. Braybon and P. Summerfield, *Out of the Cage. Women's Experiences in the Two World Wars* (London, Pandora, 1987), pp. 58 and 197.

6 Edith Summerskill 'Conscription and Women', *The Fortnightly*, 151 (March 1942), p. 210.

7 *Ibid.*, p. 213.

8 *Current Affairs*, issued fortnightly by the Army Bureau of Current Affairs, No. 44, 'Women After the War' by Phyllis Bentley, 22 May 1943, p. 5.

9 M. Goldsmith, *Women at War* (London, Lindsay Drummond, 1943), p. 200. She continued, 'After the war it will be stranger for them not to continue in this way than to carry into peacetime what has been accepted in wartime'.

10 Mass-Observation, *The Journey Home: A Mass-Observation Report on the Problems of Demobilisation* (London, John Murray, 1944), p. 58.

11 P. Scott, *They Made Invasion Possible* (London, Hutchinson, 1944), p. 147.

12 Dorothy Paterson, *The Family Woman and the Feminist. A Challenge* (London, William Heinemann, 1945), p. 13.

13 *Ibid.*, pp. 33, 5, 29.

14 *Ibid.*, p. 19.

15 She particularly criticised the Women's Institutes for acting as a political pressure group: *Ibid.*, p. 38.

16 *Ibid.*, pp. 39–40, 48.

17 See, for example, *ibid.*, p. 48. She referred to a speech by Lord Elton in the House of Lords, in which he quoted from a letter written by 'a young fighting officer', who said, 'his men were not only fighting for a brave new world, but for those things which were dear to them which they had left, and which they yearned to find still waiting for them on their return'. Paterson stated that 'those things will be homes, children, sensible friendly women; and every step should be taken to raise the status of those women who will help to make these things a shining dignified reality'. See also *Current Affairs*, No. 44, (note 8

above), specifically the editorial comments of W. E. Williams, Director of Army Education, pp. 2–3. This pamphlet was one of a series used for the purpose of educating the troops in current affairs. Bentley's text belongs within the modernising vision of the effects of war on women, but Williams' commentary which prefaced the pamphlets, countered her arguments with traditionalist ones. For a discussion of the representation of issues of gender relations to servicemen in the Second World War, see P. Allatt 'Men and War: Status, Class and the Social Reproduction of Masculinity', in E. Gamarnikow, D. H. J. Morgan, J. Purvis and D. Taylorson, *The Public and the Private* (London, Heinemann Educational Ltd, 1983), p. 47–61.

18   See also C. Gledhill and G. Swanson 'Gender and Sexuality in Second World War Films – A Feminist Approach' in G. Hurd (ed.), *National Fictions* (London, British Film Institute, 1984), p. 57, who argue that 'Through their role as mothers women, located in the home as distinct from work, became a mythical centre, expressing family, and hence national, unity'.

19   Parliamentary Debates (Hansard) 404 HC DEB 5s, 15 November 1944, Debate on Manpower (Release from Forces), col. 1989.

20   *Ibid.*, cols 2033–34

21   J. B. Priestley, *British Women Go to War* (London, Collins, 1943) argued that older women would see the war as an interruption to enduring lifestyles to which they would return. In contrast 'the younger ones have arrived at maturity during the war, and by the time peace comes will have almost forgotten what their prewar life was like' (p. 54). The expressed opinion of these young women 'that the war years have been little more than an evil dream, and that life as they remember it in 1939 is still waiting for them somewhere' would be a mere 'pretence'. After a short time they would discover that 'they themselves have changed much more than they first imagined', and would want the wider life of citizenship and part-time paid work which he depicted (pp. 56–7).

22   M. Goldsmith, *Women and the Future* (London, Lindsay Drummond, 1946), p. 15.

23   Scott, *They Made Invasion Possible*, pp. 7–8 and 147. Peggy Scott, as we have seen, posed the question of whether women released from the home by war work would want to 'go back and shut the door again' (p. 147). The tone of her writing was that they should surely not want to do so, but her explicit answer to the question was that most women *would* want to go home and that the majority did not actually want to take advantage of the wartime changes. At the beginning of the book she had reassured the reader that the woman war worker was a temporary phenomenon: 'When the war is over the job

will not be so much her concern as the home. The majority of the girls are looking forward to running homes of their own, not to running a man's job for him' (pp. 7–8). At the end, she claimed to know that 'thousands of girls are longing' to 'go back and shut the door again' (p. 147). Mass-Observation, in *The Journey Home: A Mass-Observation Report on the Problems of Demobilisation* (London, John Murray, 1944), argued in the same year that 'For better or for worse, the large number of opinionated women want to return to or start on domestic life when the war is over' (p. 55). This was especially so of those aged 25 to 39. Women younger than 25 were unsettled by worries and fantasies, and older ones welcomed the release offered by wartime work from domestic confinement. For more on M-O's contradictory messages concerning women in wartime, see P. Summerfield, 'Mass-Observation on Women at Work in the Second World War', *Feminist Praxis*, 37 and 38 (1992) pp. 35–49.

24 Kenneth Howard, *Sex Problems of the Returning Soldier* (Manchester, Sydney Pemberton, 1945), p. 63.

25 Central Statistical Office, *Fighting with Figures. A Statistical Digest of the War*, (London, HMSO, 1995), Table 3.4 (figure for March 1945).

26 Parliamentary Debates (Hansard) 404, 1944, Debate on Manpower, col. 1988. For a discussion of this debate, see Julia Swindells, 'Coming Home to Heaven: Manpower and Myth in 1944 Britain', *Women's History Review*, 4, 2 (1995), pp. 223–34.

27 Only two MPs, Lady Apsley and Lieut.-Colonel Thornton-Kemsley, questioned the government's assumptions concerning servicewomen's desires. Both spoke discordantly of evidence they had that servicewomen were concerned primarily not about how they would look or about home life as such, but about the availability of jobs after the war, and whether they would be able to use their wartime training: *Ibid.*, cols 2055 and 2060.

28 Scott, *They Made Invasion Possible*, p. 147.

29 M-O, *The Journey Home*, p. 117.

30 *Ibid.*, p. 61.

31 *Ibid.*, p. 64.

32 Edith Pargeter, *She Goes to War* (London, William Heinemann, 1942; this ed. London, Headline Book Publishing, 1989), p. 312. The book's note about the author states 'the author draws heavily on her own personal experience of the WRNS'. Edith Pargeter, as Ellis Peters, later wrote crime novels.

33 Titmuss, 'War and Social Policy' and 'The Position of Women'; Myrdal and Klein, *Women's Two Roles*; Marwick, *Britain in the Century of Total War* and *War and Social Change in the Twentieth Century*. One among a great many examples of popular treatments is

C. Lang, *Keep Smiling Through. Women in the Second World War* (Cambridge, Cambridge University Press, 1989).

34 Smith, 'The Effect of the War on the Status of Women' in H. L. Smith (ed.) *War and Social Change: British Society in the Second World War* (Manchester, Manchester University Press 1986), pp. 208–29.

35 See chapter 1, pp. 2–3.

36 Ivy Jones (362, 364).

37 Other examples include Janice Brunton, who left a routine civilian clerical job and a dominating father to become a Plotter in the WAAF. She said, 'Before I joined up I was an extremely shy, sensitive person. I over-reacted really, always thought that people were looking at me … you see I was an only child so it's quite a trauma sleeping with another twenty-four. You know, that was my first experience at Gloucester. And I think it did me a lot of good. I was really soft before' (449). Greta Lewis, a weaver before the war and the daughter of a dominant mother, who joined the ATS and worked in an anti-aircraft battery, gave a similar answer to the question 'do you think it changed your view of yourself?' 'Oh yes, because I was very quiet. I were a very quiet person then, before I went in there. So it did change you' (366). Gladys French, cost-accountant turned Wren wireless mechanic, and daughter of a stern but tolerant father, told a similar story. Referring to leaving school at the age of 17 she said 'we were terribly terribly immature … we knew nothing about the world at all' (34). She worked for seven years before joining up but nevertheless looking back it was her wartime service in the Wrens that she identified as crucial in terms of personal change: 'it gave me a lot more confidence. I was a very shy child, very diffident, quite nervous, in fact I even stammered, you wouldn't believe that now, would you. Couldn't get a word out at home … and therefore it gave me a lot of confidence I suppose, to think that we'd done all these different things and been all these different places.' (348). Marion Paul, who moved from clerical work in a mines office and a sheltering home to clerical work in the ATS for the REME said, 'I think it's made me a better person, I think it's made me more outgoing' (522).

38 Edith Dixon (440).

39 Myrna Wraith (315).

40 Marion Paul (179).

41 Janice Brunton could have been one of the women to whom Marion referred: 'Initially I think I found it quite embarrassing even getting undressed in front of somebody else, but it's amazing how – you know, you just get on with it, everybody's in the same boat' (498). Gladys French had similar memories to which she added a class dimension. Public schoolgirls in the WRNS stripped off and bathed in

front of each other, something 'us from a more prim Edwardian background weren't used to. Well we thought it was very strange, you can
imagine. But of course we got used to it, you get a bit more free and
easy when you live in that sort of society' (245). May Richards,
former clerical worker and wartime radar mechanic in the ATS said,
'when you first went into the Army, you'd no privacy of any kind, so
you probably felt a bit strange. You'd to get dressed and undressed in
front of a lot of other people and wash in a line of basins with lots of
other girls, but I think after a while you got so you didn't bother any
more' (436). Joyce Greaves, radar operator in the WAAF agreed,
although she indicated that the change was hard: 'lack of privacy
takes a lot of adjusting to really, but you get used to it. And I think
when you go into something like that, you've just got to make up your
mind. You couldn't come out again so you've got to get on with it'
(264).

42 Amy O'Connor (661).
43 Ivy Jones (364).
44 Kate Lomax (788).
45 On wartime radicalism see P. Summerfield, 'Education and Politics in
    the British Armed Forces in the Second World War', *International
    Review of Social History*, 26, 2 (1981), pp. 133–58; A. C. H. Smith,
    Paper Voices. The Popular Press and Social Change 1935–1965
    (London, Chatto and Windus, 1975), especially ch. 3; A. Calder, *The
    People's War. Britain 1939–45* (London, Panther, 1971), especially
    ch. 9.
46 Katharine Hughes (354). Marion Paul, from a lower middle-class vil-
    lage background, echoed her comment. 'I think it's given me an
    understanding of people, I think that I meet people on an equal foot-
    ing, whoever they are. I can talk to people like you or like anyone, I
    feel that they're the same as I am, and I can talk to anyone' (522).
47 Estelle Armitage (66, 312, 330). Estelle gave some graphic illustra-
    tions of both the subtle class and race distinctions fostered by her
    family in Jamaica, and the intersection of her own class prejudice with
    racial attitudes towards her in Britain. Her grandfather was a white
    man from Scotland, and her father prized the relatively light skins of
    the family. He reprimanded Estelle for walking home from school one
    day with a girl whose skin was darker, even though this girl's father
    was a doctor and her aunt a postmistress. 'That's the sort of father you
    had, that's the way you were brought up, which thank the Lord that
    I have changed my views of people' (66). She illustrated the latter
    point with a story about a London bus conductor's attitude to her in
    the 1940s: 'I could see he resented, thinking you know this is a black
    woman, or coloured as they called, you know sort of thing. Some of

them were ok, but this one, particular one, I thought what a cheek, I was thinking, and I am thinking I would not associate with you, you are thinking that "because you are black you know, you are lower than me", you know what I mean, a lot of them think that you know, but why? It is so silly, so sad' (314).

48 May Richards, grammar school educated and the daughter of a salesman (464, 468). She said of the ATS 'I[t] certainly changed the way I thought about other people .. I learned that to be rough isn't always to be bad, because when you're suddenly plonked among girls of all kinds and men of all kinds, it's a shock to begin with. Then you realise that they're still human beings and you get to know them and you probably get some sorted out – your values become right … you learned how to live with people, get on with people of all kinds, and who had come from all walks of life' (464-468). Ann Tomlinson, privately-educated daughter of a bank manager, adopted a similar tone in describing the effects on her of training with working-class Scottish women: 'I was somewhat humbled really, in a way, because I just had not realised that I would meet people like this … I think the whole thing was very very salutary. I think I learned how to like and respect other people who were not of backgrounds like mine, who had very different experiences. I learned to admire them, because of the struggles that they must have had to get where they got to' (220).

49 Barbara Wilson (225, 227).

50 Joyce Greaves (311).

51 Gladys French, pre-war cost accountant, spoke in very similar terms. 'It helped you to grow up. And I mean nothing's the end of the world after a war, is it? If things go wrong, and things go dreadfully wrong, you think well, that's nothing, you know' (348). Her growing political involvement in the war years gave her a special personal reason to want to join the fight against Nazi Germany, in spite of the fact that she 'was a bit of a pacifist': 'We honestly thought the Germans would invade Britain and we'd be taken prisoner and our families would have a rotten time … I mean, I told you, I was interested in the Labour Party and things like that, I had a lot of left wing friends, and I was quite frightened that I'd end up in a concentration camp you see' (334). Pamela Wootton charted a movement in the opposite political direction arising from the same process of maturation: 'I grew up, absolutely, I don't know how I felt about myself before, I was too young to feel anything really … But certainly we grew up, yes, we grew up with ideas of our own. We weren't easily led. We had our own points of view. And it used to be good, we used to discuss them all' (589). Exposure to different political ideas at the end of the war led to the development of her own political convictions: 'We had talks

from the various parties ... we had Labour politician candidate talks and we'd go to those, and we'd listen and their main thing was, "Now you've done your bit, you can sit back. You've done your share. We owe you this that and the other". Well, be that as it may. We had Conservative party candidates, they said, "Don't think you can sit back on your backsides now" he said, "You've got to work twice as hard to put our country back on its feet". Now that to me was the thing that turned me Blue, but my father was Red, and my brother's the same because they had similar talks' (585). French and Greaves indicated that they were less interested in politics by the 1990s than they had been in the 1940s. In contrast, Pam Wootton's wartime conversion to Conservatism and rejection of her father's left-wing viewpoint, had remained with her into the 1990s: 'I'm proud of my politics' (585).

52 For example Marion Paul followed her point about feeling equal to other people as a result of war service by saying: 'I still feel a great sense of loyalty for England – I wouldn't live anywhere else but England. I mean, it means a lot to me, England does. I'm very royalist, very royalist. And if I hear a military band all my hairs stand on end' (522). See also L. Noakes, 'Gender and British National Identity in Wartime: A Study of the Links Between Gender and National identity in Britain in the Second World War, the Falklands War, and the Gulf War' (unpublished D.Phil. thesis, University of Sussex, 1996), particularly pp. 134–46, where Noakes traces a trend among M-O's women panellists during the war, towards expressions of 'a shared, inclusive sense of national citizenship'.

53 Joyce Greaves (311); Gladys French (348); Pamela Wootton (589); Margaret Gray (578).

54 An early twentieth-century exponent of these views was G. Stanley Hall, on whom see C. Dyhouse, Girls Growing Up in Late Victorian and Edwardian England (London, Routledge and Kegan Paul, 1981), p. 122. The idea that women, because of their biological and psychological make-up, never became fully mature in the sense that men did, had implications for their attainment of citizenship.

55 Katharine Hughes (354, 404).

56 Gladys French (348).

57 Felicity Snow (256). The maturity derived from growing competence was frequently linked with the assumption of responsibilities. May Richards said, 'at the young age of 20 you had a responsibility of a radar and gun-site, even though it was an antiquated bit, it was a big responsiblity to begin while you were still young. I think a lot of us had to grow up fast' (497). If specific skills were not referred to, for example in cases like that of Mary Mackenzie, who was doing a 'woman's job', waitressing, in the WAAF, the process of maturation

was linked to managing the job and other people. Mary Mackenzie said, 'I was given responsible jobs so you know, it gave me a sense of responsibility with it too' (211). She extended her comments to refer to being 'in charge': 'I could say "Well, do this, do that", I could give orders to people without being nasty of course, you could get people to do things for you … yes, it gave me more confidence in myself' (211, 213).

58 Ann Tomlinson (359).
59 Amy O'Connor (813). Amy spelt out her feminist views thus: 'a woman is born the same way as a man, she breathes the same way as a man, she dies the same way. There's no other way about it. We're people, and there should be no discrimination between the male sex and the female sex. To my way of thinking a woman's more important than a man, because we can have a baby without a flaming man, but there's no way a man can carry on his line without the woman, and they're certainly not the gentle sex, the women – no way' (809).
60 Amabel Ingram (425).
61 Barbara Wilson (209); Edith Dixon (440).
62 Scott, *They Made Invasion Possible*, p. 147.
63 Moira Underwood (549).
64 Marianne Lloyd (351, 353).
65 Marianne Lloyd (351, 353).
66 Beryl Bramley (244).
67 Beryl Bramley (504).
68 See Scott, *They Made Invasion Possible*, pp. 147–8.
69 Emily Porter (261).
70 Emily Porter (271).
71 Evelyn Mills (297); Dorothy Rose (679); Hester Hamilton (257); Helena Balfour (655); Wilma Harrison (497); Elizabeth Little (843); Ethel Singleton (353); Fiona Thomas (443).
72 Sadie Bartlett (270).
73 Sadie Bartlett (126).
74 Sadie Bartlett (186).
75 Sadie Bartlett (126, 186).
76 Sadie Bartlett (152).
77 Sadie Bartlett (152).
78 Sadie Bartlett (275).
79 Sadie Bartlett (246). Sadie also referred to this case earlier in the interview: 'I often have a laugh when some of these girls, simply because a man brushes by them, especially that doctor – I mean he'd only brushed by her a couple of times and I thought, "you should have been in the country years ago!"' (122).
80 Sadie Bartlett (246).

81 Helena Balfour (655).
82 Nora Vickers (817–827).
83 Yvette Baynes (700).
84 Peggy Peters (227, 230).
85 Evelyn Mills (297). Hester Hamilton, progress chaser, also made it clear that she did not regard the war as a positive experience: 'I don't think war was a good thing at all' (257). She said, 'It was a very unsettling time. You never knew what was going to happen tomorrow' (254). Jean Grant, a wartime riveter, connected the question of whether war work changed her, first to her work and then to her apprehensions concerning her husband, a member of the Royal Marines whom she married in 1943 and who was away at the sea for most of the war. 'It probably made me grow up and be a wee bit more mature and look at life a bit differently, put it that way. But wartime was a strange time too, it was a worrying time, especially when your husbands were away and doing different things you know' (445).
86 Joyce Greaves (309).
87 Joyce Greaves (348).
88 For example, John Newsom, *The Education of Girls* (London, Faber, 1948), pp. 146–9. See also S. Jeffreys, *The Spinster and Her Enemies, Feminism and Sexuality 1880–1930* (London, Pandora, 1985) and A. Oram, *Women Teachers and Feminist Politics 1900–39* (Manchester, Manchester University Press, 1996), especially ch. 6.
89 Gladys French (405).
90 Women formed 31 per cent of the workforce in 1951, 33 per cent in 1961, 37 per cent in 1971 and 40 per cent in 1981. Married women were 43 per cent of all women in paid work in 1951, 48 per cent in 1955, 64 per cent in 1985. In 1951 and 1981 30 per cent of women worked full-time. In 1951 5 per cent of all adult women worked part-time, in 1981 27 per cent did so. In 1981 part-timers constituted 42 per cent of the female workforce. For discussion of these figures and their sources see P. Summerfield 'Women in Britain Since 1945: Companionate Marriage and the Double Burden', in J. Obelkevich and P. Catterall (eds), *Understanding Post-War British Society*, (Routledge, London, 1984)', pp. 62–3.
91 Katharine Hughes (356).
92 Katherine Hughes (360).
93 Janice Brunton (335).
94 Joyce Greaves (236). This man was killed within a year of their marriage.
95 Mary Mackenzie (213).
96 Heather McLaren (682). Mary Mackenzie hinted at similar feelings: 'It was sad leaving and at times I wished I'd stayed on and then other

times, no, I had my baby and that's – I always loved children' (204).

97   Katharine Hughes (350).

98   Beryl Bramley (533).

99   Greta Lewis (231).

100 Greta Lewis (201).

101 Greta Lewis (348).

102 Greta Lewis (356).

103 Greta Lewis (191).

104 Greta Lewis (416).

105 Some of the 'heroes' emphasised that their war experiences led them to take an egalitarian view of marriage. Kate Lomax, for example, recalled telling the man she married at the end of the war 'you're not going to walk in front of me or behind me, we walk together': Lomax (64).

106 Yvette Baynes (717).

107 Evelyn Mills (297, 278).

108 Joan Stanton (371, 373). Hester Hamilton said tersely that she was 'just glad it was all over' at the end of the war (319). Right at the end of the interview she started to talk about the man she married in 1948, a musician, whom she had known throughout her life: 'He was away, he was in the Royal Scots Band during the war. He was in Belsen the day after it was released. It's the one time he fainted in the Army, into his soup. He said with the smell. They dished him up with a meal. He couldn't stand it. He was six years away' (343). The interview was at an end; the interviewer turned off the tape recorder at this point rather than pursuing Hester's feelings about the return from the war of a man with such memories. But the recollections of horror vicariously experienced through the man who came back to her, put in perspective her statement that she was 'just glad it was all over'.

109 Edith Dixon (19).

110 Dorothy Rose (604).

111 Caroline Woodward (510).

112 M.-F. Chanfrault-Duchet, 'Narrative Structures, Social Models, and Symbolic Representation in the Life Story', in S. B. Gluck and D. Patai, *Women's Words. The Feminist Practice of Oral History* (London, Routledge, 1991), p. 90.

113 Kate Lomax (772). She reiterated the point later, more fully: 'married life, you might make up your mind about married life, but it's not as you imagined it. 'Cos there're too many fork roads' (788).

Appendix 1

Announcements of the project in women's magazines

Unfortunately the publishers of *Woman* and *Woman's Weekly* would not permit us to reproduce here, in facsimile, the double spreads on which our requests to women to write to us appeared, but only the announcements themselves. Since the personal, confessional style encouraged by the magazines formed an important part of the context within which women heard about and responded to our project, a summary of each spread follows.

(a) *Woman's Weekly*, 23rd July 1991

> ## Wartime workers?
>
> As part of a research project we are organising here at Lancaster University, we would be very interested to hear from women who were trained, either as civilians or service personnel, to do jobs in the Second World War. Aircraft fitters, welders, cooks, clerical workers ... we'd like to hear from any of you.
>
> Please write to me at the following address:
>
> *Dr Nicole Crockett*
> *Department of Educational*
> *Research, Cartmel College,*
> *Lancaster University,*
> *Lancaster LA1 4YL*

This letter produced over 350 replies. It appeared on page 3 under the caption 'Lovely to Hear from You'. On the same two-page spread a variety of types of writing by women appeared, stimulated by the promise of rewards: 'We so enjoy receiving letters from our readers. Share your thoughts with us and we'll pay £6 for every original contribution published on these pages'. (Nicole, of course, did not receive a reward for her letter!) The other items included the following: poems about a bad experience with a car exhaust pipe and about finding a new dentist; letters about a baby eating place mats (the lead item, illustrated by a cartoon), about eye make-up problems, about video recordings of distant grandchildren, about how to clean windows, about smiling at policemen, about a headmaster's advice from long ago and about weaning puppies. There was also a reprint of an illustrated piece from *Woman's Weekly* of 1913 about how to make a bathing tent. The spread included the contents list of 'this week's *Woman's Weekly*' as well as the weekly letter from the editor, Judith Hall. This one was about the funny habits of her eight-month-old son and referred to the place mats story and cartoon.

(b) *Woman*, 1st July 1991

Woman magazine published a brief announcement of the project, on a double spread headlined 'You and Us'.

WHERE ARE THEY NOW?

Nicole Crockett would like to hear from women who were trained for jobs during World War Two. Please contact Dept of Educational Research, Cartmel College, University of Lancaster LA1 4YL

The 'You and Us' page was similar to *Woman's Weekly*'s 'Lovely to Hear from You' spread, consisting mainly of readers' letters. However, there were more items on the spread (including a column on the magazine's Tarot phone line and a strip cartoon) and readers of *Woman* were given more editorial direction than *Woman's Weekly*'s contributors about the sorts of letters which were wanted: 'A funny story? You want to let off steam? Some good news? A cause for concern? Then tell us. We'd love to hear from you! ... We'll pay £5 for every original letter published.' There were additional special prizes for 'star letters'. Subjects of readers' letters fell into four categories: complaints; stories about children; confessions and letters about contacting people. The complaints included a mother's objections to ice cream vans parking outside schools, a man's letter about repeats on TV, and a complaint about charity organisations being based in London. Among the 'cute' stories about children was one about a small son's efforts to make the family dog live longer, and others about a small boy's desire to be a Teenage Mutant Hero Turtle when he grew up, two small sons' love of revolving doors, and a young daughter's fascination with the Stone Age. Confessions included a letter about ceasing to use an exercise bike, another about an accusation of shoplifting, and another about trying to dodge parking restrictions. 'Contact' letters included one about the pleasures of rediscovering old friends, and another inviting readers to join an Age Concern Pen Friend Club. The item about our project appeared under the heading 'Where Are They Now?', above a notice of a reunion for foster children of the 1960s, and an appeal from a woman seeking to trace a particular family. However the magazine did not print our letter verbatim, but recast it as an announcement. It produced only four replies, perhaps because, in contrast both to the other items on the spread and to the letter published in *Woman's Weekly*, its tone and the contact address given were relatively impersonal.

We entered all the replies on a database and selected our interviewees on the basis of the following criteria.

(a) Wartime occupation. Our target was ten in each of four categories of work: civilian manual; civilian non-manual; military manual; military non-manual.

(b) Geographical location. We wanted a geographical spread, so we contacted women living in urban and rural areas in Scotland, Wales and England, including the North West, North East, Midlands, South West and South East. We did not have any respondents from Northern Ireland.

(c) Availability. If someone we contacted by phone or letter was not available during the periods each interviewer had allocated to interviewing, we replaced them with someone else in the same category.

We found five interviewees through personal contacts. Three were relatives of friends or colleagues who suggested that we should interview them, and two (with whom Colin Douglas kindly put me in touch) came to Britain from the Caribbean to work in the Armed Forces during the war. This brought the total number interviewed to forty-two, of whom twenty-two did military and twenty civilian war jobs.

Appendix 2

Brief biographical details of the women interviewed

Notes:
(i) Pseudonyms are used in all cases
(ii) 'Pre-war work' is work which preceded that identified by interviewees as 'war work', but did not always take place chronologically before the war. This line is omitted in cases where women went straight into work they described as 'war work'.

Estelle Armitage

Born	Jamaica, 1921
Parents	Shopkeepers
Education	Private boarding school, secretarial college
War work	ATS clerk 1943; to Britain as ATS clerk 1944–47
Post-war	Retrained (before demobilisation) at British hospital as midwife; repatriated to Jamaica; returned to Britain 1951; midwife/nurse in Britain 1951–1980s
Marriage	1951, two children
Contact	Personal contact; interviewed by APS, January 1994

Helena Balfour

Born	Motherwell, 1919
Parents	Mother, died 1929; Father, steel smelter
Education	Elementary and high school to age 14
Pre-war work	Domestic servant
War work	Fitter, aircraft factory 1941–45
Post-war	Post office clerk
Marriage	1947, two children
Contact	*Woman's Weekly*; interviewed by NC, February 1992

Sadie Bartlett

Born	Norfolk, 1922
Parents	Mother, ex-domestic servant; Father, brick-maker
Education	Elementary school to age 15
Pre-war work	Shop assistant, hairdresser, work on land
War work	Timber Corps of Women's Land Army 1943–46
Post-war	Telephonist, cleaner, clerical worker
Marriage	1949, one child
Contact	*Woman's Weekly*; interviewed by NC, November 1991

Yvette Baynes

Born	Birmingham, 1925
Parents	Mother, tailoress; Father, Royal Navy Artificer, died 1927
Education	Elementary school to age 14
War work	Clerk
Post-war	Clerk
Marriage	1945, two children
Contact	*Woman's Weekly*; interviewed by HA, November 1991

Nadia Beale

Born	British Honduras, 1924
Parents	Separated. Mother, casual worker; Father, Chief Mechanic, Public Works Department
Education	Elementary and secondary school to age 16
Pre-war work	Trainee teacher
War work	Joined ATS as trainee driver 1943, to Britain 1944, became ATS clerk
Post-war	Retrained (before demobilisation) at British teacher training college, repatriated to British Honduras 1949, returned to Britain 1955, teacher 1965–88
Marriage	1954, three children
Contact	Personal contact; interviewed by APS, January 1994

Beryl Bramley

Born	Derbyshire, 1920
Parents	Mother, housewife; Father, mill manager
Education	Private school, girls' high school to age 16
Pre-war work	Trainee hairdresser

War work	Clerk, fitter, member of Aeronautical Inspection Directorate
Post-war	Welfare officer, personnel manager, newsagent, shop assistant
Marriage	1940, two children
Contact	*Woman's Weekly*; interviewed by APS, February 1992

Janice Brunton

Born	Liverpool, 1922
Parents	Mother, ex-professional pianist; Father, landscape gardener
Education	Elementary school to age 14
Pre-war work	Clerk
War work	Clerk SD, WAAF (filter plotter) 1941–46
Post-war	Purchase tax collector 1946–48, clerical worker 1961–c.1985
Marriage	1948, two children
Contact	*Woman's Weekly*; interviewed by HA, November 1991

Edith Dixon

Born	Ayr, 1922
Parents	Mother, housewife; Father, finance officer
Education	Private primary school, high school to age 18
Pre-war work	Bank clerk
War work	Signals Operator, WRNS 1940–43
Post-war	Clergyman's wife
Marriage	1943, five children
Contact	*Woman's Weekly*; interviewed by NC, October 1991

Gladys French

Born	London, 1918
Parents	Mother, died 1921; Father, railway clerk
Education	Elementary and secondary school to age 16
Pre-war work	Costing clerk, accountant
War work	Radio mechanic, WRNS 1943–46
Post-war	Teacher
Marriage	Single
Contact	*Woman's Weekly*; interviewed by NC, November 1991

Jean Grant
Born	Edinburgh, 1919
Parents	Mother, housewife; Father, baker
Education	Elementary school to age 14
Pre-war work	Shop assistant
War work	Riveter, then inspector in munitions factory
Post-war	Shop assistant
Marriage	1943, one child
Contact	*Woman's Weekly*; interviewed by NC, October 1991

Margaret Gray
Born	Surrey, 1923
Parents	Mother, housewife; Father, civil servant
Education	Private primary and secondary schools
Pre-war work	Telephonist
War work	Driver, ATS 1942–1946
Post-war	Telephonist; driver; publisher's editor
Marriage	Single
Contact	*Woman's Weekly*; interviewed by NC, November 1991

Joyce Greaves
Born	London, 1922
Parents	Mother, housewife; Father, factory manager
Education	Private convent school to age 16, polytechnic to age 17
War work	Ambulance attendant ARP; radar operator WAAF 1941–44
Post-war	ARP; clerical worker 1944–45; shop assistant
Marriage	1943; 1945, three children
Contact	*Woman's Weekly*; interviewed by NC, June 1992

Hester Hamilton
Born	Port Seton, 1922
Parents	Fishmongers
Education	High school to age 17; university for two years
War work	Planning officer, aircraft factory 1942–44
Post-war	Teacher
Marriage	1948, one son
Contact	*Woman's Weekly*; interviewed by NC, October 1991

Wilma Harrison

Born	London, 1922
Parents	Mother, domestic servant; Father, ex-docker, oddjob man
Education	Elementary school to age 14, trade school to age 16
Pre-war work	Upholsterer in bedding factory
War work	Centre lathe operator, engineering factory 1942–46
Post-war	Upholsterer; canteen worker
Marriage	1947, two children
Contact	*Woman's Weekly*; interviewed by NC, November 1991

Katharine Hughes

Born	London, 1921
Parents	Mother, café owner; Father, bill poster
Education	Elementary school to age 13, technical school to age 15
Pre-war work	Dressmaker
War work	Steward, WRNS 1939–40; wireless/telegraphist, WRNS 1940–45
Post-war	Receptionist; caterer
Marriage	1943, two children
Contact	*Woman's Weekly*; interviewed by NC, November 1991

Amabel Ingram

Born	Derbyshire, 1924
Parents	Mother, housewife; Father, gentleman farmer; agricultural salesman
Education	Private primary and secondary schools
Pre-war work	Nurse
War work	Decoder, WRNS 1942–46
Post-war	Poultry blood tester; speech therapist
Marriage	1954, three children
Contact	Personal contact; interviewed by NC, December 1991

Ivy Jones

Born	Cardiff, 1923
Parents	Mother, ex-weaver, casual worker; Father, public house cellar man
Education	Elementary and secondary school to age 16

Pre-war work   Librarian
War work   Meteorologist, WAAF 1943–46
Post-war   Librarian; telephonist; teacher
Marriage   1946, one child; 1952
Contact   *Woman's Weekly*; interviewed by HA, October
                1991

Greta Lewis
Born   Morley, 1920
Parents   Mother, weaver; Father, tuner in textiles mill
Education   Elementary school to age 14
Pre-war work   Weaver
War work   Anti-aircraft predictor and plotter, ATS 1941–43
Post-war   Post office worker; play school assistant
Marriage   1941, two children (plus?)
Contact   Personal contact; interviewed by APS, September
                1991

Elizabeth Little
Born   South Shields, 1919
Parents   Mother, domestic servant, char; Father, engineer-
                ing pattern maker
Education   Elementary school to age 14
Pre-war work   Shop assistant
War work   Bench fitter then gauge setter, engineering factory
Post-war   Betting shop assistant; gauge fitter, engineering
                factory; publican; shop assistant
Marriage   1953, four children (including two stepchildren)
Contact   *Woman's Weekly*; interviewed by NC, January
                1992

Marianne Lloyd
Born   Birmingham, 1923
Parents   Mother, factory worker, wartime welder; Father,
                window cleaner
Education   Elementary school to age 14, commercial school to
                age 16
Pre-war work   Clerk
War work   Draughtswoman, engineering firms 1941–46
Post-war   Draughtswoman, engineering firms 1946–48
Marriage   1945, two children
Contact   *Woman's Weekly*; interviewed by HA, November
                1991

Kate Lomax

Born	London, 1919
Parents	Separated. Mother, private nurse; Father, ship's engineer
Education	Elementary and secondary school to age 16
Pre-war work	Clerical worker, local government
War work	Photographer, WAAF 1941–46
Post-war	Photographer; clerical worker
Marriage	1946, two children
Contact	*Woman's Weekly*; interviewed by NC, January 1992

Mary Mackenzie

Born	Brighton, 1921
Parents	Mother, cooked meat shop owner; Father, musician
Education	Elementary school to age 13
Pre-war work	Shop assistant, domestic servant, waitress
War work	Waitress, WAAF 1941–43
Post-war	Shop assistant; post office assistant; civil servant
Marriage	1943, two children
Contact	*Woman's Weekly*; interviewed by NC, October 1991

Heather McLaren

Born	Glasgow, 1918
Parents	Mother, ex-printer; Father, railway carriage worker
Education	Elementary school to age 14
Pre-war work	Shop assistant
War work	Barrage balloon operator, WAAF 1941–42; Aircraft fitter, WAAF 1942–45
Post-war	Clerical worker
Marriage	1945, two children; 1982
Contact	*Woman's Weekly*; interviewed by NC, October 1991

Eleanor Matthews

Born	London, 1921
Parents	Mother died in 1920s; Father, shopkeeper, manager of billiard hall
Education	Elementary school to age 14
Pre-war work	Kitchen assistant then cook; factory worker

War work   Cook, WAAF 1942–46
Post-war   Shop assistant, cook, nursing auxiliary
Marriage   1949
Contact   *Woman's Weekly*; interviewed by NC, November
                    1991

Evelyn Mills
Born   London, 1924
Parents   Mother, ex-laundry worker; Father, council yard
                    superintendent
Education   Elementary school to age 14
Pre-war work   Clerical worker
War work   Duplicator operator in Admiralty 1942–44
Post-war   Clerical worker
Marriage   1946
Contact   *Woman's Weekly*; interviewed by NC, December
                    1991

Amy O'Connor
Born   Barrow, 1922
Parents   Mother, domestic servant; Father, owned small
                    business, died 1926
Education   Elementary school to age 14
Pre-war work   Domestic servant
War work   Signals Operator, ATS
Post-war   Laundry worker, catalogue seller, television adjust-
                    er, bread deliverer, bar maid
Marriage   1942, two children; 1958, one child
Contact   *Woman's Weekly*; interviewed by NC, January
                    1992

Marion Paul
Born   South Yorkshire, 1925
Parents   Mother, housewife; Father, colliery clerk
Education   Elementary school to age 14; commercial school
                    to age 15
Pre-war work   Clerical worker, colliery
War work   Clerk, ATS (for Royal Electrical and Mechanical
                    Engineers)
Post-war   Secretary
Marriage   1948, one child
Contact   *Woman's Weekly*; interviewed by NC, January
                    1992

Peggy Peters

Born	Portsmouth, 1921
Parents	Mother, ex-governess, housewife, wartime shop-keeper; Father, naval photographer
Education	Private primary and secondary school
Pre-war work	Secretary
War work	Secretary at naval base
Post-war	Secretary
Marriage	1949, two children
Contact	*Woman's Weekly*; interviewed by APS, September 1991

Emily Porter

Born	Manchester, 1914
Parents	Separated. Mother, dressmaker, later local government clerk; Father, soldier, died 1926
Education	Elementary and secondary school to age 16; art school to age 20
Pre-war work	Assistant teacher in private school
War work	Clerk in postal censorship 1940–46
Post-war	Civil Servant
Marriage	Single
Contact	*Woman's Weekly*; interviewed by HA, October 1991

May Richards

Born	Preston, 1922
Parents	Mother, ex-weaver; Father, sales representative
Education	Elementary and convent secondary school to age 17
Pre-war work	Clerical assistant
War work	Radar Mechanic, ATS 1941–45
Post-war	Market researcher (casual work)
Marriage	1942, four children
Contact	*Woman's Weekly*; interviewed by NC, December 1991

Dorothy Rose

Born	Manchester, 1927
Parents	Mother, housewife; Father, bus driver
Education	Elementary school to age 14
War work	Clerk, Ministry of Food
Post-war	Civil Servant; nursery nurse.

Marriage	1953, two children
Contact	*Woman's Weekly*; interviewed by NC, January 1992

Ethel Singleton

Born	Manchester, 1921
Parents	Mother, housewife; Father, lorry driver
Education	Elementary school to age 14, commercial college to age 15
Pre-war work	Clothing machinist, shop assistant
War work	Welder, engineering factory 1941–45
Post-war	Clerical worker in engineering factory; shop-keeper
Marriage	1950, one child
Contact	*Woman's Weekly*; interviewed by NC, December 1991

Felicity Snow

Born	London, 1925
Parents	Café owners
Education	Elementary school to age 14
Pre-war work	Clerical worker
War work	Flight mechanic (engines) WAAF 1942–46
Post-war	Telephonist, General Post Office; driving instructor
Marriage	1951, two children
Contact	*Woman's Weekly*; interviewed by NC, December 1991

Joan Stanton

Born	London, 1922
Parents	Mother, ex-professional pianist; Father, decorative artist
Education	Private schooling to age 16, secretarial college
Pre-war work	Secretary
War work	Secretary
Post-war	Secretary
Marriage	1948, one child
Contact	*Woman's Weekly*; interviewed by HA, October 1991

Fiona Thomas

Born	Blackpool, 1926

Parents	Divorced. Mother, dressmaker, wartime sewer in aircraft factory; Father, bus driver
Education	Elementary school to age 14
Pre-war work	Hairdresser's assistant; shop assistant; telephonist
War work	Fitter in aircraft factory 1940–43; shop assistant; bus conductress 1944–45
Post-war	Clerk; progress chaser; catering assistant; shop assistant
Marriage	1946, three children
Contact	*Woman's Weekly*; interviewed by NC, October 1991

Ann Tomlinson

Born	Lancashire, 1920
Parents	Mother, housewife; Father, bank manager
Education	Private schools to age 18, secretarial college to age 19
Pre-war work	Secretary
War work	Aircraft fitter, WRNS 1943–46
Post-war	University student; teacher; psychologist
Marriage	1946, two children; 1974
Contact	Personal contact; interviewed by APS, June 1992

Moira Underwood

Born	Lancashire, 1908
Parents	Mother, hotelier; Father, curator, book-maker
Education	Privately educated to age 14
Pre-war work	Hairdresser
War work	Explosives factory worker then storekeeper, ROF, and later aircraft factory, 1940–45
Post-war	Hairdresser; clerical worker
Marriage	Single
Contact	*Woman's Weekly*; interviewed by NC, January 1992

Nora Vickers

Born	Lancashire, 1924
Parents	Mother, ex-teacher; Father, picture restorer
Education	Elementary and secondary education to age 16
Pre-war work	Bank clerk
War work	Centre lathe operator, ROF
Post-war	Bank clerk; clerical worker; children's nanny; cost accountant; hospital office manager

| Marriage | 1964, one child |
| Contact | *Woman's Weekly*; interviewed by APS, March 1992 |

Barbara Wilson

Born	London, 1922
Parents	Mother, housewife; Father, fruit and vegetable importer
Education	Private boarding school to age 18; art school to age 20
War work	Aircraft Fitter (electrical) WRNS, 1943–46
Post-war	Architecture student; interior designer
Marriage	Late 1940s, two children
Contact	*Woman's Weekly*; interviewed by NC, November 1991

Caroline Woodward

Born	Croydon, 1925
Parents	Mother, ex-nurse; Father, musician, soldier, brewery worker
Education	Elementary school to age 14
Pre-war work	Factory worker; domestic servant; waitress
War work	Welder in engineering factory
Post-war	Laundry worker; canteen worker
Marriage	1946, three children
Contact	*Woman*; interviewed by NC, December 1991

Pamela Wootton

Born	London, 1923
Parents	Mother, casual worker, wartime factory worker; Father, trade union clerk
Education	Elementary and central school to age 16
Pre-war work	Clerical worker, local government
War work	Aircraft rigger, WRNS, 1942–45
Post-war	Secretary; private school teacher
Marriage	1951, two children
Contact	*Woman's Weekly*; interviewed by NC, January 1992

Myrna Wraith

| Born | Hull, 1925 |
| Parents | Mother, ex-laboratory assistant; Father, engineering fitter |

Education	Elementary and central school to age 14
Pre-war work	Clerk for coal merchant
War work	Clerk WAAF, 1944–47
Post-war	Teleprinter operator
Marriage	1952, two children
Contact	*Woman's Weekly*; interviewed by HA, October 1991

Bibliography

Archival sources

Public Record Office (PRO) Cab 65/20, War Cabinet Conclusions, 1941.
PRO Lab 26/130, Meetings of the Women's Consultative Committee, 1941.
PRO Lab 26/63, Women's Services (Welfare and Amenities) Committee, 'Recruiting of Womanpower'.

Films and video recordings

Brief Encounter, Cineguild, December 1945. Producers Anthony Havelock-Allan and Ronald Neame; Director, David Lean.
Caribbean Women in World War II, Caribbean Ex-Service Women's Association and Video and AV Unit, London Borough of Hammersmith and Fulham, March 1993.
The Gentle Sex, Two Cities-Concanen, April 1943. Producer, Derek de Marney and Leslie Howard; Director, Leslie Howard.
The Life and Times of Rosie the Riveter, Clarity Educational Productions, Emeryville, California, 1982. Producer and Director, Connie Field.
Millions Like Us, Gainsborough Pictures, September 1943. Producer, Edward Black; Directors, Frank Launder and Sidney Gilliat.

Newspapers and magazines

Current Affairs, issued fortnightly by the Army Bureau of Current Affairs, No. 44, 'Women After the War' by Phyllis Bentley, 22 May 1943.
Independent, 26 April 1995.
The Lancet, 5 October 1946.
Peg's Paper, 22 April 1940.
Picture Post, 11 October 1941.
Spare Rib, a Women's Liberation Magazine, 86, September 1979.

The Times, 12 November 1941.
The Times, 2 June 1947.
Woman, 12 June 1943, 1 July 1991.
Woman's Friend, 15 January 1943.
Woman's Weekly, 23 July 1991.

Official publications and parliamentary papers

Central Office of Information, *Wartime Social Survey*, 'An Investigation of the Attitudes of Women, the General Public and ATS Personnel to the Auxiliary Territorial Service', New Series Number 5, October 1941.

Central Office of Information, *Wartime Social Survey*, 'Women at Work: The Attitudes of Working Women Towards Post-War Employment and Some Related Problems. An Inquiry Made for the Office of the Minister of Reconstruction' by Geoffrey Thomas, June 1944.

Ministry of Education, *15–18. A Report of the Central Advisory Council for Education* (The Crowther Report) (London, HMSO, 1959).

Ministry of Education, *Half Our Future, a Report of the Central Advisory Council for Education (England)* (The Newsom Report) (London, HMSO, 1963).

Ministry of Education, *Report of the Working Party on the Supply of Women Teachers* (London, HMSO, 1949).

Ministry of Labour and National Service, *Report for the Years 1939–1946*, Cmd 7225 (1947)

Parliamentary Debates (Hansard), vol. 388, *House of Commons Debates*, Oral Answers, 20 April 1943.

Parliamentary Debates (Hansard), vol. 404, *House of Commons Debates*, Adjournment Debate on Manpower (Release from Forces), 15 November 1944.

Parliamentary Papers 1930–31, xvii, *Royal Commission on Unemployment Insurance*, First Report, Cmd 3872.

Parliamentary Papers, 'Marriage Bar in the Civil Service', *Report of the Civil Service National Whitley Council Committee*, Cmd 6886 (1946).

Parliamentary Papers, *Economic Survey for 1947*, Cmd 7046 (London, HMSO, 1947).

Parliamentary Papers, Home Office, *A Study of the Factors Which Have Operated in the Past and Those Which are Operating Now to Determine the Distribution of Women in Industry*, Cmd 3508 (London, HMSO, 1930).

Parliamentary Papers, *Report of the Royal Commission on Equal Pay*, Cmd 6937 (London, HMSO, 1946).

Parliamentary Papers, *Report of the War Cabinet Committee on Women in Industry*, Cmd 135 (London, HMSO, 1919).

Unpublished theses

Cox, P. 'Rescue and Reform: Girls, Delinquency and Industrial Schools 1908–1933' (unpublished Ph.D. thesis, University of Cambridge, 1997).

Crockett, N. 'Home at Work: Households and the Structuring of Women's Employment in Late Nineteenth Century Dundee' (unpublished Ph.D. thesis, University of Edinburgh, 1991).

Noakes, L. 'Gender and British National Identity in Wartime: A Study of the Links Between Gender and National Identity in Britain in the Second World War, the Falklands War, and the Gulf War' (unpublished D.Phil. thesis, University of Sussex, 1996).

Rosenzweig, J., 'The Construction of Policy for Women in the British Armed Forces 1938–1945', unpublished M.Litt. dissertation, University of Oxford, 1993.

General Bibliography

Allatt, P., 'Stereotyping: Familism in the Law' in B. Fryer, A. Hunt, D. McBarnet and B. Moorhouse (eds), *Law, State and Society* (London, Croom Helm, 1981), pp. 177–201.

Allatt, P., 'Men and War: Status, Class and the Social Reproduction of Masculinity', in E. Gamarnikow, D. H. J. Morgan, J. Purvis and D. Taylorson, *The Public and the Private* (London, Heinemann Educational Books, 1983), pp. 47–61.

Anderson, B., *We Just Got On With It. British Women in World War II* (Chippenham, Picton Publishing, 1994).

Anderson, K. and D. C. Jack, 'Learning to Listen: Interview Techniques and Analyses', in S. B. Gluck and D. Patai (eds), *Women's Words. The Feminist Practice of Oral History* (London, Routledge, 1991) pp. 11–26.

Andrzejewski, S., *Military Organisation and Society* (London, Routledge, 1954).

Arscott, C. *et al.*, *The Headmistress Speaks* (London, Kegan Paul, Trench, Trubner & Co, 1937).

Beddoe, D., *Back to Home and Duty. Women Between the Wars 1918–1939* (London, Pandora, 1989).

Bornat, J., 'Is Oral History Auto/Biography?', in *Lives and Works*, a special edition of *Auto/Biography* 3, 2 (1994), pp. 17–30.

Bousquet, B. and C. Douglas, *West Indian Women at War. British Racism in World War II* (London, Lawrence and Wishart, 1991).

Boyd, K., 'Knowing Your Place: The Tensions of Manliness in Boys' Story Papers 1918–1939', in M. Roper and J. Tosh (eds) *Manful Assertions: Masculinities in Britain Since 1800* (London, Routledge, 1991), pp. 145–67.

Braybon, G., *Women Workers in the First World War: The British Experience* (London, Croom Helm, 1981; 2nd ed. Routledge, 1989).

Braybon, G. and P. Summerfield, *Out of the Cage. Women's Experiences in Two World Wars* (London, Pandora, 1987).

Brayley, M. and R. Ingram, *World War II British Women's Uniforms* (London, Windrow and Greene, 1995).

Brittain, V., *Testament of Friendship. The Story of Winifred Holtby* (London, Macmillan & Co, 1940).

Brittain, V., *England's Hour: An Autobiography 1939–1941* (London, Futura, 1981; 1st pub. 1941).

Bryan, B., S. Dadzie and S. Scafe, *The Heart of the Race – Black Women's Lives in Britain* (London, Virago, 1985).

Burton, E., *What of the Women? A Study of Women in Wartime* (London, Frederick Muller, 1941)

Butler, J., *Gender Trouble: Feminism and the Subversion of Identity* (London, Routledge, 1990).

Calder, A., *The People's War. Britain 1939–1945* (London, Panther, 1971).

Calder A. and D. Sheridan, *Speak for Yourself. A Mass-Observation Anthology, 1937–49* (London, Jonathan Cape, 1984).

Canning, K., 'Feminist History after the Linguistic Turn: Historicizing Discourse and Experience', *Signs: Journal of Women in Culture and Society* 19, 2 (1994), pp. 368–404.

Cantwell J. D. *Images of War: British Posters 1939–45* (London, HMSO, 1989).

Caunce, S., *Oral History and the Local Historian* (London, Longman, 1994).

Central Statistical Office, *Fighting with Figures. A Statistical Digest of the Second World War* (London, HMSO, 1995).

Chamberlain, M., *Fenwomen: A Portrait of Women in an English Village* (London, Virago, 1975).

Chamberlain, M., *Growing Up in Lambeth* (London, Virago, 1989).

Chanfrault-Duchet, M.-F., 'Narrative Structures, Social Models, and Symbolic Representation in the Life Story', in S. B. Gluck and D. Patai (eds), *Women's Words, the Feminist Practice of Oral History* (London, Routledge, 1991) pp.77–92.

Cockburn, C., 'The Gendering of Jobs: Workplace Relations and Reproduction of Sex Segregation', in S. Walby (ed.), *Gender Segregation at Work* (Milton Keynes, Open University Press, 1988), pp. 29–42.

Coleman, P., 'Ageing and Life History: The Meaning of Reminiscence in Late Life', in S. Dex (ed.), *Life and Work History Analyses: Qualitative and Quantitative Developments* (London, Routledge, 1991), pp. 120–43.

Colman, P., *Rosie the Riveter. Women Working on the Home Front in World War II* (New York, Crown Publishers, 1995).

Cooper, D., *The Death of the Family* (Harmondsworth, Penguin Books, 1971).

Croucher R., *Engineers at War* (London, Merlin, 1982).

Davies, A., *Leisure, Gender and Poverty: Working-Class Culture in Salford and Manchester 1900–1939* (Buckingham, Open University Press, 1992).

Davies, B., 'Women's Subjectivity and Feminist Stories', in C. Ellis and M. G. Flaherty, *Investigating Subjectivity. Research on Lived Experience* (London, Sage, 1992), pp. 53–76.

Dawson, G., *Soldier Heroes. British Adventure, Empire and the Imagining of Masculinities* (London, Routledge, 1994).

Derracott, J. and B. Loftus, *Second World War Posters* (London, Imperial War Museum, 1972).

Douie, V., *The Lesser Half: A Survey of the Laws, Regulations and Practices Introduced during the Present War, Which Embody Discrimination Against Women* (London, Women's Publicity Planning Association, 1943).

Douie, V., *Daughters of Britain. An Account of the Work of British Women during the Second World War* (London, Women's Service Library, 1949).

Dyhouse, C., *Girls Growing Up in Late Victorian and Edwardian England* (London, Routledge and Kegan Paul, 1981).

Dyhouse, C., *Feminism and the Family in England 1880–1939* (Oxford, Basil Blackwell, 1989).

Dyhouse, C., *No Distinction of Sex. Women in British Universities 1870–1939* (London, UCL Press, 1995).

Earle J. and J. Phillips 'Equal Pay. Why the Acts don't Work', *Spare Rib*, 86 (September 1979), pp. 22–3.

Eliott, B. J., 'Demographic Trends in Domestic Life', in D. Clark (ed.), *Marriage, Domestic Life and Social Change, Writings for Jacqueline Burgoyne* (London, Routledge, 1991), pp. 85–108.

Elshtain, J. B., *Women and War* (Brighton, Harvester, 1987).

Etter-Lewis G., 'Black Women's Life Stories: Reclaiming Self in Narrative Texts', in S. B. Gluck and D. Patai (eds), *Women's Words. The Feminist Practice of Oral History* (London, Routledge, 1991), pp. 43–58.

Finch, J. and P. Summerfield, 'Social Reconstruction and the Emergence of Companionate Marriage, 1945–59' in D. Clark (ed.), *Marriage, Domestic Life and Social Change. Writings for Jacqueline Burgoyne* (London, Routledge, 1991), pp. 7–32.

Flax, J., *Thinking Fragments: Psychoanalysis, Feminism and Postmodernism in the Contemporary West* (Berkeley, University of California Press, 1990).

Friday, N., *My Mother Myself. The Daughter's Search for Identity* (London, Fontana, 1979; 1st pub. in the USA, 1977).

Geiger S., 'What's So Feminist about Women's Oral History?', *Journal of Women's History*, 2, 1 (1990), pp. 169–82.

Gledhill, C. and G. Swanson, 'Gender and Sexuality in Second World War Films – A Feminist approach', in G. Hurd (ed.), *National Fictions* (London, BFI, 1984), pp. 56–62.

Gledhill, C. and G. Swanson, *Nationalising Femininity: Culture, Sexuality and British Cinema in the Second World War* (Manchester, Manchester University Press, 1996).

Gluck, S. B. and D. Patai (eds), *Women's Words, the Feminist Practice of Oral History* (London, Routledge, 1991), Introduction, pp. 1–5.

Goldsmith, M., *Women at War* (London, Lindsay Drummond, 1943).

Goldsmith, M., *Women and the Future* (London, Lindsay Drummond, 1946).

Gordon, L. 'Response to Scott', *Signs* 15, 4 (1990), pp. 852–3.

Hall, C., 'Politics, Post-structuralism and Feminist History', *Gender and History*, 3, 2 (1991), pp. 204–10.

Hall Carpenter Archive, Lesbian Oral History Group, *Inventing Ourselves. Lesbian Life Stories* (London, Routledge, 1989).

Hamilton, M. A., *Women at Work: A Brief Introduction to Trade Unionism for Women* (London, George Routledge and Sons, 1941).

Harper, S., 'The Years of Total War: Propaganda and Entertainment', in C. Gledhill and G. Swanson (eds) *Nationalising Femininity: Culture, Sexuality and the British Cinema in World War II* (Manchester, Manchester University Press, 1995), pp. 193–212.

Hart, L., *Dynamic Defence* (London, Faber and Faber, 1940).

Hayes, D., *Challenge of Conscience. The Story of the Conscientious Objectors of 1939–1949* (London, George Allen and Unwin, 1949).

Heath, S., 'Whatever Happened to T.V.E.I.'s Equal Opportunities Policy?', *British Journal of Educational Policy*, 11, 5 (1996), pp. 543–60.

Heath, S., *'Preparation for Life'? Vocationalism and the Equal Opportunities Challenge* (Aldershot, Ashgate, 1997).

Heilbronn, C., *Writing a Woman's Life* (London, The Women's Press, 1989).

Heron, L. (ed.), *Truth Dare or Promise* (London, Virago, 1984).

Higonnet, M. R., J. Jenson *et al.*, *Behind the Lines. Gender and the Two World Wars* (New Haven, Yale University Press, 1987).

Hitchcock, G. and D. Hughes, *Research and the Teacher. A Qualitative Introduction to School-Based Research*, (London, Routledge, 1989).

Hoff, J., 'Gender as a Postmodern Category of Paralysis', *Women's History Review*, 3, 2 (1994), pp. 149–68.

Hoggart, R., *The Uses of Literacy* (Harmondsworth, Penguin Books, 1958).

Holcombe, L., *Victorian Ladies at Work. Middle-Class Working Women in England and Wales 1850–1914* (Newton Abbot, David and Charles, 1974).

Holtby, W., *The Crowded Street* (London, Collins, 1924).

Holtby, W., *South Riding. An English Landscape* (London, Collins, 1936).

Howard, K., *Sex Problems of the Returning Soldier* (Manchester, Sydney Pemberton, 1945).

Humphries, S., *Hooligans or Rebels? An Oral History of Working-Class Childhood and Youth 1889–1939* (Oxford, Blackwell, 1981).

Humphries, S., *The Handbook of Oral History. Recording Life Stories* (London, Inter-Action Trust, 1984).

Hunt, F., *Gender and Policy in English Education* (Brighton, Harvester, 1991).

Inman, P., *Labour in the Munitions Industries* (London, HMSO, 1957).

Jeffreys, S., *The Spinster and Her Enemies. Feminism and Sexuality 1880–1930* (London, Pandora, 1985).

Jeffreys, S., *Anticlimax, A Feminist Perspective on the Sexual Revolution* (London, The Women's Press, 1990).

Johansson, S. R., '"Herstory" as History: A New Field or Another Fad?' in B. A. Carroll, *Liberating Women's History. Theoretical and Critical Essays* (Chicago, University of Illinois Press, 1976), pp. 401–27.

Jolly, M., *'Dear Laughing Motorbike': Letters from Women Welders of the Second World War* (London, Scarlet Press, 1997).

Kent, S. K., *Making Peace. The Reconstruction of Gender in Interwar Britain* (Princeton, Princeton University Press, 1993).

Kirkham P., 'Fashioning the Feminine: Dress, Appearance and Femininity in Wartime Britain', in C. Gledhill and G. Swanson (eds), *Nationalising Femininity. Culture, Sexuality and British Cinema in the Second World War* (Manchester, Manchester University Press, 1996), pp. 152–74.

Lang, C., *Keep Smiling Through. Women in the Second World War* (Cambridge, Cambridge University Press, 1989).

Lant, A., *Blackout. Reinventing Women for Wartime British Cinema* (Princeton, Princeton University Press, 1991).

Lewis J., 'Women Lost and Found: The Impact of Feminism on History', in D. Spender (ed.), *Men's Studies Modified. The Impact of Feminism on the Academic Disciplines* (Oxford, Pergamon Press, 1981), pp. 55–72.

Light, A., *Forever England. Femininity, Literature and Conservatism Between the Wars* (London, Routledge, 1991).

Little, A. and J. Westergaard, 'The Trend of Class Differentials in Educational Opportunity in England', *British Journal of Sociology*, 15, 4 (1964), pp. 301–16.

Longmate, N., *The Real Dad's Army. The Story of the Home Guard* (London, Arrow Books, 1974).

Lummis, T., *Listening to History. The Authenticity of Oral Evidence* (London, Hutchinson Education, 1987).

McClintock, A., *Imperial Leather. Race, Gender and Sexuality in the Colonial Context* (London, Routledge, 1995).

Mackie, L. and P. Patullo, *Women at Work* (London, Tavistock, 1977).

Marwick, A., *Britain in the Century of Total War. War, Peace and Social Change 1900–1967* (London, The Bodley Head, 1968).

Marwick, A., *War and Social Change in the Twentieth Century* (London, Macmillan, 1974).

Mass-Observation, *People in Production. An Enquiry into British War Production* (London, John Murray, 1942).

Mass-Observation, *War Factory* (London, Victor Gollancz, 1943).

Mass-Observation, *The Journey Home: A Mass-Observation Report on the Problems of Demobilisation* (London, John Murray, 1944).

Medical Women's Federation, 'The Health of Children in Wartime Day Nurseries', *British Medical Journal*, 17 August 1946.

Miles A. and D. Vincent (eds) *Building European Society. Occupational Change and Social Mobility in Europe, 1840–1940* (Manchester, Manchester University Press, 1993).

Minister, K., 'A Feminist Frame for the Oral History Interview', in S. B. Gluck and D. Patai (eds), *Women's Words. The Feminist Practice of Oral History* (London, Routledge, 1991), pp. 27–41.

Mitchell, B. R. and P. Dean, *Abstract of British Historical Statistics* (Cambridge, Cambridge University Press, 1962).

Mitchell, J., *Psychoanalysis and Feminism* (Harmondsworth, Penguin, 1975).

Morgan, D. and M. Evans, *The Battle for Britain. Citizenship and Ideology in the Second World War* (London, Routledge, 1993).

Munton, A., *English Fiction of the Second World War* (London, Faber and Faber, 1989).

Myrdal, A. and V. Klein, *Women's Two Roles. Home and Work* (London, Routledge and Kegan Paul, 1956; 2nd ed. 1968).

Newsom, J., *The Education of Girls* (London, Faber, 1948).

Nicholson, M., *What Did You Do in the War, Mummy? Women in World War II* (London, Chatto and Windus, 1995).

Oakley, A., 'Interviewing Women: A Contradiction in Terms', in H. Roberts (ed.), *Doing Feminist Research* (London, Routledge and Kegan Paul, 1981), pp. 30–61.

Oram, A., 'Serving Two Masters? The Introduction of a Marriage Bar in Teaching in the 1920s', in London Feminist History Group (eds), *The Sexual Dynamics of History* (London, Pluto Press, 1983), pp. 134-53.

Oram, A., '"Bombs don't discriminate!" Women's Political Activism in the Second World War', in C. Gledhill and G. Swanson (eds), *Nationalising Femininity. Culture, Sexuality and British Cinema in the Second World War* (Manchester, Manchester University Press, 1996), pp. 53–69.

Oram, A., *Women Teachers and Feminist Politics 1900–1939* (Manchester, Manchester University Press, 1996).

Pargeter, E., *She Goes to War* (London, William Heinemann, 1942; this ed. London, Headline Book Publishing, 1989).

Parker, H. M. D., *Manpower. A Study of War-time Policy and Administration* (London, HMSO, 1957).

Parkin, D., 'Women in the Armed Services 1940–45', in R. Samuel (ed.), *Patriotism: The Making and Unmaking of British National Identity*, vol. II, (London, Routledge, 1989), pp. 158–70.

Passerini, L., 'Introduction', in L. Passerini (ed.), *Memory and Totalitarianism* (Oxford, Oxford University Press, 1992), pp. 1–19.

Paterson, D., *The Family Woman and the Feminist. A Challenge* (London, William Heinemann, 1945).

Pilgrim Trust, *Men without Work* (Cambridge, Cambridge University Press, 1938).

Portelli, A. 'The Peculiarities of Oral History', *History Workshop*, 12 (1981), pp. 96–107.

Price, K., *What Did You Do in the War, Mam? Women Steelworkers at Consett During the Second World War* (Newcastle upon Tyne, Open University Northern Region, 1984).

Priestley, J. B., *Postscripts* (London, William Heinemann, 1940).

Priestley, J. B., *British Women Go To War* (London, Collins, 1943).

Pronay, N., 'The British Post-bellum Cinema: A Survey of the Films Relating to World War II made in Britain between 1945 and 1960', *Historical Journal of Film, Radio and Television*, 8, 1 (1988), pp. 39–54.

Purvis, J., 'The Prison Experiences of the Suffragettes in Edwardian Britain', *Women's History Review*, 4, 1 (1995), pp. 103–33.

Reinharz, S., *Feminist Methods in Social Research* (Oxford, Oxford University Press, 1992).

Richards J., 'The Way We Were', *Guardian*, 15 August 1997.

Riley D., *War in the Nursery. Theories of the Child and Mother* (London, Virago, 1983).

Riley D., *'Am I That Name?' Feminism and the Category 'Women' in History* (London, Macmillan, 1988).

Roberts, E., *A Woman's Place. An Oral History of Working-Class Women 1890–1940* (Oxford, Basil Blackwell, 1984).

Roberts, E., *Women and Families. An Oral History 1940–1970* (Oxford, Blackwell, 1995).

Robinson J., 'White Women Researching/Representing "Others": From Anti-Apartheid to Post-Colonialism?', in A. Blunt and G. Rose (eds), *Writing Women and Space: Colonial and Postcolonial Geographies* (New York, Guilford Press, 1994), pp. 197–226.

Robinson, V., *Sisters in Arms* (London, Harper Collins, 1996).

Roper M. and J. Tosh, *Manful Assertions: Masculinities in Britain since 1800* (London, Routledge, 1991).

Roper M. and J. Tosh, 'Introduction: Historians and the Politics of Masculinity', in M. Roper and J. Tosh (eds) *Manful Assertions: Masculinities in Britain since 1800* (London, Routledge, 1991), pp. 1–24.

Rose, S., 'Girls and GIs: Race, Sex and Diplomacy in Second World War Britain', *The International History Review*, 19, 1 (1997), pp. 146–60.

Rowbotham, S., *Woman's Consciousness, Man's World* (Harmondsworth, Penguin, 1973).

Rowbotham, S. and J. McCrindle (eds) *Dutiful Daughters* (London, Allen Lane, 1977).

Sangster, J. 'Telling our Stories: Feminist Debates and the Use of Oral History', *Women's History Review*, 3, 1 (1994), pp. 5–28.

Schwartz, P., '*Partisanes* and Gender Politics in Vichy France', *French Historical Studies* 16, 1 (1989), pp. 126–51.

Schweitzer, P., L. Hilton and J. Moss (eds), *What Did You Do in the War, Mum?* (London, Age Exchange, 1985).

Scott, J. W., 'Review of *Heroes of their Own Lives: The Politics and History of Family Violence*' by Linda Gordon, *Signs*, 15, 4 (1990), pp. 848–52.

Scott, J. W., 'Experience', in J. Butler and J. W. Scott, *Feminists Theorize the Political* (London, Routledge, 1992), pp. 22–40.

Scott, J. W., 'Gender: A Useful Category of Historical Analysis', in J. W. Scott (ed.), *Feminism and History*, (Oxford, Oxford University Press, 1996), pp. 152–80.

Scott, P., *British Women in War* (London, Hutchinson, 1940).

Scott, P., *They Made Invasion Possible* (London, Hutchinson, 1944).

Settle, M. L., *All the Brave Promises. Memories of Aircraft Woman 2nd Class 2146391* (London, Pandora Press, 1984).

Sheridan, D., 'Ambivalent Memories: Women and the 1939–45 War in Britain', *Oral History*, 18, 1 (Spring 1990), pp. 32–40.

Showalter, E., 'Rivers and Sassoon: The Inscription of Male Gender Anxieties', in M. R. Higonnet, J. Jenson *et al.*, (eds) *Behind the Lines. Gender and the Two World Wars* (New Haven, Yale University Press, 1987) pp. 61–9.

Smith, A. C. H., *Paper Voices. The Popular Press and Social Change 1935–1965*, (London, Chatto and Windus, 1975).

Smith, H. L., 'The Effect of the War on the Status of Women', in H. L. Smith (ed.), *War and Social Change. British Society in the Second World War* (Manchester, Manchester University Press, 1986), pp. 208–29.

Smith, H. L., 'British Feminism in the 1920s', in H. L. Smith (ed.), *British Feminism in the Twentieth Century* (Aldershot, Edward Elgar, 1990).

Spender, S., *Citizens in War – And After* (London, George G.Harrap & Co., 1945).

Stacey, J., 'Can There be a Feminist Ethnography?', in S. B. Gluck and D.

Patai (eds), *Women's Words. The Feminist Practice of Oral History* (London, Routledge, 1991), pp. 111–19.

Stanley, J., 'Poking Around in Unspeakable Places: My Practice as Oral Historian', *Women's History Notebooks*, 3, 1 (1996), pp. 22–33.

Stuart, M., '"And How Was It For You, Mary?" Self, Identity and Meaning for Oral Historians', *Oral History*, 21, 2 (1993), pp. 80–3.

Stuart, M., 'You're a Big Girl Now: Subjectivities, Oral History and Feminism', *Oral History*, 22, 2 (1994), pp. 55–63.

Summerfield, P., 'Women Workers in the Second World War', *Capital and Class*, 1, 1 (1977), pp. 27–42.

Summerfield, P., 'Education and Politics in the British Armed Forces in the Second World War', *International Review of Social History*, 26, 2 (1981) pp. 133–58.

Summerfield, P., 'Mass-Observation: Social Research or Social Movement?', *Journal of Contemporary History*, 20 (1985), pp. 439–52.

Summerfield, P., 'Patriotism and Empire: Music-Hall Entertainment, 1870–1914', in J. M. Mackenzie (ed.), *Imperialism and Popular Culture* (Manchester, Manchester University Press, 1986), pp. 17–48.

Summerfield, P., 'Cultural Reproduction in the Education of Girls: A Study of Girls' Schooling in Two Lancashire Towns', in F. Hunt (ed.), *Lessons for Life. The Schooling of Girls and Women 1850–1950*, (Oxford, Basil Blackwell, 1987) pp. 149–70.

Summerfield, P., 'Women, War and Social Change: Women in Britain in World War II', in A. Marwick (ed.), *Total War and Social Change* (London, Macmillan, 1988).

Summerfield, P., *Women Workers in the Second World War. Production and Patriarchy in Conflict* (London, Croom Helm, 1984; 2nd ed. Routledge, 1989).

Summerfield, P., 'Mass-Observation on Women at Work in the Second World War', in L. Stanley (ed.), 'En/gendering the Archive: Mass-Observation among the Women', *Feminist Praxis*, 37 & 38 (1992), pp. 35–49.

Summerfield, P., 'The Patriarchal Discourse of Human Capital: Training Women for War Work 1939–1945', *Journal of Gender Studies*, 2, 2 (1993), pp. 189–205.

Summerfield, P., 'Women in Britain since 1945: Companionate Marriage and the Double Burden' in J. Obelkevich and P. Catterall (eds), *Understanding Post-War British Society*, (London, Routledge, 1994), pp. 58–72.

Summerfield, P. '"The Girl That Makes the Thing That Drills the Hole That Holds the Spring …" Discourses of Women and Work in the Second World War', in C. Gledhill and G. Swanson (eds), *Nationalising Femininity: Culture, Sexuality and the British Cinema in the Second World War* (Manchester, Manchester University Press, 1996), pp. 35–52.

Summerfield, P., '"My Dress for an Army Uniform!": Gender Instabilities in the Two World Wars', Lancaster University *Inaugural Lecture Series*, 1997.

Summerfield, P. and N. Crockett '"You Weren't Taught That With the Welding": Lessons in Sexuality in the Second World War', *Women's History Review*, 1, 3 (1992), pp. 435–54.

Summerskill E., 'Conscription and Women', *The Fortnightly*, 151 (March 1942), pp. 209–14.

Swindells, J., 'Coming Home to Heaven: Manpower and Myth in 1944 Britain', *Women's History Review*, 4, 2 (1995), pp. 223–34.

Tebbut, M., *Women's Talk? A Social History Of 'Gossip' In Working-class Neighbourhoods 1880–1960* (Aldershot, Scolar Press, 1995).

Thompson, P., *The Voice of the Past. Oral History* (Oxford, Oxford University Press, 1988; 1st pub. 1978).

Thomson, A., *Anzac Memories. Living with the Legend* (Oxford, Oxford University Press Australia, 1994).

Thumim, J., 'The Female Audience: Mobile Women and Married Ladies', in C. Gledhill and G. Swanson (eds), *Nationalising Femininity: Culture, Sexuality and the British Cinema in the Second World War* (Manchester, Manchester University Press, 1996), pp. 238–56.

Tinkler, P., *Constructing Girlhood. Popular Magazines for Girls Growing Up in England 1920–1950* (London, Taylor and Francis, 1995).

Tinkler, P., 'Sexuality and Citizenship: The State and Girls' Leisure Provision in England, 1939–45', in *Women's History Review*, 4, 2 (1995), pp. 193–217.

Titmuss R. M., 'War and Social Policy', in R. M. Titmuss, *Essays on 'The Welfare State'* (London, George Allen and Unwin, 1958), pp. 75–87.

Titmuss, R. M., 'The Position of Women. Some Vital Statistics' in R. M. Titmuss, *Essays on 'The Welfare State'* (London, George Allen and Unwin 1958), pp. 88–103.

Tosh, J,. 'What Should Historians do with Masculinity? Reflections on Nineteenth-Century Britain', *History Workshop*, 38 (1994), pp. 179–202.

Vincent, D., 'Mobility, Bureaucracy and Careers in Twentieth-Century Britain', in A. Miles and D. Vincent (eds), *Building European Society. Occupational Change and Social Mobility in Europe 1840–1940* (Manchester, Manchester University Press, 1993), pp. 217–39.

Waller, J. and M. Vaughan-Rees, *Women in Wartime. The Role of Women's Magazines 1939–1945* (London, Macdonald Optima, 1987).

Waller, J. and M. Vaughan-Rees, *Women in Uniform 1939–1945* (London, Papermac, 1989).

Wandor, M., (ed.), *The Body Politic. Women's Liberation in Britain 1969–1972* (London, Stage One, 1972).

Williams, G., *Women and Work* (London, Nicholson and Watson, 1945).

Wintringham, T., *New Ways of War* (Harmondsworth, Penguin, 1940).

Woolf, V., *A Room of One's Own* (London, The Hogarth Press, 1929).

Woolf, V., *Three Guineas* (London, The Hogarth Press, 1938).

Woollacott, A., 'Sisters and Brothers in Arms: Family, Class and Gendering in World War I Britain' in M.Cooke and A.Woollacott (eds), *Gendering War Talk* (Princeton, Princeton University Press, 1993), pp. 128–47.

Woollacott, A., 'Maternalism, Professionalism and Industrial Welfare Supervisors in World War I Britain', *Women's History Review*, 3, 1 (1994), pp. 29–56.

Woollacott, A., *On Her Their Lives Depend. Munitions Workers in the Great War* (Berkeley, University of California Press, 1994).

Zimmeck, M., 'Strategies and Stratagems for the Employment of Women in the British Civil Service, 1919–1939', *The Historical Journal*, 27, 4 (1984), pp. 901–24.

Zimmeck, M., 'Marry in Haste, Repent at Leisure: Women, Bureaucracy and the Post Office, 1870–1920', in M. Savage and A. Witz (eds), *Gender and Bureaucracy* (Oxford, Oxford University Press, 1992), pp. 65–93.

Zukas M., 'Friendship as Oral History: A Feminist Psychologist's View', *Oral History*, 21, 2 (1993), pp. 73–9.

Index

Note: 'n.' after a page reference indicates the number of a note on that page.